W9-AZW-908

TULIA

TULIA

Race, Cocaine, and Corruption
in a Small Texas Town

NATE BLAKESLEE

PublicAffairs

New York

Copyright © 2005 by Nate Blakeslee.
Published in the United States by PublicAffairs™,
a member of the Perseus Books Group.

This publication was supported by a grant from the Soros Justice Fellowship Program of
the Open Society Institute.

All rights reserved.
Printed in the United States of America.

No part of this book may be reproduced in any manner whatsoever without written permission except in the case of brief quotations embodied in critical articles and reviews. For
information, address PublicAffairs, 250 West 57TH Street, Suite 1321, New York NY
10107. PublicAffairs books are available at special discounts for bulk purchases in the U.S.
by corporations, institutions, and other organizations. For more information, please contact
the Special Markets Department at the Perseus Books Group, 11 Cambridge Center, Cambridge MA 02142, call (617) 252-5298, or e-mail special.markets@perseusbooks.com.

Book design and composition by Mark McGarry, Texas Type & Book Works
Set in Janson

Library of Congress Cataloging-in-Publication Data
Blakeslee, Nate, 1970–
Tulia: race, cocaine, and corruption in a small Texas town / Nate Blakeslee.
p. cm.
Includes index.
ISBN-13: 978-1-58648-219-0
ISBN-10: 1-58648-219-x
1. Coleman, Thomas Roland. 2. Drug traffic—Investigation—Texas—Tulia.
3. False imprisonment—Texas—Tulia. 4. Trials (Narcotic laws)—Texas—Swisher County.
5. Judicial error—Texas—Swisher County. 6. Police corruption—Texas—Tulia.
7. Tulia (Tex.)—Race relations. 8. Tulia (Tex.)—History. I. Title.
HV8079.N3.B55 2005   345.764'8380277—dc22   2005049220

FIRST EDITION
10 9 8 7 6 5 4 3 2 1

For Karen

CONTENTS

CONTENTS

PART FOUR

PART FIVE

TULIA

PART ONE

PROLOGUE: MARCH 20, 2003

To m Co l e m a n entered the courtroom of the Swisher County courthouse on Thursday afternoon, March 20, 2003, wearing an Italian-style black leather jacket over a blue shirt and black tie. A sea of black faces in the packed gallery craned their necks to get a glimpse of him, but he did not return their gaze. Coleman kept his eyes fixed straight ahead, his head tilted slightly downward, as he marched up the aisle toward the front of the small courtroom. It had become a familiar posture for the former narcotics officer over the preceding week. Each morning, he had been forced to run a gauntlet of photographers and reporters waiting outside the courthouse for him. They had snapped countless photos of him scurrying up the steps of the courthouse's side entrance in his black cowboy hat and dark sunglasses, but he had spoken not a word. Today was the day they were all waiting for, the day he would have no choice but to take the stand and break his silence. Four satellite trucks were in the parking lot, waiting to beam news of his testimony from this tiny west Texas town to the world.

The courtroom on the second floor of the Swisher County courthouse was not designed with great deeds in mind. It is a utilitarian facility of fluorescent lights and cheap linoleum and hard-backed church pews for the gallery, a courtroom where trials are run as efficiently and economically as the farms and ranches of the plainsmen whose hard-earned tax money built it. Yet it had been the scene of Coleman's greatest triumphs as a police officer, the place that had made him, however briefly, a hero. Posing as a down-and-out construction worker, Coleman had worked undercover for eighteen months in Tulia, during which time he reported making over 100 purchases of illegal drugs, mostly powdered cocaine. The suspects were arrested in a massive raid in July 1999. When the smoke had cleared, Coleman's one-man operation had netted no fewer than forty-seven cocaine dealers, most of them black. It was a stunning success. For his accomplishment, Coleman was named an Officer of the Year, the most coveted award among Texas narcs. He went to Austin to have his picture taken with John Cornyn, the state attorney general (later elected U.S. Senator). The papers called him a one-man wrecking crew, a lone ranger. In fact, he was the son of a Texas Ranger, the mythical corps of elite lawmen celebrated the world over for their prowess and bravery. Coleman had finally filled his father's giant boots.

The last time Coleman had appeared in this courtroom was in September 2000, when he testified against Kareem Abdul Jabbar White, the last person to stand trial in the bust. White had been sentenced to sixty years in prison in that trial, another in a long list of impressive convictions for Coleman, who by that time was already at work on a new undercover operation in another corner of Texas. Things weren't like that anymore. Coleman was no longer a cop, for one thing. He had been fired from two narcotics assignments since leaving Tulia, and was now driving a truck for a gas company, checking lines in the desolate ranching country south of Dallas. But that was just the beginning of Coleman's troubles. In the intervening two and a half years, the following facts about Coleman's past had become public knowledge: that he had no experience whatsoever in undercover narcotics work prior to coming to Tulia; that he had walked off the job as a deputy sheriff in two small west Texas towns, in each case abruptly leaving town with thousands of dollars in unpaid debts; that one of the sheriffs he'd worked for in the past had filed criminal charges on Coleman, resulting in his indictment while working undercover in Tulia; that he was widely reputed to be both a racist and a pathological liar; and that he was obsessed with guns and paranoid fantasies.

The story of the Tulia sting became a national scandal. Troublesome facts about Coleman's methods were the subject of investigative reports in dozens of media outlets, from the *New York Times*, to Court TV, to the *Independent* of London: how Coleman never wore a wire, videotaped his buys, or had a second officer observe him; how the vast majority of his alleged buys had no corroboration whatsoever; how most of the evidence was powdered cocaine, despite the fact that Coleman had infiltrated a community of low-income blacks where marijuana and crack were the most commonly used drugs; how Coleman's reports typically consisted of a few paragraphs with virtually no description of the defendants; and how Coleman grossly misidentified suspects in a handful of cases that were quietly disposed of by the district attorney after the indictments were issued.

The sheer number of cases Coleman made in Tulia, a town of just 5,000, seemed to defy logic. Further, thirty-eight of the forty-seven defendants came from the town's tiny black community, which numbered perhaps 350 people, roughly half of whom were children. In one single bust, 20 percent of the black adults in Tulia were hauled away. If every fifth person on the black side of town was dealing cocaine, some observers pointed out, then who was left to buy it? And why was so much powdered cocaine and so little crack being peddled in Tulia's hardscrabble black community, where unemployment hovered around 50 percent? This conundrum did not concern the district attorney, Terry McEachern, who prosecuted the cases with characterisic zeal. Nor did it seem to concern the jurors in the original trials.

Despite the small amounts of cocaine involved, they handed down staggeringly long sentences, even for defendants with no prior records. As the questions about Coleman began to mount, local authorities, including the man who had hired Coleman, Swisher County sheriff Larry Stewart, stood by the operation. The national press attention only seemed to harden their resolve: there would be no retrials. The sentences would stand.

Now, after two and a half years of stalemate, Coleman was back in Tulia because a small group of defendants—four of the sixteen who were still serving time—had managed against long odds to secure a postconviction hearing to determine whether or not they were entitled to new trials. It was a day that many in Tulia had thought would never come: at long last, Coleman would be cross-examined under oath on every aspect of his background and his investigation in Tulia, with the nation watching. The stakes could not have been higher. Lives were on the line, as well as careers, but something larger seemed to hang in the balance as well. After the national media took hold of the story, Tulia became ground zero in a broader debate about drug policy that had been simmering for years on talk radio, Sunday morning talk shows, Capitol Hill, and state legislatures across the country. The hearing had become a referendum on the state of the drug war itself.

Coleman's gold watch and pinky ring flashed as he sat down in the witness chair and adjusted his tie. American troops had begun their attack on Iraq the night before, and Coleman wore a flag pin in his lapel. He was slightly more heavyset than the last time he had been in Tulia, his ruddy Irish face pudgier and more florid. He also had a new mustache and haircut—the sides shaved close like a Marine's and the wavy red top grown out and slicked back. The four defendants, men he had not laid eyes on in over three years—since testifying against them in this very courtroom—had been bused in from state prison to attend the hearing. They sat on Coleman's immediate left in street clothes, their legs discreetly shackled, staring down at him grimly from the jury box.

At the end of the row of inmates sat Joe Moore, the man the prosecution had called the "kingpin" of Swisher County's drug underworld. He certainly didn't look the part of a major cocaine dealer. He wore what had been his usual uniform in the free world, a pair of crisp blue overalls, delivered to his jail cell by a local farmer friend. For his court appearance, he had added a white cotton dress shirt underneath. Even hunched over on the jury bench, he dwarfed the three young men seated at his side. At sixty, he was built like a past-his-prime George Foreman: a giant balding head stacked on top of shoulders that were almost as deep as they were broad, and a torso that only got broader as it moved down.

Moore was no stranger to the inside of a courtroom. He was the last of a long line of small-time hustlers from the Flats, the old black neighborhood west of the railroad tracks. His varied and storied career had earned him a number of different monikers in Tulia. Around the courthouse he was sometimes called the Mayor of Sunset Addition, as the Flats were officially known. In less charitable circles his name was King Nigger. To blacks he was affectionately known as Bootie Wootie, or simply Bootie. In a town where black people had always made money for other people—generally by hard labor— Moore had a knack for making money for himself. Over the years he had run his own hay-hauling crew, owned a barbecue joint, and dabbled in a variety of moneymaking schemes. What made him notorious in Tulia, however, was Funz-a-Poppin', the illicit juke joint he operated in the Flats. For over a decade, until his bar was leveled in the early 1990s, Moore was Tulia's chief bootlegger, and there was great demand for his services in a dry county like Swisher.

While the three young men seated next to him fidgeted and occasionally nodded to an acquaintance in the gallery, Moore watched the proceedings with an unblinking stare, as though his life were riding on it. And it was. He was doing ninety years.

Coleman avoided looking at Moore and his companions. There really was no safe place in the courtroom for him to rest his gaze. The front two rows of the gallery were filled with reporters, and behind them the pews were rife with other defendants busted by Coleman, men and women who had served relatively short sentences or had been placed on probation. Together with their relatives and friends, they had been in high spirits all week, watching attorneys for the defendants parse every aspect of Coleman's operation in Tulia, as they had been doing among themselves for years. Sitting in the gallery had felt at times like attending a horror film or a Holy Roller church service, with the audience murmuring and occasionally shouting in response to the action up front. Now that Coleman was finally before them, a strange, expectant silence filled the courtroom.

Donnie Smith had shown up late for the hearings that morning. He wore a clean white T-shirt and blue jeans, his hair tied down in cornrows, each short tail bound by a simple rubber band. He found a seat in the rear, about ten rows behind his mother, Mattie White. He saw that she had a new hairstyle for the hearings—bobbed short in the back and spiky on top. Mattie, a guard at the state prison west of town, had good reason to be concerned about her appearance. She had been interviewed a dozen times in the past thirty days about her son Kareem and her daughter Kizzie, who were still locked up from the bust. In the past year, her family had been profiled in *People* and in the column of a well-known writer for the *New York Times*.

Mattie rarely mentioned Donnie in those interviews, and he did not anticipate getting any airtime today, either. Donnie, a thirty-two-year-old former high school sports star, had also been busted by Coleman. Unlike his younger siblings Kareem and Kizzie, however, Donnie was a crack addict. He had been out of prison a little over a year, after serving thirty months of a twelve-year sentence. He stayed clean for about nine months, but now he was using again, and his mother was barely talking to him. Donnie would disappear for weeks at a time and then show up at her tidy frame house unannounced, asking for money. He was sleeping wherever he could find a bed. He preferred his mom's house or his ex-wife's public housing duplex in the Flats, where his two sons lived. If he wasn't welcome at either place, which was often the case, he would crash on the floor of his dad's trailer home nearby. He also had a number of girlfriends around town he could call on in a pinch.

Donnie would have made a good interview for the *Times* man or anyone else who cared to talk to him. He was not what most people would call a drug dealer, but he was one of the few defendants to actually admit spending time with Coleman. In the summer of 1998 Donnie had known him as "T.J.," a skinny, ponytailed white man who had begun hanging around the cattle auction, where Donnie worked as a day laborer a few days each month. Shortly after the two met, Coleman flagged Donnie down on the side of the road and asked him if he knew where to score. Desperate for money, Donnie acted as an intermediary for Coleman on several occasions over the course of the summer, each time purchasing tiny amounts of crack from a dealer, pinching off a bit for himself, and delivering the remainder to Coleman.

Technically that was a fourth-degree felony, punishable by up to two years in a state jail, a sort of intermediate prison for low-level offenders. Coleman called on Donnie at least two more times for this service before Donnie disappeared. His little brother Kareem had convinced him to go to a ninety-day rehab center in Lubbock. It was Donnie's second time through the center, and both times he had gone voluntarily. When he got home that winter, he went to work as a hired man on a local farm.

He had been clean for six months when the big roundup came in the summer of 1999. With no prior felony convictions, Donnie was prepared to plea-bargain. The small amounts he had gotten for Coleman, combined with his status as a first-time felony offender, he figured, gave him a good shot at probation. Then he read the indictments. He was accused of delivering cocaine to Coleman on seven separate occasions. Only one delivery was alleged to be crack cocaine. The other deliveries were said to be powder in amounts between 1 and 4 grams, making them second-degree felonies. The first plea District Attorney Terry McEachern offered Donnie was forty-five years.

In the end, Donnie managed to dodge the much longer sentences his siblings received. Yet, after a year back in Tulia, he still seemed trapped. Almost five years after he first met Coleman, he found himself right back where he was: broke, strung out, and alone. Despite his troubles, Donnie had always thought of himself as the popular, talented star he had been in high school, when the whole town seemed to love him. It was only since the bust that he came to realize how people in Tulia really felt about him. The revelations about Coleman, he discovered, didn't seem to faze most white Tulians. In fact, many of them seemed to blame him and his fellow defendants for bringing the curse of the media spotlight down on their town.

Donnie had no steady job, and being an ex-convict on parole had not improved his prospects of finding one. He was tired of the manual labor jobs he normally wound up with anyway. He wanted to become a long-distance trucker or have his own barbershop in Dallas. He wanted to reconcile with his ex-wife and move his family to some big city, far from all of this, someplace with good jobs and nice houses. He wasn't sure how he was going to do that. But he knew why he was in the courtroom today, even if nobody wanted to interview him. He had to get Coleman behind him.

The small section of the courtroom between the witness chair and the gallery was so crammed with attorneys that there was no room for the two sides to have their own separate camps. Instead they sat face-to-face across a row of three narrow tables lined up end to end, their knees practically touching underneath. On the near side with his back to Coleman sat District Attorney Terry McEachern. He was flanked by two young assistant prosecutors, a special prosecutor he had hired just for the hearing, and a fifth attorney provided by the county's insurance company.

In a part of the state where dressed up usually means a western jacket over starched blue jeans, McEachern wore an expensive gray suit and imported leather shoes. He was perhaps the only male native of Swisher County to use hairspray, and his silvering black hair was nicely complemented by gold wire rim glasses. In his early fifties, he was a big man, with a full, well-tanned neck and sensitive eyes that women found attractive. McEachern presided over one of the busiest district attorney's offices in the panhandle. In his seventeen years as the chief prosecutor for Swisher County and neighboring Hale County, he had personally tried over 500 cases. He did not believe in preparation; often he would read the case file for the first time during his opening statement. His knowledge of the law was relatively limited, and he was not particularly good at oral argument. But he knew how to pick a jury and he was an outstanding politician, and that made all the difference. He had built his career on aggressive prosecution of his two bread-and-butter charges: drunken driving and drug crimes. No matter what the charges were, he liked to tell juries that drugs and alcohol (the sale of which was still illegal in much of the panhandle) were bound to be involved somehow, along with the two other basic elements of trouble: sex and money. McEachern's rhetoric squared nicely with what jurors heard in church every Sunday, and this was not an accident. Defendants in his district usually didn't take their chances on a trial, and when they did, jurors—the righteous plainsmen and women McEachern knew so well—almost never let him down.

Things were different this time around. There was no jury to appeal
to. The defendants were in the jury box, looking down at him. A visiting
judge whose politics McEachern could only imagine sat at the top of the
dais. His career hinged on whether or not a former narc—a man he
knew next to nothing about—could hold it together on the stand for one
more day. And on the other side of the table sat thirteen attorneys,
including representatives from some of the most prestigious law firms in
the country. It was shaping up to be the worst week of his life.

Vanita Gupta was the reason the attorney's well was so full. She
was an unlikely nemesis for a career Texas prosecutor. Standing perhaps five-foot-four, with long black hair and a slender frame, she was
just twenty-eight years old and looked a good five years younger.
Born in Philadelphia to Indian immigrant parents and raised in
England, her experience as a criminal defense attorney consisted of a
single summer at the Washington, D.C., public defender's office.
Gupta first heard about Tulia in the fall of 2001. She had been out of
New York University law school for exactly four months and had just
landed her dream job: attorney for the storied NAACP Legal Defense
Fund in New York. Founded in 1940 by civil rights pioneer and even-
tual Supreme Court Justice Thurgood Marshall, LDF litigators had
argued some of the most famous civil rights cases in American history,
including *Brown v. Board of Education*, the seminal school desegregation case. The transcripts of the Tulia trials were her introduction to
the legal system in Texas, and she had never encountered anything
like it. Gupta had spent the past year and a half of her life working on
the cases for ten to twelve hours a day, poring over court documents,
visiting defendants in prison, and traveling back and forth between
Tulia and New York. Now she was surrounded by a team of top corporate attorneys from two of Washington's most prominent firms,
which she had recruited to the cause, at the turning point in a case
every civil rights attorney in the country had heard of, in the middle
of a state she knew almost nothing about.

As the only local attorney on the defense team, Jeff Blackburn knew the courts of the Texas panhandle all too well. He was a sole practitioner from Amarillo who made his living from clients who walked in off the street, mainly people facing drug or DWI charges. Coleman's operation in Tulia had been funded by an Amarillo-based drug task force that Swisher County belonged to, and Blackburn had butted heads with agents and supervisors of that same task force on many occasions. He lived with his teenage son in the back of his office building, a converted paint factory in a blue-collar neighborhood not far from the freeway. Blackburn, who was in his mid-forties and had thin brown hair that resisted styling, was not particularly handsome. But he had an abundance of charisma and never failed to put on a good show in court, where he was known as a skilled trial attorney. It was his advocacy for civil rights, however, that had made him one of the best-known defense attorneys in Amarillo. As an articulate liberal in an extremely conservative town, he had become unofficial spokesperson for the town's downtrodden. He knew virtually everybody in town, and he had a knack for interjecting himself into high-profile cases and getting his face on TV. The reporters and producers for the local news stations loved his gravelly smoker's voice and his penchant for bitingly sarcastic one-liners.

Blackburn's father had been one of the panhandle's best defense attorneys, and his idols were the great men of the Texas trial lawyer pantheon, legendary liberals who battled the forces of reaction, usually represented by the men in black robes. He considered himself a leftist intellectual. In the hall outside his waiting room were posters of great labor leaders past, figures like A. Philip Randolph and Big Bill Haywood and Mother Jones. One wall of his living room was covered floor to ceiling with perhaps 5,000 books, heavily peppered with Marxist history and philosophy. He had gotten involved in the Tulia cases shortly after the first trials and had spent countless hours working pro bono on behalf of various defendants. At times over the past two and a half years, when nothing seemed to come of the work, he had come close to abandoning the cause. Now Tulia had evolved into his biggest case ever, and he was enjoying every minute of it.

Blackburn and Gupta huddled with their colleagues as Coleman took his seat. Things were not going exactly as planned. Strictly speaking, the object of the hearing was not to determine whether or not Coleman fabricated cases in Tulia. Instead, to win, the defendants had to prove that McEachern had improperly withheld information about Coleman—such as the fact that he had been under indictment while working in Tulia, for example—from their clients, which prevented them from receiving a fair trial. This type of appeal was known as a Brady claim, after the Supreme Court case that established the precedent. Success would mean new trials for the four defendants in court today and would vastly improve the prospects for all sixteen Tulians still in prison. Failure would mean that the whole process would have to be repeated in federal court, an undertaking that might last years and offered no guarantee of success. The presiding judge, a semiretired Dallas judge named Ron Chapman, had sounded a disturbing note in his opening remarks three days earlier. The defendants should not necessarily anticipate, he warned, that each of them would get the same relief, if any, from the proceedings. The facts in each case were different, so the outcome might be different as well. Chapman had repeated that idea a couple of times during informal hallway conversations that made their way back to the legal team in ominous bits and pieces. It seemed to confirm what some on the team had feared from the outset: even if the judge agreed with their arguments, someone was still going to get screwed.

The most likely candidate was Freddie Brookins Jr. Gupta had taken on Freddie's case personally and had come to know his family well. In many ways, Freddie was the odd man out in the jury box. Seated on Joe Moore's right, he wore an expression of deep concentration, his round cheeks and shaved head reminiscent of an overgrown baby. Just twenty-two at the time of arrest, he had no prior record. He came from a solid family that was well thought of in Tulia. His father, Fred Brookins Sr., a line manager at a beef-packing plant, sat a few rows behind the attorney's well. He was a short, muscular man in his mid-fifties with a graying goatee and sensitive eyes. His air of thoughtfulness and quiet authority made him a de facto spokesman for the Tulia defendants. By contrast, the two other young men in the jury box with Moore, Chris Jackson and Jason Williams, had troubled childhoods. Williams's mother, who was also busted by Coleman, was a longtime crack addict. Jackson, known to his friends as Crazy, had several convictions and one bit in prison under his belt by the time Coleman came to town. His mother was murdered when he was young. Fred Sr. was the kind of father that Jackson, Williams, and dozens of kids on the black side of town dreamed of having. He always thought his son would be in college by now, like his older sister.

Instead Freddie was serving a twenty-year sentence 500 miles away from his family in east Texas, in the state prison that housed death row. He spent his days swabbing out the showers used by condemned men and his evenings listening for the van that arrived every other week or so to take somebody to the execution chamber. And now, four days into the hearing, Judge Chapman seemed to be signaling that Freddie had a weaker Brady claim than his three codefendants. This was because Freddie was the last of the four to be tried. The state's team was arguing, in essence, that because Freddie had the benefit of information that came out in the first three trials when preparing for his own trial, he had no valid Brady claim against McEachern. If Chapman was buying into that argument, it did not bode well for Freddie's chances for a new trial. Nor did it look good for the remaining twelve defendants still in prison, either, because most of their cases were adjudicated after Freddie's trial.

For the past three days the team had grilled Sheriff Stewart and Coleman's supervisors at the task force, and they knew they had scored some good points with the judge. But it wasn't enough. They were going to win or lose based on how well Coleman did on the stand. They had to shift the hearing from a fact-finding tour about prosecutorial misconduct to a referendum on Coleman and his character. They had to show the judge exactly what kind of man this was. The task of examining Coleman fell to Mitch Zamoff, one of the firm attorneys recruited by Gupta. Tall and lean, with an angular face and a clean-shaven head, Zamoff was a former federal prosecutor with scores of trials under his belt. He had a reputation as a ruthless and precise examiner, and he was armed with dozens of examples of Coleman's conflicting testimony in past hearings and trials. Coleman, however, had managed to dodge everything thrown at him by trial and appellate attorneys over the past three years. They had him on the ropes countless times but he always slipped away.

What they needed was a knockout. Today. Zamoff stood up and buttoned his suit. Time to go.

CHAPTER ONE

Busted

A DOZEN OFFICERS stood outside the Swisher County sheriff's office smoking cigarettes and drinking coffee in the predawn darkness of a cool summer morning on the high plains. It was July 23, 1999, and it would have been a good day to commit a crime in Swisher County. All seven of Tulia's police officers were there, including Chief Jimmy McCaslin. Sheriff Larry Stewart brought every deputy he had available, and the local state troopers had been pulled in off the highway as well. They were waiting for agents from the task force in Amarillo to arrive so they could get started with the morning's work: a stack of arrest warrants several inches high. Each had a cover sheet with the name of the defendant, his date of birth, and a black-and-white Xerox photo of the target. Under many of the photos were notes scrawled in black magic marker: "Cooker (crack)," "Fighter," "Armed: Use Caution!" The notes reflected intelligence gathered by Tom Coleman during his eighteen-month investigation.

Until the secret indictments had come down a few days earlier, none of these men, with the exception of Sheriff Stewart, had even heard of Coleman. Many had still not met him; they just knew that he was from the drug task force up the highway in Amarillo. Like most of the rural counties around Amarillo, Swisher County had technically been a member of the task force for years, but the "jump out boys," as the crooks called them, had seldom come this far south. And no agency of any stripe had ever done a roundup like this in Swisher County. Forty-seven arrest warrants for drug dealing in Tulia! This was huge. Most of the officers assembled that morning had never done a felony drug arrest. Their days consisted mainly of endless cruising around the county's perfectly flat rural roads or the deserted streets of Tulia, getting keys out of locked cars, keeping the drunks in line at football games, making an occasional arrest for DWI. A not insignificant portion of their time was spent patrolling the inside of the café at the Tulia Livestock Auction, where they enjoyed cheap coffee and marathon bull sessions. This bust was going to be on TV in Amarillo and Lubbock, maybe even in Dallas. This was going to put Tulia on the map.

The sky was turning from black to dark blue when the task force cars pulled up. A half dozen agents poured out. They were dressed all in black, like SWAT officers. They wore no badges, and their cars were unmarked. Their T-shirts simply read POLICE in big white block letters. Several of them carried assault rifles. Coleman was with them, and a few of the local officers recognized him: a scruffy, long-haired, unsavory-looking character they'd seen around town over the past year. He was the last person they'd have expected to be a cop, but then most of them had never met a real narc before. Coleman had on black as well, and he carried a black ski mask in his fist. On his belt was a pair of expensive-looking automatics. He shook hands with all of the local officers, accepting their congratulations. He didn't need any coffee; he was juiced and ready to go. This was the greatest day of his life.

Freddie Brookins Jr. woke up at dawn that morning, as he usually did, and started running his bath. He lived on the south side of Tulia, which was mostly black and Hispanic. His street was lined with small wood-frame houses, some with freshly painted porches and tidy yards, and others so weathered by the high plains sun and blowing dust that no trace of the original paint could be seen. He had no particular reason for rising so early; he had simply grown accustomed to getting up with the sun during the year he spent working in the country, just after graduating from high school. His father, Fred Sr., kept some hogs and a few calves on a piece of rented ranch property, and Freddie's job was to slop them down every morning and make sure they weren't getting into any trouble. The hogs, in turn, were supposed to be keeping Freddie out of trouble until he found a job of his own, or, as his father was quietly hoping, applied to college. Fred Sr. grew up on a farm, and he considered spending time in the country to be a wholesome influence on his kids. He still dressed like a farmer most of the time, in boots and blue jeans and a ball cap. Freddie's older siblings had spent time tending the animals when they were his age, and they all eventually settled down and found their own careers.

Freddie, on the other hand, was having trouble getting his feet on the ground. After a year or so out on the farm, he had convinced his dad to get him a job at Excel, the meatpacking plant in nearby Plainview where Fred Sr. worked as a line manager. Freddie was assigned to the processing line, where his job was to cut the bones out of a moving line of strip steaks, spending no more than ten seconds per steak. Most parents on the south side of town were pleased if their kids worked at all, but Fred wasn't crazy about his son starting a career at Excel. It was cold, it stank, and the odds of losing a finger or hand were higher than most people realized. It wasn't just that, however. Like most black Tulians his age, Fred Sr. grew up picking, pulling, and chopping cotton, and he wanted something better than manual labor for his son. Freddie didn't really have the disposition for the job anyway. He had a tendency to question authority—a trait he inherited from his dad—and there weren't many environments more heavily managed than a packing plant. After about a month on the job, he got into an altercation with a Mexican worker (Mexicans out-

numbered blacks about ten to one at the plant) and that was the end
of his career in meatpacking, supervisor in the family or no.

Now Freddie was unemployed. It was not an uncommon problem
on the south side of town, but Freddie was a Brookins, and everybody
knew that the Brookins worked. Even his grandfather, well into his
seventies, still got up every morning and put in his hours on the family farm. Freddie knew that if he didn't find something soon, it would
be back to slopping his father's hogs.

As he was stepping into his bath, Freddie saw a shadow move
across the bathroom window. "There's people in the yard!" his girlfriend Terry yelled from the bedroom. Freddie grabbed a sheet and
wrapped it around himself. Before he could get to the window he
heard a loud banging on the door. "Do you know who it is?" he asked
Terry. She shook her head. Freddie cracked the door open and saw
Sheriff Larry Stewart on his porch. Behind him were perhaps half a
dozen men with guns. Men in black with ski masks over their faces lay
prone in the yard, rifles pointed in his direction.

Freddie had grown up going to the same Church of Christ chapel
with Larry Stewart, where he'd listened to the tall, solemn-faced farmer
sing every Sunday. He hadn't said more than ten words to Stewart since
he'd become sheriff, and he had never particularly liked him—but
assault rifles at dawn? What did the man think he'd been up to?

"We have a warrant for your arrest, Freddie," Stewart said. He
slid a piece of paper through the screen door. "Delivery of a controlled substance," Freddie read. He was dumbfounded. His first
instinct was to shut the door.

"If you close the door, we'll have to shoot," Stewart warned. Freddie stepped out onto the porch, holding his sheet up with one hand
and the warrant in the other.

"Put your hands against the house!" one of the agents shouted. By
now the neighbors had come out up and down the street. Freddie
couldn't remove his hand from his waist.

"Freddie, I'm not going to tell you again," Stewart warned. Then somebody snatched the sheet off, and Freddie stood there buck naked on his front porch as they cuffed him and read him his rights. The agents began to pull him toward the car. Freddie recognized one of the Tulia cops, a man he knew as Big Otis. "Let me put some clothes on," Freddie pleaded. Otis intervened and took Freddie inside. Stewart and a half dozen cops followed. As Terry cowered in the living room, Freddie got dressed. He still had no idea what was going on.

"Larry, you've known me for years and you've never known me to sell drugs," Freddie said. Stewart's long-jowled face was like a rock. "Well, I don't know about that," he said.

"What do you mean you've never sold drugs?" one of the masked agents jeered. He stepped up close and put his gun near Freddie's head. With his other hand he pulled his mask up. It was Tom Coleman. "Recognize me now?" the man gloated. Freddie didn't.

"Take him to the car," Stewart said.

Joe Moore's house was still dark when the police arrived at 300 South Dallas Street that morning. It was not an impressive dwelling. The exterior walls were made of pocked brown stucco, repaired here and there with patches of white. The detached garage looked ready to fall over onto the rusty car parts and scrap metal strewn on either side of it. An uneven dirt yard was scarred by the hardened ruts of truck tires. The Tulia police had raided this house more than once, though the last time had been years ago. On this morning the jump-out boys left empty-handed; Coleman's prize catch was nowhere to be found.

Moore was out in the country at that hour, trying to make money the way respectable folks in Swisher County had done for a hundred years—by fattening up creatures with four legs and selling them to those with two. For the past ten years or so, Moore had run a modest hog and calf operation on a piece of land he rented from a white farmer about five miles outside of town. He started with no capital but plenty of ingenuity. He hustled cracked waste grain from Tulia's elevators and hauled off surplus milk from a local dairy to feed his first few sows. When he could scrape up enough money he'd buy a calf or two, more often than not some half-dead animal that a neighbor had all but given up on. Moore suckled them with a bottle by hand. The operation had been touch and go for years. On one occasion, when Moore was in the county jail, a fence blew down during a storm and his entire drove wandered off down the highway. A neighboring farmer rounded them up until Moore's girlfriend, Thelma Johnson, could come and collect them. Now he had over 200 hogs in his pens and the longtime labor of love was beginning to pay off.

Moore made his share of disreputable money over the years, chiefly through bootlegging. The local vice industry made Moore notorious but never rich, and he spent most of his time trying to stay out of jail, especially after the rumor spread that he was in the drug business as well. Though Moore was busted twice on minor cocaine charges over the years, Terry McEachern never managed to put him away for long, chiefly because he never caught him red-handed. It was not for lack of effort, however. For McEachern, and especially for Sheriff Stewart, Moore was the one that got away.

His past was waiting for him when he got back to town that morning. Moore parked his truck in the yard, oblivious to the pandemonium less than a quarter of a mile down the street at the small cluster of Tulia Housing Authority duplexes that housed several of Coleman's targets. Phones were ringing off the hook all over the south side of town by this point, but Moore didn't have a phone. He took off his muddy boots and settled down on the couch to wait for *The Price Is Right* to come on. Suddenly his neighbor's face darkened his screen door. "They're arresting all the black folks, Bootie!" she shouted through the screen. She was gone before he could ask what the hell she was talking about. It surely wasn't any of his people, he thought; most of them were already locked up. Thelma Johnson's son had just been arrested the month before. One of his own sons and his nephew were in prison. He figured he'd better go see who it was this time. If there was trouble, it would wind up in his lap before long anyway. A lot of people on Tulia's south side considered him a sort of godfather, and he was used to people bringing their problems to him. He would head downtown to see what was going on, he figured, and be back in time to watch his show.

Moore climbed into his old International Harvester pickup and headed for the county courthouse on the town square. As he pulled up, he saw a crowd on the lawn in front of the old brick jail on the north side of the courthouse. He could see camera crews and at least a dozen police and sheriff's patrol vehicles, more than he had ever seen in one place in the forty-odd years he had lived in Tulia. As he came to a stop in the courthouse parking lot, another patrol car whipped in behind him. Two officers barreled out, their guns drawn, and ordered him out of the truck and onto the ground. It took three sets of handcuffs linked together to get his wrists cuffed behind his enormous back. "You'll find out," the officers told him as he pleaded with them to tell him what he had done. As they entered the elevator to go up to the holding tank, someone shoved him in the back, sending him headlong into the rear wall of the car and raising a bump above his right eye that would never fully go away. They had the kingpin, at last.

Donnie Smith sat against the wall of the holding tank on the second floor of the Swisher County jail, watching in disbelief as the twenty- by thirty-foot cell filled up with his friends and relatives. Freddie Brookins Jr. was there, and Vincent McCray, and Benny Robinson, and more were coming in every few minutes. They had pretty well cleaned out the row of housing authority duplexes west of the tracks, where Donnie's ex-wife and kids lived. By 9:30 A.M., when Joe Moore shuffled in, the cell was getting crowded. Donnie was glad to see Moore. Although he had been arrested a couple of times for fighting, Donnie had never been accused of a felony. He wasn't sure what he was supposed to do. Moore's warrant had been the same as Donnie's: delivery of cocaine. But Moore didn't know any more than anybody else about what was going on; the warrant just said delivery, not when or to whom. Moore seemed to think Donnie would know. Everybody in the tank knew Donnie smoked crack, after all. "I didn't sell anything to anybody," Donnie kept repeating whenever a new person entered the tank. He hadn't smoked any for months, he told Moore, not since he'd come back from rehab in Lubbock the previous winter.

The irony of his arrest was killing him. He had been so strung out the previous fall, his mother had been afraid for his life. Now, after six months on the wagon, he had found steady work with a farmer. He was lifting weights regularly, trying to get back the compact, powerful physique he had been so proud of in high school. After spending most of the past five years trying to stay high, knowing he could have been busted by Sheriff Stewart at any time, he found he enjoyed being behind the wheel of a tractor again, making money, taking care of himself. Now here he was, stone cold sober, sitting in a jail cell.

By 10:30 there were roughly twenty men in the cell, almost all of them black. Cleveland Joe Henderson showed up wearing nothing but his pajama bottoms, his hair a wild shock of uncombed Afro. Donnie had never seen the skinny, soft-spoken Henderson without his neat Snoop Dogg–style ponytails and tiny rimless shades. Baby James Barrow, Donnie's best friend in high school, was there. All the guys Donnie used to party with were there. Timmy Towery. Chris Jackson. Jason Fry. Troy Benard. Jason Williams. Mandrell Henry. And there were men from the older (and bigger) generation too. Donnie's cousin Kenneth Powell and uncle Willie Hall—Big Tank and Big Bucket, respectively—were there. By the time 300-pound Billy Wafer, sweating and swearing, joined the mix, it was getting hot and hard to breathe in the tank, with no air conditioning.

They even got crazy old Leroy Barrow, who lived in a trailer without electricity or running water out behind the Housing Authority duplexes in the Flats. Donnie would see the old man setting out every morning on his daily search for aluminum cans, muttering to himself. Barrow's chronically unemployed younger brother Adolphus sometimes joined him. Big Brother and Little Brother they called them. The Barrows were one of the largest families in Tulia, and Leroy was not the only member considered to be a little "throwed off," as Donnie put it. The idea of Big Brother selling dope was ridiculous, however, and Baby James was just an addict, same as he was. Donnie knew just about everybody in town who smoked crack. He'd partied with them all over the years, and some of them were in the tank with him now. But as far as dealers went, Donnie knew only four or five people who really fit that description, and even they were small-time hoods, mostly playing at being gangsters. You had to go to Plainview or Amarillo to find a real dealer, and Donnie knew a few of those too. Guys like Freddie Brookins Jr. and Vincent McCray and Billy Wafer were working people. They always had jobs. Something was seriously fucked up about this.

They had all morning to speculate about who the narc was. Both Freddie Brookins Jr. and Billy Wafer had seen the man at their houses that morning, but neither had recognized him. Wafer got a good long look at him as he tossed his house looking for drugs. Nothing was found. In fact, nobody had been caught holding anything.

The mystery deepened around noon, when the sheriff came up to the second floor accompanied by an officer dressed in black. The man wore a ponytail and a red goatee, and he had a pale, puffy face. He stepped up to the bars. "How ya'll doin'?" he gloated. He was smiling. "Bet you didn't expect to see me here."

For a moment, a perplexed silence filled the tank. Then Donnie spoke up. "Shit, that's T.J.," he said. Stewart and Coleman moved on past the tank. Everybody started talking at once. Now they remembered him, a skinny guy in a black leather jacket who called himself

T.J. Dawson and claimed to be a construction contractor living ten miles up the interstate in a little hamlet called Happy. He could usually be found hanging around the cattle auction in Tulia on Monday mornings, when Donnie and a host of other day laborers showed up to work at the weekly sale, or cruising around town in a little black truck with an older black man he had befriended, a well-known alcoholic named Man Kelly. Some had met T.J., but many had only seen him here and there, hanging around with Kelly. There had been rumors from the very beginning that T.J. was a narc. "I told you that man was nuthin' but the law," Joe Moore said. Donnie remembered the rumors about T.J. but was still incredulous. "I smoked rock with that man," Donnie told them. Four or five others in the tank said they had done the same. How could he be a cop? "I sat in his truck and blew *smoke* with the man," Donnie marveled. He had been so positive the guy was an addict.

On his way out Coleman passed the tank again. "You niggers quit sellin' them drugs!" they heard him yell before he passed out of range. Everybody exploded at once, Donnie loudest of all. "Man, fuck you!" he yelled. He kicked the metal door as hard as he could, but Coleman was already gone.

CHAPTER TWO

The Richest Land
and the Finest People

IN 1890 WORD came to the fledgling town of Tulia that a party of Comanches was on the warpath in the Texas panhandle. It was an unlikely story, since the last of the hostile Texas Indians had been famously routed in 1874. The decisive battle took place about thirty miles northeast of Tulia in Palo Duro Canyon, where a U.S. Cavalry colonel named Ranald S. MacKenzie ambushed a group of 600 fugitives from the Oklahoma reservations. Most of the Indians escaped, but MacKenzie got what he was after: their enormous cache of horses. Without them the plains Indians were no threat to anyone. MacKenzie drove the herd back to his camp and selected the best 450 animals for his own men. The remaining 1,500 he ordered shot. Tulia, like each of the hamlets that popped up in the newly secured country, owed its birth to that ruthless act.

According to *Swisher County History*, a collection of anecdotes, early public records, and pioneer testimonials set down by a local historian in 1968, the rumor of the returning Comanches was brought to town by a drunken stagecoach driver from the nearby JA Ranch, the first and most storied of the giant panhandle cattle ranches. The cowboys of the JA may have been playing a joke on the newcomers, the small farmers they derisively called "nesters," whose settlements they correctly perceived as the beginning of the end of the open range. If so, it worked better than anybody could have anticipated. The news was met with hysteria in Tulia. Few of the nesters had ever seen an Indian, but they had heard the stories: children kidnapped, men murdered, crops burned. Settlers flocked to town from nearby farms, bringing nothing but their children and their guns. They dug trenches around the courthouse and the White Hotel, the only substantial buildings in town. Wood was hauled from the canyon to build ramparts. For two nights Tulia remained holed up, waiting for the pounding hooves and war whoops that never came.

Tulians tend to understand this well-worn tale not so much as a parable about fear of the unknown as a testament to the hardiness of their forebears. In the face of trouble, after all, their ancestors didn't run. They chose to stay and fight, however illusory the enemy may have turned out to be. Tulians are fiercely proud of their town's history. This may be in part because there is so little of it—the panhandle region was one of the last places in Texas to be settled by whites—or it may be due to the fact that Swisher County was carved out of the prairie by the present generation's own pioneer parents and grandparents, not some distant ancestors. What William Faulkner said of the Old South—the past isn't forgotten here, in fact, it isn't even past—is quite literally true in this county, where a few gray members of the first generation born in Swisher County are still marking time at the Tulia Health and Rehabilitation nursing home on South Austin Road.

The original settlers of Swisher County were uncommonly hardy people. Tulia sits atop an arid and windswept plateau known locally as the Llano Estacado, which forms the southern tip of the High Plains. The uncannily flat plateau, with an elevation of about 3,000 feet, ends about fifty miles east of Tulia, where the landscape drops abruptly down through rocky canyons that were all but impassable to nineteenth-century travelers. Decades after the great westward migration had reached the Pacific Ocean, this pocket of the West, which some maps still referred to as the Great American Desert, remained unsettled. The 1870 Census counted not a single citizen in a fifty-four-county swath of the Texas panhandle, an area the size of Connecticut, Maryland, Massachusetts, New Jersey, Vermont, New Hampshire, and Washington, D.C., combined. The state of Texas couldn't give the land away. The legislature eventually traded a huge portion of it—3 million acres, the better part of ten counties—to a Chicago engineering firm in exchange for the construction of the state capitol in Austin. A group of English investors ended up with the land, which became the famous XIT ranch. Few in the legislature even knew what they had given away; the XIT was as close to Denver as it was to Austin.

Even after the U.S. Army removed the Indians, settlers were slow to arrive in a land where houses had to be built of sod, streams often dried up or were too salty to drink, and almost nothing edible grew naturally. There was so little wood that cattle or bison chips were the most commonly used fuel. The settlers referred to them by grade: "round browns" burned longest and hottest, "white flats" were the worst. It was a hardscrabble existence for those who did try to make a go of it. The High Plains are bitterly cold in the winter, brutally hot in the summer. Shade is not a natural occurrence except along the river breaks; the earliest settlers had to plant saplings and wait. Every spring brings vicious thunderstorms with tornadoes and hail, and the wind is a constant presence year round, pounding dust into anything unfortunate enough to obstruct the perfect flatness of the plains. Even today, after a particularly bad dust storm, panhandle residents have reported finding dust inside their refrigerators. Still, there is a stark beauty to the High Plains, with its impossibly huge blue skies and sweeping vistas of nothing at all. The first settlers found fields of tall prairie grass dotted with herds of antelope, along with the coyotes and wolves that preyed on them. The pristine canyons were inhabited by bears and mountain lions. "If we only had water," an early cattleman once said, "this country would be a paradise." His foreman is said to have responded: "So would hell."

The frontier was rapidly closing by the late 1870s. The panhandle was one of the last places a man could bring his family for a chance at the old republican ideal of land ownership and self-sufficiency, a place where a man could start anew, no longer, as one early Swisher County brochure put it, "fettered with landlord's chains nor 'Shylock's' mortgages." Still, most of the earliest settlers were already too late when they arrived. The great cattle barons, many of them financed by eastern or British capital, had laid claim to huge expanses of the best acreage. Because the land was so dry and unproductive, only well-capitalized operations could accumulate enough land to raise a large herd. The small operators had to eke out a living on the margins, and few chose to try. The "Longhorn lords" considered anybody not working for them to be working against them, especially the Mexican traders and the small ranchers who made their living at least partly through "mavericking," appropriating unbranded cattle and calves from around the edges of the big herds. The small hamlets with their plowed fields, few and far between as they were, also threatened the economy of the open range. The Panhandle Cattlemen's Association, the closest thing the area had to a governing body, hired mercenaries to keep the newcomers in line. Thugs laid barbed wire fences between the nesters' towns and nearby roads. The farmers responded by shooting the cattlemen's fence riders off their horses. Things got so heated that the Texas legislature called a special session in 1884 to head off the class war on the range.

Life on the High Plains was about sacrifice, and it was not for everyone. Many simply gave up and went back to the world they knew. In the long war of attrition against cattlemen, wind, drought, prairie fires, and the endless armies of jackrabbits and grasshoppers, the families that remained, no matter how lonely and isolated they may have been from one another, came to depend on each other in a way no one from the city could understand. They pooled their labor at harvest time and bargained collectively with middlemen for seed and services. They printed newspapers with names like *The Stayer.* They scratched a civilization out of the dirt.

In the end, their sacrifice was rewarded. The era of the cattle kings, source of so much of the mythology of modern Texas, was a short one. By 1890, when Swisher County was officially organized, much of the open range had been fenced off, and the railroads had reached the panhandle, making the long cattle drives unnecessary. The coming of the railroads also meant that the new towns of the panhandle would not fade away. A 1909 brochure promoting Swisher County celebrated the victory of the stayers:

> It was organized in 1890, by a handful of pioneer "nesters," who, battling against great odds, with the "plow and the hoe" as their only munitions of war, began a march of invasion into a country, which had hitherto been the cattle king's dominion, each year picking up a new recruit here and a new recruit there, waging their relentless war of conquest with such vigor and determination that the "Longhorn Lord" has been completely vanquished and the virgin soil is now smiling beneath a bountiful yield of golden grain and other abundant crops for which nature intended her.

Such brochures, distributed by the railroad companies and others hoping to cash in on the real estate boom that hit so many frontier towns, were known for their hyperbole. But in this case the good news about Swisher County was true. What seemed like barren land—with only twenty inches of rain a year—was situated in the middle of what came to be known as the shallow water belt of the Ogallala aquifer, the giant underground lake that underlies much of the Great Plains. Anybody with the money for a well and a windmill could tap seemingly inexhaustible quantities of pure, fresh water at depths as shallow as twenty feet.

Tulia and the villages surrounding it slowly grew as families trickled in, drawn by the promise of cheap land. Many of them came from central Texas or southern states, including a few Civil War veterans. Others came from as far away as the Upper Midwest, and the flavor of the new communities was by no means exclusively southern. A clan of Republicans from Indiana settled northeast of Tulia. They named their town Vigo Park, after the Indiana community they had left behind. A group of German Catholic immigrants landed twenty miles west of Tulia and built a community they called Nazareth. Amarillo to the north and Lubbock in the south emerged as the commercial centers of the panhandle, though the combined population of both was still less than 100,000 by the 1930s, when things took a drastic turn for the worse. Woody Guthrie was living in the panhandle town of Pampa on April 14, 1935, the day the mother of all dust storms swept down from Oklahoma and smothered the Texas panhandle. "It fell across our city like a curtain of black rolled down/We thought it was our judgment, we thought it was our doom," he later wrote. Cars were completely buried. Thousands of farm animals were lost. Mothers covered their babies' cribs with wet blankets, but many infants and old people died of "dust pneumonia." "Black Sunday," as it came to be known, was the worst of a never-ending series of devastating dust storms, the culmination of years of drought and soil loss caused by overgrazing and overplanting on the Great Plains.

Guthrie didn't stick around to see if the area would recover, and neither did hundreds of other plainsmen, who joined the flood of refugees passing through Texas on their way to California. His ballad "So Long, It's Been Good to Know Yuh" summed up the feeling of many about their brief experiment with life in the Texas panhandle. Dorothea Lange's 1938 photo of a migrant woman stranded near the panhandle town of Childress, holding herself with one arm and shading the west Texas sun with the other, became one of the best known documents of this bitter period. Less well known is the woman's commentary, recorded by Lange, on the plainsmen she found herself thrown in with: "You can't get no relief here until you've lived here a year. This county's a hard county. They won't help bury you here. If you die, you're dead, that's all." After years of dust, drought, and the specter of starvation, the people of the panhandle had nothing left to give.

Swisher County embraced the New Deal, though you wouldn't know it from a visit to the Swisher County Museum. The New Deal is a sort of dirty secret in the modern panhandle, which became the nation's leading bastion of anticommunism in the 1950s and is still one of the most politically conservative regions in the country. But in the 1930s, things were different. Roosevelt's programs didn't really do much for farmers, but Dust Bowlers appreciated what he had to say about America's duty to the downtrodden. Swisher County went for FDR in 1932 in a landslide, 1,448 to 166. The next year county voters endorsed the state's sale of bonds for relief of unemployment, 670 to 173. (Since Texas was one of the few states in the union to explicitly cap welfare funding in the state constitution, sale of the bonds required a constitutional amendment approved by the voters.)

As the regional economy recovered in the war years, the panhandle began its hard swerve to the right, led by Amarillo. The city was undergoing a war boom, fueled by the construction of an airbase and a major munitions plant. Oil and gas had also been discovered in the panhandle, which brought an influx of new money and new people to Amarillo. Texas had been a one-party state since the Civil War, but the upheaval in the Democratic Party over civil rights and the perceived radicalism of northern "race liberals" was causing more and more Texans to begin voting Republican, at least in nationwide races. Amarillo Republicans proudly proclaimed themselves the vanguard of this shift. They were not Rockefeller Republicans, however—their creed was a new mix of fiscal conservativism, anticommunism, and fundamentalist religious fervor. In 1964, Amarillo was one of a handful of Texas cities to favor Barry Goldwater over the state's native son, Lyndon Johnson. After thoroughly trouncing Goldwater, who most Americans felt to be dangerously out of the mainstream, LBJ turned his unkind attention on Amarillo, which lost its airbase in very short order. (This is the back story to how the city came to own a municipal airport with one of the longest runways in the country.)

The bomb factory eventually evolved into Pantex, the final assembly point for the nation's nuclear arsenal. Embracing Pantex made Amarillo ground zero in the Cold War, which began to color almost every aspect of life there. The city became the breeding ground for a particularly virulent strain of American nativism, in which the chief bugaboos were Catholics, Jews, communists, and liberals. Local adherents of the ultrapatriotic John Birch Society, elsewhere a secretive and controversial group, wore their membership as a badge of honor in Amarillo; even politicians bragged of membership in campaign literature. Amarillo cemented its nationwide reputation as one of the most conservative places in America. At the height of the counterculture, when Route 66 was bringing hundreds of longhaired hippies and would-be hippies through town every month, the sheriff's office installed an authentic barber's chair in the Amarillo jail. "For a good while," the *Texas Observer* reported in 1970, "business there, if not the skill and care in grooming, was about as steady as a country barber shop's."

Led by Amarillo's defection, more and more of the panhandle jumped the fence to vote Republican. Swisher County, however, has always demonstrated an independent streak. For a generation after FDR, New Deal–style populists like Ralph Yarborough, the icon of old-time Texas liberals, fared significantly better in Swisher County than in other parts of the panhandle. In the 1957 special election for U.S. Senate, Swisher County went for Yarborough by almost 5 to 1 over Texas Congressman Martin Dies, the anticommunist crusader who led the House Un-American Activities Committee in the 1940s. Well into the 1970s, Swisher County remained the hole in the donut of panhandle voting patterns. In recent years, as the Republicans have consolidated their control over much of rural Texas, the Democrats have retained a tenuous hold on Swisher County.

Most Democrats credited one man for the enigma of Swisher County voting: H. M. Baggarly, Tulia's legendary newspaperman. Baggarly, who edited the *Tulia Herald* for nearly thirty years beginning in 1950, was the quintessential crusading country editor. Like many of his generation, he saw politics through the lens of the Great Depression and the government intervention that ended it. But Baggarly was more articulate than most and he clung to his New Deal convictions long after they became anathema in much of the panhandle. Baggarly was a deeply religious man, but what he lived for was politics. His weekly column took on what he called the Shivercrats, those Democrats who, like Governor Alan Shivers, secretly—or not so secretly—supported Republicans in national elections. Tulians' main source of news prior to Baggarly's taking over the *Herald* were the reactionary papers in Amarillo and Lubbock. Baggarly went head-to-head with *Amarillo Daily News* columnist Wes Izzard, whom he called "the Izzard of Was" for his backward-looking politics. On the visit of a prominent John Bircher to Amarillo, Baggarly wrote:

> We don't mean to be sacrilegious when we say that the Second Coming of Jesus could not hope to receive the publicity that the Amarillo papers, radio and television gave the visit of former Major General Edwin Walker to Amarillo.

Baggarly was controversial. Author J. Evetts Haley Jr., perhaps the panhandle's most prominent conservative voice, called him "one of the most . . . radical left-wingers in West Texas." That was far from true. But his advocacy for government programs like social security and his cautious support for civil rights cut against the grain in the panhandle. In the winter of 1958 an unknown party paid to have anti-Baggarly brochures mailed to almost every resident of Swisher County. The brochures singled out Baggarly's support of the Supreme Court's ruling on school desegregation. "Baggarlism is Colorism," the mailing warned. Baggarly didn't back down, and the farmers and ranchers of Swisher County, whether they agreed with him or not, came to love him for it. Baggarly became Tulia's first celebrity. His columns were read at the capitol in Austin and even in Washington, where LBJ offered Baggarly a job on his staff. But Baggarly would never leave his home; he loved Tulia too much.

And Tulia loved itself, particularly during Baggarly's reign, which coincided with Swisher County's heyday. In the postwar boom, millions more Americans could afford to eat beef on a regular basis. There was a great demand for grains such as milo to feed cattle at the big new feedlots in Colorado, Arizona, and California. Swisher County farmers began sinking irrigation wells outfitted with pumps powered by the natural gas that was so cheap and abundant in west Texas. The number of wells in the panhandle went from just 3,500 in 1945 to nearly 50,000 in 1960. Federal crop controls brought sustained high prices for wheat and other grains for the first time to the Great Plains. By the mid-1950s the panhandle was planted from corner to corner in wheat and milo, and they were calling it the "golden spread." Cotton planters were also thriving. Eventually feedlot operators began building lots in the panhandle, since much of the feed was coming from there anyway. The big slaughterhouses were not far behind, and Texas's last good cattle boom was on.

Swisher County was right in the middle of it. By the late 1950s, Swisher was one of the state's leading counties in grain harvested and cattle fed. The Tulia Livestock Auction became one of the highest volume cattle auctions in the state. Flush with cash, farmers were trading in their trucks for new models every year or two. You could buy anything you needed on the square in Tulia, and downtown was bustling every weekend. The annual Swisher County Picnic and Old Settler's Reunion featured a long parade of modern tractors and shiny new combines. For a kid coming out of Tulia High School in 1960, there were plenty of options for work on or off the farm, and the future was bright.

In the mid-1960s, however, farmers in the eastern part of the county started noticing a disturbing trend. Their wells had begun to produce less and less water, and they found themselves drilling deeper and deeper into the aquifer to sustain the irrigation levels—and the profits—they had grown accustomed to. By the end of the 1970s, what was once unthinkable could no longer be denied: mined to its limits through the boom years, the Ogallala aquifer was finally beginning to fail Swisher County. When the water began to go, more and more operators had to switch back to the kind of dryland farming their ancestors practiced—plow, sow, and pray for rain. With no irrigation, one bad year of drought was all it took to break many of the county's small farms. Rising prices—first for fuel and then for everything else—did in others, until the number of profitable farms was winnowed down to a few dozen large operations owned by prosperous families.

Tulia used to be surrounded by a constellation of tiny communities, little farming villages with their own elementary schools and post offices. These were the first to go as the money began to dry up. The final nail in the coffin was the Conservation Reserve Program (CRP). In the mid-1980s, the federal government started paying landowners to put farmed land back into pasture. A farmer could earn $40 per acre per year just for planting grass. No cattle grazing was allowed, and no hay cutting—the field had to be left alone. The idea was to boost grain prices by taking less efficient land out of production while preserving topsoil and cutting down on dust storms at the same time.

Many saw it as a sop to farmers—getting paid to grow nothing but weeds—but most farmers were not eligible to receive the payments because they did not own the land they farmed. In Swisher County, for example, about four out of five farmers, or operators as they are called, are sharecroppers or renters. To them, a section in CRP simply meant one less opportunity to earn money. The program became very popular with landowners, however, and eventually about a third of the farmland in Swisher County wound up in CRP.

Less land in production meant less of everything in Tulia. Working farms need diesel for irrigation pumps, seeds for crops, tires for tractors, insurance, loans, and tax advice; they keep money flowing through every part of a town's economy. Working farms also need labor. Farming's reliance on hired labor was already on the way out by the 1980s, thanks to bigger and better equipment, genetically modified crops, and heavier use of chemicals. The CRP program ensured it would never come back. "Used to be people could get on the end of a cotton hoe and earn enough to eat," one farmer said. "Now black kids in Tulia don't do that. They sit and watch color TV all day, even the poor people," he said.

By the early 1990s, the roads into Tulia were lined with derelict warehouses and empty storefronts, their windows covered with dust. With its abandoned railway sidings, empty grain elevators, and fields filled with rusting farm equipment, the town began to feel like a museum of the High Plains. The town square was largely deserted most weekends. The courthouse, once a prime example of turn-of-the-century Texas Renaissance architecture, had been the victim of an early 1960s renovation which removed the handsome dome and encased the entire structure in a veneer of featureless pink brick, accented by drab red panels and white vertical window blinds. The movie theater was closed, and most of the stores were gone. People did their shopping up the highway at the mall in Amarillo or the Wal-Mart in Plainview, twenty-five miles south of town. "One business would go, then another," Jeff Bivens, a third-generation Tulian, recalled. "We're down to one truck dealership; we used to have six. Down to one store, we used to have seven. Only one grain dealer left, used to have six or seven," he said. Bivens's grandfather was one of the original settlers of Swisher County, and at one time his descendants could be found all over the county. Over the years, Bivens watched them sell out, one by one, and leave town, until he was the last of his kin in the area. A thin, wispy man with a soft voice, Bivens lived alone on the northern edge of town in a trailer home with a large complex of horse stables behind it. Long past the age of retirement, he earned his living by doing custom welding and raising horses. "This'll be a bedroom town before long," he predicted. "Wal-Mart will run it the way they do the whole country, I guarantee you."

The ascendancy of Wal-Mart was a common topic of conversation at the Tulia Trading Post, another holdout of sorts a mile or so down the highway from Bivens's place. Trading Post owner Louie Edwards, who had a wry smile and a quick wit, was in his mid-eighties. He stocked steel, lumber, hardware, and just about anything else a farmer or rancher might need, selling merchandise without the benefit of price tags and making change out of an old manual cash register, just as he had since 1951. Edwards had never set foot in a Wal-Mart, though he had lost a few customers to the store in Plainview. If it had been any closer to Tulia, he probably would have gone out of business long ago. Even absent direct competition, however, the Trading Post was threatened by the high-volume business model that Wal-Mart had created. As an example, Edwards pointed to a collection of power tools resting on a dusty shelf in the Trading Post's dimly lit interior. He had sold thousands of dollars worth of Makita drills and parts over the years, he explained. Then one day the Makita rep told him he had to start ordering at least $1,000 worth of power tools and $500 worth of parts at a time—a fraction of what Wal-Mart's giant distribution centers ordered every day—to make it worth their while to keep him as a customer. "My last order was for $200 worth of parts," Edwards said. "They didn't even answer it."

The former hoe hands were on food stamps, the landowners were getting their CRP checks, and the operators were getting subsidized loans and guaranteed prices at market. Everyone in Swisher County, it seemed, was on one kind of government program or another. After a generation of promise, life in Swisher County was back to what it had always been about—getting by. More and more folks simply weren't. Bankruptcy, divorce, and alcoholism became common threads of life in the county, as they did across the Midwest. Despite the boastful slogan on the Highway 87 billboard that welcomed people to Tulia—"The Richest Land and the Finest People"—the place that had once produced America's most famous country editor retained few traces of its former charm. After Baggarly died in 1985, the *Tulia Herald* declined steadily along with the town. Now edited by a man who was more stenographer than philosopher, the paper contained scarcely any original news. Even the memory of Baggarly's greatness seemed to have faded. "I think he was a little bit queer," was all one old farmer had to say about Tulia's most famous citizen, who remained a bachelor until his death.

Some in Tulia dealt with the decline better than others. In 1993, a handful of bankrupt Swisher County farmers were indicted for filing millions of dollars worth of false liens against the judges who had presided over their foreclosure proceedings. The men were acting on the fraudulent advice of a Colorado-based organization called We the People. A financial scam masquerading as a social movement, the group was founded on the theory that the United States government went bankrupt long ago and therefore lacked the authority to enforce debt collection. The scam spread across the nation's heartland, until the FBI decided to come down hard on the group's disciples.

Sheriff Stewart's brother-in-law Jerry Herndon was one of those indicted. In the 1970s, Herndon was a local organizer for the Ameri-

can Agriculture Movement, the radical farmers' group best known for
its tractorcades in Washington, D.C., where they protested national
agricultural policies. Herndon, a soft-spoken man with gray-tinted
trifocal glasses, lived about a mile from the interstate in a modest
ranch house surrounded by hundreds of acres of pasture overgrown
with weeds. He was still proud of his activism on behalf of farmers, he
said. He narrowly avoided a prison sentence in the We the People
scam, however, and he kept a low profile around Tulia in the years
that followed. Still, he never gave up on getting his land back. On the
chrome bumper of his van, the reclusive old farmer had spelled out
the phrase "NESARA NOW" in black letters of the type used to put
names and numbers on mailboxes. The acronym referred to the
National Economic Security and Recovery Act, which Herndon
believed was a law that Congress had passed secretly. The Supreme
Court was withholding implementation, he explained, until the country returned to what he called a constitutional government and went
back on a hard currency standard. "It could really help this country
out," Herndon said.

The NESARA myth, explained in detail on Fourwinds10.com, a
website Herndon recommended, was a fantasy tailored to the ruined
dreams of thousands of American farmers. When the time is right,
the site explains, the law will be put into effect: all debts will be forgiven, including credit cards, mortgages, car loans, education loans,
and home equity loans. The entire executive branch will be forced to
resign and the IRS will fold. The worldwide banking system will be
overhauled and new currency issued, which will reprice all goods and
reverse decades of inflation. The website also features a collection of
writings from a crystal-worshiping religion, apparently of extraterres-
trial origin. A photo of a silvery UFO called a "cloud ship" appears on
the homepage.

Tulians of a certain generation seemed to view the flap over the
drug bust—which put Tulia in the national spotlight for all the wrong

reasons—as yet another test of their faith, like dust storms or Wal-Mart or farm foreclosures or the FBI. Billie Sue Gayler, who ran the Swisher County Archives and Museum, was once asked by one of the dozens of reporters who filed Tulia stories in the years after the bust how the townsfolk were holding up. She answered, "Those of us who have pioneer blood in us will survive."

CHAPTER THREE

Bootie's Empire

SHOULD HAVE gotten another lawyer. That's what Joe Moore woke up thinking on December 15, 1999, the morning of his trial. Shortly after he was arrested in Tulia, they moved him to Plainview, where he sat in jail, unable to make his enormous bond, for almost five months. During that time he saw his court-appointed attorney, Kregg Hukill, exactly twice. The first time was in August, shortly after Hukill was appointed. A sole practitioner from Olton, a small town twenty miles west of Plainview, Hukill was a short, slender man in his mid-thirties with thinning hair. He was a country lawyer, which meant he did a little of everything for his small town clients. He supplemented that income by regularly putting his name in the hat for indigent defense cases in Plainview and Tulia. It wasn't much money—he usually earned less than $500 per case—but then it wasn't much work, either. Indigent defendants virtually always plead out; trials were for folks who could afford them. Since Hukill wasn't exactly at the top of the list for high rollers in trouble in that part of the state, he didn't see many trials.

But a trial was exactly what Joe Moore wanted. Moore was accused of two deliveries: a single gram of crack cocaine on August 24, 1998, and an eight ball of powder on October 9, 1998. The powder case would be tried first. An eight ball is an eighth of an ounce of cocaine, or about 3.5 grams—not much more than a thimbleful. It is just enough cocaine to qualify as a second-degree felony, punishable by 2 to 20 years in prison. The problem, Moore told Hukill at their first meeting, was that he hadn't made either delivery. Coleman had, as he claimed, come by Moore's house. Man Kelly was in the truck with him. But Moore ran them off, he said, and Coleman did not return. "Ask Man," Moore told Hukill. "Man saw the whole thing." And Moore wasn't the only one in this predicament, he explained. Coleman had lied about other cases too. Make some calls, Moore pleaded with him. Check it out—the man was a liar.

Moore had a feeling that Hukill didn't believe his story, and it was hard to blame him. After all, Moore had two prior drug felonies on his record. Under Texas law, that meant McEachern could hit him with a double enhancement—the "Big Bitch," as defense attorneys deferentially called it. Instead of 2 to 20, the standard range for a second-degree felony, Moore would be looking at a *minimum* sentence of twenty-five years in the pen, and a maximum of ninety-nine. Hukill told Moore he would do his best to persuade McEachern to offer a deal for the minimum. If he played his cards right—and got a lucky break in front of the parole board (which, for a three-time offender, was unlikely)—Moore might make it home in as little as six years. Hukill's job, as he saw it, was to avoid a trial at all costs. Pleading "not guilty" was a bad way to start. Moore didn't have an alibi. He lived alone and didn't work a 9 to 5 job with a time clock. It was true that the case was a little light on evidence, especially for a controlled buy, where the cops took great pains to set somebody up and the case was normally a slam dunk. The DA usually had audio or video evidence of the deal, bills with recorded serial numbers, maybe a second officer to corroborate that the narc met with the defendant when he said he did. McEachern had none of that this time around. All he had was Coleman and a little—very little—baggie of cocaine.

But that didn't mean the case was weak. On the contrary. An eight ball wasn't much, but it was enough to get the job done. It was Moore's word against the word of a cop, in front of a panhandle jury. If the case went to trial, it was in God's hands, as far as Hukill was concerned. There wasn't a whole hell of a lot he could do, and he told Moore as much.

After a couple of months of Hukill's failing to return his phone calls, Moore was desperate. He wrote to the judge in the case, district judge Ed Self, asking for another attorney. He never heard back. When Hukill finally contacted Moore again, it was to tell him that his case was set for trial—in six days' time. Six days! Had he interviewed Man Kelly? Moore asked. What had he found out about Coleman? The answer was no, and nothing. Hukill had filed all the standard pretrial motions, but he had not asked the judge for an investigator, nor had he examined the other cases made by Coleman in Tulia.

The next day, perhaps stung by his client's lack of gratitude, Hukill filed a motion to suppress Coleman's identification of Moore. As a result, Moore, Hukill, McEachern, and Coleman appeared before Judge Self for a pretrial hearing, just two days before Moore's trial was set to begin. It was a shot in the dark, and desperately late in the game, but at least it would give Hukill a chance to see the state's star witness in action. Coleman did not cut an impressive figure in court. He was working on another undercover assignment in the Houston area, and he wore the same scraggly goatee and ponytail. Hukill began by holding up one of Coleman's reports on Moore. It was just three pages long, with a narrative of the delivery that was scarcely more than a paragraph and provided virtually no details of the transaction. Moore was described only as a black male, and the report did not explain how Coleman had identified him.

Did Coleman keep any handwritten notes, a daily log, or a diary of his transactions, Hukill asked? "No, sir," Coleman replied.

"This three-page report would be all there is?" Hukill asked.

The question seemed straightforward and relatively benign, but Coleman appeared to be confused. "Okay. All there is?" he hedged. Then, as though afraid of giving the wrong answer to a trick question, Coleman began to cautiously expound on his first answer.

"Okay. From my little notes that I wrote is—it wasn't like official notes," he said. "I wrote stuff on my leg, I wrote stuff on my arm, from memory, and I wrote stuff on little pieces of cigarette packs because I had subjects in my vehicle all the time," he said.

Notes on his leg? If Hukill was taken aback by this unexpected reply, he did not show it. "Are any of those notes still available?" he asked.

"Sir?"

"Are any of those notes still available?" Hukill repeated.

"No, sir, I took a bath since then," Coleman replied.

Later Coleman seemed confused about whether or not Man Kelly was present on the first occasion he reported buying cocaine from Moore, on August 24, 1998. This was the crack charge. Coleman testified he was certain that Kelly was in the truck that day; that was how he gained Moore's confidence. According to Coleman, his friendship with Kelly, who was oblivious to Coleman's true identity and purpose, was how he infiltrated Tulia's black drug community. He plied Kelly, a well-known alcoholic, with booze, and Kelly helped him get access to cocaine dealers. When Hukill referred Coleman to his report on the crack deal, which did not mention Kelly, Coleman gave a disturbing answer. "Hang on just a second," he began. "Okay. Yes, Eliga Kelly did go with me that day, because he was sitting in the truck," he said. "That's the reason [Moore] talked to me. But I didn't put it in my report because if I had put that in the report, he would have to be a witness. I remember that."

A witness would be a significant detail to omit from a report, particularly in a case with no corroborating evidence. Coleman seemed to suggest he had done it on purpose, for reasons that were not immediately clear. Yet Hukill did not follow up, instead moving quickly on to the next report. He seemed to be in a hurry to get the hearing completed.

A bit later, however, Hukill asked Coleman another fairly routine question and got another unexpected answer. Had Coleman, in the past five years, been the subject of any internal investigation by the task force or any other law enforcement employer?

"Yes, sir," Coleman replied.

There followed this exchange:

"When was that?"

"When was it?"

"Yes, sir. When was it opened?"

"I don't remember."

"Where?"

"In May, probably."

"In May?"

"I believe so."

"Of this year?"

"Yes, sir. No, '98."

"Okay. When was it closed, or is it closed?"

"Five days after it was opened."

"And what was the—what was the outcome?"

"Unfounded."

"What was the subject matter?"

"Theft."

Hukill looked at McEachern. Coleman was saying that he had been investigated for theft in May 1998, *during* his undercover investigation in Tulia. Nothing was ever turned over to Hukill in discovery about any investigation of Coleman, though records pertaining to the criminal history of the state's witnesses was a standard request he always made for his clients. McEachern had simply said that all of his witnesses were police officers, and therefore none of them had crimi-

nal histories. Again, Hukill seemed to be in a hurry. Though McEachern had made no objection to the line of questioning, he let the matter drop, without asking Coleman for any details on the matter.

That night Hukill came to visit Moore at the jail. McEachern had
called Hukill into his office after the hearing and made him an offer:
twenty-five years in exchange for a guilty plea. It was the minimum
sentence, and Hukill urged Moore to take it. Even if he wanted to follow up on Coleman's admittedly intriguing testimony that day, there
was no time to do the legwork. The judge had made it clear no continuances would be granted. If Moore didn't take the plea, he was going
to trial in two days, with no investigator and no defense witnesses.

This wasn't what Moore wanted to hear. He had tried once again
to fire Hukill in court that day, but the judge refused to assign him
another court-appointed attorney. Self did allow that Moore could
hire his own attorney, if he had the means to do so. But Moore didn't.
If he had money, he thought to himself, he wouldn't have been in the
Plainview jail for five months, waiting for Hukill to drop by. He
wouldn't have been sitting there right now, he thought, listening to
this man advising him, at fifty-seven years of age, to take a twenty-
five-year plea bargain. "I'm not takin' it," he said.

One thing Joe Moore had never been too good at was dealing
with white people. He had done it, of course, all of his life. Sheriffs,
judges, and court-appointed attorneys. Farmers, ranchers, and fore-
men. Landlords, doctors, and car dealers. He was not very articulate,
and he could read and write about as well as a first grader. With black
people it didn't matter. He understood black people. He knew who
loved him and who didn't. On the white side of town, he had to worry
about what people thought of him, particularly after he got into the
bootlegging business and his name started showing up on the scandal
sheet at the courthouse. Trouble was always in the back of his mind.
On the whole, he preferred the old days on the other side of the
tracks, when he could wake up in the morning and go to bed at night

never having to nod and smile at a white person, unless he needed to come across town for groceries. In the Flats he could tend to his business and be respected, if not admired, by everyone he met.

It was white people who brought Moore's family to the panhandle in the first place. Moore was born in the east Texas town of Coolidge, the baby of four brothers. In 1948, when Moore was five years old, his father was hired to bring a crew of hands out of east Texas to pull cotton for a big producer in Tahoka, just south of Lubbock. Moore came to the panhandle in a convoy of hay-hauling trucks full of black field hands, each with his rolled up mattresses, cotton sacks, pots and pans, and children. Moore's dad was a ramrod, or foreman, so his family slept in the farmer's car shed, rather than in the loft of the barn with the rest of the hands. Moore watched as the pullers put their 100-pound sacks on the scale, his dad checking to see that no dirt or leaves were thrown in with the bolls. At the end of the day he'd collect the day's wages from the farmer and parcel it out to his hands. "If the farmer paid $2.00 a hundredweight, Dad paid the cotton pullers $1.75," Moore explained. "That way he made his." It was Moore's first lesson in hustling—there was money to be made for the person who dealt directly with the man.

Unlike many of the hands, Moore's father decided not to return to east Texas at the end of the season. The farms of the panhandle were thriving, and there was plenty of work. The family moved from farm to farm and from town to town in the panhandle: Spade, Levelland, Morton, Olton, wherever cotton was grown. As soon as he was old enough, Moore went into the fields himself, first chopping (hoeing weeds) and later pulling cotton. School was not a consideration. "We were so poor out there in the country that we didn't get to go to school much," he said. Moore would watch the bus full of white kids pass by the fields in the morning. It did not stop for the Moores or any other black family out in the country.

Moore did not attend school regularly until the family landed in

Amarillo, when he was twelve years old. While his older brothers got jobs washing dishes, Moore's parents insisted on enrolling him in the black middle school. By that time he was far behind the other kids, and he took to playing hooky. Amarillo was a fiercely segregated city in 1955. Moore spent his days with the hookers and the hustlers walking up and down the black neighborhood's main drag, known simply as the Boulevard.

That first winter in Amarillo was a rough one. Moore's father found work killing chickens at a poultry plant. The boss allowed him to collect the discarded heads and feet and bring them home to his family. "My mom knew how to get them scales or whatever off the chicken foot and we had fried chicken foot, chicken foot dumplins," Moore laughed. "Oh man, every way you could cook a chicken foot." The family lived near an ice factory where produce was stored. Moore and his brothers would join the other neighborhood kids collecting the overripe fruit and vegetables tossed out by the plant. The brothers made extra money shoveling snow from sidewalks and driveways in white neighborhoods. Moore was only twelve years old, but already he was big and strong; he and his brothers could cover forty blocks in a day.

When it was time to move on, Moore's dad would go ahead of the family, scouting out a job and a place to live, and leaving enough money for them to get by until he sent for them. On June 26, 1956, he brought the family to live in Tulia, in two rented rooms in the back of a boardinghouse in the Flats known as the Hotel. Situated across the railroad tracks that ran along the western edge of Tulia, the Flats was a relatively new neighborhood at the time. The original black part of Tulia had been a small collection of shacks along either side of Highway 87, just outside the city limits on the north side of town. In the early 1950s, the county decided to expand the highway, and Tulia's entire black population was relocated to the Flats. Moore's dad found work as a handyman for a white man named Jeff Mussick, who owned most of the land in the Flats and built many of the fifty or so shacks that housed the black community. Eventually the Moores set up house in a couple of converted boxcars rented from Mussick.

The neighborhood was a town apart in those days, run by a handful of enterprising black patriarchs, mostly wranglers of farm labor, haulers of hay, and dealers of junk. Their names were legendary: J.D. Thompson. Black Cap. Horris Huckaberry. Wes Conti. Charlie Pimpson. After his father died in 1963, Moore attached himself to the king of them all, Earlie Smith. Smith was from the old school. When things were going against him in a card game, he would bring out a small black leather pouch, known as a "foot," which he had obtained in Lousiana. A few seconds of rubbing that foot, Moore recalled, and his luck would change. There was nothing mysterious about his methods away from the poker table, however. "Earlie Smith was at the top because he always kept everything in his hand," Moore said. Nothing happened in black Tulia without Smith getting a piece of the action. "He knew how to charm people out of their money. And he always dealt with the white folks lots better than we could," Moore said. Smith put Moore on one of his hay-hauling crews, where he worked for years. It took some time, but Moore finally realized how much money Smith was making off of him, and, it seemed, everybody who came near him.

Eventually Moore scraped together a few hundred dollars and bought his own truck. In time his crew grew to thirteen or fourteen hands and four trucks. Moore's hands could earn up to $30 per day at a time when the going rate for a day in the cotton fields was just $7.50. His older brothers were now working for him. Moore was reliable and efficient, and he kept his men in line. Eventually farmers started switching to big round bales too massive to fit in Moore's trucks, but for many years Moore's crew was one of the busiest in the county, and he was proud of it. "Sometimes we had 5,000 bales in a field and it act like it's goin' to rain," he recalled. "And we'd pull all those trucks in and say we got to clean this field out. And when we hit that field we'd clean it *out*."

What really drove the economy in the heyday of the Flats was the cafés and juke joints. Since at least the 1950s, Tulia had served as a kind of regional hub for black nightlife. Blacks looking to drink, dance, or gamble came from as far away as Amarillo and Lubbock to party all night in the Flats, which became known as "Little Dodge" for its wildness on weekends. In the 1960s and 1970s, the Flats boasted as many as five cafés running at any one time, in an area no bigger than an acre and a half. Opening a café required little start-up capital, and there were few other business opportunities for black entrepreneurs looking to make a living at something other than manual labor. The neighborhood was outside of the city limits and largely ignored by city police.

"We had Lubbock, Hale Center, Floydada, Amarillo, Dimmitt— all of them gamblers out there in the country," Moore said. "All them little ol' bitty towns in there bring money. Man, it'd be thousands and thousands of dollars even." The gambling began on Friday night, after everyone had been paid for the week, and didn't end until the sun came up Monday morning. Poker was the most common game, though other card games, such as tonk and pitty pat, were also played, as well as dominoes and dice games. Most out-of-towners didn't even rent rooms. If they had a car, they might lock the doors and curl up for a few hours. The next morning, it was time to get up and do it again. Others simply never went to bed.

In 1983, Moore and his girlfriend Thelma Johnson bought the Hotel, the boardinghouse Moore lived in briefly as a child. He knocked out the interior walls to make one large room, which he filled with pool tables and a jukebox. He christened the new place Funz-a-Poppin', and he put his brothers to work as bartenders and bootleggers. Moore's place filled a need in Tulia. After Prohibition was repealed in 1933, Texas allowed its 254 counties to choose for themselves whether to allow alcohol to be sold, and Swisher County, like many rural counties in the South and Midwest, opted to stay dry. Not that it prevented anybody from getting a drink. Officially, Tulia was against alcohol. Unofficially, there was a tremendous demand for it.

The main beneficiary of this cultural dissonance, aside from the many bootleggers in the Flats and out in the sticks, was the town of Nazareth, which by accident of geography and theology became the host of Swisher County's liquor stores. Nazareth sits just across the line in Castro County, a sixteen-mile drive due west from Tulia. The town was settled by German Catholic immigrants, for whom drinking was never a moral issue, and who wasted no time in legalizing alcohol sales after Prohibition. Thus for generations Tulians have trekked across the county line to the tiny town to stock up on beer and liquor at stores with names like The Line Shack.

Moore came to know Nazareth well, and his bar became a fixture in black Tulia. The only legal way to sell alcohol in a dry county is to open a private club, which members have to pay to join. Whites in Swisher County drank legally at two unofficially segregated private clubs outside the Tulia city limits. There was the Tule Lake Country Club, set on the grounds of a windswept and uninspiring nine-hole golf course just outside town, which was preferred by city dwellers, and Johnny Nix's Tack Shed, a few miles east of town, which catered to farmers and ranchers. Moore's bootlegging was about the only game in town for blacks. His clientele was never exclusively black, however. White ranch hands in town for the auction were not above visiting Moore's place to pick up a six-pack. Some even stayed to play cards. Funz-a-Poppin' was the worst kept secret in town. "When I took over doin' it, I had so many people. I had Spanish, whites, black, all of 'em," Moore said. "But I didn't take no sides with the black, white, none of 'em—if they's wrong, they's wrong. Everybody equal in my place."

Because vice drove the economy of the Flats, everyone who lived there depended on it to some degree. Henry Jackson, the neighborhood's most beloved pastor, would send a woman over to the Hotel every Sunday morning at 9:00 A.M. with a basket. The gambling would still be going strong, though Moore would turn the music down out of respect for Jackson. "We was givin' him lots more money than he was getting in that church," Moore said. In return, Jackson never preached against the cafés, though he would sometimes come by and try to win converts from Moore's clientele. "Jackson come around on the porch sometimes around 12 or 1 o'clock. And we'd all break off gambling and we'd all get chairs. We didn't have to but we respected him," Moore said. They sat under the trees and listened to Jackson preach. For a preacher, he was surprisingly nonjudgmental, and Moore liked that about him.

Moore had a similar understanding with Sheriff John Gayler, who presided over the county for much of Moore's tenure as chief bootlegger. Gayler, who died in the mid-1990s, is wistfully recalled in some circles as the last good sheriff the county ever had. Sheriff Gayler stories abound in Tulia. The Farmers Home Administration (FHA) is the federal agency where farmers able to swallow their pride go for low-interest loans when disaster strikes. In the 1980s Swisher County was cursed with a particularly hard-assed FHA man, a former U.S. Army colonel who had little patience for hard-luck stories. After upbraiding the widow of a deeply indebted farmer about late payments, the agent was surprised to receive a return visit from the woman's son, who promised to kill him if he was heard talking to his mother that way again. The FHA man demanded that Sheriff Gayler arrest the young man. Gayler was not impressed. "Well, I don't guess we can arrest him just for *sayin'* he's going to kill you," he supposedly replied. "But I tell you what: If he *does* kill you, we'll by God put him in jail for that."

As long as Moore kept his business on the black side of the tracks, Gayler gave him little trouble. Deputies wrote him an occasional ticket for bootlegging but made no attempt to shut down the bar. Every month, Moore reported to the sheriff's office and paid his "fines"—usually a couple hundred in cash, all of which was income from bootlegging. "They called it the 'slow payment plan,'" he laughed. Moore was selling 200 cases of beer a week.

Even when business was good, the writing was on the wall for Funz-a-Poppin'. Moore had labored in Earlie Smith's shadow for twenty years. When it was finally his turn to play the godfather, black Tulia was in serious decline. From their place at the bottom of Swisher County's caste system, blacks were the first to feel the effects of the downturn in the local economy. Seasonal work dwindled as small farms went belly up and bigger ones turned to chemicals and other labor-saving methods. Farmers were hiring fewer full-time men as well. In 1979, Tulia's garment factory, a mainstay of employment for black women, closed its doors for good. The sewing machines were packed up and hauled to Mexico, where the women expected even less for a day's work than the women born and raised in the shacks and unpaved streets of the Flats. Massive layoffs at the Taylor-Evans seed processing facility put dozens of black men out of work a few years later. Many black families relocated to Plainview or Amarillo to work in the beef-packing industry. Young people increasingly began to leave after high school and not return.

Those who stayed no longer wanted to live in the Flats, and beginning in the late 1970s they didn't have to. Federal housing programs allowed them to move into homes in Tulia proper, mostly on the south side of town. White landlords were at first reluctant to take such tenants, but as the outflow of whites from Tulia increased, they had little choice. Two small housing projects—clusters of five or six brick duplexes—were built on the south side as well. By the end of the 1980s, most of the shacks in the Flats had been torn down. Funz-a-Poppin' was the last café in business. Moore spent much of his time caring for his older brothers, as each eventually developed cirrhosis.

The political situation began to turn on Moore as well. In 1987, Sheriff Gayler was narrowly defeated by a Tulia police officer named Paul Scarborough. The consensus in the black community was that Gayler lost because he was "soft on the niggers." It didn't help that Gayler had not taken Scarborough seriously and barely campaigned. Gayler's defeat did not bode well for Moore, nor did another development at the courthouse. For two generations, the city never got around to annexing the Flats, which meant that the neighborhood never enjoyed street repair, streetlights, or any city services. (Water and wastewater lines had eventually been run, however, largely because of the rabble-rousing of H. M. Baggarly at the *Tulia Herald*.) Now, however, the council was eyeing the land for a connection to Interstate 27. The freeway had bypassed Tulia when it came through in the mid-1980s, which only added to the town's slow downturn. It ran about a mile west of town, spawning a new truck stop and motel that drained money away from the old motor courts and restaurants on Highway 87 in town. Now the city fathers wanted to connect Tulia to the highway along Northwest 6th Street, the dirt road that ran straight through the Flats—and right by Funz-a-Poppin'. It was felt highway access would make the largely abandoned area more attractive as a potential industrial site, the type of economic development the county desperately needed.

So, years after almost everyone had moved out of the area, Tulia finally annexed the Flats. Moore's bar was now under the jurisdiction of the Tulia police department, and it was officially a problem that had to be dealt with. The police wasted no time in sending a calling card. An undercover officer walked into Moore's place one afternoon when Thelma Johnson was behind the bar. Johnson slid a six-pack across the counter, as she had done hundreds of times before. This time, however, she was promptly arrested.

Johnson received a $100 fine, but that was just the beginning. By

1992, the bar—like everything else in the Flats—was leveled. The only thing left of the old neighborhood was Jackson Chapel and a single row of public housing duplexes.

Joe Moore's trial was over in a day. Hukill's prediction of a slam dunk for the state became a sort of self-fulfilling prophecy. Hukill's cross-examination of Coleman, the state's only eyewitness, was perfunctory, lasting perhaps ten minutes. Hukill did not bring up the subject of the mysterious theft investigation Coleman had mentioned at pretrial. When it was his turn to put on his case, Hukill called not a single witness of his own. He advised Moore not to take the stand, owing to his prior convictions, which would be fair game for McEachern to bring up in front of the jury if Moore testified. The entire presentation—prosecution and defense combined—took less than four hours, which included a one-hour break for lunch. "I wish I had a whole lot of facts to talk about, but the trial, the evidence didn't take very long and there is not a lot to talk about," Hukill told the jury in his closing argument. It came down to who was more credible, he argued, though he offered no reasons whatsoever to question Coleman's uncorroborated testimony. With that, he left Moore's fate in the hands of the jurors. They deliberated for twenty minutes before finding Moore guilty. The entire proceeding had the tone and efficiency of a day in small claims court.

During the penalty phase of the trial, the rules of evidence allowed the prosecution to bring up the second charge that Coleman had filed on Moore, for delivery of a gram of crack. Coleman testified that he had turned over the crack to his superiors loosely packaged in a bit of cellophane he had obtained from a cigarette wrapper because Moore had simply handed him the rocks loose. It did not sound like something a dealer would do. And Coleman had paid Moore $150, roughly twice what the tiny parcel of crack was worth. None of this struck Hukill as noteworthy. He did get Coleman to admit that Moore had run him off his property on one occasion, as Moore had claimed. Coleman said he had come back later, however, and found that Moore was more receptive. At the pretrial hearing, Coleman had testified that Moore had been mollified because Man Kelly had been with him when he returned, which allowed him to complete the crack deal. Now, however, he denied that Kelly had been present. "I didn't have the report in front of me" at the pretrial hearing, Coleman explained when Hukill asked about the discrepancy.

Coleman had alleged that the powder sale took place at 11:30 on a morning in October. Hukill called a farmer named John Eliff to the stand, who testified that Joe Moore had come to his farm almost every morning that fall to collect some surplus milk that he would have otherwise poured out. Calling Eliff was a halfhearted attempt at an alibi, which might have made an impact on the jury during the guilt–innocence phase of the trial. But Moore had already been convicted. It was too late for alibis. Thelma Johnson also took the stand to testify on Moore's behalf. Now in her late fifties, Johnson had been with Joe for over twenty years but had somehow managed to inherit none of the scandal associated with Moore's name. She had a pleasant, open face and a grandmotherly demeanor. She was widely loved by the children on the south side of town, who referred to her as "Aunt Thelma." "[Joe] is a very friendly person and he would go out of the way to help anybody if he could," she told the court. Hukill could have found any number of white farmers who would have said the same thing about Moore, the old hay hauler they had come to know and trust. But it wasn't going to help him now. McEachern countered with Sheriff Stewart, who testified that Moore's reputation in the community was bad.

"This is not Washington, D.C. This is not California," McEachern summed up. "This is our community. We have got to live in it and our kids have to live in it and you do make the conscience of Swisher County, Texas, and your signal reaches far and wide throughout the State of Texas, and I'm proud to be a citizen of Swisher County," he told the jury. By 6:30 in the evening, some seven hours after his trial began, Moore had a ninety-year sentence.

CHAPTER FOUR

The Mayor of Vigo

TEN DAYS LATER, a bankrupt farmer named Gary Gardner sat at his desk in the corner of the cold, dimly lit poolroom of his house in Vigo Park, a tiny farming community about fifteen miles east of Tulia. He was thinking about drugs. It was something he'd been doing a lot of in recent years, ever since he and his teenage son Hollister had filed suit against the Tulia school district over a new drug testing policy. The father and son team were representing themselves, without the benefit of an attorney. During the drug testing fight, which was now winding its way through federal court, an office of sorts had grown by bits and pieces in the poolroom, beginning with a pressboard computer stand and a secondhand computer. Gardner had added a couple of bookshelves, a printer, and a table, on top of which a copy of *Black's Law Dictionary* now anchored a pile of old newspaper clippings. A rifle and two shotguns leaned against the wall with their butts resting on the corner of his desk, where a table lamp might have been. A Mark Twain quote was prominently displayed on his bulletin board: "In the first place God made idiots. This was for practice. Then he made school boards."

Gardner himself had been on the school board at the time of his suit, but now he was persona non grata among the courthouse crowd

in Tulia, and he avoided going to town unless he had to. He preferred
the country anyway, where his grandfather had helped found Vigo
Park a hundred years before. The Gardners were one of the last
remaining families in Vigo, and their own hold on the land was
increasingly tenuous. Gardner was fifty-three years old and looked
every year of it. Standing about five-foot-nine, he weighed close to
300 pounds. He walked with the characteristic bowlegged amble
common to old farmers who had spent too much time aboard a tractor. Gardner's limp was exacerbated by prematurely bad feet, a sign of
his advancing diabetes. He had lost most of his hair and his face
looked permanently sunburned. He was also going deaf. But he
laughed often, showing tiny teeth set deep in his red gums like a
baby's. Gardner was fond of overalls, and when he went out he
donned a straw hat with a terrycloth hatband, on which he had affixed
a broken watch. He was an easy man to spot in a crowd.

Joe Moore's trial had started Gardner thinking again about the big
bust the previous summer. He had clipped and saved articles about
the sting from the local papers, thinking at the time that the bust was
meant somehow to be a message to him from Sheriff Stewart and his
fellow school board members. He had recognized some of the names
among those arrested, and he was not surprised to see them busted
for drugs. Some of them had been in and out of jail for years, and a
few were notorious crack addicts. Others he wasn't so sure about—it
had been a few years since he had hired any laborers, and he tended to
use Mexicans these days. Joe Moore he knew, of course. Moore had
hauled hay for just about everybody in the county at some point,
Gardner included, and he liked and trusted the man. He didn't know
many younger blacks.

The demeaning photographs and the tone of the newspaper coverage bothered him. "Tulia's Streets Cleared of Garbage," was the
headline in the *Tulia Sentinel*. Most of the suspects seemed to have
been rousted from their beds, and some were half dressed, their hair

uncombed. Sheriff Stewart or somebody had obviously tipped the papers off that something big was happening that morning. Gardener was also troubled by comments from the sheriff and district attorney, who talked about the accused as though they were already convicted. Worse, Sheriff Stewart told local reporters that the high cost of housing and trying so many defendants would surely mean a tax increase. Stewart was not exaggerating—in a normal year, the county averaged only about ten indictments for drug cases, most of them minor possession charges. There was not enough room in the county jail for all of the defendants busted in the sting, and some had to be housed in county jails as far away as Levelland, fifty miles southwest of Tulia, which was costing the county more money every day. Among the already strapped farmers of Swisher County, that alone was enough to prejudice a jury.

Gardner was all for law and order, but he didn't like Larry Stewart. The sheriff's main problem, Gardner felt, was that he was too rigid. His predecessor, Sheriff Gayler, had always exercised his authority with a measure of discretion; he knew when the interests of the community were better served by looking the other way. But Stewart, who had become sheriff in 1991, seemed to see the law the way he saw everything else in life, in black and white. He was too sure that he was right, in Gardner's mind. Too judgmental of other people's weaknesses. Too much of a Campbellite, in other words. That was Gardner's derisive term for members of the Church of Christ, of whom Stewart was perhaps the best-known example in Tulia. Stewart was a deacon in the church, and he sang in the congregation's quartet. He was such a devout follower that, despite the fact that he had been the county's chief law enforcement officer for almost a decade, most people thought of him as a church leader first and sheriff second.

Of the two dozen churches in town, the Baptists and Methodists claimed the lion's share of Tulia's professionals, politicians, and civic leaders, but no church captured the spirit of Tulia, or indeed of rural

Texas, like the Church of Christ. It is the religion of farmers and ranchers, cowboys and hired hands—the little people. The denomination has never quite shaken the stigma of being a sect, despite having churches in virtually every town, large or small, in Texas and perhaps 2 million members nationwide. The intolerance of the Church of Christ is legendary. Disciples, as they call one another, are taught that members of every other denomination, even the most fervently correct Southern Baptists, are going to hell. Gardner, a lapsed Methodist, stood little chance of making the cut.

The same stereotype that Gardner held against Stewart was his chief selling point among most Swisher County voters. Whatever else could be said about Church of Christ disciples, it was commonly held that their faith made them honest to a fault. And nobody was more faithful than Larry Stewart.

Gary Gardner came from different stock. His grandfather, C. R. Gardner, was a boxcar carpenter in Terre Haute, Indiana. Finding himself out of work in the fall of 1906, he accepted an offer from a Texas land company to come to the panhandle and build a hotel and store for a prospective town on a piece of open range about fifteen miles east of Tulia. When the job was done, C. R. Gardner decided the pioneering life was for him. He instructed his wife to sell their home, a six-room house with running water, and bring their children to the unincorporated hamlet, with no schoolhouse, roads, or grain elevator. The store is still there, as is the town, which the Gardners named Vigo Park, after a favorite spot in their former hometown. The Gardners were Republicans, who were almost as rare in the panhandle as the Catholics in Nazareth, on the opposite side of Tulia. Gary's father, Orvall West Gardner, liked to tell the story of a man who showed up at the house in his buggy one evening, having driven all the way from Plainview just to find a fellow Republican.

Orvall was a farmer, at least until impending bankruptcy and the specter of starvation forced him to look for wage work in the 1920s.

The railroad was looking for replacements to help break a strike, and the union sent representatives from their headquarters in the panhandle town of Canadian to urge the men of Vigo not to scab. The meeting ended with the union men running from the one-room schoolhouse with their dignity barely intact. Orvall took a job on the railroad, carrying a ball-peen hammer in his pocket to protect himself from the picketers. His family was hungry and he needed the money—but more than that, he was a Gardner, and nobody was going to tell him what to do. Over the next generation, Vigo Park developed a well-earned reputation around the county for contrariness, and its residents were quietly viewed as something akin to the hillbillies of Tennessee or the Cajuns of Louisiana: inscrutable and maybe a little dangerous.

Orvall finally got married in his mid-forties to a schoolteacher, the only reliable source of marriageable young women in the tiny towns of the panhandle, and Gary was the couple's first child, born in 1946. By the time he was old enough to go to school, most of the rural schoolhouses had closed, and Gardner rode a bus into Tulia with the other farm kids. The consolidation of the school districts, almost as much as the slow decline in the farming economy, eventually decimated the Swisher County countryside. More and more country families moved off the farms and into the larger towns of Tulia, Happy, and Kress to be closer to the schools their children attended. But Vigo Park was still a thriving community in the 1960s, and Gardner lived the farming life to its fullest. Every summer from the time he was thirteen, he hired out as a field hand, harvesting wheat on a custom combine crew. Spending a few days on each farm, the crews followed the harvest north across the Great Plains. At first Gardner's father allowed him to go only as far as the panhandle town of Silverton. But by the time he was in high school, Gardner and his younger brothers followed the crop all the way to Canada, living out of a bus outfitted with sleeping quarters.

Gardner graduated from high school in 1964. After a semester studying engineering at a community college in Amarillo, he quit school and joined the harvest again. He returned to Vigo one night in the fall of 1965 at 2:00 in the morning—he had driven his pickup straight in from Kansas—only to find every light in the house burning and his brothers singing "You're in the Army Now." Gardner had been drafted. Everyone else was going to Vietnam, but Gardner was sent to Germany, where he spent two years on the front lines of the Cold War. Although he agreed to an extended enlistment, in the end army life did not match up well with the antiauthoritarian Gardner streak. He entered officer's training school as a mechanical engineering student and found that he enjoyed the coursework, which was fast-paced and thorough. Nevertheless, he found himself ejected barely six months into the program for, among other things, a "lack of tact." He didn't blend well with the GIs, either. For one thing, he didn't drink beer, which was a major pastime of enlisted men. It wasn't a moral thing—the Gardners were fairly easygoing Methodists, though his mother was a teetotaler. Gardner just didn't enjoy being drunk. One of his first experiences with booze had been on the wheat harvest, where he was often called on to drive his hard-drinking boss around when the man got too drunk to steer his car. He bought a used car and took to driving around Germany, seeing the sights by himself.

Gardner returned home in 1968 to find hard times on the family farm. The entire maize crop had been lost to insects, and with two brothers already working at home, there was not enough work for Gardner to justify joining them. He went to Amarillo to work on trucks. One afternoon, while picking up a load of car parts in a blizzard, he noticed a highway patrolman sitting on the side of the road snug and warm in his leather coat, with the heater running in his nice modern cruiser, doing, it seemed, very little of anything. He decided to sign up. The Department of Public Safety, as the state's highway patrol is known, has always prided itself on being a modern, professional civil service, with high standards and little tolerance for scandal. It was also known as a good way to meet women, and Gardner wasn't disappointed. He met his wife, Darlene, after a few months on the job. Not long after, he quit. "I knew if I got married and had kids, I'd never change; I'd have stayed highway patrol forever," he said later. He found he missed the freedom of being self-employed. He missed the farm.

By the 1970s, when Gardner went back to farming, people were going broke in Swisher County at a frightening pace. Gardner supplemented his modest farm income by repairing wells and dusting crops. Wedged into the tiny cab of his Piper Cub, with his World War II leather bomber's cap on his head, he had hit most of the phone lines between Tulia and Vigo at one time or another. He was never a stickler for rules and regulations. An old farmer once thought to ask him if he had a license to do septic work, after Gardner had nearly completed repairs on his system. "Yep, got it the same time I got my pilot's license," Gardner told him.

Gardner loved the country. He couldn't understand "city people," as he called Tulians. There was no adventure to city life. They had lost the pioneer spirit. Out on the farm, if something broke, you didn't call a plumber, or an electrician, or a welder, or a mechanic. You fixed it yourself. Gardner had a full machine shop and a woodworking shop, and he could make or repair almost anything he or his family would ever need. He loved being the center of town, having people count on him. His neighbors took to calling him the Mayor of Vigo.

Until the mid-1980s, Gardner could take off in his crop duster from an empty field near his house, turn the nozzles on, and just fly for miles, watching the dollars flow. But then CRP came in, and the water started running out, especially in the eastern portion of the county where Vigo lay. Gardner's well-pulling business boomed for a time, as his neighbors replaced eight-inch water lines with six, and then four. But with every well he pulled and every pipe he replaced, he knew he was digging his own grave. The water was never coming back. At one time, the area around Vigo had a family on every quarter section. Now the official population on the voting rolls was forty-five, and Gardner could count the number of viable operations in his part of the county on one hand. The rest was grass. Gardner's yellow Piper Cub sat in his garage under a thick layer of dust. His machine shop and woodworking shop were locked and quiet.

"You can always tell when things are gettin' rough in farm country—you stop seein' beer cans in the gutter and start seein' whisky bottles," Gardner was fond of saying. He had seen many of his neighbors in Vigo ruined by alcoholism. It was always the same story: people lost their land, then they started drinking, then they got divorced. Gardner believed that if any one vice could be eliminated, it should be alcohol. Instead, increasingly since the early 1990s, Gardner's fellow plainsmen were fixated on another vice: narcotics.

In the summer and fall of 1995, a group of church and civic leaders in Plainview, including Terry McEachern, organized a series of antidrug marches through the city's minority neighborhoods. Carrying bullhorns and waving signs—and on one occasion a Confederate flag—as many as 100 people at a time participated in the nightly marches. The Plainview police provided an escort and pointed out suspected crack houses, into which the marchers shone their flashlights and channeled their derision. Suspicious characters scurried away, to the cheers of the angry crowd. The marches were hugely popular; even Wal-Mart and Cargill, the agricultural services conglomerate, got into the act, pledging money to support the district attorney's antidrug efforts.

The marches were inspired by Turnaround America, an antidrug campaign founded in the early 1990s by a Philadelphia community activist named Herman Wrice. The former high school coach pioneered the confrontational tactic after watching many of his best student athletes become addicted to drugs. Marching in a brightly colored hard hat, Wrice became something of a folk hero as his efforts gained nationwide publicity. He eventually formed a nonprofit and became a sort of drug war consultant, chiefly to small and medium-size towns. The model was duplicated in a number of cities in the mid-1990s, most notably St. Petersburg, Florida. The Plainview movement began after a local church invited a Turnaround America member to give his pitch to city leaders.

"He came and made a presentation to city council and got us really pumped up," Plainview city council member Irene Favila recalled. Favila, who is Hispanic, attended the first march with her husband, Ray Rosas, the leader of the local chapter of the League of United Latin American Citizens (LULAC). She later regretted it. Billed as a form of community empowerment, the marches seemed more like scapegoating to Favila. The marchers focused only on the poor side of town, just as the Plainview police did in general when it came to drug enforcement, a complaint Favila heard regularly from her Hispanic and black constituents. Plainview, like many small panhandle towns, was in the midst of a demographic upheaval in the 1990s, as thousands of recent Mexican immigrants settled in town. Many of them worked at the rapidly expanding Excel meatpacking plant, which employed some 2,500 workers, perhaps 90 percent of them Hispanic. High turnover meant the plant had to hire 100 people per week just to stay at full production levels. Others worked at the giant Wal-Mart distribution center or at Azteca, a large flour milling plant owned by a firm based in Monterrey, Mexico. By 2000, Plainview was almost 50 percent Hispanic. The elementary schools, bellwethers of short-term demographic change, were 75 percent Hispanic. Under threat of a lawsuit by LULAC, the city adopted single member city council districts, resulting in the election of Rosas, the first Hispanic city council member. Favila was the second, and the first woman. By the end of the decade, Hispanics could reliably count on two city council places and roughly half the school board.

The power of the old guard, mostly white men in their seventies and eighties, was gradually eroding in the face of change, but they were not going without a fight. Many of the immigrants spoke little English and were functionally illiterate. Favila and her colleagues fought to get more Spanish-speaking teachers into the schools and build affordable housing. They also lobbied to bring in a community college to train the newcomers for something better than wage labor, a move staunchly opposed by the local four-year university, Wayland Baptist, a bastion of old-money power in the county. "This is how stupid they are, how racist," Favila said. "The bottom line is that they don't want our people getting educated because they know that eventually Hispanic people will take over the leadership of this town." Favila came to see the antidrug marches as part and parcel of the broader racial struggle going on behind the scenes in Plainview.

Editor Mike Garrett of the *Tulia Sentinel* covered the Turnaround Plainview campaign in person. He was so moved by what he saw that he joined in with the marchers, chanting "Up with hope, down with dope" and "Save the children." Several employees of the *Plainview Daily Herald* were also marching, Garrett informed his *Sentinel* readers, so he did not feel bad about joining in himself. "We found the march exhilarating and fun, and we got to meet a lot of nice people who view drug dealers as just plain scum," he wrote. Of the neighbors who turned their lights on to show their support Garrett wrote, "Those lights are symbolic of the lights of freedom that shone in a Boston harbor steeple church during Paul Revere's famous midnight ride." Earlier that year, an undercover drug sting centered in Plainview had nabbed a couple of Tulians as well. In light of the recent arrests, the marches seemed to be exactly what Tulia needed, Garrett wrote. "God seems to be involved in this campaign," he added. "Let's continue to let Him work through us as our voices get louder and louder: 'If you keep sellin' crack, we'll keep comin' back.'"

The Tulia papers, particularly the *Sentinel*, kept up a steady antidrug drumbeat. In the fall of 1996, a group of school officials led by Superintendent Mike Vinyard proposed a drug testing program for students at Tulia's junior and senior high schools. They were bolstered by a 1995 Supreme Court decision upholding a testing policy in the small town of Veronia, Oregon. But the Veronia program tested only students participating in the high school athletics program. The court found that because the district had demonstrated that drug abuse was prevalent in the sports program and because the athletes were role models to their peers, the district had a compelling reason to administer the tests. Tulia proposed to test not just athletes but all students involved in extracurricular activities, which included a majority of the student body. And the school board's data on drug abuse in the schools, such as it was, was far from convincing. Proponents of the program pointed to a 1994 survey in which 27 percent of Tulia students admitted using illegal drugs at some point in their lives. Just 10 percent had used drugs in the month prior to the survey. That put Tulia below the state average, and lower even than fellow panhandle school districts, where drug abuse lagged behind other areas of the state. "We took the position that any amount of abuse was too much," school board member Scott Burrow said.

It quickly became evident that Gary Gardner was the only dissenting voice on the board. The night of the vote, the hearing room was filled with over 100 parents, overwhelmingly in favor of the program. Gardner argued vehemently that the district was only inviting lawsuits. It had not shown the compelling interest that the court looked for and found in the Veronia case. Gardner's own son Hollister was a drum major in the band and a leader in the Future Farmers of America chapter. Gardner had no intention of giving the district permission to test Hollister, he warned the board.

But the community wanted something done. Board member Sam Sadler, a prominent insurance salesman, spoke up in response to Gardner. He was neither as pithy nor as direct as Gardner, but his stumbling explanation captured the mood of the assembled parents:

> First of all, I see my son. He has entered the sixth grade this year, and he is easily influenced, [a] follower, not a leader. . . . I take him to school mornings, [my wife] picks him up evenings. The other evening when several bigger kids, some colored kids—not trying to pick on anybody—but they had him all huddled up in a huddle there. You know just really talking to him when she picked him up. She stopped and they all kind of looked, you know, and then they kind of turned and went the other way. And you know you do your best at home and you try to explain, you tell and do everything you know how, but if this is another step we can do to help our kids . . . be in a drug free and protect his health, his safety, I think that's a pretty compelling interest for me to protect my son, and to me it's a compelling interest.

The policy was adopted by a vote of 6 to 1. In January, Hollister Gardner filed suit against the school board in federal court in Amarillo, alleging a violation of his Fourth Amendment right to protection from unreasonable search. Gardner and his son went to the Texas Tech law library in Lubbock to study and prepare their filings. Gardner found he had a knack for the law. "The law's a simple deal," he told his friends. "If you can take an engine apart and you can read a Bible, you can be your own lawyer." Gardner's fellow board members weren't sure what to make of his intransigence. He became an object of ridicule around Tulia, though some were careful not to underestimate his abilities. "He's got a powerful mind," said Louie Anderson, the owner of the Tulia Trading Post. "He's not to be made fun of, I don't believe."

Bemusement turned to resentment when Gardner obtained a trial setting in federal court, forcing Swisher County to hire outside legal help to prepare a defense. "He cost the taxpayer plenty, and I don't think that's right," said Delbert Devin, the Swisher County Democratic Party chair. Devin once counted Gardner as a friend. But Gardner changed, according to Devin, in the early 1990s, when his youngest son, Charlie, was diagnosed with brain cancer. The medical bills nearly broke the Gardners. When Charlie died in 1996, Gardner built the boy's casket himself and buried his son in the family plot. After that, Devin said, Gardner became bitter. "He didn't want to help nobody. Just fight all the time," he said. His brother Danny, who had a son and daughter in high school, had joined the suit and had retained Jim Harrington, a well-known civil rights lawyer in Austin, who was now devoting considerable time to the case. Gardner felt vindicated by the results of the most recent round of drug testing at the high school: of 954 tests administered in the 1998–1999 school year, only ten students tested positive, and six of those were kids who had been volunteered for testing by their parents. Nevertheless, the school board was still vigorously defending the program against Gardner's efforts to shut it down.

Gardner had been fighting for almost three years. Now, sitting alone in his poolroom, three days before Christmas, he had to make a decision. On his computer screen was a draft of a letter to the defendants busted that summer. The letter urged the defendants to seek a change of venue for their trials and offered to testify in support of such a motion. Gardner had written it months ago but never sent it. It was too late to help Joe Moore, but there were over three dozen others still locked up, awaiting trial. It wasn't just what the sheriff and district attorney had said, Gardner explained in the letter. He also had a bad feeling about the narc, Tom Coleman, who had spoken to the papers as well. The articles never failed to mention that Coleman had won the Officer of the Year Award. "I have no facts to base my feelings upon," Gardner wrote the defendants, "other than in reading the article, the officer reminded me of a cow buyer I knew several years ago whose checks were never any good and always talked too much about his personal accomplishments." He went on: "Since a lot of people's lives are going to be affected by this man's veracity on the stand . . . I think perhaps someone outside of the local law enforcement system should investigate this man's background."

Gardner sat and stared at the screen, debating whether or not he should print the letter and launch yet another war with the powers that be in Tulia. Not that he minded a fight. On the contrary, it was what he did best. He just wasn't sure if this one was worth the trouble.

At that moment the phone rang. It was Tommy Abbott, a man Gardner hadn't heard from in years. Abbott was a farmhand who had "gone outlaw" in the mid-1980s and stolen some cattle in a nearby county. It was a serious enough offense to get hard time. But what many didn't know about the case was that Abbott had gotten on the wrong side of the county's most powerful rancher prior to going on his spree. The rancher was bound and determined to see Abbott sent away for a very long time and had the connections at the courthouse to get it done. Gardner intervened on Abbott's behalf and helped him get a change of venue. He had never done anything like that before, but it seemed like the right thing to do. Abbott wound up serving a few years in prison, but nothing like the stacked sentences he would likely have faced in his hometown. When he got out, he went to school to become a nurse practitioner, settled down, and made a life for himself. Something, maybe the holiday spirit, had moved him to call and thank Gardner for helping him out when he needed it most. Just calling to say thanks.

Gardner put down the receiver and clicked print on his word processor. Tulia would never be the same.

PART TWO

CHAPTER FIVE

"Deep Cover"

WORD OF Joe Moore's ninety-year sentence spread quickly among the small pool of lawyers who handled indigent defense cases in Swisher County. Shortly after Moore's conviction, Kregg Hukill got a call from a Plainview defense attorney named Paul Holloway, who had picked up four clients from the Tulia bust. Holloway assumed that Terry McEachern must have had something special on Moore, something more than what little evidence the state had against his clients. What Hukill had to say about the trial was sobering. The charge was delivery of a single eight ball, Coleman was the only witness to the offense, and the prosecution presented no corroborating evidence. It was over in a day. Two prior felonies equaled a double enhancement equaled ninety years. End of story.

Holloway hung up the phone. That was the same case McEachern had on his clients, the same flimsy case for which he had thus far refused to offer anybody a plea. Now McEachern was in the driver's seat; if he'd won once on those facts, he could do it again, and the people of Tulia were clearly in a hanging mood. A bad deal had just gotten a lot worse.

Paul Holloway began his career as a corporate attorney with a downtown Houston law firm, representing deep-pocketed clients like General Electric. Holloway's wife was from Plainview, and in the mid-1990s, the family moved there to be closer to her family. In time Holloway opened his own office in an attractive one-story brown adobe across from the Hale County courthouse. He bought a respectably large house in the comfortable west side neighborhood favored by Plainview's small professional class. He developed a reputation as a careful, thorough attorney who could be trusted to handle a complicated civil suit or get a wayward son or daughter off the hook. In his early forties, he had a slightly boyish face and an earnest, self-deprecating manner that belied his confidence in his own abilities. He compensated by dressing in conservative suits and driving around town in a gold Mercedes. In court he was deferential to the judge and went out of his way not to embarrass cops on the stand. Nobody had ever described him as flamboyant.

Yet he had a reputation as a troublemaker at the courthouse, principally because of the way he played—or rather refused to play—the indigent defense game. Like most of his colleagues, Holloway sought to keep his clients from getting in front of a panhandle jury whenever possible. What distinguished his work was his exhaustive pretrial preparation and his refusal to take the standard plea bargains McEachern's office handed out. In Hale County, the standard plea offer for first-time DWI cases was the maximum sentence: 180 days in jail. The "deal" defendants got in exchange for their guilty plea was two years of probation. Holloway let it be known, to the infuriation of the DA's office, that he would never advise his clients to take a plea for the maximum sentence, even if it was probated. He would fight Breathalyzer evidence with expert testimony, file continuances, drag cops through pretrial hearings, whatever it took. Holloway believed in doing the job right, regardless of who was paying the bills.

That did not sit well with the philosophy of indigent defense in Hale and Swisher counties. When Holloway began his practice in

Plainview, fees in the Sixty-fourth District Court were capped at $400 for time in court and $500 for work done out of court. It didn't matter whether an attorney did ten or a hundred hours of work on a case, he or she was not going to be paid more than $900, unless an exception was made, which was entirely at the discretion of the judge. Attorneys were given a strong incentive to plea out, for which they routinely billed less than $400 per case. Holloway, on the other hand, once billed the county $6,000 in a felony case that eventually plead out. The county commissioners were outraged, but it was hard to argue that Holloway hadn't earned it—he routinely spent weeks working on cases that other attorneys disposed of in a day. In a system set up with pragmatism in mind, Holloway was a wrench in the cogs.

The situation in Hale and Swisher counties is not unusual. Texas has one of the least-regulated systems of appointing attorneys to represent poor defendants in the country. At the time of the Tulia bust, Texas was one of a handful of states that provided no state funding or standards for indigent defense; each county devised its own system and provided its own funding, which varied widely from county to county. Very few counties in Texas have a public defender system of the sort used by many states and the federal government, which employ full-time, salaried defense attorneys who do nothing but represent indigent defendants. Instead, attorneys are most often appointed by judges, who also set rates of compensation and make rulings on budgets for expert witnesses and investigators. Particularly in rural counties, the pressure on judges to keep costs down results in compensation that is generally poor and sometimes completely inadequate. Most judges set hourly rates, sometimes with informal caps on the total amount an attorney can bill for a case. Some, however, set flat rates for various tasks. A 2000 study of indigent defense by the Texas Appleseed Fair Defense Project found, for example, that the going rate for felony jury trials in Titus and Smith counties, both in rural east Texas, was $1,500 and $750 respectively, regardless of how many hours an attorney worked on the case. In counties where hourly rates are used, judges routinely reduce attorneys' billings at their own discretion. The disincentive for court-appointed attorneys to put in extra work for their clients is obvious.

Holloway had his doubts about the Tulia sting from the moment he read the police reports on his cases. The narrative portion of Coleman's report on each of his clients was less than 500 words long. Holloway had never read a felony report that was so brief or so devoid of detail. A good attorney can pick a police report apart—even a perfectly legitimate account can generate ammunition to create doubt in a juror's mind. But here there was almost nothing to work with. The suspects were barely described. There was no corroborating evidence of any kind. Holloway had defended his share of cases made by undercover cops, but the narcs in most of his cases had been hired by the state police force, the Texas Department of Public Safety. Reports filed by DPS narcs were nothing like Coleman's work. They almost always had audio or video of the suspects making the sale. They made detailed chronologies of the deals, documenting everything they heard or observed. Tom Coleman gave him a single paragraph. How did he defend that?

To make matters worse, the state was seeking enhancements of the charges against three of his four clients because the drug deals allegedly took place in a "drug-free zone" near Conner Park, which was located just across the street from the black section of town and was where a good many of Tulia's young people could be found playing basketball or hanging out on any given evening. Pitched by legislators as a way to keep dealers from preying on vulnerable schoolchildren, drug-free zones—usually within 1,000 feet of a school or park—became commonplace across the country beginning in the mid-1980s. In a town the size of Tulia, which covers little more than a square mile, the policy meant that literally half of the town was in one drug-free zone or another. It had the effect of officially codifying what every defense attorney already knew to be true: that being busted for drugs in a small town was much more dangerous than being busted in the nearest big city.

Delivery of between 1 and 4 grams of cocaine was supposed to be a second-degree felony, punishable by 2 to 20 years. Instead, because of the enhancement, his clients would be facing first-degree charges, a class of felonies that included rape, murder, and kidnapping. For allegedly delivering a few grams of cocaine, his clients were facing possible sentences of 5 to 99 years.

On the day he collected the files, Holloway walked across the street to the courthouse and confronted McEachern. "This is a joke, right?" Holloway asked. McEachern was indignant. There was no audio or video or any of the other corroboration normally associated with drug stings, he explained, because this operation was different: this was "deep cover." Coleman had lived and worked among his suspects, and it was too dangerous for him to wear a wire in a situation like that. This was an argument Holloway hadn't encountered before.

"I know I'm not your friend, but to the extent that I am, I'm telling you something is wrong with these cases," Holloway said. McEachern wouldn't budge.

"They're good cases," he insisted. "And don't ask me for a deal. They're going to trial."

After Holloway interviewed his four defendants, his doubts multiplied. Each of them adamantly denied the charges. That was not unusual, but there was something different about this bust. All four were arrested at dawn in their homes, yet no drugs were found during the arrests. Even without a search warrant, the "plain view" doctrine—one of the most widely abused prosecutorial standbys—allows officers to seize drug evidence they happen upon in the course of an arrest. Cops can also simply ask permission to search during the arrest or convince suspects to give written permission during booking, as many Tulia defendants did in the hours following the bust.

Holloway had handled dozens of warrantless drug possession cases over the years.

Three of his clients, Yolanda Smith, Vickie Fry, and Joseph Marshall, were black, and the fourth, Daniel Olivarez, was Hispanic. All of them were poor. Only Vickie Fry managed to bond out. Both Fry and her husband, Vincent McCray, had been picked up, leaving their two small children alone at the house. A sympathetic Hispanic family living next door loaned Fry's mother some money for bail the day after the bust. Fry had no prior offenses of any kind. Her husband, Vincent, had several DWI convictions but no record of selling drugs. He worked at the Grandy's fast-food restaurant at the truck stop on I–27. Yolanda Smith, who was on welfare, had a previous offense for selling crack. Daniel Olivarez, who was twenty, had nothing on his record. Marshall, who was just twenty-one, had a previous arrest for possession of crack. Holloway had taken plenty of cases with clients fitting this profile in his career, but the drug involved was almost always crack cocaine. Each of the Tulia cases involved delivery of powder.

It didn't make sense. And Holloway wasn't buying McEachern's "deep cover" explanation about the lack of corroborating evidence, either. Olivarez, McCray, and Smith were each accused of multiple deliveries. After successfully completing the first buy without a wire, why couldn't Coleman have worn one during subsequent deals? He had already established their trust, presumably. Undercover narcs working for the state police did it every day.

Holloway requested an investigator shortly after he picked up the cases but was denied funding by Judge Ed Self. When Joe Moore got the Big Bitch in December, Holloway knew he couldn't go into court empty-handed. He began his own investigation in earnest. He attended the next two trials, those of Chris Jackson and Jason Williams, both held the second week in January in Tulia. The facts were depressingly similar to his own cases, and the results were devastating. Jackson received twenty years for delivery of an eight ball. Williams was accused of four separate deliveries of eight balls, two of which were alleged to have occurred in a drug-free zone. He had no prior convictions and was just nineteen years old at the time of the offense. The jury gave him forty-five years.

The state produced no corroboration of any kind for Coleman's testimony, which was perfunctory, and, to Holloway's mind, not very convincing. Yet after watching the defense attorneys in action, Holloway wasn't surprised at the guilty verdicts. Both trials were slam dunks for the prosecution, with the defense putting up little fight. Holloway cringed as Chris Jackson's court-appointed attorney, Angela French, allowed McEachern to get away with abuse after abuse without objection. McEachern improperly bolstered Coleman with references to his "deep cover" status during jury selection and his supposed "outstanding" reputation as a cop during the trial itself. French did not even cross-examine Coleman when McEachern put him on the stand, though she did call him back during her presentation, which was painfully short. Jason Williams had drawn Joe Moore's attorney, Kregg Hukill, who hardly made the most of his second crack at Coleman.

Still, Holloway listened carefully to Coleman's testimony and took notes. He was intrigued by a seemingly offhand comment Coleman made about the sheriff of Cochran County, for whom Coleman had worked as a deputy prior to coming to Tulia. In Jackson's trial, and again two days later in Williams's trial, Coleman called the sheriff a crook. In both cases the testimony was essentially unsolicited. In Holloway's experience, cops were extremely reluctant to criticize other cops, particularly on the record in a public venue. It was part of their code. Yet Coleman, who described himself as coming from a law enforcement family, seemed cavalier about it. Holloway didn't know the sheriff of Cochran County; he wasn't even sure where Cochran County was. But it was something to start with.

A few hours after twelve Tulians sent Jason Williams away for the remainder of his youth, Holloway was on the phone to the tiny town of Morton, county seat of Cochran County. After some searching he had located it on his road atlas about fifty miles west of Lubbock, on the way to nowhere. The man he was looking for was Ken Burke, he was told, but Burke was no longer the county sheriff. The dispatcher was happy to give out his home number, however. Morton, a tiny farming town about half the size of Tulia, was that kind of place.

Holloway hung up and phoned Burke at home. "You don't have any reason to talk to me," Holloway admitted, after explaining who he was, "but I wanted to ask you what you remember about a deputy you had named Tom Coleman."

There was a slight pause. "Good cop," Burke said. It was the standard response, the one Holloway had heard cops give many times on the stand and the one he expected now. Still, there was something about the way Burke hesitated. Holloway decided to take a chance.

"That's funny," Holloway said, "because he said you're a lying crook, and he said it twice, under oath."

Burke went off. "That sunovabitch!"

It was Coleman who was the liar, Burke said. "I'm not supposed to be tellin' you this, but we had him indicted after he left here. Talk to J. C. Adams, the county attorney," Burke said. "He'll tell you everything you need to know."

Morton is a dusty, one-stoplight town about fifteen miles from the New Mexico line that makes Tulia seem hectic and bustling by comparison. Like Tulia, it is cotton and cattle country, but no major roads go anywhere near it. Adams, like many rural county attorneys in Texas, maintained a private practice in addition to his official duties. Holloway parked his Mercedes in front of Adams's law office on the deserted town square. It was bitterly cold, and it looked like snow. The reception area was empty, except for a pair of live prairie dogs, gopher-size rodents indigenous to the High Plains, which Adams kept in cages like pet rabbits. Holloway sat down beside the cages to wait.

Adams finally emerged and invited Holloway into his office. He was a large man with a brusque, businesslike manner. It was obvious he didn't like Tom Coleman, but he didn't know much about the Tulia sting and seemed to suspect that this conversation was going to lead to a subpoena and a court appearance. They had indeed indicted Coleman, Adams explained. The charges were theft and abuse of official capacity. He had the file open on the desk before him. "You didn't get this information from me," he warned Holloway. Coleman had stolen gas from the county pumps. Adams himself had witnessed him illegally filling his pickup truck. That was the night Coleman skipped town, Adams explained. It wasn't because of anything Sheriff Burke had done, however. Coleman left to chase after his girlfriend, who took off one evening with her child to return to her parents' home in Illinois. He didn't even turn in his patrol car, Adams told Holloway. He just walked into the sheriff's office after his dinner break that evening and told the dispatcher that his wife had left him and he had to go find her. They found the patrol car parked in front of his empty house fourteen miles outside of town.

He did leave a note for the sheriff, Adams said, pulling a piece of paper from the file in front of him and pushing it across his desk to Holloway. The half-page note was filled with grammatical errors and mark outs, and the handwriting resembled that of a teenage girl. It read:

Dear Sheriff,

Its been a year, I have work in Cochran County, I wan't to thank you for the job,

But it time to move on,

My family + myself hate the blowing dirt here and all the crap that with have to go thru,

You're a pretty good person, I have enjoyed being your friend, I
wish you well, and hope you can win the election in Nov. 1996.
   Tom R. Coleman
   (signed)

   The tone of the letter didn't suggest Coleman had anything
against the sheriff. It was more like the other way around—in the mar-
gin someone had scrawled, "Worth 30 gal. of gas to be shed of him."
   In the weeks prior to Coleman's disappearance, Adams explained,
the sheriff had heard from several local business owners that the
deputy was behind on his bills. Burke spoke with Coleman about it,
and he had promised to make good on the debts. After Coleman was
gone the sheriff realized the full extent of Coleman's deceit. His tab at
the supermarket was over $1,200. The First State Bank in nearby
Whiteface was holding long overdue notes for $2,000. He owed $400
to the propane company, over $1,000 to the phone company, and he
was two months behind on his rent. The list went on. Coleman had
been trading on his status as a cop to get credit all over town, and he
burned them all. Altogether, his debts came to over $6,900, a consid-
erable sum in a town where the per capita income was less than
$25,000. Burke also discovered that the woman Coleman had been
living with was not his wife, as he had claimed, and the boy was not
his son. Burke fired off an angry letter to the Texas Commission on
Law Enforcement Officers Standards and Education (TCLEOSE),
the state licensing agency for peace officers, to serve as a warning in
his permanent file for future employers to read.
   The sheriff promised to help everyone get their money, but Coleman was gone for good. Finally, in May 1998, just prior to the two-
year statute of limitations for theft, the county decided to file charges
on Coleman for stealing the gas. In August, county officials got word
that Coleman was working in Swisher County. A Teletype was sent
informing Sheriff Larry Stewart of the warrant for Coleman's arrest.

"So what happened?" Holloway asked.

"They arrested him," Adams said.

Holloway couldn't believe it. The sheriff's department had to arrest the county's undercover agent *during the operation.* Not only did Coleman keep his job, but the district attorney didn't tell the defense attorneys about the incident. This was beyond the pale. At the very least, Holloway figured, it should mean a new trial for the three defendants who got hard time on this man's testimony. For his own part, Holloway was now certain that the cases should not have been brought in front of a grand jury in the first place.

Coleman never returned to Morton to deal with the charges. In mid-August, Adams explained, Coleman's attorney showed up in Morton with a check for the full amount he owed, $6,900. The money was put in a restitution fund, and the theft charges against Coleman were dropped. That was the end of the story, as far as Adams was concerned.

"Where did he get the money?" Holloway asked. Adams just shrugged.

Holloway had an idea of where it might have come from. Before he left, he persuaded Adams to give him his entire file on Coleman.

Bad apples tended to bounce from town to town in rural areas in Holloway's experience. Every small town had been burned by a new football coach or math teacher who came with a good recommendation but turned out to be a pervert or a closet alcoholic. More often than not, administrators preferred to pawn problem employees off on a district in another county rather than blow the whistle and endure the scandal that followed. It was unfortunate, but it happened.

But this was a cop. Sheriff Stewart or somebody from the task force must have called Cochran County during the background check on Coleman. Checking the TCLEOSE file and calling the most recent employer is the minimum they could be expected to do. Holloway couldn't believe Cochran County hadn't warned them off after the way he left town. Cops, reluctant to criticize one another, had developed a sort of code for bad actors: "Not eligible for rehire." Surely Coleman qualified for that label.

Back at his office, Holloway began methodically examining the file. There was no doubt that Coleman had been arrested. It was all there in black and white—the charging document from Cochran County, the arrest warrant, the bond Coleman had secured pending trial. Holloway quickly found one of the reasons Coleman may have had money problems in Cochran County. He had an ex-wife named Carol Barnett who sued him for unpaid child support in the mid-1990s. By court order, his county paycheck was being garnished $480 per month. Holloway developed a theory. The arrest warrant out of Cochran County had put Coleman's back against the wall. He had to come up with almost $7,000 fast, or his new job in Swisher County, not to mention his career in law enforcement, would come to an abrupt end. His salary as an undercover task force agent was only $23,000 per year, which meant he was taking home perhaps $1,500 per month; after the garnishment, Coleman was making around $1,000 a month. He'd be lucky to pay his current bills, much less his old ones.

He had a steady source of funds in the task force, however, which provided him with cash every week to make drug buys in Tulia. He had supposedly bought cocaine from dozens of people, and he was making several deals per defendant—usually eight balls, if Holloway's cases were typical. That meant the task force must have given him thousands of dollars in buy money over the course of the investigation. Holloway suspected that Coleman was stealing money from the task force by reporting buys he never actually made.

It was a scam Holloway had heard about from time to time but never personally encountered. One eight ball of cocaine (or a few grams of ground-up crack) can easily be made into ten eight balls or more by mixing the cocaine into a batch of baking soda or any white powder and then parceling it back out. The result was a diluted product that was too weak to use but that still tested positive for cocaine in the lab. The fake eight balls go into the evidence locker, along with the names of the supposed dealers, and the buy money goes into the narc's pocket. With nobody monitoring Coleman's movements and no corroboration of the alleged deals, who would know the difference? It was outlandish, sure, but so was Coleman's story of dozens of cocaine dealers in tiny Tulia. The more Holloway learned about Coleman, the more plausible it seemed. He had to tell Judge Self. Even if he didn't buy into Holloway's theory, Self had to be told about Coleman's arrest. It changed everything.

Judge Ed Self, who was in his mid-fifties, had been on the bench less than two years, but Holloway had known him much longer. Self's square jaw and ruddy complexion made him look vaguely German, an effect bolstered by his severe demeanor. He had helped Holloway get his practice off the ground when the two attorneys worked out of the same building in Plainview. At one time, Self did criminal defense work, but he eventually shifted his practice to civil matters. He became disillusioned with defense work, he once told Holloway, because of a case he lost before a judge in Plainview. Self was representing a client who had been beaten by the police and coerced into giving a confession. The judge granted a hearing on Self's motion to have the confession thrown out, and he made the most of it. Self ran circles around the prosecutor that day; there was no doubt in his mind that he had won convincingly. At the end of the hearing, the judge calmly ruled against him. It was a game you couldn't win, and Self decided not to play any more.

That is, until Governor George W. Bush appointed him to a vacant judgeship in 1998. Nine months later, Self had to face election for his first full term in the district, which included Hale, Swisher, and neighboring Castro County. Answering to the law and order voters of the panhandle seemed to make him see things in a different light. Not long after Self took the bench, Holloway found himself in front of the judge in a hearing to quash another dubious confession. Halfway through the hearing, Holloway discovered that the officer produced by the prosecution to testify on the collection of the confession hadn't even been present at the interrogation. The cop turned beet red when Holloway caught him in the lie. It was a nifty piece of lawyering, and it made Holloway's day—right up until Self's ruling. Motion denied. "He was becoming exactly what he despised," Holloway said.

Still, Holloway felt confident that Self would not be able to hold his nose on the Tulia sting, once he heard what Holloway had to tell him. To bolster his case, he decided to join forces with Tom Hamilton, another Plainview trial lawyer, who, along with his partner and son, Brent, had also taken on some court-appointed Tulia cases. Tom Hamilton, who was in his late fifties, was a former district attorney, so his opinion carried weight at the courthouse. He was a lean man and a bit on the short side, but he had a commanding presence and a quiet authority that made people listen carefully to what he had to say. His son Brent, who was in his mid-thirties, was more muscular and handsome, and he had inherited his father's sense of gravitas.

As a prosecutor, Tom had a reputation for playing it by the book. He once dismissed a case after he happened to witness a highway patrolman beating a defendant. He told the outraged officer that he couldn't risk having the defendant's attorney question him about the beating on the stand—the result would either be perjury or an indictment for assault.

Hamilton's cases were almost identical to Holloway's. No drugs were found when his clients were arrested, there was no corroboration of any kind for the alleged buys, and, though none of the deals was for more than an eight ball, several of them were said to have occurred in drug-free zones, making them first-degree felonies. Hamilton had already spoken with McEachern about the poor quality of the cases, but the DA wouldn't budge. He had also called some other court-appointed attorneys in town and heard much the same story as Holloway. Some of their defendants denied ever meeting Coleman and others claimed to have sold him crack only. Hamilton was impressed with what Holloway discovered in Cochran County, and they resolved to do their pretrial work together. They would have to work fast. One of Hamilton's clients, Billy Wafer, had a probation revocation hearing set for February 11. It was already January 25. Hamilton was also representing Donnie Smith, who had a trial setting a few days after Wafer's hearing.

They would in all likelihood not be able to use the Cochran County charge at trial. Under the Texas rules of evidence, specific instances of past misconduct by witnesses were not admissible unless they involved a final conviction for a felony or "a crime of moral turpitude." These provisions were commonly referred to as Rule 608 and Rule 609. Theft was a crime of moral turpitude, but Coleman technically had not been convicted. (He paid restitution, which usually went hand-in-hand with a conviction, but his attorney had worked out a special deal.) In a perverse way, Holloway almost felt his clients would have been better served if he had discovered the charge *after* they were convicted, if that was in fact to be their fate. The prosecution's failure to reveal Coleman's arrest to the defense would have made an excellent basis for an appeal. That type of appellate argument was known as a Brady claim, after the case that established the legal precedent in U.S. law. In the Brady case, the Supreme Court found that the prosecution had an affirmative duty to turn over evidence in its possession that might be used to prove a defendants innocence. Subsequent case law had firmly established that such information included the criminal history of the state's witnesses. Now that the defense team had found the information themselves, however, that appellate avenue was closed off to their clients. They could not argue that they didn't have the benefit of the information as they prepared for trial. They had to find a way to win the first time around.

The theft charge itself might have been inadmissible, but the evidence of Coleman's debt, how and when he paid it off, and the garnishing of his paycheck was all fair game and potentially useful, provided the judge gave them the latitude to present it to the jury in a way that supported their theory of the cases. Plus, their knowledge of Coleman's indictment was the perfect lever to pry some concessions out of the judge. Tom Hamilton had been practicing law in Hale County for over thirty years. He knew all the rules of evidence, but he was from the old school, where such things took a backseat to considerations of common sense. "If something doesn't smell right, the judge in my opinion had the obligation to try to find out what it is," he said later. "And I just felt like something didn't smell right in this case and if we could get enough information before the judge, the judge would finally say, look, you know, something's not right here. I'm gonna have some hearings outside the court and I'm gonna find out what's goin' on."

The next day, January 26, the fourth trial of the Tulia sting got under way in front of Judge Jack Miller, who shared jurisdiction over Tulia with Judge Self. The defendant was a young man named Cash Love, one of the few white suspects busted by Coleman. Love was the longtime boyfriend of Donnie Smith's little sister, Kizzie White, and the two had a child together. He was represented by an Amarillo attorney named Van Williamson. Holloway was not surprised when he learned a few days later that Love had been found guilty. The sentence, however, was a shocker. Love had been convicted of eight separate deliveries, some of which had been found to have occurred in a drug free zone, and the jury had instructed that the sentences for each conviction be served consecutively. The total time was 361 years. Love's sentence brought a new sense of urgency to the pretrial work. Together with Tom and Brent, Holloway drafted a motion to Self, outlining what they had already discovered about Coleman and renewing the request for an investigator. The motion sought Self's permission to bring witnesses from Cochran County to testify about the charge or, if that was inadmissible, at least to testify about Coleman's reputation for veracity. Testimony about a witness's general character was less tightly controlled under the rules of evidence than was testimony about specific incidents of misconduct.

The team also needed access to documents to further develop their theory: records of cash advanced to Coleman for purchases in Tulia, payroll records for Coleman from Swisher County and the task force, documents related to the Cochran County charge and the debts he owed in Morton. The team prepared subpoenas for them all, along with demands for Coleman's handwritten notes about the investigation, copies of random drug screens he was allegedly given by his employers, documents related to missing or stolen cocaine at the task force (the cocaine had to come from somewhere, they theorized), and copies of withholding orders that might show how much Coleman's paycheck had been garnished while he worked for the task force.

The motion to Self also requested funding for expert testing of the drugs—not just the evidence in their own cases, but every eight ball purchased by Coleman during the entire operation. The idea was not just to determine whether or not the cocaine was suspiciously weak, though Holloway certainly hoped that would be one result of the testing. If Holloway's theory was correct, an expert, by analyzing the amount and type of cutting agent in each sample, might also be able to demonstrate that all of the cocaine, allegedly bought from over forty different individuals, actually came from the same source. It wouldn't conclusively prove that the cases were bogus, but it would go a long way toward supporting the notion that Coleman had made the eight balls himself. The motion was ex parte, meaning the prosecution would not see it. It was for Self's eyes only.

Holloway poured himself into the pretrial work. In the back of his mind, however, he thought it wouldn't be needed. Just finding the

Cochran County charge had been the real breakthrough; Judge Self hadn't known about it during the first trials. For all Holloway knew, McEachern hadn't been told, either. "I think I thought that if somebody knew about Tom, it would all be stopped," he said later. The motion laid it all out for Self. The judge was not going to be pleased to hear this new information, particularly with four trials already in the can. There was also the considerable investment in time and resources the county had put into the investigation, which would all go out the window if the cases were thrown out. Still, even in the panhandle, this couldn't stand, Holloway thought. "Maybe I was being naive," he said later.

CHAPTER SIX

Officer of the Year

AFTER FIRING OFF the motion to Judge Self, Holloway decided to call Carol Barnett, the woman who had sued Coleman for unpaid child support and received a portion of his paycheck while Coleman worked in Tulia. Barnett worked in the dispatcher's office of the Pecos County sheriff's department in Fort Stockton, one of the lonely outposts that dot the never-ending stretch of I–10 between El Paso and the Hill Country of central Texas. The nearest metropolis (by west Texas standards) was a two-hour drive northeast to Midland/Odessa, the heart of Texas oil and gas country. Lubbock was another two hours beyond that. Holloway reached Barnett at home on the evening of February 7. "Start with the ex-wife" is an old trial lawyer axiom, and this time it did not disappoint. Barnett had plenty to say about her former husband. But she was not just bitter about Tom Coleman, she was afraid of him. By the time Barnett finished with her story, Holloway was too.

Carol Barnett married Tom Coleman on February 22, 1990. The two met in Fort Stockton, where Coleman had begun working as a sheriff's deputy the year before. Coleman grew up about fifty miles away in the small town of Pecos. His father, Joe Coleman, was the Texas Ranger for the area. That made the Colemans a very special family in Pecos. The Rangers are an elite division of the state police force; there are only a 118 of them in the entire state. Few institutions are as venerated in the hagiography of Texas. For generations, school-children across the state have learned how the Rangers conquered the frontier, relying on their bravery and their prowess with a gun. "One Riot, One Ranger" is one of their mottoes. Now the unit prides itself on the investigative skills of its officers. In rural areas, sheriff's offices that lack experienced detectives frequently turn to the Rangers to investigate murders. The Rangers also investigate police corruption, which lends to their reputation for integrity and independence. Although the force covers the entire state, for most of its history it has been an extremely clubby institution. Long after the state police department was forced to diversify its ranks, the Rangers continued to select their members through a system more akin to a fraternity than a civil service, with kinship and social ties trumping merit and ability. Even though lawsuits in recent years have marginally opened the selection process, the Rangers remain an overwhelmingly white, male institution, one of the last in the state.

Joe Coleman was considered an outstanding Texas Ranger. His wife, Ermadine, worked in law enforcement as well. Tom was his old-est son. Ever since he was old enough to wear a cowboy hat, Tom had dreamed of becoming a Texas Ranger like his father. But whereas Joe wore the customary white hat of the Rangers, Tom always insisted on wearing a black hat. It always bothered Joe somehow that his son wanted to look like an outlaw. As Tom grew up, it became clear that the differences between father and son went far deeper than the color of their hats. Tom was constantly in trouble in school. He developed a reputation as a juvenile delinquent and was frequently in trouble with the police. As embarrassing as this was for Joe, he never failed to bail his son out. In private, however, Joe could be cruel and abusive. As a form of punishment, he would sometimes take Tom and his little brother Mark out behind a shed in the backyard and hold them in headlocks until they passed out.

Tom dropped out of high school in the eleventh grade and went to work in the oilfields that surrounded Pecos. But he never gave up on his dream of following in his father's footsteps. He finally got his GED at the age of twenty-seven, barely passing the exam, and his father rewarded him by getting him a job as a guard at the Pecos County jail. But things soon turned sour for Tom in Pecos. He was lazy and inattentive at work and in constant danger of being fired. He considered guarding prisoners to be beneath him, and he wanted the sheriff to commission him as a patrol deputy, a true cop. His personal life was a mess as well. It was widely known around Pecos that Tom abused his first wife, Regina Culberson, whom he married shortly after he left high school. In 1989, she fled to Alabama. Tom abruptly quit his job and followed her there. Eventually he returned home, divorced, unemployed, and by now deeply in debt. With Tom's bridges burned in Pecos, his dad managed to get him a job as a deputy in nearby Fort Stockton, where the sheriff was a friend of his.

There he met and married Carol Barnett. The counties in the trans-Pecos region of west Texas are large and sparsely populated, and Coleman was assigned to patrol the area around Iraan (pronounced Ira-Ann), a tiny hamlet in the far eastern corner of the county. Coleman was finally a cop, and he threw himself into his job with gusto. He took to sleeping in his car so he would be the first on a crime scene. Despite the couple's meager income, he began buying guns of all kinds, and sometimes carried as many as three on his person at one time. But Iraan, with a couple of stoplights and a population of 1,300, didn't provide the kind of excitement Coleman was looking for. He began making up excuses to patrol Fort Stockton instead, which put him in trouble with the sheriff. In fact, Coleman was often caught lying by his coworkers, Barnett told Holloway. He would lie about anything.

In 1991, Joe Coleman died of a heart attack. After that Tom's behavior became increasingly erratic. Cleaning out his father's office, Tom found an enormous arsenal, including thousands of rounds of ammunition, live World War II–era grenades, and tear gas canisters, which he brought home and stored in a closet in the bathroom. Coleman's father also had an old fully automatic assault rifle, which he had kept hidden for years. The illegal gun was a family heirloom, and Tom could not bring himself to get rid of it. He tucked it away in his attic. After the divorce, Barnett called the Bureau of Alcohol, Tobacco, and Firearms, who came to the house and confiscated the gun. Despite having so many guns around, Coleman never seemed to feel safe. He became increasingly paranoid and hid guns in various locations around the house and booby-trapped the front door when he and Carol went out of town. He began carrying a KKK card in his wallet, although there was no genuine KKK movement in Pecos County. Coleman just liked showing it to people, Barnett said.

Tom and Carol began having serious marital problems. Coleman doted on the couple's first child, a son, but wanted nothing to do with a daughter born with albinism. He became increasingly violent toward Barnett and convinced that she was cheating on him or planning to leave him. The couple was also deeply in debt, and local creditors called regularly. Finally, after Barnett told him she wanted a divorce in February 1994, Coleman cracked. In a scene that prefigured what he would do in Cochran County just two years later, he wrote a note to the sheriff informing him that he was quitting and blaming all of his recent troubles on his wife. Leaving his patrol car at his house, Coleman put his two-year-old son in the family car, pawned a gun for gas money, and drove to the north Texas town of Sherman, where his mother had moved following his father's death. Barnett eventually recovered her son in a vicious divorce and custody battle. After years of dodging his child support payments, Coleman gave up his parental rights to both children.

Barnett told Holloway she was not surprised that Coleman had managed to land another deputy job, despite his checkered past. The name Joe Coleman continued to carry a lot of weight in west Texas law enforcement circles even after his death. "He's been riding on his daddy's shirttails for years, tryin' to be like his daddy," she said. When she heard about the big bust in Tulia and Coleman's newfound fame, Barnett told Holloway, she assumed he was lying about his undercover work. But he was still Joe Coleman's son, and that meant the Rangers would watch out for him, she warned. In fact, Holloway had found a couple of mysterious references to a Ranger named Larry Gilbreath in Jay Adams's file on Coleman. He now began to wonder if Gilbreath hadn't helped Coleman work his way out of the Cochran County mess. Before hanging up, Barnett gave Holloway a list of names and numbers of past coworkers of Coleman's, and a warning to watch his step if he planned on going after her ex-husband. "Ask anybody about him," she said. "The guy is a nut."

On February 9, Tom Hamilton, Brent Hamilton, Donnie Smith, and Terry McEachern appeared before Judge Self in a pretrial hearing for Donnie, who was set to go to trial in six days. The previous day, McEachern had filed motions to quash all of the subpoenas the defense had delivered. It was unclear whether McEachern had known about the theft charge against Coleman before he looked at the subpoenas for Cochran County's records on the case. In any case, he seemed to know enough about it now to argue that it was inadmissible in court. Coleman may have paid restitution, but technically there had not been a final conviction, he told Judge Self. Citing Rule 609, he asked the judge to instruct the defense not to mention the charge in front of a jury. As far as the rest of the subpoenas went, McEachern argued, it was a fishing expedition. The defense hadn't shown how any of the information they sought was material to the case; they were just digging for dirt.

Self, of course, knew the theory that the defense was putting together from reading the ex parte defense motion, information that the district attorney did not have available to him. Yet he now agreed with McEachern. He did not see how Coleman's character was at issue, he said. The sheriff and the supervisors of the task force had testified in previous trials, as they no doubt would in the upcoming case, that they had conducted a background check when Coleman applied for the job and found nothing amiss. There would be no mention of the theft charge and no testimony about his reputation from his past associates, Self ruled. The documentary evidence the team had already collected would be sealed. Self did not rule on the subpoenas, but he made it clear he considered the whole episode closed. With respect to the analysis of the drug evidence, Self said he was not prepared to rule. He instructed Hamilton instead to do some research on where such testing could be done and, crucially, how much it would cost. It was a total washout.

After the hearing, Tom and Brent met with McEachern in his office, where Tom took a last stab at bringing McEachern around. When Tom was district attorney in the early 1970s, he always made it a point to know everything he could about his witnesses. "If I'm the DA then I'm gonna have to vouch for somebody that's on that stand. It's my ass that's on the line; it's not theirs," he said later. Hamilton knew that McEachern was not that type of prosecutor, and he wasn't surprised that McEachern seemed to know very little about the charges against Coleman. All he seemed to know was that Coleman passed a polygraph test at some point, according to his commander at the task force. McEachern seemed unclear on the specifics.

"Terry, there's something wrong with these cases," Tom told him again. McEachern's response was devastatingly pragmatic. "Tom, let me ask you something: I have tried four cases already—am I gonna go in and say that these cases were improperly convicted?" McEachern said. "One of 'em got over 300 years. What am I gonna do?"

That evening Holloway called Hamilton. He had just interviewed

Carol Barnett the night before, and he was excited. She had spilled her guts on Tom, he said. The guy was worse than a bad apple—he was certifiable. They had to get somebody down to Pecos County to pick up the divorce file. According to Barnett, there were documents in the file that would sink Coleman if they were ever shown to a jury. Then Hamilton told Holloway what had happened in court that day. Holloway was crushed, but he wasn't ready to give up, not after what Barnett had told him. They had to get down to Pecos County and start doing interviews. Hamilton was dubious. Self had made it clear he wasn't interested in hearing about Coleman's past. Besides, there was no time to drive to Fort Stockton to chase after witnesses. Billy Wafer's hearing was in two days.

Billy Wafer was in his early forties, married with two children. He had short salt-and-pepper hair, a large, square head, and a frame almost as big as Joe Moore's, though he was not as tall. He had worked as a forklift operator in Tulia for most of the past ten years. In the late 1980s he had been given ten years' probation for marijuana possession. At the time of his arrest in the Tulia sting, he had done nine and a half years without violating. Not that it mattered now—if his probation were revoked, he'd be sentenced to the entire ten years. A revocation hearing is not a full-fledged trial, and the differences favor the prosecution. There is no jury. The standard of evidence is also lower: the state must only show "by a preponderance of the evidence" that the defendant has violated the terms of his probation. By the time a revocation reaches the hearing stage, it is usually too late for the defendant.

The case against Wafer, however, was weak, even by the standards of Coleman's investigation. Wafer was alleged to have met Coleman and Man Kelly at the Allsup's convenience store one morning, agreed on a deal for an eight ball, and then directed a third party to deliver the drugs to Coleman later that morning at the sale barn, where Coleman sometimes hung around. They didn't even have Wafer handing Coleman the drugs. Plus, Wafer had a pretty good alibi. At the time of the alleged meeting at Allsup's—between 9:00 and 9:30 on a weekday morning—Wafer was at his job at Seed Resources, where he served as the warehouse foreman. He had time cards, and his boss had agreed to testify on his behalf.

Beyond that, there wasn't much to the case. Wafer's fate was probably going to hinge on whether or not Judge Self found his alibi credible. Brent Hamilton was representing Wafer, but Tom attended the hearing as well. Despite Self's ruling in the pretrial hearing earlier in the week, Tom wasn't ready to give up on Coleman just yet. At a minimum, Wafer's hearing was a chance to do some more fact-finding while Coleman was under oath. If Self would allow it, Tom wanted Brent to use his time with Coleman to fill in some gray areas in their theory of the cases. But Tom also felt that they stood a good chance of catching Coleman in a lie on the stand. If they could dirty him up a little in front of the judge, he thought, maybe Self would reconsider his decision.

On cross-examination, Brent tried to flesh out the short description of the alleged deal in Coleman's police report. It soon became clear that Coleman could not remember exactly how his exchange with Wafer occurred. "It was just a conversation," Coleman said. "He said something, I said something; he said something else. Okay? I'll do the deal, see you later."

"You're the only officer that can testify about this transaction," Brent pointed out. "There's no audiotape."

"Well, if Mr. Kelly could testify, sure make things a lot easier around here," Coleman said. Coleman had alleged that Kelly made some of the purchases on Coleman's behalf, which put Kelly on the hook for several felonies of his own and precluded him from testifying in other defendants' trials. So far, McEachern had not seen any reason to make Kelly a deal to become a state's witness. It was just Coleman's word in Wafer's case, as it had been from the beginning.

Brent began to back his way into a discussion of the Cochran County theft charge. He began a line of questioning on Coleman's hiring by the task force. Coleman testified that he had to fill out an application for Sheriff Stewart as well.

Q: Did it ask you about prior employment?
A: I believe it did.
Q: Prior experience with law enforcement?
A: Yes, sir, I believe it did.
Q: Prior drug investigation?
A: I don't believe so.
Q: Arrests?
A: Arrests?
Q: Yes, sir.

Coleman was visibly nervous. "How many arrests I have made?" he offered. "No," Hamilton corrected. "Did it ever ask whether *you* were ever arrested?"

"I believe so," Coleman replied. McEachern did not object, so Hamilton pressed on.

Q: Did it ask you whether you were ever charged with any offense?
A: I believe so.
Q: Did you list any previous charges?
A: Of being arrested? Nope, I don't believe so.
Q: Being arrested or being charged.
A: Huh-uh. No, sir.
Q: You were required to, weren't you?
A: Yeah, but I've never been arrested or charged for nothing except [a] traffic ticket way back when I was a kid.

Brent paused. What Coleman had just said was clearly false, and everybody present knew it, including the judge. McEachern said nothing. Brent elected not to try to call Coleman on the lie; he would give him some more rope, to see what the man would do with it.

"Have you ever been required to post bond for any case other than a traffic ticket?" he asked. There was a long pause. Coleman seemed to be weighing his options, or perhaps rethinking the wisdom of his previous answer.

"I don't recall," he finally said.

"What does—What does you don't recall mean? You don't remember whether you were, or—"

"I don't remember," Coleman interrupted. "What—What are you getting at here? I don't know what you—I've been arrested for murder or what? I mean what's your deal here?" Coleman's outburst seemed finally to bring McEachern to life. He objected to the line of questioning as irrelevant. In the back-and-forth that followed, Self quizzed Brent on where he was headed: was he trying to impeach Coleman with something other than a conviction of a crime? Brent couldn't deny it, and Self sustained the objection.

Self later shut down Brent's efforts to ask about Coleman's personal finances, after Brent declined to explain why it might be relevant, citing the need to preserve the secrecy of his defense strategy for the time being. Instead, Brent requested a bill of exceptions, which allows a line of questioning to be continued on the record, even though it has been ruled inadmissible by the judge, so that an appellate judge can assess whether or not the material should have been allowed. During the bill, Coleman testified that during the time he was employed by Swisher County, probably in April or May 1998, he had received between six and seven thousand dollars from his mother to pay some bills. Brent tried to dig further into Coleman's employment history, but the bill was limited to questions about his finances, and Self held him to it. Coleman admitted that he had left debts in both Pecos County and Cochran County, but that was all Brent could get from him.

After the state rested, Brent put on Wafer's boss and Wafer himself. Wafer's alibi was not rock solid. His boss testified that Wafer could and often did leave the warehouse on company business or personal errands. Like the other cases, the contest basically came down to a swearing match between Coleman and the defendant. Fortunately Wafer made a good witness. He was articulate, and he projected an aura of quiet confidence. More importantly, he was one of the few people Coleman had accused who was steadily employed and could reliably say where he was at any given time. His boss clearly liked and trusted him. Wafer even had men working under him at his job.

Wafer must have made a good impression on Self or Coleman— who for the first time was seriously challenged by a defense attorney and came across as rattled and defensive—must have made a bad one. It may have been Coleman's lie on the stand, unchallenged though it was, that Self could not stomach. At the end of the day, he declined to revoke Wafer's probation and Wafer was free to go.

It was Friday afternoon. Donnie Smith's trial began on Tuesday. Tom and Brent had the weekend to prepare.

CHAPTER SEVEN

Donnie Smith

THE EARLIEST THING Donnie Smith can remember is riding through downtown Tulia in his mother's car. He was about four or five years old, standing in the backseat looking over his mother's shoulder. As she turned left from Second Street onto Austin Avenue, Donnie fell over and rolled right out of the unlatched rear door, landing on the street in front of the Hale County State Bank. His mother, Mattie White, immediately scooped him up and took him to the drugstore to get him patched up. Donnie learned two things that morning that stuck with him: the red-bricked streets of downtown Tulia are hard, and your mother is all you really have in this world.

Mattie White was born and raised in the Flats, one of eight children fathered by Earlie Smith, the longtime godfather of black Tulia. Mattie was never close to her father. "He wasn't nothin' but a crook. I didn't fool with him much," she said. The Smith family always seemed to be in the middle of whatever trouble was brewing in the Flats. Mattie had a particularly notorious stepbrother, Earlie Smith Jr., who was in and out of prison from an early age. She watched several of her aunts and uncles die of cirrhosis. Mattie found Jesus late in life, but in her early years she was wild too. Mattie had a son, Cecil, at sixteen and a daughter, Tonya, at eighteen, each by a different father.

Eventually she settled down and married Ricky White, and had four more children, Donnie, Ricky Jr., Kizzie, and Kareem.

Ricky White's childhood had been spent shuttling back and forth between the family home in West Dallas and Tulia, where his father wrangled farmhands during the cotton harvest. In Dallas, his father shined shoes in barbershops during the day and hustled pool at night. He was not much of a family man, and the circles in which he ran, in both Tulia and Dallas, required him to carry a gun. He would sometimes disappear for weeks at a time. When Ricky was about eight years old, his mother took the family to Tulia for good, and his father stayed behind. Ricky's mother provided for the family by opening a café in the kitchen of her house in the Flats. (She sold fried chicken sandwiches that people still marvel about in Tulia, years after her death.) A gambler named B. J. Williams took Ricky under his wing. "He was just a real good dude, man—a hard, street dude," Ricky said. "He taught me how to shoot dice and pool, how to get girls. You know how old dudes pick up young guys—in those days it was the whole package."

Life in the Flats was not so different from life in segregated Dallas, except that Ricky was now attending school regularly for the first time, across town in Tulia's newly integrated elementary. He was a smart kid, and he quickly caught up with his peers. He was a member of Tulia's first generation of blacks to attend high school as a matter of course, and it seemed to open up a new world of possibilities. Ricky was charismatic and good-looking and ambitious, a natural leader. He excelled in high school sports, where he played football alongside the future county judge, Harold Keeter, and many of the men who wound up running Tulia. After graduation, he got a two-year degree in engineering technology from Amarillo College and later spent several semesters at Texas A&M University, the state's premier engineering school.

But by that time he had already started a family with Mattie, and the pressures of providing for them brought him back to Tulia without a degree. Still, he had more education than most of the white men he wound up working for, which made him unusual in the black community. He got a highly sought-after job at the highway department, one of the first black men in Tulia to do so. The Whites moved out of the Flats earlier than most, purchasing one of the new houses that went up on the south side in the early 1970s.

As young fathers in the early 1980s, White and Fred Brookins Sr. put together a sports team for the city league, mostly to give black teenagers and young adults something to do. The Lobos, as White and Brookins called the team, recruited many of Tulia High's former sports stars, but the team also adopted talented kids who didn't have a chance to shine in high school. Some didn't have the grades to qualify or dropped out of school completely. Others had been kicked off teams for drug use or simply had attitudes that, in the minds of Tulia's coaches, made them not worth the trouble, regardless of their talents on the field. The Lobos quickly became one of the best softball squads in town, though the team was as much about mentoring the young men, many of whom grew up in households without fathers, as it was about playing ball. Ricky became a respected leader in the black community, and in the mid-1980s, he ran for city council.

Yet Ricky never seemed to live up to his expectations for himself. Tulia was not ready for a black city councilman, and he could not seem to get ahead at work either. In Tulia in the 1970s and 1980s, the prospect of a black man supervising white men was still a foreign idea. He experimented briefly with running a bar in nearby Dimmitt but never made much money. He eventually settled into a job at D-A Manufacturing, a small valve factory just outside of Tulia. Though he was trained as a draftsman, he wound up working as a machinist, a position he held for about twenty years.

His family life turned sour as well. Ricky's relationship with Mattie was rocky from the start. "My dad always had ladies, he had ladies younger than me," Donnie said. In fact neither spouse was faithful to the other. They quarrelled constantly, though they were never physically violent. Donnie lived in fear that his dad would disappear. One morning he went into his father's room and noticed that all of his clothes were gone from the dresser. "He was gone and I thought I'd lost him forever," he said. But Ricky just went to work for a brother-in-law in Louisiana for a few months.

More often it was his mother who left. When Donnie was eleven, Mattie took the kids and moved to Wichita Falls, about seventy-five miles northwest of Dallas, to live with a boyfriend. Unable to afford a place of their own, Mattie and her boyfriend moved into his mother's house, which was already crowded before Mattie and her six kids arrived. It was the kind of ill-considered decision Mattie was known for in Tulia. Donnie's oldest brother, Cecil, who was then fourteen, refused to stay and moved back to Tulia to live with Ricky. After six months, the arrangement fell apart and Mattie moved the entire family back home. Before she did, however, her boyfriend introduced Donnie to a man named Robert Collins, who worked as a plumber in Wichita Falls. "That's your real dad," he told Donnie.

Mattie's boyfriend thought he was doing Donnie a favor by telling him the truth, but Donnie took the news hard. He had always taken pride in being the son of Ricky White, a man so many people respected. Now he wasn't sure who he was. Back in Tulia, he began to spend more and more time away from his family. He spent countless hours hanging around Jackson Chapel in the Flats or at his grandmother's house. Cecil, who was beginning to get in trouble with the cops, would not have much to do with Donnie, and he took to walking the streets of the south side or the Flats by himself, dribbling his basketball for hours at a time. He failed sixth grade. "Donnie was just different," his older sister Tonya said. "He just kinda strange. He does stuff like people don't love him. He'd rather go to a stranger before he come to his own family. That's just Donnie." Donnie eventually insisted on changing his last name to Smith.

Ricky and Mattie split up for good when Donnie was fourteen. Ricky took up with a younger woman who had kids of her own. Mattie worked long hours sewing jeans at the Levi's plant in Amarillo or at the Royal Park garment factory in Tulia. She sometimes moonlighted at a convenience store as well, leaving the children unsupervised. "Those kids basically raised themselves," said Kent Brookins, who went to high school with Donnie.

Donnie poured himself into sports. He spent all of his time after school in the park, playing basketball and football. His uncle Tony Powell had been a football star in his day, and he showed Donnie how to run good patterns and how to cut with the ball. In high school, Donnie became a standout in basketball, football, and track. He was hoping to get a scholarship to West Texas A&M University just up the highway in Canyon. Though he was only five-foot-nine, Donnie averaged twenty-two points a game for the Tulia Hornets basketball team and was named a captain of the squad. The whole family was gifted. Donnie's little brother, Ricky White Jr., was one of the fastest sprinters ever to run track at Tulia High, and many thought he had an outside chance at qualifying for the Olympics. "They should all be in the NBA or somewhere doin' something," Tonya White said.

Sports had always been a huge part of the lives of Tulia's black teenagers. With so few black families in Tulia, there are only a handful of black students in every grade. Yet over the years black athletes who make the football team have been disproportionately found in the skill positions, such as quarterback, halfback, and receiver. Although this is a source of pride for black families, it is also a cause for resentment. Conventional wisdom in black Tulia holds that the bar is set so high for black players that only the very best—those whose natural ability simply can't be denied—are allowed to play at all. Those whose mediocre abilities only merit a place on the line inevitably lose out to white kids, especially those with parents in the booster club. For those who do make the cut, the glory is like a drug. "As long as you're winning for them, you're cool," Thelma Johnson said. "Oh, you need money for a uniform, you need help getting to practice? No problem, we can take care of that for you." Once they graduate, however, it's a return to anonymity on the south side of town, and a future in manual labor.

The summer after Donnie's junior year, Mattie moved to Pampa, an oil town of about 20,000 about an hour and a half northeast of Tulia. Donnie and his younger siblings went with her, but when school started again, Mattie sent them back to Tulia. There was no room in Ricky's house for four more kids, so it was decided that Tonya, who had graduated the year before and was living and working in Amarillo, would move home and watch the kids. Losing his mother was the hardest thing that had ever happened to Donnie. Most of his friends already knew that Ricky was not his father, and now every-body on the south side was talking about how Mattie had abandoned him and his three younger siblings. Donnie had never felt more alone. Tonya was bitter about the new arrangement, feeling that she was being punished by Mattie for being responsible. Donnie knew he could count on Ricky in an emergency, but Ricky had a new life now, with a new family to look out for. As usual, he responded to the pain in his life by redoubling his efforts to be the best athlete he could be. Because he had missed summer workouts that year, Donnie was passed over for quarterback. He was still made a captain of the team and became an outstanding receiver and kick returner. At graduation, he was named male athlete of the year, the highest honor at Tulia High. He was proud, but it was not the happy occasion it should have been because his mother was not there to see it.

Just graduating from high school made Donnie exceptional. If Tulia's experiment with secondary education for blacks were charted on a graph, it would resemble something like a bell curve. Beginning at zero, the number of black high school graduates climbed slowly after Tulia High was integrated in the 1950s, reaching a peak in the mid-1980s. In the early 1990s, however, the numbers began to drop, particularly for young men. The current graduation rate for black male students, according to an informal tally kept by a teacher at Tulia High, is somewhere in the range of 1 in 4. The majority of the dropouts wind up serving time, often for drug-related charges. This has led in part to another demographic phenomenon in Tulia, one that is somewhat harder to quantify but is evident to anyone who spends time in the black community: a shortage of black men in their twenties and early thirties. By the 1990s, the incarceration rate for young black men in Tulia rivaled that of inner-city neighborhoods in any of the state's metropolitan areas.

Donnie's older brother Cecil was kicked out of high school midway through his junior year for smoking pot. He is currently in a state penitentiary in Beaumont, serving a fifteen-year sentence for robbery. He recalls the day he realized that he was the last of his friends who had not been locked up. "I remember I was in Canyon and this dude I knew from Happy said, 'Man, all them cats in Tulia have been to prison but you.' And I was like 'Yeah, they have, huh?'" he said. That was in 1988. Later that year, Cecil was sent to the pen for the first time on a burglary charge.

Now in his mid-thirties, Cecil's smooth face looks several years younger than that of his little brother Donnie. His demeanor is mild and suave, and he has a resonant, soothing voice like Ricky Sr.'s. He has a tendency to laugh reflexively when he realizes he's said something thoughtful. Like Donnie, he was a star athlete in high school, where he was twice named the basketball defensive player of the year. By the start of his junior year, he was receiving recruiting letters from colleges, including Texas Tech in Lubbock and West Texas A&M in Canyon, as well as a number of junior colleges in the panhandle.

Cecil entertained thoughts of a college career, but his life outside of school was catching up with him. He was breaking into houses and stealing, chiefly to get money to buy pot.

Cocaine started appearing in Tulia a few years after Cecil was kicked out of high school. At first it was powder, but by 1985 crack became the drug of choice, at least in the black community. Cecil was among a small group who started selling it, mostly to friends and relatives in the Flats and on the south side of town. It was a network that came to include some of the best athletes in Tulia. "The minute they got out of school, they'd go to messin' with it," Cecil recalled. If they weren't selling it, they were using it. The most notorious of the early dealers was Dock Casel, who was about three years older than Cecil. Casel had the connections in Amarillo that most of the small-time dealers lacked. But even the nickel and dime players were making money, and that was the attraction, Cecil said. "It's the money, man, they go to making all that fast money," he said.

Crack wasn't like marijuana, which you could smoke all weekend and still make it to work on time Monday morning. "After that crack come through, that changed everything. It changed everybody. Even the old people, they went to smokin' it," Cecil said. But mostly the market was the younger generation. The long fall from high school standout athlete to crack addict became a familiar story in black Tulia. In the mid-1980s, Tulia was known for its boxing club, which trained several young black men who eventually turned pro. One of them, Edward "Pee Wee" Parker, won a few belts in Houston before he wound up serving time for drugs. Another promising boxer, Ford Jennings Jr., wound up on the streets of Amarillo, addicted to crack. In the early 1990s, he was shot in the face in a deal gone bad. There were basketball stars like Dock Casel, and later Donnie and Donnie's little brother Ricky Jr., who went to prison in 1995. Donnie's cousin, Michael Smith, was sent to prison a year later. Donnie's best friend in high school, James Barrow, was a dominating middle linebacker, a bone-crushing hitter who had the size and the meanness to get some attention from college scouts. He wound up an addict as well.

The older generation seemed powerless to stop it. "I know I 'bout broke my mom's heart," Cecil said. "She wanted me to do something with my life and I turned out a drug head."

After Cecil got out of prison in 1989, he moved to Fort Worth, where he settled down and got a good job building swimming pools at $800 per week, more than he ever dreamed of making in Tulia. He and his girlfriend bought a house and had two daughters. He completed nine years of parole without violating, an almost unheard-of accomplishment among Cecil's old crowd. But then he and his girlfriend began having trouble, and one day Cecil cashed his paycheck and bought a bus ticket back to Amarillo. He hadn't been home in years, but it was like nothing had changed and he quickly took up with his old friends again.

One thing was different: Donnie was using crack now. Cecil remembered being surprised at how it had changed him. "Donnie was a smart youngster, man. That tripped me out when I heard he was smokin' that dope. And then the way he got after he was on it. I used to come down there and we'd be smokin' together and I's like, 'Man, gimme some of that, man.' And he's, 'Oh, man I cain't do it man,'" Cecil said. "That dope make you evil, make you ornery, man. He ain't never been that way. I seen some sides of him I ain't never seen in my life. He did some treacherous things."

Cecil will be locked up on his current bit until at least 2009. He's clean and sober again, but now he's worried he'll come home with hepatitis C, which is rampant in Texas prisons, or worse. "If only I'd stayed in Fort Worth, man, maybe none of this would have happened this way," he said. He thinks the next generation should do what he did, or almost did. "I just think when they grow up and get old enough and get out of school, they've just got to get away from Tulia, man. There's no jobs or nothin' there for 'em, you know. And if they don't, they going to be caught up like the rest of us. I think that's the answer: when you get old enough, if you don't go to college, just move away man. Because if you don't you're going to be right down here," he said. "Tulia's just a dead-end town now, man."

Donnie Smith almost made it out. Recruiters did not eye him the way they did his older brother; he was on the small side, even by the standards of regional schools. It didn't help that—despite his B average in high school—he failed to make the minimum score most schools require on the college entrance exam for their scholarship athletes. Still, he was determined to play football or basketball for somebody, and he enrolled at West Texas State University in Canyon, about fifteen miles north of Tulia, where he was allowed to take 099-level classes in lieu of passing the entrance exam. He spoke to the basketball coach about trying out as a walk-on in the spring semester, and the coach was agreeable, provided he kept his grades up and made himself eligible. Donnie found the classes manageable, and he enjoyed college. The campus of WT was a cosmopolitan world by his standards. He lived in a dorm with a white kid from up north, who came to the school on a wrestling scholarship. The two used to listen to "Stairway to Heaven" every night as they went to sleep.

Donnie was still going home on weekends and running with his old friends, including Michael Smith and James Barrow. One night Donnie and his friends got into a fight with a group of white boys cruising on Dip Street, the main drag that runs through the town square. Fights were common on Dip Street, where high school kids with money cruised their new trucks and drank beer. But this one was different. After Donnie knocked one of the kids down, Michael Smith gave him a kicking vicious enough to scare the other white boys off. A few days later, Donnie got word that the cops in Tulia were looking for him. He turned himself in and was charged with a misdemeanor, for which he received probation. He failed to report to his probation officer or pay his fees, however, and he was eventually rearrested. He was in jail in Tulia for two weeks at the end of the semester and missed most of his final exams.

He dropped out of school and moved back to Tulia. He became a regular at the sale barn and found farm work when he could. In the fall of 1994, Donnie and his little brother Kareem played semipro football for a team based in Dimmitt. The league was mostly made up of former high school athletes like himself who either didn't have the grades or didn't get offered a scholarship to play college ball out of high school. Because the players were technically unpaid—they had to sell tickets and merchandise to support themselves—they were still eligible to play in college, on the outside chance of being spotted by a scout and offered a second opportunity somewhere. Donnie was still in excellent shape, and the coaches made him a starter at cornerback. Kareem was made the backup quarterback. Donnie played a few games, traveling as far as Houston and San Antonio for road contests. It was fun to be playing again, but it wasn't the same as playing in front of his friends and family back in Tulia. And it was no way to make a living. He was now twenty-four years old, and he knew in his heart that no scholarship was in store for him. He quit the team and went home to Tulia again.

Later that year he married Lawanda Ward. Shortly after their second son was born, Donnie and Lawanda began having marital problems. Money was a constant issue. She was working as a waitress and pursuing a nursing degree at Amarillo College. Try as he might, Donnie could never land anything that paid more than $5 per hour, usually manual labor jobs that lasted a few months at most. He became depressed. Donnie had tried crack once in high school, but the lifestyle never appealed to him, especially after his older brother Cecil and his younger brother Ricky Jr. got deeper and deeper into it. Now, however, he began hanging out with the partying crowd and—unbeknownst to Lawanda—spending all of the family's money on crack.

After Lawanda kicked him out, Donnie hit rock bottom. When he turned to his uncle, O'Neal Yarbrough, for advice, O'Neal took him to see Harold Keeter, the county judge. Keeter was one of the few officials in Tulia who really seemed to believe in drug rehab, and he helped Donnie get into a facility in Lubbock. But a year later, he was back on crack. He was perhaps the lowest he had ever been when Coleman found him, back at the sale barn, shoveling shit, trying to make enough money to stay high.

Donnie's trial began in the Swisher County courthouse on the morning of February 15. Tom Hamilton was the lead attorney, and his son Brent was present to assist him. Tom had elected to defend each of Donnie's seven cases separately. He considered it his good fortune that the least serious case, delivery of less than a gram of crack cocaine, had somehow come up first. Now he would have a chance to test out his defense strategy with considerably lower stakes—the penalty range for delivery of less than a gram was up to two years in a state jail. The rest of Donnie's cases involved delivery of eight balls of powder, which carried 2-to-20 year sentences, and at least one of those charges was enhanced to a first-degree felony by virtue of allegedly occurring within 1,000 feet of Conner Park. If that one went to trial, he would be looking at 5 to 99.

As a first-time felony offender, Donnie was eligible for probation on the crack charge. But after the win in Wafer's case, Tom was shooting for an outright acquittal. Donnie admitted to Tom at their first meeting that he was a crack addict when he met Coleman and had gotten crack for him on several occasions. But he adamantly denied getting powder for the man. Donnie told Tom that he wasn't a dealer at all, and the incident reports—suspect as they were—seemed to support his claim. In several of the buys, he allegedly took Coleman's money and bought the drugs from a third party, out of Coleman's sight. It was an alarmingly simple—if lazy—way for a narc to make cases, but it didn't surprise Hamilton. Narcs weren't paid to make penny-ante possession cases, which carried relatively mild penalties. They were paid to find dealers. The trick Coleman had pulled on Donnie—setting up an addict as a so-called street-level dealer—was a specialty of drug task forces like the one in Amarillo, and it happened every day somewhere in Texas.

The three-paragraph report for this case had Coleman picking up Donnie—it did not say where exactly—and riding around in his truck looking for crack. After Donnie spotted an unidentified black woman in a small blue pickup on Parmer Street in the Flats, he collected $120 from Coleman (which included a $20 finder's fee) and delivered it to the woman in exchange for 0.6 grams of crack. Coleman took the crack, dropped Donnie off, and drove away. Donnie claimed that this particular deal never occurred, and Tom planned to put on alibi evidence to rebut the report. By a stroke of luck, Coleman claimed to have met Donnie on a Monday afternoon, and Donnie always worked the Monday cattle auction at the sale barn.

McEachern seemed slightly rattled as the two sides prepared for jury selection that morning. After four easy wins in a row, things had gone off the rails in an unexpected way at Wafer's hearing. Still, that had taken place in Plainview, with no jury present. There was no reason to think that anybody in Tulia had gotten wind of what happened. He reminded Judge Self of his ruling in the pretrial hearing the week before: no mention of Coleman's "history," as McEachern called it, in front of the jury, even during jury selection. When the jury pool was brought in, McEachern began by showing them his standard overhead projection lesson on the standard of evidence they must use to decide guilt or innocence. As was his habit, he emphasized the portion of the law that says that a reasonable doubt is "one that is based on reason and common sense," underlining those two terms for the jurors with his felt pen. Common sense, a notion that appealed to rural jurors, was really what being on a jury boiled down to, in McEachern's view. He was a master, Paul Holloway said later, at "changing 'beyond a reasonable doubt,' to something more akin to a gut instinct."

Then McEachern began to carefully and subtly coach the pool for what was about to follow: a case with very little evidence and only one witness, whose character, despite the judge's ruling, was undoubtedly going to come under attack. It didn't matter if only one witness could testify to the events of the crime, he told them; the law allowed a conviction with only one witness. It didn't matter that there might not be much cocaine involved. He likened the drug to a rattlesnake. "It doesn't matter if it's a little rattlesnake or a big rattlesnake; if a rattlesnake bites you, it's going to kill you," he told them. Nor did it matter how concentrated the cocaine was. Under the law, even a trace of cocaine was enough. There had been no independent testing of the cocaine yet, but McEachern didn't want to be caught by surprise.

He also prepared them for the attack he knew was coming on Coleman, a strategy he planned to portray as a scurrilous and unfounded assault on law enforcement by a desperate defendant who knew he was guilty. In rural America in 2000 there was no better known or more widely despised example of that phenomenon than the trial of O.J. Simpson. The case had become a standby in McEachern's repertoire in recent years. "Now, it's all right if you have read or heard something about a case in the paper. I give you strictly this: There's a real famous case—I give you this as a hypothetical—out in California that people might have read or heard and disagreed with. I'm not going to name any names. Okay? Just as a hypothetical. But, see, those jurors were the same as you."

When the trial began later that afternoon, Tom Hamilton wasted no time in attacking Coleman's credibility. McEachern's first witness was Roy Murphy, a chemist from the state police, who certified that the evidence in the case was cocaine. On cross-examination, Tom began a line of questions about how and why cocaine is cut by dealers. When McEachern objected to the relevance, Tom explained the defense's theory that Coleman cut the cocaine and pocketed the money. Self sustained McEachern's immediate objection and ordered the jury to disregard the comment.

But Tom persisted, and it paid off. Murphy testified that he had examined the evidence in each of Coleman's cases as they were made, and that virtually all of it was powder cocaine. "In your analysis of the powder cocaine, sir, did you find it to be . . . rather weak—in other words, it had been cut, it had been cut more than would be normal on the street?" Tom asked. "It was," Murphy replied. "A number of the other cases were weaker than I normally received." Now Tom was on a roll. He steered Murphy back into a general discourse on how cocaine was adulterated. Eventually McEachern objected again and Self sent the jury out of the courtroom. Self asked again how it was relevant, and Tom laid all of his cards on the table, describing his entire theory of the cases for the record:

> We believe it goes to his motive, his intent and opportunity. We believe that the fact that he was charged with a criminal offense that involved moral turpitude and lied about it at the last hearing in Hale County, the fact that he had an opportunity to acquire the cocaine, himself, maybe in another purchase from somewhere else, under circumstances that he didn't report, used that money that he was given by Swisher County and the task force for the purpose of cutting the cocaine and thereby making a profit, and that profit was used to pay off some $7,000 worth of obligations that he had in the county where he was filed upon for abuse of official capacity and theft, where he managed, with the assistance of Texas Ranger Larry Gilbreath, to get the charges dismissed, and he used the funds for the purpose of paying off some $7,000 worth of debts where he was seen and charged with the offense of theft after stealing gas for the employer that he formerly worked for at the time he left in the middle of the night, and we believe that these are circumstances which raise an issue as to his motive

and his intent and his operation and his opportunity to acquire funds to relieve himself from the liability with which [he] was confronted on these charges.

Tom went on in the same vein for another minute, spelling out everything they had discovered in one long gush. He wanted it all in the record. Self may have sealed the documentary evidence on Coleman, but anybody reading this transcript—an appellate judge or an appointed counsel for another defendant—would have a road map to collect the evidence for himself. If the judge would allow it, Tom went on, he wanted Roy Murphy to describe for the jury how Coleman, in theory, could have done what the defense suspected he did, and how a chemist could detect such a deception by examining the chemical composition of all of the evidence samples. Tom conceded, of course, that such a test had not yet been done.

Self didn't like the sound of it in court any better than he had in the pretrial hearing. "I'm going to sustain the objection, counsel. I'm not going to let you go into those matters. I don't think any of those matters are relevant or material to the issues before the jury in this case," he said. Tom sat down, frustrated.

When the jury was brought back in, McEachern called Coleman's supervisors at the task force, Lieutenant Mike Amos and Sergeant Jerry Massengill of the Amarillo police department. Amos, a tall man in his early sixties with a military bearing, was the task force commander. There were about four dozen regional task forces across the state, and each had a complex chain of command. The Amarillo police department was the host agency of the panhandle task force, which employed perhaps a dozen narcotics officers, most of them hired directly by Amos. Others, like Coleman, were hired by one of the task force's many participating counties and assigned to the task force. Amos explained that Coleman had been sent to a two-week narcotics training school in Houston, sponsored by the U.S. Drug

Enforcement Agency, and had then been given on-the-job training with task force narcs working in Amarillo. Massengill, who had white hair scalloped by a textbook case of male-pattern baldness and a thick cop mustache, was Coleman's immediate supervisor—though, strictly speaking, nobody was actually supervising Coleman when he was on the job in Tulia. Coleman, who lived in Happy at the beginning of the operation and later moved to Amarillo, reported to the task force offices every morning, Massengill explained, and then drove down to Tulia at least two or three days a week to make buys. Massengill testi-fied that he came to Tulia perhaps five to six times to check on Cole-man but never actually observed him make a buy.

Sheriff Stewart, who took the stand next, testified that his contact with Coleman was limited to providing him with photos of suspects when Coleman requested them. When Tom got his chance to cross-examine Stewart, he handled him as gently as possible. He knew how well respected Stewart was in Swisher County, and how revered law enforcement was in general. In reality Hamilton was appalled by Stewart's handling of Coleman's investigation. "The sheriff in Tulia is a good guy," he said later. "But he's a farmer; he knows absolutely nothing about law enforcement, as far as how you conduct an investi-gation, how you check out your agents." Tom's effort to get Stewart to talk about Coleman's theft charge in front of the jury was rebuffed by Judge Self, and he requested a bill of exceptions.

After Self sent the jury home for the evening, Brent got up to do the examination of Stewart for the bill. Under questioning, Stewart was slippery and evasive. Brent asked if he would fire one of his deputies if he discovered that the man had stolen gas. Stewart said it would depend on the circumstances. Brent then showed Stewart the charging document from Cochran County and had him read a por-tion of the dismissal agreement. "Restitution has been made," Stew-art read.

Judge Self interrupted. If Brent was going to submit the document for the bill, Self said, then he should just do it. "You don't need him to read it," he said impatiently. He clearly considered the matter a waste of time.

Stewart testified that he found out about the charges against Coleman when he received a Teletype from Cochran County on August 7, 1998. Coleman told him the charges were false. Beyond that, Stewart's memory of the incident seemed strangely hazy. Had Coleman said anything negative about his former employers, Brent asked? He may have, but Stewart could not specifically remember what it was. He understood that restitution had been paid shortly after the charges were discovered, and that a longtime friend had given Coleman the money to cover it. Who gave him the money? Stewart had been told but he did not remember. He had been told that Coleman had been given a polygraph about the charges and had passed it. Did Stewart ever tell the district attorney about the charges? Stewart said he had but claimed he couldn't remember exactly when.

Brent grew more frustrated every time Stewart's memory failed him. How could he not remember the details of something so extraordinary? It was not as if arresting one of his own deputies was something he did on a daily basis. Stewart was equally fuzzy about his background check of Coleman. He testified that he may have made a couple of calls but basically relied on the task force to check Coleman out. Earlier in the day, Lieutenant Amos had made it sound like more of a joint effort. It was obvious, in any case, that somebody failed to contact his most immediate employer, Sheriff Burke of Cochran County. If that most basic step would have been taken, presumably none of this ever would have happened. Clearly Stewart was not interested in taking the blame for it, or, for that matter, admitting in any way that Coleman might not have been a good candidate for undercover work.

"Your remembrance of it is that he had, at least to your knowledge, such an unblemished past that it didn't bother you a bit, did it?"

Brent asked. Self interrupted. "I will let you make your bill for purposes of appeal, but we're not going to sit here all day for you to just argue with this witness," he said. Brent apologized and then asked the same question again. Self sternly ordered him to move on. "Are you saying he cannot ask that question?" Tom interjected from his seat at the defense table. "I'm saying he's already asked that question at least three times," the judge retorted. Brent sat down.

Brent then called Lieutenant Amos back to the stand. He testified that Sheriff Stewart had brought Coleman's arrest warrant to his attention, and that Coleman had been taken temporarily off the street, "till the problem had been clarified or rectified or taken care of." Amos seemed only slightly more informed than Stewart about the details of the incident. It was his understanding, he said, that the criminal charge was trumped up to get Coleman to pay his debts in what should have been a civil process, not a criminal one, and that Coleman and his attorney worked out "some type of agreement." He testified that he did no independent investigation of the incident. He did not talk to the sheriff's office in Cochran County or to the district attorney or county attorney there.

Brent then asked how the task force accounted for the funds issued to Coleman for drug purchases in Tulia. Under repeated questioning, Amos admitted that, with nobody to actually observe Coleman making the buys, it was possible for him to deceive his supervisors. If an officer lied, Amos said, it would be hard to catch him, unless he did it over and over again or reported paying way too much for a small amount of narcotics. "That would be a certain flag that would alert us," he said.

"Were there any flags in this case?" Brent asked.

"No," Amos said.

At the end of the day, Tom urged Judge Self to consider admitting some of what they had covered in the bill, so that the jury would be aware of it. Self declined to admit any of it. In a hearing the next morning, out of the presence of the jury, he quashed all of the sub-poenas that Brent and Tom had prepared in conjunction with Paul Holloway. Coleman's personnel file, records of task force funds issued to him, records of drug screens run on him—they would get none of it. Self ordered that the documents be produced for his review only, and then sealed and attached to the record. "I'm going to anticipate that counsel understands those matters are not admissible," Self said.

Coleman took the stand at about 10:00 that morning. Donnie was struck by how different he looked. He still had the ponytail and goatee, but he had gained weight, and he looked much healthier than he had in the summer and fall of 1998. McEachern did his best to bolster his star witness's credibility. Why couldn't he wear a wire? Too dangerous, Coleman replied. Was "deep cover" different from simple undercover? Oh yes, very different. Had he been periodically drug tested? Certainly. On cross-examination, Tom Hamilton went straight to Coleman's work history. Asked why he had left Cochran County, Coleman said, "Well, I was working in Cochran County, there was a few little things going on there, and the sheriff was using the sheriff's office for personal gain." It was the same story Paul Hol-loway had heard him tell in court back in January. In light of the pre-vious week's revelations, however, the tale took on a new light. In essence, Coleman was accusing the sheriff of the very same transgres-sion for which he himself had been indicted. In any case, McEachern didn't want to hear any more of it from his witness. When Hamilton asked Coleman to elaborate, McEachern jumped up. "Judge, may we approach?"

Self sent the jury out again. McEachern argued that the defense was headed toward an area already ruled inadmissible. Hamilton countered that Coleman was changing his story—in an earlier trial he had said he'd left the county because of financial trouble—and that the defense had a right to try to impeach him with the inconsistency. Self sustained the objection but allowed Hamilton to continue the questioning with the jury out, as another bill of exceptions. An increasingly large portion of the trial was taking place outside of the jury's earshot, and it did not bode well for Donnie's chances.

As Hamilton began the bill, Coleman immediately amended his last response. He left because of the sheriff's behavior *and* because he had outstanding bills. "I don't have nothing to hide," Coleman said. Coleman then claimed that because he was currently suing Cochran County, his personal attorney had advised him not to discuss the sheriff's illegal activities. Self instructed him that he would have to answer anyway. Coleman then told a long, rambling story about how the sheriff had charged an oil change on his personal pickup to the county, and how angry the sheriff had gotten when Coleman confronted him about it. Asked for another example, Coleman said the department's mechanic had charged an alternator to the county, even though it was for his personal vehicle. "I wasn't about to get involved in that," Coleman said.

Coleman denied stealing the gas from the county. He said he was forced to pay restitution because the county was threatening to file charges on him. Hamilton pointed out that charges were in fact filed on him. "Oh yes, sir, they was," Coleman said. "Like I say, this is under litigation, and when this lawsuit comes about, we'll all know what's going on over there as soon as the Texas Rangers and attorney general finds out what's going on in that county." They began to move into a discussion of the theft charge, but Self wanted to bring the jury back in to move on with the cross-examination; the bill would be completed later.

In front of the jury, Hamilton moved through the rest of Coleman's employment history. Prior to Cochran County, Coleman had been a deputy in Denton County, and before that in Pecos County, he testified. He said that his contentious divorce from Carol Barnett had caused him to leave his position in Pecos County, since his wife also worked for the sheriff's office. Ongoing matters related to the divorce also caused him to move on from Denton County, he said, though McEachern's objection prevented Hamilton from delving into that curious response.

Hamilton then moved on to the transaction with Donnie. Coleman was not able to add much detail to what was in the report. Hamilton did get him to discuss "pinching," the practice by which an intermediary in a drug deal will take a bit of the product for himself before delivering it to the buyer. Was that unusual, Hamilton asked? "No, it wouldn't be unusual," Coleman replied, "because they're getting their narcotic—if you bring me an eight ball, if you tell me, 'I'll meet you back here in thirty minutes,' that gives you time to go talk somebody into fronting you an eight ball to bring me, and you're—if you pinch off of it, you give it to me, well, you just got your high free without me knowing about it." Was that common among people who had a drug habit? Hamilton asked. "Yes, sir. It's a lot—if a people—if people have habits like that, it's a lot of their motivation." Coleman seemed oblivious to what Hamilton was driving at: that Donnie, and perhaps others caught up in the sting, weren't dealers at all, but addicts using Coleman as a cash cow to get high. Hamilton hoped that wasn't lost on the jury as well. In the aftermath of Self's rulings, he was becoming increasingly certain that Donnie was going to have to take the stand in his own defense. The jury had heard only the barest snippet of the defense theory of the case, and the attorneys had not been able to get to Coleman at all, at least not when anybody was watching.

When Hamilton finished with Coleman, McEachern rested his case. For his first witness, Hamilton called the office manager from the sale barn, who had records showing that Donnie worked eight and a half hours the day of the alleged buy. He then called Donnie's mother, Mattie, who testified that she drove Donnie to work that morning. During the jury's lunch break, Self allowed Brent to continue his examination of Coleman for the bill of exceptions. Once again, the bill proved more revealing than the trial itself. Brent began questioning Coleman about the charge in Cochran County. Perhaps recalling his unfortunate testimony in Billy Wafer's hearing the previous week, Coleman would not concede being formally charged with a crime. "If you run a CCH [criminal history search] on me right now, I don't have anything on my record," Coleman said. "If I was charged, it would be on my CCH."

Brent didn't know if Coleman's arrest was on his record or not; it certainly should have been, if Sheriff Stewart had followed procedure. If it wasn't, then somebody had some explaining to do. Brent handed Coleman the charging document for the theft count and asked him to read the first page of it. Coleman acted as if he'd never seen it. "Can I get a copy of this?" he asked. "Just answer the question," Judge Self coached him. Brent walked him through the documents: order of dismissal, payment of restitution. How much did you pay, Brent asked? Coleman would not answer, he said, without seeing what the records indicated he had paid. Self interrupted him: "Just answer his question, sir, right now." The judge seemed frustrated with Coleman's hedging, which, left unabated, tended to veer toward perjury, as it had in Wafer's hearing a few days before. Catching Coleman in a lie was part of the defense strategy, but Self clearly had had enough of the defense and its strategy. Coleman's memory quickly improved. "It was approximately sixty-seven hundred dollars, wasn't it?" Brent asked. "Approximately, yes, sir," Coleman replied.

Coleman confirmed that he had left other debts outstanding in other places he'd worked. He testified he'd left bills in his hometown of Pecos, where he began his law enforcement career. He blamed those on his first wife, Regina Culberson. He was not sure if they'd ever been paid. He had also left debts in Pecos County, which he attributed to his second wife. Coleman admitted to knowing Texas Ranger Larry Gilbreath and talking to him about the trouble he was having in Cochran County. Did he ask Gilbreath to intervene on his behalf? "I don't believe so. I don't know. I don't recall," Coleman replied. Well, was Gilbreath a family friend of his father's? At the mention of his father, Coleman seemed to lose what was left of his composure. "I have no idea. I imagine my dad knew him. All the Rangers know each other pretty much," he said. Then he began to ramble again. "All it is—all it is a—a—get-me-back deal because I wouldn't go along with their program in Cochran County," he said. "And they was afraid I was going to open my mouth and call the Texas Rangers. And all this come out in the lawsuit." The charge was no big deal, he insisted. He testified that he found out about it on a Monday, hired an attorney out of Lubbock, and had it resolved by the end of the week. The money was given to his mother by a family friend, Coleman said, though he was vague about how the loan was arranged and claimed not to know the friend's name. His mother, in turn, gave him the money in cash, he said.

As quickly as he could, fearing that Self would lose patience at any moment, Brent then ran through as many of the allegations Carol Barnett had made to Paul Holloway as he could. Had Coleman ever represented himself as a member of the KKK? "Not that I know of," Coleman replied. Not unless it was in an undercover capacity, he clarified. It was a strange answer—Coleman had previously testified that his work in Tulia was his first undercover assignment. He admitted to having the automatic weapon confiscated but said he had inherited it and didn't know what to do with it. He denied having grenades or other explosives in his possession. This was getting far afield, and Self let Brent know that he needed to bring the bill in for a landing. The journey through Coleman's recent past had the effect Tom and Brent had hoped for—Coleman came across as defensive and evasive. He looked, in other words, like a liar. It was an amazing hour of testimony. The only problem was that nobody on the jury had been present to witness it.

When the jury came back that afternoon, there was nothing left to do but call Donnie to the stand. The night before Tom had told Donnie it might be necessary. It was a gamble any time you put a defendant on the stand, but this time Tom was really going for broke. He told Donnie to tell the truth, the whole truth: that he had been a crack addict, that he had scored crack for Coleman, though not on the occasion Coleman had claimed in this case, and that, crucially, Coleman had lied about the alleged powder deliveries. It was a desperate move, one that Tom had second thoughts about later. At the time, though, he felt Donnie had no chance unless he rolled the dice. "I said you know these guys that have already been convicted, and they didn't take the stand. Or if they did, [the jury] didn't believe 'em," Tom recalled later. "I said I just want you to tell the truth. Just get up there and tell the truth. I thought maybe we stood a chance by getting the jury to say, 'Well maybe this guy's a damn crook, and Donnie's tellin' the truth.'" Donnie reluctantly agreed.

Donnie did well on the stand. Testifying, he discovered, was a lot like rehab—it was a matter of talking about your problems in front of strangers. He had taken two trips through rehab in the past three years, and though he knew it probably wasn't something he should have been proud of, he felt like he was getting pretty good at it. As Tom questioned him gently, Donnie told the jury about his first experience with drugs, his leaving college after a semester, his troubles with his wife, and finally his addiction to crack. He realized he needed to do something about his problem one day, he said, when he was sitting at home alone with his two boys. "I was—I was using that dope, and, you know, I had no life, you know. And I could just sit there and see my boys looking at me, and I didn't feel no love for them because, you know, the drugs had me," he said. Donnie told them about his two trips through rehab and his chance meeting with Coleman sandwiched between them.

Donnie testified that Eliga Kelly had asked him to help Coleman buy some drugs. Then Tom took the plunge.

"Now, on several different occasions did you, in fact, go and help them locate some drugs for this guy. Is that right?" Hamilton asked.

"Yes, sir."

"And what kind of drugs was it?"

"We got him some rock, rock cocaine."

"Did you ever at any time get any powder cocaine for anybody?" Hamilton asked.

"No, sir," Donnie replied.

McEachern was taken aback by Donnie's admission. He picked up the state's only exhibit, a small baggie of crack, and held it in front of Donnie's face. This was not the crack he delivered? Donnie replied that it was not. He had been at work on the afternoon in question, not riding around the Flats with Coleman. What about all these other dates that he allegedly delivered powder? Were they all complete fabrications? They were, Donnie said. McEachern seemed uncertain how to proceed. "So, if I understand you right, just to be perfectly clear, you're freely, voluntarily and intentionally admitting that you delivered to Tom Coleman at least on four or five occasions crack cocaine," McEachern said. "Is that correct?"

"Yes, sir," Donnie replied.

McEachern was momentarily stumped. Then he switched gears. "All right. Now the question I'm most concerned with is: Where did you get the cocaine?" he said. Donnie didn't answer immediately. In fact, McEachern had never asked him that question in the six months since his arrest, nor had he ever discussed Donnie's giving up any names during any of his discussions with Tom and Brent Hamilton about Donnie's case. Now McEachern began peppering Donnie with questions.

Q: What's this dealer's name?

A: (No response.)

Q: Where does he come from?

A: One come from Lubbock.

Q: What does he drive? What does he look like?
A: (No response.)
Q: Is he brown?
A: (Pause) I can't answer that question at this time.

Here Self told Donnie that if he knew the answer, he'd have to give it.

A: Yeah, he's brown.
Q: What's his name?
A: I feel if I said that something, I couldn't go around and look at the kids and their family, and I'd have to say that I sent their parents off, their child off, you know, for a long time. I can't do that.

When, after several more attempts to pry a name out of him, it became clear that Donnie would not answer, McEachern sat down. Donnie walked slowly back to his seat next to Tom. "We rest, Your Honor," Tom said.

But McEachern was not quite done. He called Man Kelly as a rebuttal witness to Donnie's testimony. This was an unwelcome surprise for the defense. McEachern had just let Kelly out of jail the day before. In exchange for agreeing to testify as a witness for the state, he had been given a deal on his charges: ten years' probation. He was sixty-one years old and he'd been an alcoholic for years; six months in jail without a drink had left him looking worse, if possible, than when he went in. He appeared tired and unhappy to be in the courtroom, yet he had a certain defiance about him. Kelly may have been a drunk, but he was not a pushover. He had a reputation in the black community as a brawler.

"I've told you to do one thing concerning these offenses. Is that correct?" McEachern asked him.

"Just tell the truth about it," Kelly replied.

There was no mention of Kelly in Coleman's report for the case at hand, but Kelly testified that he had accompanied Coleman on several occasions to pick up Donnie and ask him for drugs. In no case, however, did Donnie ever have any drugs on him, he said. Instead he would have Coleman drop him off on a corner, and then Donnie would walk away, to whose house Kelly did not know. McEachern tried to refresh his memory. Was it ever by the Church of Christ? Not that Kelly recalled. How about 101 North Floyd, where Cash Love lived? No, not there. McEachern pressed on. Did Donnie ever take Coleman to see Kizzie or Creamy White? No. Kelly did say that he and Coleman had met separately with Kizzie and Creamy, but only one time apiece. (Coleman had filed a half dozen cases against each of them.) Did Kelly know if the cocaine in Donnie's cases was crack or powder? He did not.

McEachern was asking about extraneous offenses that had nothing to do with the case being tried, but since Donnie had himself alerted the jury to the existence of the other cases filed against him, Tom could not object. In any case, the testimony was not particularly damaging thus far. If anything, it was comical, Tom thought. McEachern had just made Kelly a deal to get his testimony. Hadn't he interviewed him before today to see what he knew?

McEachern then embarked on a wide-ranging survey of Kelly's knowledge of Coleman's investigation in Tulia. Did Kelly know who the major dealer in Tulia was? No, he couldn't say. McEachern began listing names of people Coleman had allegedly made deals with, deals that Kelly had supposedly helped set up.

Had he introduced Coleman to Jason Williams? Yes, he had. Christopher Jackson? Not that he recalled.

Daniel Olivarez? Yes.

Kenneth Ray Powell?

"No, sir, Kenneth, he didn't run no dope," Kelly replied. "What he done, he did to himself. He wasn't no dealer or nothing that I know of."

Tom watched in quiet fascination. McEachern seemed to have left considerations of trial strategy behind; he seemed, at this late date, almost to be on a fact-finding mission about the investigation.

Benny Lee Robinson? No.

Fred Brookins? No.

Jason Fry?

"Who's that?" Kelly asked.

Bootie Wootie?

"No sir, never did get nothing from Bootie Wootie, I didn't. I never did."

McEachern listed a half dozen others, eliciting only one more positive response.

Finally McEachern got to Billy Wafer, the man whose narrow escape a few days prior had prompted McEachern to pull Kelly out of jail and put him on the stand in the first place.

"Okay, do you recall the time that Billy Don Wafer waved y'all over and then Yolanda Smith met y'all later after you went to the sale barn?" McEachern asked.

Kelly answered slowly. "I remember talking to Billy," he said. "But Billy told me to get out of his face."

"Okay—" McEachern began, but Kelly wasn't done.

"Told me he didn't do nothing, just get away from him," he said.

Tom was elated. The district attorney had just made a liar out of Coleman, his star witness. But McEachern still wasn't done. He rattled off six more names, all "no's," before he finally passed the witness and sat down.

Tom jumped in. "What about Denise Kelly?" he asked. Denise was another of Tom's clients. As long as we're taking the man's deposition, Tom figured, he might as well get in a few questions of his own.

"No, sir."

Finaye Shelton? Another client.

"No, sir."

Kelly told Tom that Coleman had given him money or alcohol, mostly alcohol, to introduce him to people he knew who used drugs. After he made the introductions, Coleman would give them the money, and they would take it to somebody else to buy the dope, Kelly testified. Did Coleman ever get to the big dealer in town? Kelly had no idea.

"I don't know a big guy from a little guy," he said.

Under redirection by McEachern, Kelly testified that he was with Coleman twice when they got drugs from Donnie. McEachern noted that Coleman could have gone back alone and made deals after Kelly's introduction, and Kelly agreed. Kelly also testified, under questioning by McEachern, that workers at the sale barn occasionally punched each other in and out, undercutting Donnie's alibi for the case at hand somewhat.

In his closing statement, Tom tried as best he could to lay the blame for what had gone wrong in Tulia on the task force. The sheriff was a good man, he told the jury, but he trusted these guys to bring in an expert and to do the job right. It seemed nobody had taken the time to thoroughly check him out. The issue was Coleman's credibility; he was a rotten apple. Tom knew that the jury had been present for precious little of Coleman's most damning testimony, but there was nothing he could do about that now.

McEachern was practically raving during his closing. "He wants to attack Commander Amos, and he wants to attack Sergeant Massengill, and he wants to attack Tom Coleman, and he wants to attack all the people that are in law enforcement," he began, waving his arm in the direction of Tom Hamilton.

"And when our sheriff takes the stand, he wants to attack our sheriff. But when he gets up on closing argument, he wants to go, 'We've got one of the best sheriffs in the whole world, and he is a good guy," McEachern sneered. "Well that's just wrong," he said. And don't feel sorry for Donnie, he told the jurors. He made the decision to turn to drugs.

"Had everything going for him, had the world on a string, and just gave it away, was even offered a second chance ... didn't even take the opportunity of that," he said. "And [Hamilton] wants to talk about the Constitution and everything else like that. I want to talk about reason and common sense. I want to talk about Swisher County common sense, because we're not New York, and we're not Los Angeles, and we're not in Kansas, and Dorothy is not here. And don't let anybody click their heels, and we follow down the yellow brick road."

An hour and a half later, the jury came back with a guilty verdict. During the sentencing phase, Tom put on Judge Keeter, who agreed to testify about Donnie's willingness to go to rehab and get his life back together. His old boss Ken Dawson also stood up for Donnie, telling the jury what a good worker he had been. Hamilton urged the jury to consider probation for Donnie. But it was no good. McEachern brought out Sheriff Stewart, who testified that Donnie's reputation in the community was bad. That was all the jury needed to hear. They gave him the maximum of two years in state jail.

After the conviction, Tom came to see Donnie in the county jail. McEachern was offering a plea bargain for the remaining cases: twelve and a half years, to be served concurrently with the two he had just received. It was a much better offer than anybody had received to date, especially considering that Donnie was accused of so many deliveries. Also, as in so many of the cases, the state was seeking to enhance one of the remaining charges to a first-degree felony because Coleman alleged it had occurred in a drug-free zone. If he chose to go to trial and lost, the sky was the limit on the time he would serve. Donnie wasn't sure what to do. Gary Gardner, who attended the trial and visited with Donnie afterward, told him that on a level playing field he would have had the case beat. "All these people are giving you advice," Tom said. "But you're the one that's going to have to do the time."

Mattie came to see him later that afternoon and advised him to consider taking the plea. It was less than half the time McEachern was offering his siblings Kizzie and Creamy, whose trials were still to come.

"I think you're just gonna have to do this little bit of time," she told him. Donnie took the deal.

CHAPTER EIGHT

Freddie Brookins Jr.

ON THE LAST DAY of Donnie Smith's trial, Freddie Brookins Jr. and his father drove to Amarillo to meet with Freddie's attorney, Mike Hrin. Freddie's trial was set to start the next morning, February 17. Hrin, who was in his early forties, was an unusually short man with a full beard. He had surprising news for Freddie: McEachern had called that afternoon and offered a plea of five years. Freddie had professed his innocence from the day of the bust, but Hrin urged him to take the deal in light of the sentences handed down in the previous trials. He was accused of delivering a single eight ball, which carried a maximum sentence of twenty years. He had no priors, which meant he would be eligible for probation if convicted, but gambling on the jury's goodwill was a huge risk to take, Hrin told him. If he took the plea, with a little luck he could be home in a year.

Freddie didn't have much experience with the courts in Tulia. He knew the juries hadn't been kind; his high school friend Cash Love had just been sentenced to over 300 years, and it had him scared. But in the back of his mind, Freddie was thinking he was not like Cash, who had been in trouble since he was a teenager. He was different. Freddie said he'd have to talk to his dad about it.

Fred Brookins Sr. was born on a farm in Swisher County during the cotton harvest of 1953. He was the fifth of seven children, and his father, a migrant farmhand from east Texas, named him after the farm's white owner. When Fred was five, the family moved to Swisher County for good. They lived and worked on a farm, and Fred was put to work with his brothers and sisters pulling cotton. Even before he was old enough to drag a sack, Fred was in the fields, pulling the bolls he could reach and pitching them into the rows for his older siblings to collect. The family moved into town during the mid-1960s, renting a modest house on Tulia's south side, about a block from where Fred would eventually raise his own family. Fred's father was a rock, a fiercely proud, independent man who believed in the merits of hard work, sobriety, and prayer. His mother found work as a janitor at the elementary school. After twenty years in that job, she earned her GED and began a new career in nursing at about the same time Fred was graduating from high school. She finally retired for good in the mid-1990s. Fred's father never stopped farming.

As a child, Fred learned to hate the cotton fields. Summer meant long hours under the sun on the end of a hoe, fighting a never-ending battle against the Johnson grass that covered Swisher County. Harvest in the fall meant trudging through the chest-high rows in the cold dawn, with the desiccated plants scratching at his arms. His mother wanted him to move on and do better. The first job Fred held that didn't involve cotton was at the Dairy Queen, where he was made an assistant manager and given the keys to the store at the tender age of fifteen. In high school, Fred worked at the nursing home. He would get up every day at dawn, arriving at the home just as the residents were waking up. Many of them were the sons and daughters of Tulia's original pioneer families, now bent and broken from a lifetime of hard work. Fred helped the men bathe and shave themselves and fed them breakfast. In the evening he returned and put them to bed. In the summers he worked as a welder for Roll-A-Cone, a manufacturer of tractor accessories a few miles northeast of town. The company's namesake, invented by owner Wally Bird, was a device for harvesting milo, and it had made Bird a successful and relatively well-off man. Bird took a liking to his earnest, hard-working welder, and one day he led Fred out behind the plant and showed him the tiny building, no bigger than a well house, where he had built the prototype of his invention, where the entire enterprise had started. "A person can be anything he wants to be," Bird told him. "The key to success is to find something that works and stick with it."

Even as a young man, Fred already believed that. "Stick with it," might have been the family credo. The Brookins family, Fred believed, was evidence that the system worked: hard work pays off in the end, for black or white, rich or poor. Fred knew there were people like him who couldn't seem to get ahead in Tulia, people living in shacks in the Flats without running water. And there were crusty old cowboys and farmers who called him pickaninny and nigger. They sometimes thought it was funny, when he was still in grade school, to give him a kick in the ass with their pointed boots when he walked through the courthouse square on weekends. He never told his dad about those incidents. Partly he was afraid of what his dad would do to the men, and partly he was ashamed that he didn't seem to inspire the respect his proud, hard-working father always did. The answer, he always thought, was to work harder.

And that was what he did. Six months after graduation, Fred got a job on the line at Missouri Beef Packers in Plainview. Almost thirty years later, he was still working for the company, now called Excel. It's about a twenty-minute drive from Tulia to the company's sprawling plant on I-27, though if the wind is blowing the right way it can be smelled much sooner than that. Over the course of Fred's career, meatpacking became one of the panhandle's major industries. Modern packing plants are highly mechanized facilities that can slaughter and process several thousand animals per day. Carcasses move through the processing side of the plants on huge chains past workers armed with various cutting tools, like assembly lines in reverse. The packing-houses are among the few unionized workplaces in the panhandle, though they are not known for the high job satisfaction of their workers. On the contrary, meatpacking is the most dangerous job in America. Workers make the same cuts hundreds of times per day, leading to repetitive motion injuries; accidents, caused in part by pressure to keep the line moving as fast as possible, are common. Annual injury rates run as high as one employee in four in some plants, and amputations are not uncommon. Not surprisingly, turnover is high. In the panhandle, the plants are staffed chiefly by Mexican immigrants.

Fred started out on the processing side of the plant as a trimmer. He stood at a moving belt with a sharp knife and trimmed cuts of meat as they came past him. The work was hard on the joints and the plant was cold and noisy and foul-smelling. But the money was better than he could make as a farmhand. He married his longtime girl-friend, Patty, at nineteen and started a family. In time the couple had four children—John, Kent, Mary, and Freddie Jr. Responsibility just seemed to fall naturally on Fred. He became a union steward, helping his fellow workers navigate the pitfalls of a work environment that was both ruthlessly efficient and dangerously insensitive to their safety. Fred found himself down on his knees one morning looking through trimmings for a coworker's fingers. It was just something a person got used to.

One day in 1995, Fred got into an argument with a supervisor who felt Fred had questioned his authority. Fred tried to walk away, but the supervisor followed him down a long hallway, berating him every step of the way. When Fred finally had enough, he turned and took a swing at the man. The union managed to keep him from being fired, but he was suspended for a year. Patty had recently lost her job as well, and the family was broke. Patty went down to the welfare office to apply for food stamps, and Fred did not try to stop her, though he was too proud to go there himself. Patty came back empty-handed—the caseworker told her to sell one of the family's two cars for food money. Patty was disconsolate. "What are we going to do?" she said. Fred's answer was the same one he always settled on when trouble came. Work harder. "Get a bucket," he told Patty the next morning. "We're going to slop some hogs." Over the past few years, Fred had kept a few hogs and calves on a piece of rented property near Happy. He had bought them mostly so his kids would have work in the summer, though the operation never made much money. Now it would have to replace a steady paycheck for the family to get by.

The union finally called one morning and told him he had his job back. There was one hitch: after twenty years on the job, the company wanted him to work the night shift. Fred agreed. He threw himself into his work. In short order he was made a green hat, a leader of his department. A few years later he was offered a job as a supervisor. He hated to leave the union, but he took the promotion. Fred never complained about conditions at the plant. Meatpacking had allowed him to raise a family. But he wanted something more for his kids.

Although they lived on the south side of town like most black families, the Brookins family had always moved easily between white and black Tulia. In the 1970s, the Tulia Church of Christ decided to close its mission to the black community for financial reasons. The black congregation, of which the Brookins were devoted members, was folded into the larger white church. Most black families didn't feel comfortable with the arrangement, but the Brookins family stuck it out for years. When they finally decided to leave the church, they were the last black family attending regularly. Larry Stewart was a deacon in the church, and Fred's children grew up hearing him sing in the church quartet every Sunday.

There were some things about black Tulia that Fred could not stomach. As a young man, Ricky White had been one of his closest friends. The times Fred spent with Ricky working with the Lobos in all its various incarnations were some of his favorite memories, outside of his own glory days in high school football. By the early 1990s, however, the two families seemed to be on divergent tracks. Fred found himself spending less and less time with Ricky and worrying more and more about his children associating with Ricky's kids and that crowd of friends. Ricky was living in a house a few blocks from Fred on Briscoe Street, in a part of the neighborhood that had long hosted a number of popular party hangouts. With Mattie in and out of their lives and Ricky involved with a new woman who had kids of her own, the White kids were beginning to fall through the cracks. Fred knew that Ricky's oldest son Cecil was rumored to have dealt drugs in high school, along with a cousin named Michael Smith. And it was no secret that Donnie and Ricky Jr., high school football teammates of Fred's son Kent, were using drugs. Soon the cops were after Ricky Sr., allegedly because he was dealing marijuana.

Fred did everything he could to keep his older sons Kent and John from running with the Briscoe Street crowd. "He didn't mind us talking to them," Kent recalled, "but if we did anything with them he'd bust our butt." Kent always marveled at how Ricky and Mattie's kids could get away with anything. At his house, there were consequences for getting caught. Kent, John, and their sister Mary were model students and athletes. Kent was a star running back and John made second team All-State as a cornerback. Mary was a key member of a celebrated women's track team that went all the way to the state tournament in Austin. They always did what the coaches asked on the field and in class they were deferential and polite.

But playing by the rules had its own special price. Kent was a star on the football team, which made him popular in school. Yet he never seemed to fit in with the kids in his own neighborhood. Kent spent countless hours working out with his black teammates, including fellow standouts Donnie Smith and James Barrow, and they got along well enough on the field. But he seldom partied with them or shared a joint after practice, and his companions resented him for it. The bottom line,

Kent said looking back on it, was that he wasn't black enough for them. "Their attitude was, 'you don't belong with us,'" Kent said. "Still today, they don't like me for that reason." The way Kent carried himself in school and around town, the way he kept to himself, the way he always had something to do when the other kids were just hanging out: it all seemed to say that Kent was going places and they weren't.

In the end, Kent didn't go too far. Slowed by a shoulder injury in his junior year, he never reached his full potential as a football player, and he was passed over for a scholarship, though few believed that the handful of boys who did get offers were more talented than Kent. Without a scholarship, there was no money for college, although Kent had the grades to go. He applied for jobs all over Tulia but found that the goodwill he accumulated as a high school star had evaporated. When his dad questioned his diligence, Kent challenged him to apply for a city job himself, to see what kind of reception he got. Fred Sr. came back chastened by the experience. In the end, Kent went to work at Excel. Eventually he settled down, married his white girlfriend, and got a job as a maintenance man at West Texas A&M University in Canyon. His younger brother John, an even bigger star at Tulia High, joined the service after graduation.

Freddie idolized Kent. He was crushed when his older brother wasn't offered a scholarship. But he still believed that he himself would make it, and he listened to Kent's counsel to always give 110 percent on the field. By the time he was a freshman in high school, it was clear he would be another star Brookins. He made the varsity track, basketball, and football teams that year. By his junior year, he was the starting tailback, the most coveted spot in all of high school sports. Like his older brothers, Freddie navigated white Tulia with relative ease. His best friend was a white boy named Donald Lones, whom Fred Sr. had coached in little league. Donald's parents were divorced, and he spent as much time at Freddie's house as he did at his own. He called Fred Sr. "Pops" and referred to Mary as "Sister."

Yet Freddie saw the world differently than Kent did. He found time to hang out with his teammates after practice. His friends included Kareem White, Donnie's younger brother, who was the team's quarterback, and Cash Love, another outstanding athlete. Freddie went to parties and he smoked a little marijuana. He was funny and a great dancer and he had a way with the ladies. But he inherited his father's stubborn streak and his tendency to be plainspoken to a fault, which got him in trouble with his teachers. His grades were a notch below his older siblings'. He still bragged about his family, and his relationship with his father was the secret envy of his friends. But he was more accepted by his black peers than Kent ever was. He somehow managed to straddle the line between what his father wanted him to be and what his peers demanded of him. He sometimes had to go against his dad's wishes to do it, but as the baby in the family he received a measure of latitude. He snuck out of the house to attend Tulia's annual Juneteenth party, which had been started by a brother-in-law of Ricky White's in the 1970s, during a period of high feeling in the black community.* Over the years it had evolved into a party with an exuberance that Fred Sr. no longer found appropriate.

But Freddie never bought into the gangster culture so many of his peers seemed to admire, and any illusions he had about the heroes of that crowd in Tulia did not last into manhood. When he was younger, Freddie looked up to Dock Casel, another notorious cousin of the White's, who was about ten years older than Freddie. Casel was a player. He drove around town in a nice Mercedes. He always had plenty of cash in his pocket and he was generous with it. Fred Sr. had coached Casel on his Lobos teams, and the kid was undeniably tal-

---

* Juneteenth is a traditional Texas celebration of the end of slavery. The name refers to the approximate date in the summer of 1865 that slaves in Texas finally learned of the Emancipation Proclamation, signed by Abraham Lincoln on January 1, 1863.

ented. He was forced out of high school athletics for smoking pot, and he dropped out of school not long after that. Fred and Ricky White convinced him to go to trade school, but Casel wound up dealing cocaine. Before long he was the biggest-volume dealer in Tulia, at least on the black side of town. Freddie had heard the rumors about Casel, but to Freddie he was just a suave, funny guy with a lot of friends. As he was leaving a party one evening, however, Freddie heard the sounds of a struggle coming from the side yard of the house. He and a friend went to investigate, and they found Casel forcing himself on a high school girl who happened to be a good friend of Freddie's. "Man, what the hell are you doing?" Freddie demanded, inserting himself between Casel and the crying girl. The two almost came to blows, before Casel decided it wasn't worth the effort and left the party. Freddie never spoke to Casel after that, and he wasn't sorry to see him go to prison a few years later.

Freddie had problems of his own. In the middle of his senior year, his girlfriend Tara became pregnant. Tara was a white girl, but her parents seemed to like Freddie and got along well with Fred Sr. and Patty. Both sets of parents were unhappy with the turn things had taken, but after Jaycee was born, things seemed to go all right for a time. Fred Sr. and Patty spent a lot of time watching the baby. But the two teenage parents started having problems, and one night, after a terrible fight, Tara locked Freddie out of her house. In a fit of anger and frustration, Freddie took a screen off a window and made his way back into the house, prompting Tara to call the police. Freddie was still at the house when the police came, and they made a rougher than necessary arrest. When Fred Sr. called the jail the next morning, angry at how his son had been treated, he was surprised at how Stewart's opinion of his son had hardened in the few years since the two men had stopped seeing each other regularly in church. "Oh, Freddie messed up bad this time," he told Fred Sr. Stewart claimed that Freddie had physically assaulted Tara, a charge she later denied. Unable to get Tara to pursue the case against Freddie, the authorities could only file a misdemeanor on him. Because he had no previous record, he was given deferred adjudication, meaning the charge would be dropped altogether if he did not reoffend in the immediate future.

There were no scholarship offers for Freddie. He had a lot of natural ability, but his chances were hurt by the fact that the program was not that good. The quality of coaching had deteriorated since the school's heyday, and area colleges were not used to looking for talent from Tulia. Freddie worked briefly at Excel before his dad got him into the Job Corps, a federally funded job-training program for young people who are not college bound. Freddie went to the central Texas town of San Marcos, not far from Austin, for six months to learn auto body repair and painting. It hardly guaranteed Freddie's future in Tulia, since there were only two body repair outfits in town. Still, it was continuing education, and Fred Sr. greatly preferred it to Freddie's starting a career at Excel. In a stroke of luck, when Freddie got back to Tulia, he heard from a garage employee that the owner was looking to hire another man. But when Freddie stopped by to inquire, the man told Freddie he didn't need anybody. He wouldn't even give Freddie an interview. Freddie felt it was because he was black.

Back in Tulia, Freddie rekindled his relationship with an old flame, Terry Basaldua. Terry was a smart girl with a quick smile, who had always admired Freddie's sense of humor. She was a few years younger than Freddie and had a toddler, Serena, who was born when Terry was fourteen. Serena's father, also just fourteen when the baby was born, was no longer in the picture, and Freddie treated Serena like his own child. He settled into working for his father, slopping hogs and tending the same piece of ranch property the family had once worked together. After his arrest, knowing that juries looked favorably on defendants with a steady paycheck, Freddie took a job at a cotton baling company just outside of town. One of Fred Sr.'s kids was back in cotton, after all.

The night before the trial, Freddie and his father discussed McEachern's plea offer. Freddie told his dad what Hrin had said about possibly being home in a year. Freddie did a month in the county jail before his parents could raise the $2,000 to bond him out. It had been the most miserable month of Fred Sr.'s life. He couldn't imagine his son being locked up for an entire year. And he wouldn't be in Tulia but in some state prison, for all they knew off in Huntsville, hundreds of miles away from his family. Freddie had maintained his innocence from the day he was arrested, and his father believed him. In his heart Fred Sr. believed his son would get a fair shake in Tulia, just as he felt Tulia had given him a chance to succeed. Cash Love and Joe Moore and the others had gone down, but they didn't play by the rules. Freddie didn't belong in prison, and there was only one possible answer to his dilemma.

"Did you do it?" Fred Sr. asked. Freddie knew his dad was trying to make a point.

"No, I didn't," he replied.

"Well, then," Fred Sr. said, "don't take the deal."

Even though he was paid cash upfront for his services, Mike Hrin did less work preparing for trial than many of the appointed counsels. He seemed to think that Freddie was going to accept whatever deal McEachern offered him. His pretrial work consisted of reading Coleman's report and examining McEachern's file. He filed no pretrial motions, not even a standard discovery motion for Brady material. He did not interview any of the state's witnesses or talk to the other defense attorneys who had Tulia cases, with the exception of a brief visit with Van Williamson, who shared a building with Hrin in Amarillo. Williamson was the attorney in the disastrous Cash Love trial. He mentioned to Hrin a rumor he heard that Coleman had been in some kind of trouble in Pecos County, but he didn't know any of the details.

Freddie had difficulty getting Hrin to return his calls and met with him only twice. He wanted Hrin to subpoena an alibi witness for

him. Freddie remembered being in Amarillo at a relative's house the
day Coleman allegedly bought cocaine from him. It was Easter weekend, and a cousin of Freddie's had asked him for a ride so that he
could go visit his family. The boy's mother, Fred Sr.'s sister, was reluctant for her son to get involved in the trial, however. He was on probation, and she was scared of angering Terry McEachern. In any
event, no subpoena was ever filed. All Freddie could do was plead
with his cousin to show up in court for him.

Freddie's trial, presided over by Judge Self in Tulia, lasted two
days. As usual, Coleman was the only witness to the alleged transaction. He filed a report that was barely a paragraph, alleging that he
had come to a duplex on East Broadway Street in Tulia looking for a
man named Bennie Robinson. Nobody was home, Coleman wrote,
but before he turned to leave a young man came out of the back half
of the duplex and waved him over. "I'm Brookins," Freddie allegedly
said. "What do you need?" Coleman claimed that Freddie already had
the baggie of cocaine in his pocket, even though he was presumably
not expecting anyone. Coleman said he had never had a conversation
with Freddie prior to that day, nor did he ever speak with him again.
Freddie did live in the rear unit at the time, but he never had a conversation with Coleman, he told Hrin. He had only seen him driving
around town in his truck with Man Kelly.

Sheriff Stewart was the first witness to testify for the state. Early
on, Hrin asked what kind of background check Stewart had done on
Coleman, and McEachern immediately requested a bench conference. Self sent the jury out and then allowed Hrin to proceed with his
questioning. Stewart explained that Sergeant Massengill of the task
force had made most of the inquiries, and he did not remember hearing that Massengill received any negative comments about Coleman.
Hrin then asked if Stewart had learned any new information about
Coleman subsequent to his hiring and the beginning of the investigation. Stewart replied that he had.

"The new information that you have obtained, or learned, would you characterize any of that as negative or marginal?" Hrin asked.

There was a pause. Two days ago, in this very courtroom, with Self and McEachern looking on, Stewart had admitted that he'd arrested Coleman himself during the investigation, and that the authorities and at least a half dozen creditors were after him in another county. Hrin had no way of knowing that, so he could not appreciate the significance of the carefully parsed answer that Stewart gave.

"With what I know right now today, I do not believe it's negative," Stewart said.

Hrin had no idea he had come close to uncovering the Cochran County charge. He was still blindly groping for something having to do with Coleman's time in Fort Stockton. He pressed Stewart on whether he had heard of any incidents involving Coleman in that city. Stewart answered vaguely that he thought he had seen a subpoena for documents having to do with Coleman's employment there. In fact, Tom Hamilton had subpoenaed the sheriff's office for a copy of the income withholding order that Carol Barnett filed in Fort Stockton. Stewart told Hrin that he couldn't remember specifically what type of records the subpoena was after, even though his office had been ordered to turn the information over to the judge just the day before.

Hrin was done. Having determined that he knew absolutely nothing about any of the allegations against Coleman, Self invited him to repeat his line of questions in front of the jury. Hrin did not see the point, so he let it go. Later that morning, however, Sergeant Massengill took the stand and testified that something troubling came up subsequent to Coleman's hiring. Massengill hadn't been present for Stewart's response to the same line of questioning, and he was apparently in a more candid mood than the sheriff. McEachern cut him off, and in a bench conference Self ordered Hrin to stop the questioning. Hrin would have to save it for a bill of exceptions later, outside the presence of the jury.

After lunch, McEachern called Coleman to the stand. On cross-examination, Hrin asked Coleman why he left his last law enforcement position. Coleman testified, as he had in past trials, that the sheriff of Cochran County had been using his office for personal gain. McEachern objected when Hrin asked Coleman to elaborate, but Self overruled. Coleman had brought it up, after all. "You can go ahead," Self said.

"Like charging stuff to the county that he was using for his personal stuff, and, you know, just things that I shouldn't have been around," Coleman explained.

"Okay. So you weren't involved in it, the sheriff was and made you uncomfortable to work?" Hrin asked.

"Well, I can put it to you this way," Coleman said. "My whole family is in law enforcement, and I wasn't about to put a black mark on my career like that, so I left the department."

By four o'clock, the state was done with its case. Hrin was to put on his defense beginning the next morning. In the time left that afternoon, Self allowed Hrin to make his bill of exceptions. He began with Massengill, who quickly admitted that Coleman had been charged with theft during the investigation. Even with Self allowing the witnesses to answer, however, firm information about exactly what transpired was difficult to come by. Was the charge the reason Coleman left Cochran County? It was not, but Massengill couldn't say what the reason was. Was the charge a misdemeanor or a felony, Hrin asked? Massengill thought it was a misdemeanor, but he wasn't positive. Massengill testified that the task force sent Coleman back to Sheriff Stewart to "get it cleared up." He understood that Coleman was placed on annual leave for a week and that the case was eventually dismissed. Had he ever seen an order of dismissal? He wasn't sure. Did Coleman make restitution? He couldn't say.

"You were his immediate supervisor?" Hrin asked at one point. Massengill was. He just didn't know much about it, it seemed.

"But the sheriff could have that information?" Hrin asked. "Possibly," Massengill allowed. "Maybe his memory is better than mine. I am not real sure."

As it happened, Stewart's memory was not much better. Called back to the stand by Hrin, he testified that he was reasonably sure the charge against Coleman was a misdemeanor. He did the arrest himself and obtained a personal recognizance bond for him, he said. He never called Cochran County to discuss the charges with anyone. Coleman hired an attorney, and in a week's time he had a dismissal on the case. Coleman was then given a polygraph by the Amarillo police department, which he passed. As soon as the dismissal came in, Stewart said, he put Coleman back on the street.

Did Stewart actually see the dismissal, Hrin asked? Stewart replied that he did not. Hrin was mystified:

Q: I can't understand this. You give him a leave of absence for a week.

A: Yes, sir.

Q: Tell him he can't work until it's disposed of.

A: Yes, sir.

Q: He comes back and tells you it's been dismissed, and you let him go back to work without any verification from Cochran County that it's been dismissed.

A: No, I don't remember anything past that.

Hrin wasn't sure what to make of Stewart's laconic answers to the astounding revelation that the only witness in this case had been arrested during the investigation. The man was either very cagey or very stupid. Hrin now asked him if, after discovering the warrant in the first place, he had called the Cochran County sheriff's office to find out why Coleman had left that department eight months before coming to Tulia.

A: No, sir. I don't think anything ever came about to make me think anything except that he left on his own. That's what he told me, and there was no—no indications otherwise.

Q: Well, Sheriff, with all due respect, if you have an individual who is handling hundreds of dollars of task force money—

A: Uh-huh.

Q: —to make these drug buys on a weekly basis, and it's brought to your attention that he's charged in another jurisdiction with stealing that county's property—

A: Yes, sir.

Q: —that wouldn't cause you some concern, just a little concern about having access to these funds and accountability and that sort of thing? That just never crossed your mind to worry about that?

A: When this—this came—when this warrant come in—came in, yes, sir. Very obviously it was a concern.

Q: Okay. But not enough so to pick up the phone and call his ex-employer and say, "Is this the only problem with this guy? Is there anything I need to know?"

A: I did not do that.

Q: Okay. Just didn't think it was important?

A: I don't know as I would say that I didn't think it was important. It was not the step that I took.

When his bill was completed, Hrin asked that he be allowed to rehearse at least a portion of the questioning in front of the jury. Coleman had given a different account of why he left Cochran County than the one given by his supervisors, Hrin argued, and he ought to be allowed to explore that inconsistency before the jury. He further asked that he be allowed to impeach Coleman with the charge itself. Self asked if Hrin could cite an authority, something in the case law or the rules of evidence that supported his position. Hrin was not prepared to answer; he did not know about the charge, after all, until that afternoon. In fact, Texas case law holds that specific instances of conduct by a witness can be invoked by an attorney to correct a false impression created by a witness's previous testimony. This certainly seemed to be such a situation, but Hrin was apparently unaware of that exception to the rules. McEachern cited Rules 608 and 609, regarding incidents of specific conduct by witnesses. Self ruled the entire bill inadmissible.

After the trial recessed for the day, Fred Sr., Kent, Patty, Mary, and Freddie gathered in the Brookins' living room. Freddie's girl-friend Terry was there as well. Fred Sr. was grim. They had to be prepared for the worst tomorrow, he told them. Inside he was furious. How could Coleman testify against his son, if Stewart had to arrest him during the operation? He was the only witness the state had. Couldn't the judge see the man was a liar? Couldn't everyone see that?

That night Freddie and Terry lay awake talking in bed. Freddie was impressed that Terry wasn't crying. Still, he could tell she was scared.

"I could still get acquitted," he told her.

"Don't even say that," Terry said. "Your dad's right, we have to be ready for the worst."

If he did get sentenced to prison, Hrin had told Freddie, they would take him straight from the courtroom to jail. There would be no time to go home and get ready. No time for good-byes. Anything they were going to say to one another, they had to say it now. Freddie asked if Terry would wait for him. In anticipation of this night, Terry had been asking around about how much time Freddie would actually have to do if the jury gave him the full twenty years. The consensus seemed to be that Freddie would have to do five at least. Five years. Terry had just been accepted to Wayland Baptist University in Plain-view. She would be a twenty-four-year-old college graduate by the time Freddie got out. Her daughter Serena would be eight. That was even harder to imagine.

Thinking about Serena as a third grader—coming home from

school with a backpack full of homework, getting her ears pierced, playing softball—Terry realized for the first time just how much she had begun to count on Freddie's presence in not only her life but Serena's as well. Her own father had died when she was young, and she and her brothers and sisters had been raised by her mother and a series of boyfriends. She had grown up fast. She wanted Serena to have a real childhood. There was no doubt in her mind that Freddie was the dad her daughter needed. She told him yes, she would wait, no matter how long it took. And she would write him every day.

Eventually they stopped talking, but neither of them fell asleep that night. They lay next to each other in silence, as Freddie's fate slipped up on him with the morning sun.

It did not take Hrin long to present his case the next morning. Freddie's cousin, his potential alibi witness, was a no-show. Hrin had nobody else to call, except for Terry and Freddie himself. Terry testified that Freddie left for Amarillo at 9:30 in the morning and was gone until 7:00 in the evening. Then Freddie took the stand. He was dreading facing McEachern. He had always been feared in black Tulia, but in the past six months his legend had grown enormously. McEachern didn't spend much time examining Freddie, but he did score two points. One was a low blow and the other demonstrated once again his knowledge of panhandle juries.

"You ever been convicted of anything?" McEachern asked right out of the gate. Hrin immediately objected, but the damage was done. McEachern knew that Freddie had been given deferred adjudication on his only previous charge. By definition, deferred adjudication means that no final conviction was entered, so under the rules of evidence such a charge could not be used to impeach a witness. It was the same rule that had saved Coleman's skin twice in the past week. Self sent the jury out, and a discussion was had. The charge had never been properly expunged from Freddie's record, McEachern said, and he claimed to know of a case that would allow such a charge to be used. In the end, he could not produce it, and the jury was brought back in. Hrin forgot to ask the judge to instruct the jury to disregard McEachern's question.

McEachern then began to quiz Freddie about the "party house" he lived behind. Didn't Creamy, Cash Love, Kizzie, and Donnie hang out at the front house? Hadn't he seen a lot of police cars coming by? Freddie testified that he went to high school with those people but didn't hang out with them anymore. McEachern pressed: didn't he see Creamy coming around a lot? Yes, Freddie said, because his girlfriend lived there. There followed this exchange:

Q: And who's his girlfriend?

A: Her name is Chandra. I don't know her last name.

Q: Well would Van Cleave ring a bell?

A: No, sir. I don't know her last name. I never associated—I never really associated with them. You know, we speak. You know, they have their life and I have mine.

Q: And he has a child by her too, doesn't he?

A: No, sir.

Q: Doesn't?

A: Not that I know of.

Q: And she is white, Caucasian. Is that not true?

A: Yes, sir.

Q: And she is also charged in this?

Hrin finally jumped in and objected to the obvious irrelevance of the questions. In just two minutes of cross-examination, McEachern had imputed to Freddie a criminal record he did not have, raised the specter of interracial sex, one of the most sensitive social issues in rural America, and tied Freddie to one known crack user and one alleged dealer who had just received 361 years in the pen. When

McEachern was done with Freddie, Hrin took one last look in the hall for Freddie's cousin. Unable to locate him, he rested. He had presented his entire case in one hour and fifteen minutes. It took the jury less than an hour to find Freddie guilty, and another hour to assess him the maximum term of twenty years.

CHAPTER NINE

One Riot, One Ranger

PAPER PILED UP like snowdrifts in Gary Gardner's makeshift office that winter. It began with a flurry of responses to the first round of letters he had sent out back in December, urging the sting defendants to seek a change of venue. They all told a familiar story: either they had never met Coleman or they hadn't sold him what he claimed they had. After that Gardner had become a fixture at the county clerk's office, where he collected every scrap of paper he could get his hands on about Coleman's investigation. As Paul Holloway and Tom Hamilton were digging into Coleman's past, Gardner set about trying to learn what he had really been up to in Tulia. He meticulously recorded every case made by Coleman in Swisher County, including the amount and type of drug purchased. He compiled these into a document he labeled "Indictments by Name, Race, and Social Background." His desk was covered with well-thumbed trial transcripts, tabbed here and there with Post-it notes covered with Gardner's uneven scrawl. Gardner discovered, among other things, that Coleman had made only one purchase larger than an eight ball during the entire eighteen-month operation in Tulia, and that buy was for just five grams of powder. With all the huge sentences, Gardner thought, where were the big-time dealers? He interviewed the defendants' family members, beginning with Mattie White and Thelma Johnson. His experience with the ongoing drug testing lawsuit had taught him to be methodical and to record everything he did, so he typed up summaries of his interviews. He labeled them as affidavits and had his subjects sign them at the bottom.

Mattie told Gardner that in addition to Kareem, Donnie, and Kizzie, her oldest daughter Tonya had also been indicted. That had to be a mistake, she said, because Tonya had been living for years in Oklahoma City, where she worked as a nurse's aid. As far as Mattie could tell, Stewart had made no attempt to locate her so far.

Mattie also said that in her conversations with Sheriff Stewart he had mentioned a list of suspects provided to Coleman early in the operation. Gardner had heard this list referred to before. In the back-and-forth over the school drug testing policy, a Tulia police officer had bragged that the department had compiled a list of "sixty known drug dealers" in Tulia. He was beginning to suspect that this list of so-called dealers was really a tally of everybody on the south side of town who had ever given the authorities any trouble, and that Coleman's operation had been a convenient way to finally run them all out of town.

In time a retired minister named Charles Kiker joined Gardner in his advocacy. Born and raised in Tulia, Kiker had returned home in March 1999 after a forty-year career as a pastor, most recently at a Baptist church in Kansas City. With his long, thin frame and long-jowled face, he called to mind a more avuncular version of Sheriff Stewart. He was chagrined to read the biased coverage of the busts in the *Tulia Herald*, the once-proud paper that was still edited by H. M. Baggarly when Kiker last lived in Tulia. His daughter and son-in-law, Nancy and Alan Bean, had also recently relocated to Tulia. They had been living in a small town outside Wichita, Kansas, where Alan, a thoughtful, mild-mannered Canadian with a Ph.D., was a minister. Nancy now taught at the high school in Tulia.

Together with Fred Brookins Sr., Thelma Johnson, Mattie White, and Billy and Carolyn Wafer, Gardner and Kiker began meeting regularly at Alan and Nancy's house to discuss the busts. They called themselves the Friends of Justice. They were soon joined by Lili Ibara, an enthusiastic young college graduate from Boston who had volunteered with VISTA, a national community service program, and found herself placed with Texas Rural Legal Aid in Plainview. As they were pondering how to begin fighting the convictions, however, everyone else seemed to be giving up. After Freddie's trial resulted in yet another maximum sentence, defendants started pleading out in droves. They were encouraged to do so by increasingly reasonable offers from McEachern, who seemed eager to get the whole affair behind him. Coleman testified one more time, in the trial of Donnie Smith's younger sister Kizzie White. Despite having no prior record, she was sentenced to twenty-five years.

It was the most difficult decision of his career, but Paul Holloway eventually instructed his clients to plead out as well, as did Tom Hamilton. Holloway and his twelve-year-old son had just watched *To Kill a Mockingbird*, he recalled later. "I told him the difference between me and Atticus Finch is this: At the end of the trial—this complete railroading of an innocent man—Atticus turned to his client immediately and said, 'Don't worry, we're going to appeal.'" But Holloway's conscience would not allow him to do that in Tulia. "I took an oath as a lawyer not to piss on this system, but I knew in my heart they would win no appeals."

By mid-April, virtually all of the remaining three dozen defendants had plead out. Many were offered probation, but others were forced to take pleas for prison time. Almost twenty people were now in prison or on their way to prison, so many that simply compiling a list of where each of them was incarcerated was a considerable task for the Friends of Justice. Lili Ibara was given the job of contacting the media about the story. She wrote a letter outlining everything that had happened in the bust and mailed it to every major media outlet in the state. The initial arrests had produced a round of stories the previous summer, some of which noted that the racial makeup of the defendants had raised eyebrows in Tulia. But the publicity soon died down, and nobody seemed willing to do an investigative story about the bust itself. The Amarillo and Lubbock papers, which had treated the bust as big news when it first broke, seemed uninterested in revisiting it now. Weeks went by, and Ibara got no bites on her letter.

Among the media outlets Ibara wrote to that spring was a small-circulation magazine in Austin called the *Texas Observer*, where I was working as a reporter. The *Observer* was primarily known for its coverage of the Texas legislature, which it delivered from a decidedly left-leaning perspective. Despite its small staff and limited budget, however, the magazine also did investigative reporting around the state. I called Ibara in April 2000 and spent a week in Tulia shortly thereafter, interviewing defense attorneys and defendants' family members and reviewing Gary Gardner's voluminous files. At that time, both Joe Moore and Donnie Smith were incarcerated in a transfer facility in the west Texas city of Abilene, and I interviewed each of them there. In June, the *Observer* ran an 8,000-word story exploring Coleman's background in considerable depth and outlining some of the problems with his trial testimony.

In addition to the information Paul Holloway and Tom and Brent Hamilton tracked down, the story brought to light another incident that seemed particularly damaging to Coleman's credibility. A court-appointed attorney for a sting defendant named Yul Bryant discovered that Coleman had filed two separate police reports on his client. They were almost identical, except for Coleman's description of Bryant. In the first report, Coleman described Bryant as a tall black man with bushy hair. Bryant is five-foot-six and completely bald. A later report described Bryant in more generic terms. It looked like a clumsy effort by somebody to cover up an obvious mistake by Coleman. Bryant, who said he was in Amarillo at the time of the alleged buy, believed the man described in the report was an acquaintance of his named Randy Hicks. At the request of Bryant's attorney, Kerry Piper, McEachern's investigator called Coleman in, showed him pictures of Bryant and Hicks, and asked him to identify Bryant. Coleman pointed to the picture of Hicks. The case against Bryant was quietly dismissed. If Piper had not been fortunate enough to discover the discrepancy in the reports, Bryant would have been prosecuted for a crime he apparently did not commit.

The *Observer* story also reported another peculiar fact about Coleman's investigation that had been previously overlooked: in a roundup of roughly forty suspected cocaine dealers, not a single gram of cocaine was recovered on the morning of the bust or in the days that followed. Although most of the defendants had been rousted at dawn and taken completely by surprise, not one of them was caught holding cocaine of any kind, crack or powder.

The most sensational material in the article was culled from a document created during Coleman's divorce from Carol Barnett. A judge assigned an investigator to interview associates and family members of both parents to determine who should get custody of the couple's two children. The image that emerged of Coleman in the investigator's report was far from flattering. Rick Kennedy was a Pecos County deputy assigned to work with Coleman when he was stationed in Iraan in the early 1990s. Kennedy told the investigator that the sheriff was having trouble with Coleman and wanted Kennedy to help straighten him out, but Kennedy didn't have much luck. Coleman would not listen to or follow orders, and he had some disturbing tendencies. He was obsessed with guns, for one thing. On an overnight fishing and camping trip with Kennedy, Coleman brought a small arsenal and insisted on having a machine gun with him at all times—on the boat, in the tent, and in the truck. He struck

Kennedy as paranoid, an observation that was echoed by several other former associates interviewed.

The other common thread that leaped out from the investigator's report was Coleman's dishonesty. "Tom can lie to you when the truth would sound better," Kennedy reported. Nina McFadden, the wife of another deputy Coleman worked with in Pecos County, described Coleman as "an idiot," "paranoid," and "a compulsive liar." Susan Coleman, Carol Barnett's sister, called him a pathological liar.

Larry Jackson, another former Pecos County law enforcement colleague of Coleman's, told the *Observer* that Coleman was widely known around the county as a liar and a paranoid gun nut.* Over the years, Jackson had worked with Coleman's father on a number of murder investigations and had come to revere the man, as most area cops did. The son was another matter. Patrolling tiny Iraan, Coleman carried as many as three guns on his person at one time. "I could cut a switch and police Iraan," Jackson laughed. When Coleman abruptly left Pecos County, nobody was sorry to see him go. Consequently, when news reached the sheriff's office that Coleman had been named Officer of the Year for his work in Tulia, the reaction was utter disbelief. Jackson himself marveled that Coleman had even been hired in Swisher County. "Some people called me and said, 'Well, the sheriff [in Tulia] is high on him,'" Jackson recalled. "And I said, well, it looks to me like you need to elect a new sheriff then. Something's wrong."

For many of the defendants' families, the *Observer* story confirmed what they had long suspected. Coleman was no good, and McEachern and Stewart had been covering for him from the beginning. "Get a dirty man to do a dirty job," Fred Brookins Sr. said. On a Sunday morning shortly after the article was published, Lili Ibara and a friend made dozens of copies and put them on the windshields of

---

* Jackson asked that he not be identified by name in the *Observer* article. He has since passed away.

cars in the parking lots of the Baptist Church and the Church of Christ in Tulia. It was a declaration of war. Charles Kiker and Alan Bean began mailing the *Observer* story to anybody they could find who might be able to help their cause. Joined by Gardner, they began writing a steady stream of letters to the papers in Tulia, Plainview, and Amarillo.

The backlash in Tulia was immediate. Having publicly identified themselves with the defendants, Kiker, Gardner, and Bean became the targets of opprobrium in both of the local newspapers, where letter writers tagged them as the "KGB." They were accused of dragging Tulia's name through the mud and sullying the reputation of Sheriff Stewart. "Any attack on the undercover investigation, the officers involved, and subsequent trials and convictions," Sheriff Stewart's daughter Angie wrote in a letter to the *Herald*, was "an attack on our entire community." Friends, neighbors, and even some family members shunned the organizers. Nancy Bean, who grew up in Tulia and had relatives all over the county, was devastated. Her great aunt banned the Beans from all future family reunions and let Nancy know that her children's photos had been removed from her refrigerator. In its letters column, the *Herald* ran a bizarre screed about the bust, supposedly authored by Coleman himself, in which he described witnessing neglected crack babies and automatic weapons in the homes of Tulia defendants. "Have you ever seen a little girl having to perform oral sex to get drugs?" the letter read in part. "Have you ever stood in the driveway of a drug dealer's house listening to him brag about his new boat or fancy truck he bought on the misery of these children?" The notion of Joe Moore or Donnie Smith buying a nice truck, much less a boat, brought some laughs from the defendants' advocates. The letter made Tulia sound like South Central Los Angeles.

That summer, a copy of the *Observer* story landed on the desk of a drug war reform advocate and former stand-up comedian in New York named Randy Credico. Credico hit his professional peak in the early 1980s, when the twenty-seven-year-old comic appeared on *The Tonight Show* with Johnny Carson. There was a lot to like about Credico; with his boyish good looks and wiseacre persona, he called to mind young David Letterman. But just when things seemed to be going well—Carson and Ed McMahon were both laughing—Credico pushed it too far. He told several jokes about the Reagan administration, including one in which he compared U.N. Ambassador Jeanne Kirkpatrick to Eva Braun, Hitler's mistress. Very few laughs. To make matters worse, Credico, who routinely did impressions as part of his shtick, then did a few brief, nervous moments of Carson himself, despite warnings from his colleagues in the New York comedy clubs. He was never invited back. It was typical of a self-destructive streak in Credico's nature. Discretion and decorum did not come naturally to him. Further hampered by problems with drugs and alcohol, Credico's career began to slowly decay.

His pugnaciousness served him well in his next career as an activist, however. Credico became active in New York left politics at a time when U.S. meddling in Central America was the cause of the day. He became a staunch supporter of the Sandinista cause, visiting Nicaragua on many occasions and doing his anti-Reagan shtick at fund-raising parties and rallies. In the mid-1990s, he turned his attention to the drug war. Credico had befriended the great civil rights lawyer and liberal icon William Kunstler late in the attorney's life. After his death, Credico was selected by Kunstler's widow, Margaret Kunstler, to head the William Kunstler Foundation. It was an impressive title, but Kunstler had died largely insolvent, and the underfunded foundation was essentially a one-man show.

Yet Credico's tireless energy made him a force to be reckoned with in New York politics. Repeal of New York's drug laws—among the toughest in the nation—became his main cause. New York, that great bastion of liberalism, introduced the concept of mandatory minimum sentences to American jurisprudence in the early 1970s with the so-called Rockefeller drug laws. What Credico lacked in resources, he made up for with his uncanny knack for generating publicity. He was a natural at working the press, and reporters loved his comedian's mug and facility with snappy one-liners about local politicians.

Credico got a lot of letters like Kiker's—all drug war activists did. But this one was different. Once he finished reading the *Observer* article, he couldn't stop thinking about the case. It was the most egregious injustice he had encountered in a long time. In August, he made the first of what became many trips to the Texas panhandle.

By the time Credico landed in Tulia, the situation seemed to have reached a stalemate. Coleman had not testified in a proceeding in months, and McEachern did not seem eager to get him back in front of a jury anytime soon. But there were still a few unadjudicated cases that had to be dealt with, and a showdown of sorts was beginning to materialize around the case of Donnie Smith's younger brother, Kareem White, who had thus far refused to accept a plea. White had been assigned a court-appointed attorney out of Amarillo named Dwight McDonald, a black attorney in his mid-thirties, whom Kareem's father Ricky had met previously and admired. He didn't have many actual trials under his belt, but he had a reputation for thoroughness and he recognized Kareem's upcoming trial for what it was: a turning point in an ongoing struggle in which a great many young people's lives—as well as a number of law enforcement careers—hung in the balance. He regarded it as the biggest trial of his career. Randy Credico brought McDonald out to visit Gary Gardner, who by now had an extensive collection of trial transcripts, as well as all of the relevant documents relating to the Cochran County charge. Gardner laid out the complex chronology of the charge for McDonald and highlighted some of Coleman's inconsistent testimony in past trial transcripts. McDonald had also been in contact with Paul Holloway and Tom Hamilton.

Kareem's trial was set for September 6 in Judge Jack Miller's court. He would be tried for the first of five eight ball deliveries, and the state was seeking a drug-free zone enhancement, making the charge a first-degree felony punishable by five to ninety-nine years. The Texas ACLU had taken an interest in the case, and Credico was doing his best to raise national media interest in the story. He managed to land Kiker and Gardner on a nationally syndicated radio show out of New York called *Democracy Now!* The host, Amy Goodman, was not sure what to make of Gardner, who had to be warned not to refer to the defendants as "niggers" on the air. That was the term used by most white Tulians of Gardner's generation, and he saw no reason to hide that fact. "It doesn't matter what I call 'em," Gardner told Goodman during the interview. "What matters is that they didn't get a fair trial."

In the weeks leading up to the trial, Credico was everywhere. Sarah and Emily Kunstler, the college-age daughters of William Kunstler, had begun following him around Tulia, shooting a documentary about the bust. Credico's mere presence seemed to disrupt the normal power relationships in Tulia. He was not intimidated by Stewart or McEachern, and he made sure everybody at the courthouse knew it. One afternoon, Credico spotted McEachern coming across the courthouse parking lot following a pretrial hearing for Kareem's case. "Hey McEachern," Credico yelled. "I saw your boy Coleman—I told him 'Nice job, maggot!'" Momentarily stunned, McEachern stopped to consider this foul-mouthed stranger in a rumpled suit, with a well-chewed cigar stump hanging from his mouth. He shook his head and kept moving.

McEachern guessed that Credico meant trouble, and he was right. A producer for the ABC news program *20/20* had contacted McDonald about the case, and Credico was desperately trying to get somebody from the *New York Times* to come to town and cover the trial as well. It was beginning to look like the next time Coleman testified, he would be performing for a much larger audience.

Dwight McDonald's representation of Kareem got off to a disastrous start. Kareem, known to his friends as Creamy, was a tall, muscular twenty-three-year-old. Like Donnie, he had been a star athlete in high school; unlike his older brother, he had grown into a brooding, taciturn young man who rarely smiled. Kareem told McDonald that the cases were fabricated, and McDonald saw no reason to doubt his client, given what he had learned about Coleman. Indeed Coleman claimed to have made one of the buys at high noon less than a block from the courthouse square.

In a conference call with Judge Miller and McEachern, McDonald offered to submit Kareem to a lie detector test, provided the state would agree to three conditions: first, that McDonald be present for the test—if not in the room, then at least nearby where his client could consult with him if necessary; second, that Kareem be asked specifically if he had sold *powdered* cocaine to Coleman, not merely if he had sold narcotics; and third, that Coleman himself be tested if Kareem passed the polygraph.

To McDonald's surprise, McEachern consented to the conditions. Things did not work out that way, however. One afternoon in March, Kareem was picked up from the jail in Levelland, where he had been held since the bust the previous summer, and driven seventy miles to the Plainview jail, where he was told he would be given a polygraph. McDonald was nowhere to be found. When Kareem asked to see him, he was told not to worry, that McDonald had okayed the test. Kareem reluctantly agreed to proceed, and the operator began asking a series of preliminary questions, ostensibly to help him craft the actual questions to be used when Kareem was hooked up to the machine. Right off the bat, the officer asked Kareem if he had ever sold narcotics. The answer was yes, but without McDonald present, Kareem wasn't sure whether to respond. He decided to tell the truth.

Just before Kareem was wired up for the test, another officer stepped in and reported that McDonald was on the phone, demand-

ing that the test be stopped. He was out of town and had only heard
that Kareem was in Plainview because his secretary had gotten wind
of the proceedings. Kareem was driven back to Levelland, but the
damage was already done: he had admitted to selling drugs in an
interview with the police.

In preparation for the trial, McDonald contacted Van Williamson,
the attorney for Cash Love. After Love's conviction, Williamson filed
a motion for a new trial, based on information that Paul Holloway
and the Hamiltons had brought to light about Coleman. Though
ultimately unsuccessful, Williamson did at least get a hearing on his
motion, in which he questioned members of the prosecution team
about the Cochran County theft charge, among other things.
McEachern swore that he knew nothing about the charge until after
Love's trial. Coleman, however, testified that he knew about the theft
charge in May 1998, months before Sheriff Stewart received the warrant for Coleman's arrest on August 7. Williamson contended that
none of the cases made by Coleman during that May through August
interval—which totaled almost fifty, including several against his
client—should have been considered legitimate. Stewart himself said
in previous testimony that he would not allow an officer with charges
hanging over his head to make cases under his command. At a hearing
for another defendant a month later, however, Coleman changed his
story, claiming that he did not learn about the charges until his superiors did, on August 7, when the arrest warrant came over the Teletype in the Swisher County sheriff's office.

The only problem with Coleman's claim was a document in
Cochran County's files. It was a waiver of arraignment, signed by
Coleman on May 30, 1998, acknowledging that charges had been
filed against him. Williamson encouraged McDonald to go after
Coleman and Stewart on the date discrepancy, especially since one of
Kareem's cases fell within that May to August window. The date of
the signed waiver also supported the defense theory that Coleman,

knowing he had trouble looming in Cochran County, stole money from the task force all summer long by fabricating cases.

At the hearing for Cash Love, McEachern had told the judge his own understanding of how Coleman came up with the money to settle the theft charge. A Texas Ranger by the name of Larry Gilbreath, whose jurisdiction covered Cochran County, loaned Coleman's mother the money to pay off the creditors. This was the same Larry Gilbreath that Coleman had talked to about his troubles in Cochran County, the one whose name Holloway had discovered in Jay Adams's files. None of the defense attorneys had ever actually seen or spoken to Ranger Gilbreath, but he was emerging as a shadowy guardian angel figure for Coleman.

In addition to having the waiver of arraignment in his arsenal, McDonald also won a major victory in a pretrial hearing. He had been in contact with several of Coleman's former associates, in Cochran and Pecos counties, names he had found in the *Texas Observer* story and in documents collected by Tom and Brent Hamilton and Paul Holloway. He was astounded by their stories of Coleman's reputation and behavior, yet he knew that finding a way to get these people in front of a jury was going to be a challenge. As he had in the previous contests, McEachern moved preemptively to prevent mention of the Cochran County charge, or any other specific acts of conduct on Coleman's part, under Rule 609. Judge Miller sided with McEachern, but he also granted McDonald's motion, under a related rule, to allow witnesses to testify about Coleman's general reputation in the communities in which he had lived and worked. Under the seldom used rule, McDonald's witnesses would not be allowed to mention specific reasons for their opinion of Coleman, but they could say whether he was known for being honest or dishonest. If Kareem's case, like most of the cases in the sting, came down to a swearing match, then having those character witnesses—many of them fellow cops—line up against Coleman would be a tremendous boost. When

McEachern lost that ruling, he announced that he would bring his own reputation witnesses to counter McDonald's. After what he had learned about Coleman's career in law enforcement, McDonald could not imagine who McEachern could find to vouch for Coleman's credibility.

As the day of the trial approached, McDonald tried every trick in his playbook. He filed over a dozen motions. He tried to have the case dismissed because of McEachern's duplicitous maneuver on the polygraph. When that failed, he tried unsuccessfully to have Judge Miller removed and a new judge assigned to the case. Ten minutes before jury selection was to begin, McDonald filed a motion for a change of venue. He had affidavits from Gary Gardner, his brother Danny Gardner, Charles Kiker, and Alan Bean, all contending that biased media coverage in the local press, along with a general feeling of animosity toward the defendants and their families, meant that Kareem could not receive a fair trial in Tulia. McEachern was livid, but Miller granted McDonald a hearing, despite the eleventh-hour filing.

Bean and Kiker testified about the sensationalism of the local coverage, particularly that of the *Tulia Sentinel*, which had referred to the defendants as "scumbags." When McEachern's turn to cross-examine came, he seemed less interested in the merits of the motion than he was in demonstrating to Judge Miller, who did not live in Tulia, that McDonald's witnesses were not important people in town. He got Bean to admit that although he called himself a minister, he did not have a congregation in Tulia and his most recent job was selling cookware. He inquired about the size of Kiker's old congregation in Kansas City, which was not very big.

Then Gary Gardner took the stand. McEachern was to blame for the local bias, he told McDonald, because of statements he made to the local papers. "In one of them, the newspaper quoted him as stating in Swisher County we use Swisher County law," Gary said.

"What did you take that to mean?" McDonald asked.

"I took it to mean that the law is a little different in Swisher County than it is other places," Gardner responded.

When McEachern's turn with Gardner came, he did not bother to hide his disgust. More than anybody else, he blamed Gardner for the trouble the Coleman bust was now causing him. And that wasn't the only thing he had against the loud-mouthed farmer from Vigo. Over the summer, Gardner had been responsible for a series of reports in the *Dallas Morning News* criticizing McEachern for his handling of an arson case in which the suspect was a twenty-two-year-old mentally retarded Hispanic boy, the son of a former employee of Gardner's. A psychiatrist found that the boy was not a danger to the community and was not competent to stand trial, but McEachern refused to release him from jail. In the wake of the coverage in the *Morning News*, McEachern finally let him go, more than a year after his arrest. McEachern was also singled out by name that summer in an exhaustive investigative series on the Texas death penalty by the *Chicago Tribune*. The report examined the case of David Wayne Stoker, whom McEachern had prosecuted for the murder of a convenience store clerk in the mid-1980s. In winning a conviction against Stoker, McEachern's office apparently conspired to conceal a deal it had cut with the key witness in the case and reportedly refused to accept the retraction of another witness's statement prior to the trial, despite the fact that he now claimed to have made it up. At least one member of the notoriously conservative Texas Board of Pardons and Paroles felt that Stoker might have been innocent of the crime. He was executed in 1997.

The embarrassing *Tribune* report, part of the paper's review of the record of then presidential candidate George W. Bush, was hardly Gardner's doing. But it was a bad summer for McEachern's reputation, and his anger crystallized around Gardner, his chief persecutor, whom he now had on the stand and under oath. McEachern asked Gardner if he owned the land he farmed in Vigo. "I have my name on a note to Farmers Home Administration," Gardner cracked. "I couldn't go as far as to say that I own it. I get to pay the taxes on it."

McEachern was getting angrier by the minute. "Are you a member of any group or a part of a court watch, watch group, or proceeding?" he asked.

"I'm a member of the Vigo Fire Department and I vote in the Democratic Party," Gardner replied.

"Did you threaten to sue me in my official capacity as a district attorney for legal proceedings in a court of law here in Swisher County, Texas?" McEachern demanded, referring to the arson case.

"First, I don't make threats, Mr. McEachern," Gary began. "And if I sue you...I will sue you in your personal capacity, because I don't think that you are in your official capacity a week after you dismiss a case on the kid and then you slander him."

McEachern seemed to be amused by the legal lingo Gardner had recently made his own. "Do you have any degree in law?" he sneered. "Are you licensed to practice in Tulia?"

Gardner was not easily embarrassed. "I don't have no degree in law," he said.

Miller denied the motion and the jury was selected.

Kareem's trial lasted two and half days, making it one of the longest of the sting trials. A half dozen reporters from the local papers and the Associated Press were in attendance, as well as a producer from 20/20. Credico was in the gallery, as were all the members of the Friends of Justice. For the most part, McDonald performed well. He was obviously well prepared, and he seemed firmly in control—right up until the very end, when things took a turn he had not anticipated.

McEachern put on his case much as he had in the previous trials, with Stewart, Amos, and Massengill explaining how the operation worked and setting up Coleman's eyewitness testimony. Unlike most of the cases, however, McEachern actually had a corroborating witness for this particular sale. Coleman claimed that Man Kelly was with him and observed the deal. McDonald was ready for Kelly's testimony, however. In Donnie Smith's trial in February, Kelly denied ever seeing Kareem sell dope to Tom Coleman. McDonald had Donnie's trial transcript with him. Over McEachern's objection, he pulled it out and had Kelly read what his prior testimony had been. Kelly could not explain the discrepancy. Perhaps he hadn't seen Kareem sell drugs to Coleman after all, he said—he had just seen him hand something to Coleman. Later, under questioning by McEachern, Kelly reported that he had seen Coleman with Kareem many times. Yet this too was contradicted by what Kelly had testified in Donnie's case. He said he had only seen them together once, McDonald reminded Kelly, who seemed hapless and confused throughout his testimony.

McDonald did well in his cross of Coleman too. Under questioning from McEachern, Coleman testified that he never bought from more than one defendant without first going back to Amarillo to deposit the evidence in the vault. Yet McDonald had discovered a second report from the same morning as Kareem's case, in which Coleman claimed to have bought an eight ball from a defendant named Willie Hall in Tulia at 9:30 A.M. The time on Kareem's case was 10:35 A.M., roughly an hour later. There was no way he could have made the hundred-mile round trip from Tulia to Amarillo and back again in one hour. Confronted with the second report, Coleman simply changed his story.

McDonald also caught Coleman in an apparent lie in front of Judge Miller. Outside of the presence of the jury, McDonald questioned Coleman on the Cochran County charge. As Van Williamson had predicted, Coleman claimed that he did not learn about the charges until August 1998, when the warrant came across the Teletype machine in Sheriff Stewart's office. McDonald produced the waiver of arraignment and had Coleman read the date on it. Coleman first made as if he could not find the date. After McDonald pointed it out to him, he claimed, despite all evidence to the contrary, that he still did not know about the charges until August. He was not even sure what a waiver of arraignment meant, he said, though just minutes earlier he had testified that he was familiar with the term. He had merely signed it as a precautionary measure at the urging of a friend, he said.

Finally, just before the close of the trial's second day, McDonald brought out his character witnesses. As McDonald had known it would, the trial had come down to a test of who was more credible, his client or Tom Coleman. He had saved these witnesses for the very end; their testimony against Coleman was to be his kicker. First to take the stand was Ori White, the district attorney from Pecos County. He testified that he knew Coleman from his days as a sheriff's deputy in Iraan and Fort Stockton. Under the rules of evidence, McDonald was strictly limited in what he could ask.

"And with regard to Mr. Coleman," he began, "what's his reputation as far as truthfulness or untruthfulness, in your part of the world?"

"It's bad," White replied.

"So you are saying that he is an untruthful person?" McDonald asked.

"I believe so," White said.

That was as far as McDonald was allowed to go, and White stepped down. He was followed by Clay McFadden, a former Pecos County deputy who had worked with Coleman. "Mr. Coleman was constantly untruthful," McFadden said. The next witness, James Dewbre, the president of a bank in Cochran County that had loaned money to Coleman, also testified that Coleman was untruthful. Last, McDonald called Ken Burke, the sheriff of Cochran County who had written to TCLEOSE warning future employers about Coleman. Burke was the man Coleman had accused so many times of being a crook, and he was clearly itching to say much more than the one word assessment he gave of Coleman. "Untruthful," he said. None of the men was on the stand for more than five minutes, yet the impact of the testimony was considerable.

McDonald was done. He had impeached Coleman's corroborating witness, Eliga Kelly, with his own previous testimony. He had induced Coleman to tell an apparent lie on the stand in front of the judge. And best of all, he had produced four witnesses, three of them from law enforcement, to testify that the only real witness for the state, the man on whom the entire case was built, was a liar. He felt good about his case.

After McDonald rested, McEachern called his rebuttal character witnesses. Stewart and Amos took the stand and, somewhat predictably, vouched for Coleman's honesty. Then McEachern played his ace in the hole. A tall man in cowboy boots, tan chinos, and a gleaming white dress shirt strode purposefully up to the witness stand. Even before he opened his mouth, the distinctive circle-on-star badge gleaming on his chest told everybody in the courtroom that they were in the presence of a Texas Ranger. "Would you state your name, please?" McEachern said.

"I'm Larry Gilbreath," the Ranger replied. McDonald winced. Here at last was the mysterious Ranger Gilbreath, the man who intervened to save Coleman's neck in Cochran County. McDonald could sense the awe coming from the jury box. The Rangers were legendary, and not just because of their supposed prowess as detectives. A key part of the Ranger legend was that their word was gold. They were the cops, after all, who investigated police corruption. They were above reproach, the elite of a state police force that prided itself on professionalism.

Gilbreath testified that he had met Coleman when he was a deputy in Cochran County and had known him for several years.

"Just one question," McEachern said. "Do you have an opinion as to Tom Coleman's truthfulness?"

"I know him to be truthful," Gilbreath replied without a moment's hesitation. McDonald could almost feel Kareem's acquittal slipping through his fingers.

For good measure, McEachern brought in several more character witnesses the next morning. With the exception of Bruce Norman, Coleman's current partner at a task force in southeast Texas, all of them were friends of the family. Two of them, Jerry Byrne and Bob Bullock, were Texas Rangers. Byrne had gone to high school with Coleman. Bullock was a Ranger in Midland who had worked with Coleman's father for years. A third, Pecos police chief Clay McKinney, was the son of a former Texas Ranger from the border area, Clayton McKinney Sr. For the past decade, McKinney Sr. had been the chief deputy under Midland County Sheriff Gary Painter, one of the state's best known drug warriors and one of the major political power brokers in his part of the state. This was the royalty of west Texas law enforcement, a far-flung but tightly knit community. Coleman was extremely well connected—far better connected than McDonald or anybody else understood.

It took the jury an hour and a half to find Kareem guilty. Though he had a right to have a jury decide his punishment, McDonald preferred to throw his client on Judge Miller's mercy. Miller's judgment was sixty years in prison.

PART THREE

CHAPTER TEN

Black Cards and White Cards

KAREEM'S ADVOCATES were crushed. His father, Ricky, left the courtroom immediately after the verdict was read; he couldn't bear to stay for the sentencing. Of his six children, five were now in prison— three of them because of Tom Coleman. Dwight McDonald was so shaken that he resolved that very afternoon never to try a case in Swisher County again.

Nobody was more stunned than Randy Credico. Throughout the trial, and in particular during Coleman's testimony, he scoffed at how ridiculously weak the state's entire case was. At one point, he laughed so loudly that McEachern complained to Judge Miller, who briefly stopped the proceedings and threatened to throw Credico out of the courtroom. It wasn't until he heard Miller pronounce the words "sixty years" and watched Kareem being led away in handcuffs that Credico fully realized what he was up against in Tulia. It didn't matter that the truth about Coleman had finally come out. Jurors in Tulia weren't interested in the truth. Credico went back to New York and began faxing the *Texas Observer* story to every reporter and activist in his Rolodex. Tulia was ground zero in the national debate over the war on drugs, he thought; the country just didn't know it yet.

On September 29, Alan Bean and Gary Gardner drove two van-loads of people from Tulia to the capitol in Austin, where Will Harrell, the young director of the Texas ACLU, had arranged a press conference at Credico's urging. Among the Tulians were a half dozen children whose parents had been arrested in the sting. Standing on the steps of the capitol with the children—dressed in identical black and gold "Friends of Justice" T-shirts—gathered around him, Harrell introduced them as "orphans" of the drug war. He announced that the ACLU, with Amarillo attorney Jeff Blackburn as the lead counsel, had filed suit against Sheriff Stewart and Tom Coleman for civil rights violations. A *New York Times* reporter named Jim Yardley was in the audience, and that afternoon Credico convinced him to come to Tulia to follow up on the *Observer* story. Credico had been trying for some time to coax a *Los Angeles Times* reporter into covering the story as well. Once he had Yardley on the hook, he began inundating the L.A. reporter with cell phone messages. "You're about to get scooped on the story of the century," Credico warned.

On October 7, the story appeared on page 1 of the *New York Times* and the *Los Angeles Times* on the same day. A feature segment on CNN followed soon after, and the media circus was on. As one story after another was filed that fall and winter, each following essentially the same script, the town took a severe beating in the nation's newsstands and living rooms. Jurors were made to look like uneducated bumpkins, and Tulians in general like insensitive racists. Asked her opinion of the sting, one woman told a reporter that there was less of a line at the convenience store after the bust, which she appreciated. For its Tulia segment, *20/20* assembled a room full of jurors and questioned them about the verdicts and the long sentences they had handed down. Few of them seemed to have any second thoughts, even when told of Coleman's background.

Just as the media frenzy was hitting its peak, U.S. District Judge Mary Lou Robinson issued her long-delayed ruling in Gary Gardner's lawsuit against Tulia's school drug testing program. Citing the school district's failure to demonstrate the existence of a serious drug problem in Tulia's schools, Robinson ruled that the program was unconstitutional. Gardner had won. The ruling, which prompted another round of stories critical of the drug war in Tulia, felt like salt in a wound to local authorities.

Tulia responded by circling the wagons. The school board voted to appeal Judge Robinson's ruling to the Fifth Circuit Court of Appeals. Supporters of Sheriff Stewart, meanwhile, staged a rally at the Swisher Memorial Building, where an overflow crowd listened to several of the town's most prominent pastors express their confidence in Stewart. One of the most outspoken defenders of the sting was Lana Barnett, the head of the Tulia Chamber of Commerce and Tulia's chief promoter. The avalanche of negative publicity was Barnett's worst nightmare. She took every new round of articles or TV news stories personally. Out-of-state reporters inevitably remarked on the number of churches in Tulia (more than 20), as though that reflected poorly on the town in some way. Many of the stories commented on how down-and-out Tulia was, how the roads into town were lined with closed businesses and rusting junk. She responded with a Clean Up Tulia campaign, urging businesses and homeowners to pay a bit more attention to how the town appeared to outsiders. (Later she commissioned a new bumper sticker: "Hallelujah, I'm from Tulia.")

As for the bust itself, Barnett, like most of her fellow Tulians, had no doubts about the defendants' guilt. "We know these people; we grew up with them. And we know what they sell," she said angrily. She had no patience for their claims of unfair trials. If anything, Barnett felt the system was stacked in the defendants' favor. She resented her tax dollars being spent on providing attorneys for indigent defendants, for example. "If you can't afford insurance, then you don't go to the doctor," she pointed out. "If you can't afford to hire a lawyer, then you go without," she said.

Barnett held to a particularly fundamentalist version of the pioneer ethic, but the basic tenets of the pioneer worldview—that survival is a product of hard work and nobody is entitled to anything beyond the fruits of his or her own labor—were widely held in Swisher County. Equally prevalent was the belief that blacks in Tulia did not adhere to the pioneer ethic, that they were in fact the great counterexample to the ethic: many of them did not work but did not starve, either; they paid no rent yet they had shelter; they seemed to assume that they were entitled to things that other people had to work for, though they did not pay their fair share of taxes.

This helped explain the curious dissonance in the rhetoric of many whites in town, who insisted in one breath that they had been miscast as racists and in the next listed a litany of reasons why the black community was deservedly despised by the good people of Tulia. "They've grown up doing nothing but cheating and stealing and that's all they know," said Delbert Devin, the Democratic Party chair for Swisher County. By way of example, Devin told the story of a hired man who asked for an advance to pay his utility bill and then didn't show up the next morning to work. "[He said,] 'Oh, I'll be there, Mr. Delbert.' Well, I haven't seen him since," Devin recalled bitterly. Devin said he did not know of any instance of a white person cheating a black person in Tulia.

Such blanket statements were common in white Tulia, particularly among those of Devin's generation. Devin, who was in his early eighties when the bust took place, could recall a time when there were no blacks in the county, or at most a handful living and working on white-owned farms out in the sticks. He had been present for the entire history of black and white relations in Tulia, and it was not a racist history, he insisted. "This was one of the only towns where a black person could spend the night in those [segregation era] days," he said, repeating what became something of a mantra after the nation's attention was drawn to Tulia. He recalled going to the Flats with a Methodist church group in the 1960s and delivering presents at Christmas. He remembered the tiny shacks, some with dirt floors. "This town takes care of its own," he said.

Other stories from that era paint a less rosy picture. In the 1950s, one white farmer recalled, Tulia hosted a traveling rodeo that employed a clown known for one particular crowd-pleasing gag. When the show began, barefoot black children would line the fences of the fairgrounds, unable to afford a ticket to get inside. He would pick two of the smallest, cutest kids he could find—"pickaninnies" as they were commonly called—and convince them to climb inside a giant gunny sack, which he then hauled out to the center of the arena. In his other hand he carried a shotgun. "What are you up to now?" the rodeo announcer would ask over the public address. "I'm huntin' coons!" the clown would yell, at which point he would drop the sack and fire a deafening blast from the shotgun into the air. The kids would run as fast as they could for the fence, to the laughter of the crowd.

Over the years Tulia was no better or worse on issues of race than the average panhandle town. The Swisher County Museum does not record when the original black neighborhood, located just outside Tulia's northern boundary, was erected, but most agree that the first few shacks were built sometime in the 1930s. (*Swisher County History*, for its part, devotes exactly three paragraphs to the history of blacks in Tulia.) Tulia sided with the conservatives on the big civil rights issues of the 1950s and 1960s. In 1956, the statewide primary ballot asked Democrats to take a position on several hot-button issues of the times, including "specific legislation exempting any child from compulsory attendance at integrated schools attended by white persons and negroes"; "specific legislation perfecting state laws against intermarriage between white persons and negroes"; and "for use of interposition to halt illegal federal encroachment." (Interposition, which referred to the ostensibly sovereign right of a state to reject unconstitutional federal mandates, was a buzzword of segregationists.) Tulia's voters approved all three propositions overwhelmingly. Later, in 1962, county Democrats soundly rejected a ballot proposal to abolish the poll tax, a notorious method of keeping black voters away from the polls.

Yet Tulia's school system was integrated in the 1950s without incident. White Tulians were fond of pointing out that Tulia's first black high school graduate, Billy Wayne Dick, was named Mr. Tulia High in his senior year. Dick, who was persuaded to write a supportive letter in defense of the town in the *Tulia Herald* after the story broke nationally, was a celebrated local football hero. "Ask him if he rode on the same bus to the games," was Thelma Johnson's rejoinder to Dick's letter to the editor, in which he fondly recalled his days at Tulia High. Long consigned to eating in the kitchen and entering Tulia's cafés through the back door, blacks eventually became a common sight in dining rooms in the years following the Civil Rights Act of 1964. But it took a few years. In an often retold story of the era, Joe Moore and a friend tested the act out shortly after its passage by taking a seat in one of Tulia's most popular cafés. "I'm sorry, we don't serve niggers here," the waitress told the two men. "That's all right," Moore's friend replied. "We don't eat 'em neither."

As Terry McEachern was fond of pointing out, Tulia was not Los Angeles, with its openly racial politics and history of violent racial unrest. Nor did Tulia have the legacy of slavery that continued to hang over similar towns in east Texas, where some African American families still lived in shacks of the kind once found in the Flats, and where a person could still find out, if he really wanted to know, which black families in town had once belonged to which white families. Because of its small size, Tulia was in some ways a model of integration. Everybody used the same schools, parks, and stores, and anybody could, in theory at least, live anywhere in town they chose. Yet race was a central organizing principle of life in Tulia, and you didn't have to scratch deeper than the surface of almost any topic of conversation to get to the racial issue underneath. The subject of taxation, one of the most popular topics of conversation in rural Texas, is a good example. Swisher County is one of the few in Texas to levy what is known as a personal property tax—essentially a special tax on automobiles. The measure was intended to make up for the devastating loss of county and city revenue from foreclosed farms and bankrupt businesses, and from tax exemptions on cattle passed at the state level. It was sold to Swisher County farmers, privately at least, as a means of forcing poor, non–property owning blacks and Hispanics to pay their share of the county's bills.

Talk about the government tended to come around to the preferential treatment of minorities. A commonly held belief is that Swisher County is known as an easy place to get welfare, which tends to attract poor minorities to Tulia. Like much of the panhandle, it was becoming increasingly Hispanic by the late 1990s. In fact, while the county does have an admirable network of church and United Way–affiliated charities, food stamps and welfare checks are doled out by a state agency in Texas, and the amounts are uniformly low from county to county. In the past, when welfare was handled chiefly at the county level, Swisher County, like most rural counties, had a well-earned reputation for stinginess. Even when tax revenues were high and the county was relatively fat, caring for the poor was considered a low priority for county officials and left largely to church-sponsored charities.

In the 1960s, one farmer recalled, the solution to the problem of poverty in the county was often a simple one. The farmer once fired a black farmhand who had been stealing from him. The man immediately left town, leaving behind a wife and several children in a trailer on the farmer's land. It seemed the family would become wards of the county. Instead the county judge offered a typical panhandle solution, which the farmer gratefully accepted: a county truck loaded up the woman and her kids and drove them, along with all of their possessions, to the New Mexico border. On the black side of town, the complaint was frequently reversed: that their kids were not getting the benefits of government grants and scholarships that white kids enjoyed.

The total tax dollars invested in poverty programs in Swisher County, controversial though it may be, is dwarfed by the subsidies the county receives through the various federal farm programs. In 1999, farm subsidies totaled $28.7 million for Swisher County. Much of that money subsidized cotton and wheat grown for the export market, where U.S. farmers would otherwise be unable to compete with low-cost operations in Latin America and Asia. The farms that keep the county alive would likely be gone in a generation if the government checks ever stopped arriving, which means that almost everybody in Swisher County, regardless of race, relies on a handout of some kind, either directly or indirectly. Most American taxpayers are unaware of the extent of such programs; if they were, it would be a hard pill to swallow. Indeed, critics of farm programs have observed that in some counties (including many in the panhandle) the government could simply buy out most of the farms in the county—land, buildings, and equipment—for roughly what it will spend on subsidies over a ten- to fifteen-year period.

Conversations about sports in Tulia often meant talking about race as well. The existence of a largely black team, the Lobos, in the city league had for years meant that softball was more than just a game in Tulia. Ricky White, now in his fifties, was still coaching and playing for the Lobos, though his old friend and fellow cofounder of the team, Fred Brookins Sr., stopped participating long ago. In recent years, Freddie Brookins Jr., Jason Williams, James Barrow, and White's own sons Creamy and Donnie had been some of the team's best players. The bust had left White barely able to field a team.

The subject of the Lobos still generated excitement in Tulia, but the significance of the team depended on whom you asked. For Fred Sr., the Lobos were an effort to get some troubled kids turned around before they wound up in prison. He still spoke with pride about several Lobos who went on to junior college or college while he was coaching the team. For Ricky White, it was about respect, and that meant winning. An all-black team was a rarity when the Lobos were founded, and the team began to earn a reputation as they played in tournaments around the area. They were not always welcome. "In Nazareth, their left fielder was like 'nigger, this' and 'nigger, that,'" White recalled. "[A Lobos player] went to climb the fence and fight, but I said, 'No, beat 'em with the bat,'" he said. And they did. "They didn't feel like they should be losing to us, but they did. We dropped a bomb on them."

In the mid-1980s, when the Lobos started winning regularly, the black community turned out in large numbers to watch them play. The games took place at Tulia's lone softball field in a large park on the southern edge of town. The park lay in a shallow valley between Tulia's black neighborhood to the north and a subdivision of mostly white-owned brick homes built in the 1960s on a gentle rise—sometimes referred to as Snob Hill—that overlooked the park from the south. The black spectators naturally began to sit on the third base side, which they reached first in their walk down the hill, and the whites sat on the first base side. Like everything else that mattered in Tulia, softball had become a racial contest.

The best team in Tulia for years had been sponsored by R&R Spraying, a local crop-dusting company. The team boasted many coaches and staff members from the high school, as well as some of the best former players from the school's baseball program. The team was almost exclusively white. As the Lobos became better and better, each game against R&R became charged with symbolism. Consciously or not, Tulians seemed to read all kinds of meaning into the contests. At the broadest level, the games were a referendum on whether blacks could ever match up with white Tulia. If R&R won, it meant that the coaches had been right about the kids they ran out of their programs. Or it meant that the sheriff was a fair man; that the boys he targeted as troublemakers over the years really were no good. If the Lobos won, it proved the sheriff and coaches wrong. To some it meant that the high school teams would have been better off with black coaches, who had been few and far between over the years.

Softball games, normally sparsely attended, became major events in Tulia. "Every time we played R&R it seemed like stores and banks and everything would close and everybody was there," said Fred Brookins's oldest son, Kent, who played on the team as a teenager. "Anybody can tell you, when the Lobos and R&R played, there was no seats, no parking spots, the bleachers were full, people were standing around the fences and stuff watching the game."

In the late 1980s, the Lobos faced R&R in the qualifying round of a national tournament. The winner would go on to El Paso to compete against teams from across the country in a sort of world series of amateur softball. In one of the most celebrated events in the history of black Tulia, the Lobos won that game. Afterward, the R&R coach approached Ricky White about the tournament. He knew most of the Lobos players couldn't afford the 400-mile trip to El Paso, and he offered to make White a deal: let R&R go to the national tournament in their place, and his team would pay for the Lobos to attend another tournament in Houston or Dallas. "We don't need your money," White told him. The Lobos scraped together the money, went to El Paso, and beat some of the best teams in the country, finishing fifteenth overall out of over 150 teams.

In recent years, White had moved back to the Flats, where he lived with his girlfriend, Michelle Williams, and her children in a trailer home. He had laid out the rough outlines of a softball diamond in an open field where the shacks of the Flats once stood. It was not an ideal location to play ball. The ground was an uneven patchwork of weeds and hard-packed dirt. In a previous life a portion of the infield had been Earlie Smith's junkyard, and while most of the big trash had been hauled away, little bits of rusted metal and rotting two-by-fours worked their way up through the dirt in places. Jackson Chapel stood in not very deep center field, and a copse of mostly dead mesquite trees posed a thorny obstacle in left. Fifty feet behind homeplate sat White's own trailer, alongside a ramshackle set of plywood and chicken wire pens that housed the greyhounds White bred.

Since the bust, the diamond had seen little use. On any given night, White had a half dozen neighborhood kids over at his trailer, though his girlfriend Michelle—who pled to a two-year sentence in the sting—wasn't around to cook for them as she usually did, and his heart wasn't really in teaching softball as it used to be. Increasingly, he preferred spending his evenings alone in the fields behind his house, hunting jackrabbits with his dogs. "He arrested my whole team, man," White said of Sheriff Stewart. "It was just a group of kids havin' a good time," he said. "They couldn't handle that, I guess."

Despite its small size, the black community in Tulia has long been considered a problem for law enforcement. The Tulia police did not regularly patrol the Flats for over thirty years, and things could get wild in the neighborhood, until the mid-1970s at least. In the 1950s and 1960s, the biggest cotton gin in the county maintained a migrant labor camp in a long barn in the southwest corner of Tulia. On weekends, field workers would walk down to the Flats looking for some entertainment. If they wanted to drink and gamble, Joe Moore recalled, that was all right, but when it came to romancing the local women, that was another story. "They come out and they leave they women at home. They think they going to come down in Sunset, the Flats down there, and take our women—and that's why all hell breaks loose there," he said. With so little law enforcement presence, the neighborhood had an element of the Old West to it. Many gamblers packed guns, and shootings and stabbings were not unheard of in the cafés. Whoever was considered the unofficial boss of the Flats—Earlie Smith for many years and later Moore himself—was expected to keep people in line. Most of the trouble, at least in Moore's memory, came from unscrupulous out-of-towners. "If they *win* they money, they can leave with they money. But they think they gonna come there and *take* they money, they probably be layin' out dead. 'Cause they would kill you here," he said. "One thing about it, they would kill you."

Stories of violence and debauchery in the Flats percolated out into Tulia at large, where the black neighborhood became synonymous with vice and lawlessness. The stories mean something else altogether in the black community, where they have been told so many times over the years that they have become like fables, history lessons for a generation that lost most of its past when the old neighborhood was demolished. "Bad actors" ended up badly in the old stories. Irresponsible young cops got their guns taken away. People who gave respect got respect in return.

For twenty years, beginning in the early 1950s, official justice in the Flats resided in one figure, Swisher County sheriff Darrell Smith. A kind of paternalism permeated law enforcement in the Flats during Smith's reign. In retrospect at least, it seemed more or less benevolent to many of the older generation of blacks in Tulia. If Smith ran somebody in for fighting, or worse, the matter could often be resolved the next morning with a visit to the jail from the perpetrator's employer. The farmers and ranchers of Swisher County didn't elect the sheriff to lock up their hired hands with crops in the field and precious hours—and dollars—slipping away. Trials in which both the perpetrator and the victim were local blacks or Latinos were generally considered a waste of time and resources.

By and large, Smith was content as long as the cafés respected the hours he set for them, which meant lights out and everybody off the street at midnight. Around 11:30 the foreman at the labor camp came down to round his men up, if the locals hadn't run them out of the

Flats already. The gambling went on all night, often with a blanket pinned over the window to hide the light. The gamblers paid a kid to keep an eye out for Smith's cruiser. "We knew we had to be out of sight, the windows closed," Moore said, "because Darrell Smith would get out of his car and walk and if he see a light in there he gonna kick the door down." Anyone caught out after midnight could be fined $7.50 for vagrancy, a considerable sum in the 1950s, when rents in the Flats ran $5 per week.

The crimes that Smith did investigate had an almost nostalgic, Andy Griffith quality to them. One night in 1972, after a long session of gambling and drinking in the Flats, Earlie Smith Jr. and two of his young friends hit upon an idea for making some extra cash. They took a trailer out to a local hog farmer's pens, loaded it full of hogs, and set out for a neighboring town first thing in the morning to sell them. It's not clear from Sheriff Smith's carefully typed police report how he knew who the perpetrators were, but one clue may have been the stop the young men made to have a new tire put on the trailer, a service for which they paid one live hog. In any case, when they got back to town, the sheriff was waiting for them. The men still had $1336 of the $1426 they made off the hogs. Smith had the money in the farmer's hands and a signed confession twenty-four hours after the hogs went missing.

Things weren't like that anymore. The Flats were essentially gone and everybody lived together now, for better or worse. Surveying the lot where Funz-a-Poppin' once stood, empty now except for a concrete slab, Mattie White remembered something the old black minister Henry Jackson used to preach when she was a young woman. "He said all of this—the cafés, everything—would be gone one day," she said. "And now we've seen it." The ironic thing, Mattie said, was that it wasn't until all that sinfulness and lawlessness was gone that the authorities in Tulia started to take an interest in the doings of the black community. "This new generation didn't have nothing on us," she laughed.

Over the past generation, law enforcement had become a constant presence in the lives of most black families. Even before the Coleman sting, so many young black men had been sent to prison—for longer and longer sentences—that the demographic makeup of the south side of town changed. Thelma Johnson wondered who her teenage granddaughter Sheena was going to marry when she got old enough. "There just aren't that many black men in Tulia," she said. With the help of Thelma Johnson and Mattie White, Alan Bean drew up a list of every young black man who had passed through Tulia High in the past fifteen years. Of the seventy names on the list, only twelve were still walking the streets in Tulia. Twenty-seven of them were incarcerated (fifteen from the Coleman sting), one had died of AIDS, one had been killed in a shooting, and the rest had moved away. After the bust, one of Ricky White's young grandsons, Laramie Kelly, stayed for a short while at Alan and Nancy Bean's house. His mother, Denise Kelly, pleaded to a short prison sentence in the sting. His father, Ricky White Jr., had been in prison for most of his son's life. Laramie, who was about to enter junior high, was a handsome, quiet boy, loved by his teachers. The coaches already had their eye on him for football. He reminded a lot of people of his uncle Creamy as a child. Putting him to bed every night, it was hard for Alan and Nancy not to imagine what might be in store for him in a few years. "They're getting his cell ready for him," Alan said.

It wasn't hard to find people on either side of town who preferred things the way they used to be, when the Flats were still standing. Many in the black community saw the sting as part of a reaction against racial mixing in Tulia. "The young white kids are so intrigued by the slang, the talk, the way of life, how them young black kids walk the street all the time," Billy Wafer said. Racial boundaries seemed much more fluid among the younger generation in Tulia. "That's what they're so fearful of, the influence on their kids, and that's the reason things are happening the way they are now," Wafer said. He noted that all four of the whites caught in the sting ran with the black crowd. The sentiment in the black community was that Cash Love in particular, a young white man who spent most of his life in the company of blacks and had a child with a black woman (Mattie White's daughter Kizzie), was singled out to send a message about his lifestyle choice. "When we saw Cash, we didn't see white. We saw black," Billy Wafer explained. "They don't want 'em crossing over."

Interracial sex, marriage, and child rearing were hot-button issues in Tulia. Many of the black defendants dated white women, and some had biracial children. "Creamy, he pretty much just did whatever he wanted," Gary Gardner said. "They ought to have put that boy in a calf cradle and castrated him." Gardner's solution may have been tongue-in-cheek, but the sentiment underlying it was not. Most white Tulians had no qualms about expressing their opposition to interracial dating, which was virtually unheard of in Tulia twenty years ago.

"Runnin' around getting white girls pregnant? In the middle of the Bible Belt, we don't cater to that," Donnie Childers said. A talkative, friendly man in his late thirties, Childers worked at the Tulia Trading Post. "I believe we're equal as far as we work together, but I don't believe in the interbreedin'. If God had wanted us to intermingle, he'd have made us all the same color, and that's the way I preach to my kids," Childers said. Mixed-race childbirth was no good for anybody involved, least of all the child, he said. Childers echoed a widely held sentiment in Tulia—that when it came to race, a person had to be one thing or another, or risk being nothing at all. "Those kids are gonna be lost when they grow up. They won't fit in with the whites, or the blacks either. They'll just be there. And I hate to see it because it sure ain't their fault," he said.

The controversy over interracial dating was stoked by several widely talked about incidents in recent years. In the fall of 1994, Ricky White Jr. and Kareem White were arrested after a woman read an entry in her daughter's diary in which the girl described having sex with the two young men. Although the sex was consensual, the girl, who was white, was under eighteen. Her mother went to the police, and both brothers were charged with statutory rape. Kareem, who was just seventeen, beat the charge when his court-appointed attorney, Paul Holloway, showed that he was less than three years older than the girl at the time of the incident. His older brother Ricky, who was on parole for a drug charge, was not so lucky. Facing an imminent parole revocation, he saw little point in fighting the rape charge and pled to ten years in the pen.

If the case of the unlocked diary was bizarre, stranger still was the prosecution of Thelma Johnson's son David in the summer of 1998. David Johnson, then thirty-six, was arrested for the murder of Anthony Culifer, the infant son of his former girlfriend, Rhonda Fore. Anthony had been dead nine years when the police arrested Johnson. At the time of the infant's death, the medical examiner ruled that he had died of pneumonia. Four years later, in 1993, Johnson and Fore, who is white, had a falling out. That's when Fore went to the police, claiming that she had a dream about Anthony that prompted her to remember the actual circumstances of her baby's death: Johnson had smothered him. Fore claimed to have witnessed the act, though she could not explain why she had not come forward sooner. The police believed Fore's unlikely story, but a grand jury declined to indict Johnson, seemingly ending the investigation.

Not long after, however, Dr. Ralph Erdmann, the medical examiner for much of the panhandle, was forced to resign after he was accused of faking an autopsy. The scandal prompted the reexamination of a number of deaths in which Erdmann was the examining doctor, including the case of Anthony Culifer. A Texas Ranger named Dewayne Williams reopened the case. Williams found a pathologist in Lubbock willing to testify that photos taken by Erdmann of the corpse showed what could have been signs of trauma. Johnson was rearrested and held on $500,000 bail. With Terry McEachern's cooperation, Williams had Anthony's body exhumed. There wasn't much to look at after nine years, but the state pressed forward with the case anyway. The prosecution was aided by the eyewitness testimony of Fore's daughter, who claimed she was present when Johnson killed her baby brother and testified against Johnson at trial. She was less than an ideal witness, however—at the time of the alleged incident she was just two years old.

Rhonda Fore's testimony on the stand was far from compelling. She wavered over whether she actually witnessed the crime and gave conflicting testimony about her baby's health at the time of his death. In fact, the baby's health was poor. Medical records showed that Anthony visited the doctor seven times from December 1988 to March 1989, suffering from fevers, coughs, difficulty breathing, and vomiting. On March 13, one week before his death, Anthony was placed on a ten-day course of antibiotics.

One thing the jury never got to hear was the transcript of a conversation between Johnson and Fore, secretly recorded by Ranger Williams, in which Johnson steadfastly protested his innocence. "We already know they're deciding one way or the other to convict you or me of it," Johnson told Fore, "and the main reason I think it's me is because I'm a black man."

As a potential witness in her son's trial, Thelma Johnson was required to wait outside the courtroom for much of the proceedings. As he left the courtroom one afternoon, Ralph Erdmann, the former medical examiner, paused beside her and whispered, "You had better get some legal help, because they're railroading your son in there." Thelma knew Erdmann was right, but there wasn't much she could do about it. In the end, despite the problems with the state's case, the jury convicted Johnson of manslaughter and gave him the maximum sentence of ten years.

About six months after David Johnson was arrested, Jamie Moore, the seventeen-year-old grandnephew of Joe Moore, was arrested for the rape of a white teenager. Moore, a high school dropout who had been in trouble with the law before, insisted the sex was consensual, and prosecutors originally indicted him for statutory rape. (The girl was not 18.) Under pressure from the girl's parents, however, McEachern reindicted Moore for forcible rape shortly before trial. Tellingly, the trial turned less on the facts of the alleged crime than it did on the question of whether or not the girl "ran with blacks" prior to the incident. The defense produced several witnesses who testified that the girl had previously spent time with Moore and his friends, an assertion that she consistently denied, even to the point of undermining the credibility of her own account of the night of the crime. She claimed that Moore had come to her house uninvited at 1:30 in the morning and asked her for a ride home, which she for some reason agreed to provide, even though the two were not acquainted. It strained credulity, but it seemed more important to convince the jury (and perhaps her own parents) that she did not associate with the wrong crowd, even at the risk of losing the case. In the end it didn't matter. Moore was convicted and sentenced to seventy-five years.

Incidents like these even overshadowed seemingly innocent cases of young love between teenagers of different races, which were becoming increasingly common at the high school. "They lost control of their daughters, is what happened," Fred Brookins Sr. said. The trials of Ricky Jr. and Creamy, David Johnson, and Jamie Moore became referendums on the morality of interracial sex (a perspective that Terry McEachern did little to discourage) and forced parents to take a stand on a taboo that seemed in danger of slipping away in Tulia. Interracial relationships threatened a long-standing tradition, the same tradition Alan Bean and Gary Gardner broke by speaking out against the bust: you looked out for the interests of your own race first. Your card, to use a metaphor common in the black community, was either white or black—there was no in between.

One Tulian who remained conspicuously unafraid to straddle the fence was Ike Malone. After the story of the sting broke nationally, Malone, a black man in his early fifties, gave a number of on-camera and print media interviews in which he defended local law enforcement and Sheriff Stewart in particular. Malone, who had been divorced for many years, was an assistant manager at a farm supply store called Big N. Standing about six feet tall, he had a thin, wiry frame, a bulbous, slightly upturned nose, and big round eyes that gave his face an elfin appearance. At one time he had been good friends with both Fred Brookins Sr. and Ricky White, even playing catcher for the Lobos, but he had fallen out with both of them over the years. Now, as a result of his vocal support of law enforcement in the wake of the drug bust, Malone was on the outs with the majority of the black community, though most were not surprised at his behavior. "Ike Malone lost his black card years ago," Thelma Johnson said. "He ain't never gonna get a white card neither, but don't try to tell him that."

Malone believed that of all the cases Coleman made, only one had been fabricated, and that was Joe Moore's. Even Malone, as judgmental as they come, had respect for Moore. "Now when it came to the sentencing phase, in hindsight, we might agree they gave them too many years," he said. "I was not in the jury room. Those people have to sleep at night, and right now I'm glad I was not in there."

The problem in Tulia was not with the white people, according to Malone; it was with the black people. "Right now I could call the mayor of Tulia, the county commissioners, the judge, anyone, and say I need some help," Malone said, and he would get it. He had little that was good to say about the sting defendants and their families, however. "There's no cohesiveness in the black community now," he said. "Back in '75, you could tell the good people from the bad. The workin' people from those who would never work. Now women are havin' extra babies to add $75 to their check because they're too damn lazy to get up and get a job," he said. "What you hear in Tulia is gonna be half true because the people in the affected families are mostly lying and they're embarrassed to admit what damn near every-one knows."

More than anything, Malone seemed to resent being portrayed as part of a community that was powerless and victimized. "I had just got my Hennessey in a bar in the Salt Lake City airport, and this guy starts tellin' me how bad Tulia is," he said. Even the airport shoeshine boy was taking pity on him, Malone said with an exasperated sigh. He let them all know he didn't need their sympathy. "Want to see what I got on?" Malone told the shoeshine boy, drawing his attention to the silk tie he was wearing at the time. "Want to put a price on it?"

Malone prided himself on his knowledge of city politics and eco-nomic trends, knowledge gleaned through his friendships with Tulia's most important people. Malone had no patience for the cries of racism in Tulia. "I meet no strangers. The difference between a stranger and an acquaintance is a conversation. That's how it goes here. And I'm sorry if it doesn't sell magazines," he said. "But if we as a species don't start livin' together we can hang it up."

If Malone's efforts in defense of the establishment were appreci-ated at the courthouse, where he stood in the white community at large was difficult to discern. As Thelma Johnson observed, if a white card could turn black almost overnight, exchanging a black card for a white card was a much more difficult task. Malone's name came up one afternoon at the Tack Shed, one of the county's private drinking clubs, in a wide-ranging discussion of the bust and its aftermath. Joe Borchardt, whose family once owned Big N, the store where Ike now proudly served as an assistant manager, said he knew Ike but didn't recall that he ever worked there in the old days. "We didn't hire none of them druggies," he said.

CHAPTER ELEVEN

The Jump Out Boys

THE SHABBINESS and hypocrisy of the Texas drug war made good copy for national reporters who came to Tulia, but most of them could have found similar stories closer to home. In New Jersey, for example, a former task force narc was convicted in 2000 of running a brothel while on duty; he later also pleaded guilty to selling protection to drug dealers. In the summer of 2001, the FBI began investigating a narc accused of stealing funds from a Tucson, Arizona, drug task force; he and his wife were eventually indicted for embezzling $615,000 over a four-year period. In 2003, thirty convictions were overturned in rural central Missouri after a task force narc was indicted for perjury. Also in 2003, authorities discovered that a man convicted of selling cocaine to an undercover officer and sentenced to five years in prison was allowed to go free after he agreed to make a $200,000 payment to the suburban Atlanta drug task force that set him up. Each of the narcs in this sampling of recent drug war scandals was employed through the same U.S. Department of Justice program as Tom Coleman, the Edward Byrne Memorial State and Local Law Enforcement Assistance Grant, which funds drug task forces in mostly rural and suburban areas across the country. Launched in 1988, the little-known program has quietly become the lifeblood of a troubling new model of drug enforcement, one that has operated largely outside the attention of Congress or the national media.

The program was named in memory of Edward Byrne, a New York City police officer shot dead by drug dealers in 1988, at the height of the national crack epidemic. Byrne, a rookie officer, had been assigned to guard a house in South Jamaica, a part of Queens known for its talented rap stars and violent street gangs. The home belonged to a witness in an ongoing narcotics investigation of Howard "Pappy" Mason, one of the most infamous crack kingpins in New York City. As Byrne sat outside the house in his patrol car early one morning, a gunman walked out of the darkness and shot him three times in the head. Seven months later, George H. W. Bush, nearing the end of a bitterly fought presidential race against Massachusetts Governor Michael Dukakis, visited New York City, where he had arranged to receive the endorsement of a major police union. For months, Bush had been hammering away at Dukakis for being soft on crime. His notorious Willie Horton ad, which criticized Massachusetts's prison furlough program, was devastatingly effective. In a moving ceremony in New York, Edward Byrne's father presented the candidate with his dead son's badge. Bush first declared that he could not in good conscience engage in politicking on such a solemn occasion, but then he apparently thought better of it. Holding Edward Byrne's badge in his hand, he challenged Dukakis to come out in support of a bill before Congress that would, among other things, allow the death penalty for high-volume drug dealers.

The gauntlet had been thrown down, and the Democrats, who then controlled both branches of Congress, did not blanch. The result was a piece of hastily conceived legislation passed with shamefully little debate on the eve of an election. The Anti-Drug Abuse Act of 1988 is a document of its time, filled with the Manichean rhetoric of a moral war: "For the future of our country and the lives of our children, there can be no substitute for total victory," the authors announced in one section. The act created a cabinet-level department in the White House, the Office of National Drug Control Policy, to be overseen by a new national drug czar who would coordinate the burgeoning federal drug war budget. (William Bennett became the first to wear the title.) "It is the declared policy of the United States to create a drug-free America by 1995," the act read. As preposterous as that language sounds in retrospect, by creating the Byrne grant the bill had a drastic impact on the lives of hundreds of thousands of Americans, though not in the way most members of Congress envisioned.

The federal government could not put a narc in every town in America, the thinking went, but it could try to convince every local sheriff and police department of the need to hire one of their own. As usual, this was done with the promise of money. The Byrne grant, as it came to be known, offered states funding for several categories of crime-related programs, among them "multi-jurisdictional task force programs." The idea of teaming federal and local efforts in street-level drug enforcement had its genesis in the Nixon-era Office of Drug Abuse Law Enforcement, one of the precursor agencies of the Drug Enforcement Agency. Nixon's idea was to get experienced federal agents, who had been limited mainly to drug interdiction at the nation's borders, out into the heartland to train local sheriff's deputies and police officers, most of whom had little or no experience with the rapidly growing underground drug trade. The task force model envisioned by the Byrne grant program was different. This time the federal government provided only the money; the manpower would come from local police forces, county sheriffs, and district attorney's offices, which would band together with forces in neighboring counties to form new outfits solely dedicated to drug enforcement. The money was distributed to the states by the Department of Justice's main grant-making arm, the Bureau of Justice Assistance, which offered few guidelines for the program. The states in turn set up their own policies and procedures for the new task forces.

Nearing the end of its second decade, the Byrne task force program has long since been eclipsed by better-funded and more publicized endeavors, such as crop eradication in Colombia and Afghanistan and interdiction along the nation's borders. Yet the Byrne money has not stopped flowing, and back in rural America, out of the limelight, the task forces have quietly flourished. Nationwide, there are now over 750 Byrne task forces, employing somewhere in the neighborhood of 5,000 to 7,000 narcs. (The Justice Department does not know the exact number.) For comparison, the U.S. Drug Enforcement Agency, the nation's premier antidrug bureaucracy, has about 5,300 agents. In a relatively short span of time, the Byrne grant, an ambitious experiment conceived in the heat of a political campaign, created an entirely new tier of law enforcement nationwide.

In Texas, drug enforcement outside of the major cities was traditionally handled by the state police force, known as the Department of Public Safety (DPS), which has maintained a narcotics unit since the early 1970s. Despite its historic role, DPS Narcotics was bypassed entirely when Texas created its first Byrne grant task forces, which were administered by the Texas Narcotics Control Program (TNCP), a new entity created inside the governor's office. This was no accident: Byrne money was seen from the beginning as a form of pork, a valuable way for the governor to seek favor with rural and suburban communities. By the standards of the federal government, the amount of money involved was modest; in the late 1990s, roughly $500 million per year in Byrne money was allocated nationwide, a little less than half of which was spent on drug task forces. (The total federal drug war budget, while difficult to quantify, is roughly $20 billion per year.) But in cash-strapped rural Texas, the Byrne money was a gold mine. It is not uncommon for rural sheriff's deputies and police officers in Texas to earn less than $20,000 per year. Many are forced to moonlight at second jobs, and some even qualify for food stamps. (In Tulia, prior to a pay raise in 2003, a city police officer started out at a base salary of $16,000; with normal expenses and a family of three, new Tulia officers qualified for $200 per month in food stamps.) Inevitably turnover is high. Likewise, many rural district attorney's offices have trouble keeping their offices staffed with prosecutors and investigators, who can earn up to twice as much by moving to the nearest medium-size city.

The governor's office was flooded with applications for the new source of funds. Ambitious sheriffs and district attorneys vied with one another to recruit neighboring counties into their new outfits. The program required the task forces to come up with matching funds equal to one-quarter of the total budget; the federal grant money covered the remaining three-quarters. The more counties a task force project director could sign up, the more sources of matching funds he had access to, and the bigger the potential grant from Washington. In west Texas, the new task forces tended to be huge, encompassing as many as two dozen sparsely populated counties. All that was required, however, was an agreement between two neighboring counties, and a new task force was open for business. By the late 1990s, there were four dozen outfits employing over 700 officers. The narcotics division of the state police, with fewer than half that many officers, had gradually become a stepchild in the Texas drug war.

It soon became clear that the jump out boys, as they came to be called, were not like state police narcs. The Texas Department of Public Safety has always prided itself on its professionalism. Applicants must pass written, physical, and psychological tests, and the officers are relatively well compensated, by Texas standards. Within the department, as in most state police forces and urban police departments, an assignment to the narcotics division is a highly sought after promotion and carries a certain amount of prestige. For task force agents, by contrast, the trip from patrol deputy in a one-stoplight town to undercover narc might involve a single two-week training course.

As a result, the standards of narcotics enforcement across the state have gradually eroded. "These narcotics task forces are the antithesis of every good law enforcement management technique," said Texas State Representative Terry Keel, a Republican from the Austin suburbs. "Anyone in police management will tell you that narcotics interdiction is where you must have your tightest operation. You have to have close supervision of your people," he said. "The officers in the narcotics task forces do not have a chain of command that watches them carefully. Typically the chain of command that hires and fires them is not even nearby. They may not see them for months. They are left undercover and loosely supervised in some cases. They have unbridled discretion often on their interdiction decisions, and they deal with large amounts of cash," he said. "Now all of that is a formula for disaster."

Because they often operate in rural areas, far from major media markets, stories of task force malfeasance tend to stay beneath the radar. Read enough clips from small town papers, however, and a pattern of corruption begins to emerge. Rogue officers, missing drugs, stolen cash, fabricated cases, failed drug tests: every small town in Texas seems to have a story of corruption involving the jump out boys. "People don't understand," a former task force narc-turned-whistleblower named Barbara Markham said in the wake of the Tulia scandal. "Everybody's talking about Tom Coleman—well, there are whole task forces of Tom Colemans out there."

Prior to Tulia, the state's most infamous task force scandal involved the Permian Basin Drug Task Force and its flamboyant director, Midland County sheriff Gary Painter. Located about 120 miles south of Lubbock, Midland, hometown of George W. Bush, is the oil and gas capital of Texas. (Its sister city, Odessa, was the setting for *Friday Night Lights*, the classic account of Texas high school football.) From the day he was elected in 1986, Painter displayed a knack for getting face time in his local media market, where his big white cowboy hat, thick glasses, and vaguely porcine features became a fixture on the evening news. But Painter's outsize ego demanded a bigger stage. In 1987, he somehow convinced a crew from *Nightline* to cover his purported investigation into an international arms dealing scheme involving a Portuguese arms dealer and the country of Iran. Working with two temporarily deputized mercenaries, Painter set up the deal himself, crashing into a Midland warehouse with news cameras rolling just as the dealer was taking possession of his "contraband"—barrels filled with sand, labeled as missile parts. Federal authorities, who considered Painter something of a loose cannon, declined to prosecute. Nor were they impressed by Painter's claim a few years later to have discovered, also with the use of undercover mercenaries, the existence of "terrorist training camps" in northern Mexico. Painter returned disappointed from his meeting with CIA officials in Washington, D.C. "It's just very mind-boggling that this credible information is being ignored," he complained to an Associated Press reporter.

In 1989, following a national trend, the Texas legislature rewrote state asset forfeiture laws to allow a greater percentage of money and assets seized during drug busts to go directly into law enforcement agency budgets, rather than city or county general revenue funds. Painter was one of the first task force directors to understand that the drug war had the potential to become a money-making enterprise, and it turned him from a buffoon into one of the most powerful politicians in his part of Texas. Together with his righthand man, former Texas Ranger Clayton McKinney, Painter grew Midland's task force into one of the biggest in the state, covering a wide swath of west Texas stretching from the Big Bend of the Rio Grande up to the New Mexico border. But it wasn't big enough for Painter, who sent his agents on far-flung investigations across the country. Wherever there was revenue potential, Painter kept a hand in the game, ensuring that when the proceeds from confiscated cash and assets were divided, his task force would get cut in. By 1990, hundreds of thousands of dollars were moving through the task force's forfeiture accounts.

Almost from the beginning, however, allegations of misconduct swirled around the Permian Basin drug task force. Neither Painter nor McKinney was ever charged, but indictments seemed to fall all around them. In 1991, Rick Thompson, the sheriff of Presidio County, a border county that belonged to the task force, was busted for smuggling a horse trailer full of cocaine. Over a ton of cocaine, worth an estimated $20 million, was confiscated, making it the largest drug bust in west Texas history. Painter had served as a deputy under Thompson before moving north to Midland, and the two remained close. (After Thompson got a life sentence, Painter hired Thompson's wife to work for him at the Midland sheriff's office.) A grand jury investigation following Thompson's bust resulted in indictments against Hal Upchurch, a district attorney in Ward County who worked closely with Painter's task force, and Ronald Tucker, one of Painter's many "temporary deputies."

Later that year, the Midland County commissioner's court, led by county judge Charles W. "Bro" Seltzer, moved to rein in Painter. Citing fiscal constraints and unacceptable liability risks, the court directed the sheriff to confine his operations to Midland County. Seltzer told the *Texas Observer* in a 1991 interview that the court was also making a statement about the turn law enforcement had taken in west Texas. "Law enforcement is not, never has been, and never should be a for-profit enterprise," he said. Seltzer knew the commissioners were threatening a sacred cow. "There is a whole industry of people out there—professional snitches, informants, and worse—who do nothing but get in good with dopers or anyone else they think they can set up, and then go peddle their deals . . . to the highest-bidding law enforcement agency," Seltzer said. "And frankly, some of these people are downright scary." Seltzer had good reason to be worried.

Painter responded by suing the commissioners for infringing on his constitutional authority. A judge ordered Painter to temporarily limit his out-of-county activities. But the ruling also reasserted Painter's control over forfeiture funds, which allowed his task force a measure of independence from the commissioners' budgetary authority.

When Midland County declined to continue sponsoring his task force, Painter convinced officials in neighboring Ector County to host it. It was later revealed that Painter had apparently greased the rails for the transition by secretly putting one of the Ector County officials on his task force payroll, using forfeiture money to hire the man as an "informant." Finally, in June 1998, after state and federal authorities investigated allegations ranging from evidence tampering and fraudulent reports to bribery and theft, the governor's office cut off funds to the Permian Basin task force. Despite the investigation, a grand jury returned no indictments, and Painter wasted no time getting back in the drug interdiction business. Governor George Bush commissioned a new, DPS-led task force based in Odessa to replace Painter's old outfit. Most of the surrounding sheriff's offices joined, but not Midland County. Instead, Painter mustered a new posse from the remains of his old one, renaming it the Trans-Pecos Drug Task Force. Rather than establish the task force at home in Midland, where his own commissioner's court had turned against him, Painter set it up 100 miles away in Pecos, where chief deputy Clayton McKinney's son served as chief of police. (This was Clayton McKinney Jr., who testified on Tom Coleman's behalf at Kareem White's trial.) Inexplicably, the governor's office signed off on the move, and the Byrne Grant check was in the mail.

Painter did not make most of his money through undercover work, but by stopping and searching couriers on the highway, where countless trunk loads of drug cash were being hauled south every day. By the mid-1990s, when virtually every county in the state had joined a task force, such roadside searches became a familiar sight across

Texas. Priorities quickly became skewed, recalled Frank Brown, who for eight years served as the main prosecuting attorney for cases made by the Rio Concho drug task force, based in San Angelo. "I'm proud to say we were the only task force in the state that didn't have a [drug-sniffing] dog in a car stopping every car on the highway," he said. For years, Brown advised local agents not to make unconstitutional stops, despite the overwhelming incentive to do so, and the increasingly commonplace occurrence of such stops in other parts of west Texas. When the Texas Court of Criminal Appeals ruled in 1995 that drug arrests stemming from traffic stops made without probable cause were not necessarily invalid, Brown decided to get out of the business for good, moving to Alpine to become a defense attorney. The ruling, he believed, gave the jump out boys a license to run amok. "I always thought it would be an interesting experiment to put a black man in a brand-new Corvette with Miami plates, and have him drive from Beaumont to El Paso," Brown said. "It'd take him six months."

The money doesn't come only from highways. A former prosecutor affiliated with the North Central Texas narcotics task force, near Dallas, freely admitted that he offered lighter sentences to suspects who agreed not to fight forfeiture of cars, cash, and other items of value confiscated during drug investigations. "If we don't have enough money by the end of the grant year, we're all out of a job," he told the *Dallas Morning News*.

Gary Painter's flameout and resurrection, spectacular as it was, did not cause state officials to reevaluate the task force program. Apart from the crisis in Midland, which forced Governor Bush to act, the TNCP essentially ran on autopilot. The only real authority the governor's office exercised was through the grant application process, which task force directors had to navigate each year to renew funding for their projects. In Texas, as in many states with task force pro-

grams, the scramble for Byrne money is a zero-sum game: one task
force's funding increase is another's loss. The TNCP developed a
complex system of rating the relative success of the various outfits,
weighing such indicators as number of cases opened, buys made, suspects arrested, drugs confiscated, and assets forfeited. In 1999, for
example, thanks in large measure to Coleman's bust, the Panhandle
Regional Narcotics Trafficking Task Force was the top-ranked task
force in the state.

Under this model, statistics translate directly into money. More
arrests, the logic holds, proves a need for more money to hire more
agents, which, if granted, means still more arrests in the following
quarter, and the cycle gains momentum. The spread of this statistics-
driven model of law enforcement has meant a dramatic increase in the
number of drug arrests in Texas. At any given time, one in three Texas
inmates is doing time for drug-related charges, and chances are good
that the jump out boys—who arrest some 14,000 Texans every year—
put him or her inside. Not surprisingly, the growth of the task force
system coincided with a massive acceleration in prison construction in
the state. In what amounted to the largest public works project in
modern Texas history, the state more than tripled its prison capacity—from 40,000 to 150,000 beds—in just ten years. (Texas now has
more inmates than California, even though Texas has 40 percent
fewer people. Only Louisiana and Mississippi incarcerate a greater
percentage of their populations than Texas.) There were many factors
driving this expansion, including stricter parole guidelines and over-
crowding lawsuits, but the task forces were central by any reckoning.
The same is true across the country, where drug prosecutions, chiefly
for low-level crimes, have pushed the national inmate population over
the unprecedented 2 million mark.

High-profile agencies like the DEA get the headlines and inspire
the gritty Hollywood dramas, but it is the thousands of Byrne
grant-funded narcs in rural and suburban America who do the dirty

work of the day-to-day drug war. The type of operation Tom Coleman was directed to set up in Tulia—"buy busts" from low-level dealers—has long been the bread and butter of Byrne grant task forces because the relative simplicity of the method allows big numbers of arrests to be racked up in a short period of time. A focus on street-level buys more often than not means targeting black suspects, which helps explain a couple of striking statistics in Texas. Blacks account for 12 percent of the state's population but 40 percent of prison inmates. Most of them are young men: on any given day in Texas, roughly 1 in 3 black men between the ages of twenty and twenty-nine are in jail, on probation, or on parole.

"It's just too easy—they never go up the chain," defense attorney Walter Fontenot of Liberty, a small town in east Texas, said of the task forces. "I have never understood the reason for their existence. It just seems to be a governmental bureaucracy that's in existence for appearance only," he said. Fontenot, who is black, said the drug war is caught in a vicious cycle. "If you dig into this stuff, you will find that most people are black, most people are poor, and they just cop out and get probation, and a couple of years later the probation is revoked, because they go back to the same thing because that's all they know," he said.

"It's all about numbers," said Anahuac defense attorney Ed Lieck. "More numbers means more money. I've been doing this for ten years, and law enforcement is about money," he said. "Anybody who tells you different is lying to you." For those who have become addicted to the annual grants, keeping the program alive has become an end in itself, as President Clinton discovered in 1994 when he tried unsuccessfully to convince Congress to scale back the Byrne program. Nearly a decade later, the Heritage Foundation, a conservative Washington think tank, published a critical report on the Byrne grant, in which the authors noted that the program had made no discernible impact on drug crime. Still, the money keeps flowing. "Let me tell you what the political reality is," Texas legislator Terry Keel said. "You've got a whole bunch of these brother-in-law types out there running around with ninja suits and sunglasses, cars and guns and cash. That is a valued law enforcement lifestyle by those persons, and there are lots of them. And they tend to turn up the political heat on their local elected officials, including legislators, who they lead to believe that the sky is gonna fall if their job is eliminated," Keel said.

The problem, according to civil rights advocates like Texas ACLU executive director Will Harrell, is that the emphasis on statistics has overshadowed more pressing questions. "Nobody is looking at quality control. We're simply looking for quantity," he said. "That's what the drug war is about: how many people have you arrested and locked up today? Nobody is concerned with whether or not they got a fair trial. Nobody is concerned with the police methods used to capture somebody and nobody is really concerned with whether the people are innocent or not. That's not a part of the equation when determining which of these agencies are going to get funding."

CHAPTER TWELVE

Sin and Redemption

BY THE SUMMER of 2001, when national media attention tapered off, surprisingly little had changed in Tulia. Lobbied heavily by the Texas ACLU, the Texas legislature had passed a package of so-called Tulia bills meant to prevent a recurrence of the scandal. Jeff Blackburn's civil suit was slowly winding its way through the courts. Yet little notice was taken of the twenty Tulians serving time, most of whom were approaching the end of their second year of incarceration. As Paul Holloway had predicted, their appeals were unsuccessful, and now, nine months after the story broke nationally, virtually none of the defendants had any legal representation at all. Fed up with waiting for someone to step forward, Gary Gardner began writing a writ for Joe Moore on his own. Tulia seemed to be reverting into a small, unremarkable, unknown town on the Texas plains, to the relief of most residents.

Thus, when one of Tulia's biggest secrets came undone that summer, it was the *Amarillo Globe News* that got the scoop. On a cool evening in June, Charles Sturgess, the owner of the Tulia Livestock Auction, went for a drive in his pickup through his ranch property west of town. With him was a strapping young high school boy who had once worked for Sturgess at the auction. The sun had gone down and Sturgess was unwinding. He had the cruise control set at five miles per hour and a bottle of whiskey handy. They were on their way to pick up some baby pheasants Sturgess had promised the young man, but Sturgess had suggested a detour to check on some cattle first, and the young man reluctantly agreed. He was less interested in Sturgess's next suggestion, which came in the form of a reach across the truck's bench seat for the young man's crotch. Sturgess, by this time fairly loaded, took the rejection well. "I must be out of my mind," he said. He drove the boy home.

But the incident was not swept under the rug. The boy, whom Sturgess had propositioned before, told his parents about the incident, and they went to the police. Two nights later, a Texas Ranger named Garth Davis wired the boy up and instructed him to arrange another meeting with Sturgess, who readily accepted. The two went for another nighttime drive through Sturgess's ranch, with Davis listening to every word that was said. When Sturgess made another pass, Davis closed in on the pickup and arrested him.

It was no small thing to accuse Charles Sturgess, a married man and one of the wealthiest and most respected cattlemen in town, of chasing after underage boys. In the culture of the panhandle, homosexuality was the only vice that rivaled illegal drugs in the hierarchy of sins. In many ways, "the homosexual agenda," as evangelicals called the gay rights movement, had become the new communism—a more up-to-date version of an amoral worldview that served as a foil for Christian ethics in sermons and editorials. Much of the antigay legislation that was perennially debated in the state legislature in Austin originated about 100 miles from Tulia in the Pampa offices of state representative Warren Chisum, a diminutive old rancher who made homosexuality his signature issue when he was elected in the late 1980s. The idea that someone as well-respected as Charles Sturgess—whose family was active in the Church of Christ—had been a secret homosexual would be a tough pill to swallow.

But there was more news to come. When Sturgess's truck was searched the next day, officers found—along with porn mags, pills, and marijuana—three and a half ounces of powdered cocaine. In one single bust of a prominent white man—and a completely fortuitous one at that—many times more cocaine had been seized than in any single buy during Coleman's entire eighteen-month undercover operation. Sturgess was charged with possession with intent to distribute, a second-degree felony.

It was an astounding turn of events, and the Amarillo paper covered the bust prominently. The *Tulia Herald* found the bust less newsworthy. There was no front-page story, no comment from Larry Stewart, no photo of Sturgess in cuffs. Not that it mattered. Almost before Sturgess bonded himself out, everybody in town was talking about the bust. In the weeks to come, the rumors were running wild. Homosexuality, drugs, corruption of youth: it was hard for many Tulians to imagine a more despicable scenario. There was a billboard on the edge of town with a picture of a giant fishhook and a message for Tulia's youth: "Porn, Drugs, Sex, Alcohol, Tobacco: Don't Take the Bait." Sturgess, who was an avid smoker, had hit five out of five. How long had it been going on? Tulia never got any answers out of Sturgess. A few months later, while his case was still awaiting trial, he drove his truck out to a piece of deserted ranch property and—as many anticipated he would—shot himself dead.

Sturgess's friends found his homosexuality difficult to fathom. In the weeks following his arrest, Sturgess chalked the incident up to booze and drugs. "He said he was messed up and talked a lot of shit to this kid," said Johnny Nix, a horse trainer and farmer who had known Sturgess for decades. Nix was willing to give him the benefit of the doubt. "I'm not saying he didn't really do those things," he said. "I'm just saying he didn't know what he was doing." The cocaine use, on the other hand, wasn't such a surprise after all. Nix was the owner and operator of the Tack Shed, the popular bar a few miles east of town, and Sturgess would occasionally drop by for a beer. He was often high as a kite when he did. "He used to come in and buy everyone a round, blowin' and goin' like an eight-day clock," Nix remembered. Drugs were not welcome at Nix's place—a sign behind the bar reminded patrons of this—but nobody ever ran Sturgess off. He could be loud and abrasive, and his brand of humor usually involved giving all of the farm and ranch hands present a hard time, one by one, until he had razzed them all. He was worth more than most of the Tack Shed regulars put together, and he wasn't afraid to let everybody know it. But people still liked him.

But that was all before. Nix forgave Sturgess for what he did, but he had no illusions that Tulia ever would. "Nobody ever thought about how many people depended on Charles," Nix said later. He was widely regarded as one of the best auction managers Tulia ever had. Everybody depended on Sturgess to get them the best prices possible for their animals, and he almost always delivered. A horse Nix trained for Sturgess was named a champion by the American Quarter Horse Association not long after Sturgess died. Yet Nix wasn't surprised by Sturgess's decision to kill himself. Even if he had beaten the rap in court, he would have lived out his days ostracized in the town where he grew up. A man like Sturgess had the means to live anywhere he wanted, but Tulia was his home, and things would never be the same again. "He was caught in a trap," was how Gary Gardner put it.

Nix knew firsthand how unforgiving Tulia could be. His decision to open the Tack Shed in 1990 made him an official outsider in town. Tulia's love–hate relationship with vice is as old as the town itself: the town had a bar before the first church was ever built. A man named Briggs Hopson was the county's first bartender. But the church was not far behind, and bartending became an underground profession in Swisher County. Civilization on the High Plains meant Christianity, and Christianity in turn-of-the-century America, more than anything else, meant prohibition. Rallied by one of Tulia's first papers, the anti-whiskey *Tulia News*, edited by a Church of Christ member named Thomas T. Waggoner, Swisher County voted itself dry on December 7, 1901, by a tally of 119 to 28. The only place the referendum was even close was in the tiny hamlet of Love—a community of sixteen registered voters—which split exactly half for and half against. The decision made by Swisher County's founding fathers has stood for over a hundred years, as the nation went from wet to dry to wet again. The last local option vote in the county, taken in 1946, ran more than three to one against.

Powerful as they were in city politics, Tulia's churches could never get a handle on the purveyors of vice out in the country, where cock-fighting, crap games, and other forms of gambling have always been popular ways to pass the time. And wherever there was gambling, there was booze. Nix was simply following in a long line of country bootleggers, though he was enterprising enough to try to make it legal. The Tack Shed, which was housed inside a modest-size barn a few yards from Nix's horse stables, was popular with the rural crowd, though it never made much of a profit. It had a pool table, a jukebox, and a big-screen satellite TV that Nix usually kept tuned to the simulcast from the racetrack in Ruidoso. On one wall was a big Confederate flag.

Nix seemingly opened the bar mostly because he liked having people around to drink beer and play dominoes. He was divorced and lived alone, though he had been dating the same woman for the past twenty years. He had a beer belly and his swollen nose had turned just a bit red from drink. But he was not a drunk. In his mid-fifties, he still farmed several hundred rented acres by himself, with no hired help. He had large, gnarly hands and classic plainsmen eyes—cobalt blue irises with pupils reduced to pinpricks by many thousands of hours aboard a tractor in the bright panhandle sun.

He almost lost his land to unpaid taxes in the 1980s, and the experience left him with a grudge against the county tax assessor and the entire courthouse crowd. He did not back down when the powers that be opposed his bid to open a bar, not even when the Baptists sent a busload of members down to Austin to formally oppose his license application in front of the Texas Alcoholic Beverage Commission. Nix was not particularly religious, and he liked to tell people that he was an ecumenical horse trainer: he had trained race horses owned by ministers of three different faiths. The city fathers had stopped an earlier attempt at opening a private club in the Conestoga Restaurant by putting up a few swing sets on a lot next to the restaurant and calling it a park. How could you have a bar next to a park? For good measure they also passed an ordinance: no drinking clubs inside city limits.

Nix got his license in spite of the local opposition, but the fight was far from over. State police troopers began camping out on the stretch of highway between the Tack Shed and town, pulling over all of Nix's customers and testing them for DWI. Eventually Nix himself was arrested for DWI in the mid-1990s. There was no breathalyzer evidence, just an officer's testimony and a number of empty beer cans collected from Nix's truck. Still, it was not his first offense and he was looking at jail time if convicted. He beat the rap, in no small part because Fred Brookins Sr. was on his jury. A black patron was a rarity at Nix's bar, and Fred Sr. did not really know Nix. ("Colored people have to get drunk first to have the balls to come in here," Nix liked to say, and by that time had likely spent all their money anyway.) But Fred Sr. knew Tulia, and he had suspected all along that Nix was really being prosecuted for owning a bar. In his quiet, thoughtful way, he steered the jury toward a not guilty verdict. Years later, he was still proud of what he had done that day, though he also recalled that Nix shook every juror's hand but his after the verdict was read.

Nix thought the drug sting was a disaster. "There didn't have to be but one innocent person in the whole bunch for it all to be screwed," he said. The cost of the entire operation should be added up and charged to McEachern and Sheriff Stewart, he said. More than anything, Nix opposed the philosophy behind the bust. "A sheriff, he needs to know everybody by their first name," he said. "That ought to be his job: ask him how he's doin' and help him out." Under Sheriff Gayler, deputies had rarely written tickets; they left that to the Tulia police department, Nix said. But Stewart was different.

After driving on the dirt roads that ran between his and his neighbors' farms for forty years, Nix had only recently learned that they had a speed limit, courtesy of one of Stewart's deputies. "They don't have to go out and look for trouble," he said.

As demonized as alcohol was in official Tulia, the use of narcotics, particularly since the late 1980s, occupied a special place in the pantheon of the town's most despised vices. "Drugs have touched everybody in some way somewhere down the line," Tulia police chief Jimmy McCaslin said. "We all know everybody in this town and we all know somebody who's had to deal with it. Maybe they felt like this was a way to put a stop to it," he said of the long sentences that jurors gave to Moore and his fellow defendants. "Maybe they felt we've got to find something that works."

One thing Tulia has not tried is rehab. Despite the county's longtime obsession with sobriety, Tulia has no licensed drug and alcohol rehab facility. In the county annex building is an office for a counselor from the Texas Department of Mental Health and Mental Retardation, but the door is almost always locked. Swisher County authorities referred so few clients for services over the years that the Plainview-based counselors simply stopped coming to town. What Tulia has instead is the Driskill House, a halfway house located on Highway 87 on the north side of town. At first glance the Driskill House looks as dead as every other business along this desolate strip of highway. Set between an empty lot and an old real estate office lately taken over by the Alpha & Omega Assembly of God Church, the one-story building has no signage of any kind. One hot afternoon in July, a couple of trucks and a line of muddy boots outside the entrance were the only indication that the building was inhabited. A young man in a three-quarter sleeve rock band T-shirt and sunglasses and an old cowboy in a gimme cap sat in the shade of a free-standing brick wall that shielded the building's glass entryway from the sun and blowing dust. Two stray dogs, one bleeding from the head, lay nearby in a swarm of flies, contemplating the air-conditioned interior on the other side of the glass.

Driskill House was named after a popular former county judge, Jack Driskill, who helped found the place after being hounded out of office for a DWI conviction in the early 1980s. At one time the state had supported the program, but the facility lost its funding in 1999 because the director was not a licensed therapist. (Virtually all of the publicly funded drug rehab clinics in the panhandle closed or dramatically curtailed services in the 1990s as a result of a drastic reduction in state funding.) The county helped out when it could but did not have a contract with the facility. Now Driskill was limping along with one part-time counselor and one full-time administrator. They took donations from food banks and grocery stores, and pooled the food stamps of residents who were eligible to receive them. Residents worked during the day, mostly as day laborers, to pay for their rooms.

Driskill was run by a cattle buyer from Vigo Park named Greg Culwell. An earnest, handsome man in his mid-forties, Culwell was a recovering alcoholic himself. He led the group of fifteen or so residents in morning meditation and evening counseling sessions, and made sure they didn't stay in bed all day. On Sundays, he drove them all to Amarillo to attend services at a big nondenominational evangelical church. Despite the current fixation on drugs, Culwell said, it was alcohol that had long been the bane of farm and ranch country.

"There's people around Swisher County who drink like a fish and just manage it well enough to get by," he said. It had taken years for the ranchers and farmers of Swisher County to come to think of alcoholism as a disease. Abuse of alcohol was considered a moral problem more than a physical one, and rehab was commonly considered a form of coddling or a way to weasel out of a jail sentence. The answer was to just leave it aside and come to Jesus, as George W. Bush famously did on his fortieth birthday. But not everybody could do it the way Governor Bush did. Jack Driskill helped people understand that.

Attitudes about drugs were slower to shift. There was still a great deal of fear about drugs, Culwell said. But it was not a fear of the unknown anymore. By now, almost everybody had a friend or relative caught up in it. If the great country music icon George Jones (who battled cocaine addiction for years) was not immune, Culwell liked to tell his clients, then who was? In fact, some well-known names in town walked down that road. A longtime resident of Driskill House was Bobby Keeter, the younger brother of Harold Keeter, the county judge. The Keeter family owned Keeter's Meat Company, which did custom butchering for Swisher County ranchers long before the big meatpackers came to the panhandle. The company didn't employ many men, but the business remained a fixture of Tulia's economy through good times and bad. People were not surprised to see Harold become a fine lawyer and eventually the top elected official in the county. Bobby was another story. A juvenile delinquent in high school, he went into professional bull riding after graduating and seemed to get his life on track. But then came the drugs, which had become common on the professional rodeo circuit. The most frequently abused were speed, for the long overnight hauls between fairgrounds, and pain pills, for the breaks and bruises that came with the job. Keeter became hooked on both.

It was easy to imagine Keeter riding a bull. He was several inches short of being tall, but everything about him was meaty, from his ham hock hands to his thick, tanned neck, to his flattened nose, which looked like it had been beaten with a tenderizer. He gave the impression of spending too much time in the family meat lockers. Around Driskill House, he usually wore a dirty PBR (Professional Bull Riders) T-shirt, jeans, and worn leather work boots. He did not look like a speed addict. His face was still boyish at forty and counting, though his short, curly hair was turning silvery gray. He was a notoriously persuasive smooth talker, a talent he had put to effective use over the years, whether promoting PBR events at cattle auctions around the panhandle or passing bad checks at out-of-town convenience stores.

The cause of Bobby's downfall was all too familiar to many in Tulia's black community, but his treatment in the criminal justice system did not match their experience, to say the least. Keeter's first bust was for possession of marijuana in Amarillo in 1979, at the age of twenty-one. That case was eventually dismissed through the efficient work of the Keeter family attorney. Four years later he was arrested for theft in Lubbock but again did no time. In August 1983, he was caught breaking into a car in Plainview. On the same night he was also charged with possession of marijuana, this time over four ounces, which made it a felony. Two months later, while out on bond, Keeter was arrested again in Plainview, this time for breaking into a house. He had begun shooting speed, and he was out of control.

Keeter eventually pleaded guilty to breaking into the car and got ten years probation. The marijuana charge and the second burglary charge were simply dismissed. As part of the deal, which was approved by district judge Jack Miller (the same judge who gave Kareem White sixty years), Bobby was sent to a private drug rehab facility in Houston, with his father paying the bill. Before long he was back in court, however. After a failed urine test, Keeter threw himself on the mercy of Judge Miller, admitting that he was still using speed and could not stop. Although it had been only fifteen months since Miller had sent Keeter to rehab, he obliged the young man's pleadings once again. He declined to revoke Keeter's probation—which would have meant ten years in prison—ordering instead that Keeter be committed to the state mental hospital in Vernon for drug treatment. In committing the habitual offender, Miller told him:

> And again, I hope that you can take advantage of this, and this will be some incentive to try to get all the help available for you because you've got a long time to go in this life, hopefully. And the quicker you can straighten yourself out where you can function in our society as a free, productive, law-abiding citizen, the better, because that's what all of our desires are. So good luck on that, and thank you.

Free was something Keeter understood, but productive and law-abiding continued to elude him. A year after receiving Miller's second dispensation, Bobby was arrested in Lubbock for possession of speed. The case didn't stick, but his probation officer told the judge that Keeter had not reported for his monthly urine tests in over a year. Still, no revocation. Finally his luck ran out. He was arrested in Lubbock once more for possession of speed. It was just two weeks before Christmas, 1987. Bobby's dad finally had enough. As the family gathered in Tulia for the holidays, Bobby was left to his own devices: no bail money, no family lawyer. Keeter sat in the Lubbock jail for four months. Finally, after four arrests in four years of probation, two failed drug tests, and scores of technical violations, Judge Miller revoked Keeter's probation and sent him to prison in April 1988. He was home by October.

"They may not have understood it, but I was raised here. They knew my father and my brother. They knew I was brought up right," Keeter said of his many trips through the local court system. "I did a lot of right things in my life, along with the wrong things." He drew out a scrapbook from his bedside table. Inside were posters from rodeo events he had promoted, photos of him receiving prizes, photos of his wife and daughters. He flipped through the pages quickly, narrating as he went, not distinguishing between the good and the bad, in the manner of someone who had compiled and confessed his sins in front of countless therapy groups and counselors. Here he was with Ken Henry, who used to hold the record for the most money earned in a single bull ride ($18,500). Here was a congratulatory letter from the managers of the Tulia Livestock Auction for his work with kids. Here was his old house, in a shot taken shortly before Bobby accidentally burned it to the ground. He looked at a smiling shot of his daughters. "Those were better times," he said.

Nobody knew what to do with Bobby Keeter, but most people liked him. Keeter had spent his share of time in the Flats as a young man, where he used to sell Joe Moore discount cuts of meat stolen from the family business. ("You just had to call him and put in your order—steak, ribs, whatever—and he'd bring it right to your door," Moore fondly recalled.) Keeter wondered where the sense of sympathy and mercy he benefited from so regularly had been in Moore's case. "I just know a whole lot of good people got caught up in a bad deal," he said.

Keeter was not the only white Tulian to have sympathy for Joe Moore, who enjoyed a surprising amount of goodwill on both sides of town. It was one of the reasons he insisted on a jury trial. Moore had worked for almost all of Swisher County's old-time farming families over the years, mostly as a hay hauler. Virtually all of them remembered him as reliable, efficient, and honest. "I would loan Joe Moore twenty dollars today," one old farmer said, months after Moore's conviction in the Coleman sting. Even some Tulia police had a grudging respect for him. Moore's nickname in the white community, "the mayor of Sunset Addition," was more than just a joke. At least until the Flats were torn down, he was the head of a community that had no official voice in the white government.

In the early 1980s, when most blacks moved across the tracks, the job passed to an assistant pastor at Jackson Chapel named Melvin Tatum. Tatum, a brother-in-law of Ricky White, served as the black representative to a number of boards and commissions and once worked for the county as a sort of all-purpose social worker for the black community. He spent most of his time mentoring black teenagers without fathers. In 1985, Tatum left to become a full-time pastor at a small church in Liberal, Kansas. It was the kind of opportunity that simply did not exist in Tulia, and Tatum was just one of many talented people leaving town in the 1980s. When he announced that he was moving on, Tulia's mayor predicted that the community would suffer. "He told me our people seemed to need a leader they could turn to," Tatum recalled.

There wasn't another Melvin Tatum waiting in the wings, but Joe Moore was still around. He may not have been a leader, but he was loyal and he cared about people, and they loved him for it. Moore had hired a number of Tulia's young men, Donnie included, for one job or another over the years. He also had a number of women who depended on him to varying degrees, though Thelma was the only one he considered his wife, and he always made sure that she was okay even after the pair stopped living together. ("I think he thinks I'm his mother," she said.)

Thelma, in turn, had good reason to be loyal to Moore. In the early 1990s, a raid on Moore's house turned up a single rock of crack in a tube of Chapstick. Moore was not home at the time, but Thelma was, and McEachern had them both indicted for conspiracy to distribute cocaine. It was a fancy charge built around very little evidence. McEachern didn't have much on Moore, but he did have Thelma. As the two sat in jail, unable to raise the collateral for a $50,000 bond, McEachern went to work on Moore. He threatened to send Thelma away for twenty-five years if Moore didn't cooperate. Finally Moore caved in. He pleaded to a short prison term, with the understanding that Thelma would get probation. It was his only trip to the pen. Nobody in the black community believed that Moore sold cocaine to Tom Coleman, chiefly because nobody could believe that Joe Moore, of all the defendants, would have been that stupid. "Joe's no angel," Thelma said. "But he didn't do what they said he did, and that's the bottom line."

Tucked away in prison in Abilene, Moore didn't learn about Charles Sturgess's suicide for months. When he finally heard the story from a visitor, he was amazed by every detail, except for the cocaine. Moore had worked for Sturgess on occasion, just as he had for Sturgess's father. "I been around hustlin' and gamblin' all my life," he said. "I know what someone looks like when they've been using something."

The question that occurred to Moore was why Coleman, who hung around the sale barn almost every week, never tried to set up Sturgess.

Johnny Nix thought he had a pretty good idea. Sturgess ran in a good crowd. The cops, including Larry Stewart, didn't mind going out to the sale barn to drink Sturgess's coffee every morning, despite the rumors about him. In fact, Terry McEachern was one of Sturgess's drinking buddies, and it was no secret that McEachern had sobriety issues of his own. Stories of the district attorney's drunken exploits abound in Tulia. McEachern pulling his car out of a ditch with his tractor early in the morning, after a night of drinking. McEachern showing up drunk late at night on a woman's doorstep, crying. One of the sting defendants, Vincent McCray, once lived in a trailer near McEachern's house in the country. McEachern had inadvertently driven through his yard so many times that McCray, whom McEachern prosecuted for DWI on more than one occasion, eventually got fed up and made him pay for a sprinkler he ran over.

There were important people in Tulia who had more in common

with Charles Sturgess than they cared to admit, and his connections afforded him a measure of impunity. Once Sturgess's secret was out, however, it was a different story. "You know you can be a drunk and get over it and they're okay with you," Nix said. "But with drugs, nobody wants to be around you."

"Just hypocritical, the whole batch of 'em," he said.

Tulia, a Texas panhandle farming and ranching community of 5,000, is the biggest town in one of the fastest shrinking counties in Texas. (Artie Limmer)

In the late 1950s, Swisher was one of the state's leading counties in grain harvested and cattle fed. Now most of the shops in downtown Tulia are closed, victims of the steady decline in the state's rural economy. (Corbis/Andrew Lichtenstein)

LEFT Freddie Brookins Jr. was the starting tailback for Tulia High's football team in the mid–1990s. Though he had no prior offenses, he was given the maximum sentence of twenty years for allegedly selling an eight ball (less than 3.5 grams) of cocaine to undercover agent Tom Coleman. (Courtesy of Fred Brookins Sr.) RIGHT Donnie Smith was named Tulia High's male athlete of the year in 1988. He was sentenced to twelve and a half years in the Coleman sting. Three of his siblings were also indicted. (Courtesy of Mattie White)

Joe Moore, called a "drug kingpin" by the district attorney, in front of his house in Tulia. He was sentenced to ninety years for allegedly selling a single eight ball of cocaine to Tom Coleman. Moore's trial lasted seven hours. (Alan Pogue)

Fred Brookins Sr.'s son Freddie was sentenced to twenty years.
Fred Sr., a manager at a meat-packing plant, became a leader of
the local opposition to the bust. (Corbis/Andrew Lichtenstein)

Joe Moore, 60, in state
prison in Abilene, 2002.
(Artie Limmer)

Swisher County District Attorney Terry McEachern prosecuted the cases made by Tom Coleman in Tulia, which resulted in indictments against forty-seven people—thirty-eight of whom were black—for dealing cocaine. Twenty-six defendants were sent to prison. (Amarillo Globe News)

Swisher County Sheriff Larry Stewart hired Tom Coleman and was one of a handful of people in the county who knew about the undercover operation. As the bust became a national scandal, he remained one of Tom Coleman's staunchest defenders. (Getty)

Tom Coleman, the son of a well-known Texas Ranger, was named Officer of the Year following the bust in Tulia. This photo of Texas Attorney General John Cornyn (left) presenting the award appeared on the website of the Texas Narcotics Control Program. (Cornyn is now a U.S. Senator.)

During the trial of Kareem White, the last defendant tried in the sting, three Texas Rangers came to Tulia to vouch for the reputation of Coleman (second from left), including Ranger Jerry Byrne (far right), a long-time friend of Coleman's. (Courtesy William Kunstler Fund for Racial Justice)

Tom Coleman (Dan Sellers)

Alan Bean, Gary Gardner, and Thelma Johnson, local opponents of the Tulia drug bust, at Bean's house in Tulia. Their organization, the Friends of Justice, helped bring media attention to the bust in Tulia, and made them targets of local scorn. Gardner, a local farmer, was the first person to publicly question the bust in Tulia. (Artie Limmer)

Texas ACLU Director Will Harrell speaks at a press conference at the state capitol with Tulia "war orphans"—the children of defendants arrested in the sting. The scandal brought legislative scrutiny to federally-funded multi-jurisdictional drug task forces, like the one that funded Coleman's operation in Tulia. (Alan Pogue)

Gary Gardner on the steps of the Swisher County Courthouse. Behind him are drug war reform activist Randy Credico (left) and Alan Bean. (Alan Pogue)

Jeff Blackburn and Vanita Gupta, who organized post-conviction representation for the Tulia defendants, talk to reporters on June 16, 2003. Behind them are State Senator Rodney Ellis (left) and Mitch Zamoff, of Washington, D.C., one of the attorneys who worked on the case pro bono. (Alan Pogue)

Freddie Brookins Jr. talks to reporters on June 16, 2003. Behind him from left to right are Donnie Smith, Joe Moore (obscured), Fred Brookins Sr., and Ted Killory, a member of the defendants' legal team. (Alan Pogue)

Joe Moore. (Corbis/Andrew Lichtenstein)

PART FOUR

CHAPTER THIRTEEN

East Meets West

JEFF BLACKBURN got his first glimpse of Tom Coleman on June 29, 2001, nine days after Charles Sturgess was arrested, when Coleman arrived in Amarillo to have his deposition taken. Coleman's deposition was the crux—or so Blackburn was hoping—of the civil suit he had filed the previous fall, when the glow of the national spotlight was still on Tulia. It had not been a good summer for Coleman. In April, he was fired by a task force in the north Texas town of Waxahachie after the commander discovered that he had been having sex with a truck stop prostitute and crack addict who worked as a snitch for the task force. It was the third task force he had worked for in the eighteen months since he left Tulia. He had become what the police unions derisively called a gypsy cop, and now he was unemployed.

Billy Wafer was the plaintiff in the suit, which alleged that Sheriff Stewart and Tom Coleman had conspired to violate Wafer's civil rights. The suit focused narrowly on Wafer's case, but the proceedings had obvious implications for every defendant in the sting. The fact that the national media attention had turned elsewhere in the intervening months only heightened the pressure on Blackburn to score a big win for Wafer and put the injustice in Tulia back in the spotlight. Blackburn had joined forces with an earnest young medical malpractice attorney named Chris Hoffman and his father and law partner, Tim Hoffman. The elder Hoffman, who had a full beard and kind, twinkling eyes, was a widely respected veteran trial lawyer who mentored Blackburn when he began working on civil rights cases. The three had been meeting for months with a small team of volunteers, including Blackburn's legal assistants Virginia Cave and Margaret Barras, and a semiretired attorney named Jack Swindell. Randy Credico had become a fixture at Blackburn's house, sleeping on the couch in his rumpled suit and driving back and forth to Tulia in his rented car. Blackburn called the loosely knit group the Tulia Legal Defense Project.

Blackburn didn't mind having Credico living out of his house, despite his cigar smoking and his endless string of shouted cell phone conversations. (Blackburn himself smoked more than a pack a day.) The two had become close friends, and besides, Blackburn's work was his life. Like Credico, he had always considered himself an activist, yet he also believed in getting paid for what he did whenever possible. He did not take court appointments for indigent defendants, and he considered most of his colleagues who did to be beneath his level as an attorney. In Blackburn's experience, whoever put on the best show for the jury usually won, no matter who the client was or what the facts were, and the stingy fees paid for court-appointed cases did not allow the art to be practiced the way he believed it should be. It hadn't always been that way. When he started out in Amarillo, he shared a reception area in an office suite with a well-known criminal defense attorney named Seldon Hale, who had made a name for himself as a defender of Amarillo's downtrodden. Hale taught Blackburn that even "street lawyers" without big-name clients could make money. Hale would wade into the small crowd of people waiting to see him every morning and select his clients by asking everyone the same question: "How much cash have you got on you right now?" When Hale was done, Blackburn often wound up representing the unlucky souls left out in the hall.

Now, after years of paying his dues, Blackburn had reached a level of comfort. He drove a Lexus sports car and spent thousands of dollars on audio equipment. He had a weakness for handmade, one-of-a-kind turntables from England and old-fashioned vacuum tube-driven amplifiers. His personal life was a wreck; at forty-four, he had been divorced four times. Lawyering was the only thing he had ever been good at, and his practice had brought him all of his proudest moments. But the work was never just about the money. It was about fighting a legal system that routinely railroaded the weakest defendants and a local culture that only paid lip service to equal justice.

In other words, it was about fighting Amarillo. It wasn't that Blackburn would have preferred living somewhere else. He was proud to be from the plains. It was the last place in America where people smoked when they felt like it and ate red meat for lunch and dinner—and sometimes for breakfast too. Blackburn loved to host out-of-town guests and regale them with stories of Amarillo's local eccentrics, such as Stanley Marsh III of Cadillac Ranch fame. Blackburn was regarded as something of a curiosity himself. He allowed neighborhood graffiti artists to use the long adobe wall around his courtyard as a canvas for elaborate murals, and his office became something of a landmark in his part of town. He enjoyed all the perks that came with being a big fish in a little pond: the way everyone knew his face from TV and how all the waiters knew his name at his favorite restaurants. But he also found a lot to hate about the culture he grew up in: the closed-mindedness and paranoia of his fellow Amarilloans, the tiresome conformity of their daily lives—"going to church and working at the bomb factory," as he put it. Cops, prosecutors, and judges were among the daily enforcers of that culture, and over the years Blackburn had won more than a few rounds against them.

Now that he was involved with the Tulia struggle, however, he was beginning to have some doubts about his colleagues, particularly Gary Gardner and Alan Bean. Blackburn met Gardner in 1996, when Gardner tried to convince him to join his fight against Tulia's school drug testing plan. Blackburn told him it was a losing cause, and Gardner, who went on to file the suit himself, had held a grudge against him ever since. Shortly after Kareem White's trial, Gardner paid another visit to Blackburn's office in Amarillo. Gardner made no secret of the fact that he considered Blackburn an opportunist, jumping into the fight only after the national media began paying attention. With characteristic bluntness, he told Blackburn that he was welcome to join his cause, provided Blackburn understood who was the trail boss of the operation and who was just a cowhand. Blackburn told him, in essence, to get off of his ranch.

It didn't help that in the intervening months Gardner, in Blackburn's eyes a right-wing redneck and meddling amateur, was quoted in media coverage of the controversy at least as often, if not more, than Blackburn. Now Gardner, the self-taught lawyer, had taken up Joe Moore's case and was filing motions on his behalf. Alan Bean, meanwhile, was planning a rally in Tulia to mark the second anniversary of the sting. Tulia had become a cause célébre in the drug war reform movement, and Bean was inviting every activist in the country to come to town in a few weeks. Blackburn, who would have to pick a jury for Wafer's civil suit from Swisher County or a nearby county, could just imagine how the spectacle of long-haired marijuana legalization activists parading around Conner Park in support of Wafer and his fellow defendants would play in the local papers.

Tom Coleman showed up for his deposition accompanied by Sheriff Stewart and two attorneys hired by Swisher County's insurance carrier: Jon Hogg, who was from San Angelo, and Charlotte Bingham, from Lubbock. Tim Hoffman, who had considerable expertise in taking depositions, began the questioning of Coleman. Blackburn, Chris Hoffman, and Billy Wafer sat beside him at the conference table. The day before, Tim Hoffman had deposed Sheriff Stewart in the same room. Hogg did most of the talking for the other team, but Blackburn had a feeling it was the silent, scowling Bingham, a slight woman with thin lips and close-set eyes, who was actually running the show. Defending government agencies from discrimination suits was her bailiwick, and she seemed to regard the Tulia scandal as a charade. Her subtle coaching of Stewart made it clear in Blackburn's mind where she was coming from. It was the task force that hired and supervised Coleman, not Stewart, so it was the task force that was on the hook for anything that went wrong, not Swisher County. Under this defense strategy, the less Stewart knew about Coleman's operation, the better, and Blackburn suspected that Bingham was at least partly responsible for Stewart's frustratingly vague answers and failure to recollect many details of Coleman's background check or the circumstances surrounding his arrest in Tulia, even though Stewart himself had personally done the arrest. For his part, Stewart seemed determined to maintain a front of extreme courtesy and humility. (During a break in his deposition, Stewart asked for time to pray.) Even when pressed by Hoffman, Stewart played the part of the elderly country sheriff, somewhat befuddled by the intricacies of the task force's chain of command and the procedures of a narcotics investigation. Blackburn had already begun to despise both Stewart and Bingham.

Like Blackburn, Stewart had never seen Coleman testify at trial, since he had always been required to leave the courtroom following his own testimony. Now he watched impassively as Hoffman dragged Coleman through four hours of testimony about his methods in Tulia, his dealings with Billy Wafer, and his background in law enforcement. It was by far the most methodical examination of Coleman anybody had ever done. After lunch, Hoffman turned up the heat. The day before, he had managed to get Stewart to agree that he would have fired Coleman if he had reason to believe that Coleman was dishonest. As far as Stewart was concerned, however, Coleman had never lied about anything. Now, as Stewart looked on, Hoffman tried to force Coleman to admit that he had lied to Stewart's face. Stewart had testified the day before that Coleman had acted surprised when Stewart confronted him with the Cochran County arrest warrant. Now, under questioning from Hoffman, Coleman claimed he found out about his indictment in Cochran County at the same time Stewart did, when the arrest warrant came across the Teletype machine on August 7, 1998. Just as Dwight McDonald had done in Kareem White's trial, Hoffman showed Coleman the waiver of arraignment he had signed on May 30, 1998, acknowledging that charges had been filed against him. Why would he pretend not to know about the charges in August? Didn't that make him a liar?

This time Coleman had a new answer. He didn't know he was charged when he signed the waiver, he explained, because the waiver was blank at the time that he signed it. Coleman told Hoffman that he got a call in April 1998 from Larry Gilbreath, the Texas Ranger who later vouched for Coleman at Kareem White's trial, warning him that officials in Cochran County were considering filing charges against him. He had gone to see an attorney in Lubbock named Garry Smith, who advised him to sign a blank waiver of arraignment as a precautionary measure, so that Smith would not have to find him if charges were ever actually filed. In fact, Coleman had told this "blank waiver" story once before, in a postconviction hearing for Kizzie White the previous summer. Blackburn had read the transcript. Smith had appeared at the hearing and offered a tepid endorsement of Coleman's account, testifying that he might not have known the exact charges at the time he had Coleman sign the waiver. Even if that were true, however, Coleman clearly knew he was being charged with something, or he wouldn't have hired Smith and signed a waiver at all.

Coleman acknowledged that this differed from accounts he had given in court before. Coleman had, however, told the blank waiver story to Terry McEachern in the past, he said.

"So you gave him basically the same explanation that you've given us here today?" Hoffman asked.

"Probably, yes, sir. Pretty close to it. Pretty close that I can. Today—today has been more—today has been more of what's really happened," Coleman replied. He had been answering questions for over four hours by this time, and he was becoming more and more rattled, as Blackburn had guessed he would. "I mean, if—if today could be back in them other trials without the defense lawyers twisting everything around like they do," Coleman said, "things probably wouldn't be as bad as they are right now, because there's an explanation to everything."

Hoffman asked if he stood by everything he had testified to in the trials. "That can be questionable," Coleman replied, "It's—just depends on how hard—or how the defense attorney twisted the truth. I mean, I—I have read over my testimony, and—and some of that stuff in there is, like, totally out in left field."

Blackburn was elated after Coleman's deposition. The blank waiver story struck him as an obvious lie—another in a long line of ridiculous stories Coleman had told over the years. He felt certain that Bingham, after seeing how poorly Coleman did under oath, would be ready to talk settlement—anything to keep him off the stand and limit the county's liability. Blackburn's celebratory attitude ended abruptly the next day, when it was Billy Wafer's turn to give a deposition. Blackburn had done very little coaching of Wafer prior to the deposition. He merely told him to tell the truth. If Stewart suffered from a fuzzy memory, Wafer seemed to have the opposite problem—he remembered too much for his own good. Wafer did fine under Bingham's questioning about the facts of the case Coleman had filed against him. He stuck to his story, which had been good enough to get him off the first time around and still held up well. He saw Coleman with Eliga Kelly at the Allsups' one morning, he testified, but he never made any deal with him.

Things began to go south, however, when Bingham started a line of questioning about Wafer's history of drug use. Blackburn knew she would mine that area; after all, Wafer was on probation for possession of marijuana at the time of his arrest. What he didn't know was how productive it would be. Wafer admitted that he smoked pot four or five times a year, usually with his brother-in-law Tony Powell. Asked if he ever used cocaine, Wafer mentioned one time that he could recall, about a year ago, with Tony Powell. Blackburn cringed—that was just a few months after Wafer beat his sting case. It didn't have any bearing on whether or not he had been falsely accused by Coleman, but it wouldn't look good to a panhandle jury if Wafer went right out and celebrated his acquittal by doing some cocaine. Blackburn detected a smug sense of self-satisfaction coming from Bingham as she furiously scribbled notes. Under further questioning, Wafer recalled using cocaine on two other occasions, once over Christmas of 1998 or 1999, and another time, many years before, when he inadvertently smoked some crack somebody had put in a joint.

But that wasn't all. Wafer also admitted using speed as a young man, every week for about five years. He had always wondered whether or not the pills he took were illegal, he said, as Blackburn struggled to conceal his dismay. Finally Wafer testified that he was arrested in March 1999, some four months before the sting, for being delinquent on his probation payments, and subsequently failed a urine test. He was in jail for ten weeks and lost his job at Seed Resource at that time—not, as he had told reporters, when he was later arrested in the Coleman sting.

It was as disastrous a deposition as Blackburn could have imagined. He knew it was his own fault, for not fully exploring the issue with Wafer beforehand. Over the preceding nine months, Blackburn and his team had accumulated the most complete accounting of the sting anybody had yet put together. They had Coleman and Stewart conspiring to keep secret damning evidence that defense attorneys should have been entitled to. They had Coleman apparently lying in a deposition, and they had every reason to believe they would skewer him in front of a jury. But it was all worthless without a client a jury could believe in. Wafer was not a drug dealer, but, fairly or not, he was now damaged goods, and the other side knew it.

In mid-October, Blackburn settled the case for $25,000. It was a paltry sum; they had spent half that amount preparing for the suit. Under the terms of the settlement, the county admitted no wrongdoing, a fact that Tulia authorities gleefully shared with the local press, despite the supposed confidentiality of the agreement. Technically Wafer had won, and Blackburn's team had greatly expanded the factual record, but everybody knew it was really a loss. There would be no media bounce from a result like this.

Later that month, Vanita Gupta watched Sara and Emily Kunstler's short documentary about Tulia at an NAACP banquet in Washington, D.C. She'd heard of Tulia before, but she knew virtually nothing about the case. Now she stared, transfixed, at the stark images of young black men and women in their pajamas being led by stone-faced Texas deputies into an old red-brick jailhouse that looked like something out of a Louis L'Amour novel. A long shot from the window of a moving car showed inmates chopping weeds along a rural highway, guarded by a man in a big white cowboy hat. It was a common enough sight in Texas, but for Gupta it was a window into another century, and it put the hook into her. "The only difference from 1920 and now is they can't take us out and hang us on a tree," an earnest black teenager said into the camera. "They can just send us to prison for life. It's the same thing: we ain't never gonna be free again."

A few weeks later, Gupta was on a plane to Amarillo.

Gupta was born in Philadelphia, the second daughter of middle-class Indian immigrants. Her father, an engineer, had left India along with thousands of professionals during the "brain drain" of the 1960s. When Gupta was still an infant, the family moved to England, and she was raised in a town just outside of London. She came of age in the 1980s, when England, mired in a recession, was convulsed by an anti-immigrant backlash. Especially in London's blue-collar suburbs, which had a large Indian community, gangs of unemployed white youths roamed the streets, looking for trouble. South Asians were the scape-goats of choice, and "Paki" became one of the most loaded words in the nation. Gupta heard it often. She did not have a white friend until she came to the United States to attend Yale University in 1992.

Despite her experiences growing up in Margaret Thatcher's England, Gupta was unprepared for the racial dynamics of New Haven, Connecticut. Yale is one of the great bastions of privilege and power in the United States, filled with the progeny of senators and CEOs. Outside the ivy-covered walls, however, sits one of the poor-est—and blackest—cities in New England. Most students never ven-tured into the blighted neighborhoods just a stone's throw from their dormitories. Like her fellow students, Gupta had grown up in relative privilege, yet she found herself wondering where she fit into this new environment. In England, she had been part of a despised minority; now she was safely ensconced at the top of an entirely different kind of caste system.

When Yale's janitors and other service employees—mostly minorities from New Haven—began organizing for higher wages, many progressive students rallied to their cause, and Gupta joined the fight. A black professor and activist named Cathy Cohen became a mentor to Gupta, who began spending more and more time outside the classroom. She became involved in campaigns to counter the anti-immigrant and anti–affirmative action policies coming out of the Newt Gingrich–led Congress in the mid-1990s.

After graduation, Gupta got a job in Boston working for another black mentor, Dr. Deborah Prothrow-Stith, the assistant dean of the Harvard School of Public Health. A leading expert on juvenile crime, Stith believed that youth violence, especially killings associated with inner-city gangs and drug dealing, should be considered a public health issue rather than strictly a criminal justice matter. A rash of school shootings put Stith's observations in high demand, and Gupta helped prepare congressional testimony and op-ed pieces for national newspapers. Stith advocated intervention at an early age, teaching life skills and building the emotional capacity of inner-city kids.

Two years later, as a law student at NYU, Gupta got her first taste of the American South and her first sobering lesson in the value of cutting-edge Harvard theories in a Texas courtroom. Gupta signed up for a capital defense clinic sponsored by the NAACP Legal Defense and Education Fund (LDF). George Kendall, a giant in the thankless field of death penalty appellate work, was representing Delma Banks, a Texas man who had been on death row for over twenty years. Banks, who is black, was accused of the 1980 murder of a white teenager in Texarkana. There was no physical evidence linking him to the crime. Banks, who had no prior record, was convicted chiefly on the testimony of two witnesses, Charles Cook and Robert Farr. At the time of Banks's trial, Cook had an arson charge pending, which the district attorney agreed to drop in exchange for his testimony. Yet Cook testified at trial that there had been no deal. He also claimed—falsely, as defense attorneys would later discover—that he had not been coached in how to testify. The prosecutor stood by quietly as Cook perjured himself. Kendall and his team also discovered that Robert Farr, contrary to his testimony in court, was a paid police informant. Banks's court-appointed attorney, meanwhile, was completely ineffective.

Kendall won Banks a new trial, only to have the victory reversed by the Fifth Circuit Court of Appeals, one of the nation's most conservative federal tribunals. The Fifth Circuit ruled that whatever the merits of Banks's claims, he had brought them forward too late in the process. They ruled, in effect, that actual innocence was not necessarily sufficient grounds for a new trial. The Supreme Court intervened minutes before Banks was to be executed—he was already strapped to the gurney—and eventually overturned his death sentence.

For Gupta, this crash course in Texas justice was devastating, but it was exhilarating to work with Kendall and the LDF—they were simply the best in the business. After graduation, Gupta got her wish: she was hired on full-time with the LDF in the fall of 2001. Her assignment was to work on drug war cases, but she had only a general idea of how to get started. Gupta had only been on the job a little over a month when she saw the Kunstler video, but she knew she had found her first case.

Gupta made it to the Texas panhandle the first week of November 2001. On the flight down, she grew more and more nervous, especially after she changed planes in Dallas and found herself, aside from a salesman or two, unmistakably surrounded by plainsmen and women. She couldn't help but think of the long sentences she heard about in the Kunstler video; these were the men and women who served on those juries. She listened to the thick accents of the women chatting amiably, many seemingly returning from shopping trips to Dallas. The men seemed taciturn and gruff, like cooped-up cowboys who couldn't wait to get out of the city and back to the ranch. She suddenly felt self-conscious, as though everybody on the plane knew she had come all the way from New York, just to stir up trouble for them.

Gupta had arranged to meet with Jeff Blackburn and Chris Hoffman at Hoffman's law office in Amarillo. Officially she was on a fact-finding mission, but in her mind she was ready for LDF to take over the cases immediately. She was already formulating her pitch to Blackburn and his team and was apprehensive about how she would be received. She had been out of law school less than six months, and she looked even younger than she was with her petite frame and long, brown hair, which she styled with a simple part down the middle. She knew that Blackburn had been working on the cases for over a year. Who was she to parachute in and shake things up?

Still, to her the next step was obvious: filing writs of habeas corpus for each of the twenty-two defendants still in prison. A habeas writ is an appeal directly to the highest court in the state arguing that a conviction has been unjustly obtained. It is the last option available to a defendant who has already exhausted his direct appeal. Indigent defendants in Texas are not entitled to court-appointed attorneys for habeas appeals (unless they have been sentenced to death), so habeas writs tend to be of the shot-in-the-dark variety, scrawled in pencil on ready-made forms, sometimes with the assistance of jail-house lawyers. Habeas petitions that are denied in state court can be refiled in federal court, which is the last course of action available to any convicted felon in the United States. There were strict time limits on filing such writs, and Gupta couldn't understand why, after all the publicity the previous fall, none of the defendants had postconviction representation. It was time to start filing some paper for these people before it was too late. It was time to get the ball rolling.

Everything about Amarillo seemed to discourage just such a mission. Nobody in the airport was in a hurry. There was no line of cabs waiting outside; an old man in a golf cart drove people from the airport's single terminal to the rental car lot. Gupta saw rabbits foraging not 200 yards from the terminal entrance. Along I–40 into town, a billboard advertisement for one of the local TV news stations loomed over the freeway. It showed the anchors, three men and two women, standing in a line and staring down at the tiny cars that passed beneath, like gatekeepers to the city. They were five of the whitest people Gupta had ever seen, and they were not smiling, not even the weatherman.

When Gupta arrived at the Hoffmans' office, she felt a sense of disarray. Gupta was not the only outsider there; an attorney named Alicia Young from the national ACLU office and a radical young organizer from the Drug Policy Alliance named Deborah Small had also come from New York to attend the meeting. There was still great interest in the case, despite the fact that Tulia had been out of the headlines for some time. Nobody seemed to be in charge, and Young had taken it upon herself to foster harmony between the two main groups working on the cases—Blackburn's Tulia Legal Defense Project in Amarillo and the Friends of Justice in Tulia, whose relationship had deteriorated over the previous year. Chris Hoffman and Van Williamson, who also attended the meeting, seemed receptive to Gupta's interest in filing habeas writs. The truth was, now that the Wafer civil suit had petered out, they were running out of ideas.

Blackburn came in late, out of breath. He struck Gupta as warm and friendly, but her mention of habeas petitions sent him into a theatrical diatribe against the Texas Court of Criminal Appeals (CCA), to whom such writs would be presented. The CCA has ultimate jurisdiction over all criminal cases in Texas. The Texas Supreme Court, the court of last resort for all civil matters, is the state's better-known high court, having been the subject of an unflattering report on the CBS show *60 Minutes*. The report examined how campaign contributions to the justices, who are elected in partisan races, had affected the court's decision making over the years.

The CCA is also selected through partisan elections, and over the previous ten years, as the Republican Party took over the state, it had become a bastion of law-and-order conservatism bar none. The reversal rate for death penalty appeals heard by the CCA—about 3 percent—is lower than any other state high court in the country. In a case that came to symbolize the intransigence of the court's pro-prosecution bias, in 1998 the CCA denied a new trial to Roy Criner, who was serving ninety-nine years for rape and murder, despite the fact that DNA evidence tested after the trial proved that he was not the perpetrator. In her ruling on the case, Judge Sharon Keller made the unlikely argument that the new evidence would not necessarily have made a difference in the jury's verdict. After the case created a national scandal, Criner was pardoned by the governor—two years after the DNA evidence was first presented. Equally infamous was the El Paso death penalty case of Cesar Fierro, who was induced to confess to murder after the Mexican police in neighboring Juarez arrested his parents and threatened to torture them if he didn't comply. Keller, writing for the majority, termed the police tactic "harmless error."

"They're not a court," Blackburn said. "They're some kind of uber–police force." Going the habeas route would be a waste of time, he said. Blackburn favored working through political channels to influence the Texas Board of Pardons and Paroles, which had the power to recommend pardons to the governor's office. If the defense could show that Coleman had conclusively lied in one case, then perhaps they could build enough momentum in the media and among sympathetic public officials that the board and the governor would be forced to act. Blackburn saw the work they had done on the Wafer lawsuit as step 1 in a multiyear plan toward this end. Gupta was unconvinced. Even if appealing to the CCA was futile, it was a necessary stop on the way to federal court. All of a defendant's remedies at the state level had to be exhausted before a federal judge would even consider a habeas appeal. There was no way around it.

Gupta spent the next day with Blackburn and Randy Credico, getting to know them and learning about the cases. Blackburn was witty and smart and well read, the last person she expected to find in the Texas panhandle. He knew his civil rights history and had a deep respect for the legacy of the Legal Defense Fund. Though he remained unconvinced of the wisdom of the habeas strategy, he agreed to share everything he had with Gupta, including the lengthy depositions of Tom Coleman and Sheriff Stewart taken by Tim Hoffman in Wafer's lawsuit. Her next stop was Vigo Park, where she planned to meet with Gary Gardner. Blackburn told her not to bother. Gardner was doing more harm than good, he said. He also hinted vaguely that visiting Gary in Vigo might not be 100 percent safe.

Gupta was not sure what to expect as she made her way through the straightedge farm-to-market roads of Swisher County toward Gardner's house, struggling to follow his directions to Vigo Park. The sky was impossibly high and blue and the November fields were mostly an empty expanse of brown mud, allowing her to see for miles in every direction. After spending the past six months working in Manhattan, she found the stark emptiness of the plains beautiful and exhilarating. Gardner lived in a sort of compound, his modest farmhouse surrounded by a big yellow school bus, windmills, tractors, motorcycles, and a large shed housing a yellow crop dusting plane that looked like it had not moved in years. Two giant hound dogs bounded up to the backyard gate and bellowed at her as she stepped cautiously from her car. Gary ambled out of the kitchen door wearing a pair of blue denim overalls and waved her up the driveway. Before she could even introduce herself, he began exclaiming about how beautiful she was and how lucky he was to meet her. Jolly and self-deprecating, Gardner was not at all what Gupta expected from Blackburn's warning.

Gardner ushered her into his poolroom and showed her his stacks of files. Gupta was amazed by the amount of work that he had done.

Gardner, who had been studying the cases for almost two years, had obtained virtually every document from every case. He proudly rattled off some of the discoveries he had made along the way, including an effort to cover up an obvious mistake in a police report on a defendant named Romona Strickland, from whom Coleman claimed to have bought an eight ball of powdered cocaine. Strickland, a young black woman whose home had a reputation as a party house during the time Coleman was in Tulia, maintained her innocence, even after McEachern told her she had failed a lie detector test administered at her insistence. After McEachern declined to show her the charts from her test, Strickland, who was out on bail, had her Plainview lawyer, Eric Willard, arrange another test, which she passed easily.

McEachern decided it was in his interest to dispose of Strickland's case quietly. He eventually allowed both Strickland and Kareem White's girlfriend, Chandra Van Cleave, another client of Willard's who passed a lie detector test, to plead no contest and pay a fine. The cases were lost in the shuffle, or would have been, had Gardner not discovered that somebody crossed out a phrase from Coleman's description of Strickland in the report of the alleged buy. It was an unprofessional way to correct a report, but that wasn't nearly as damaging as the nature of the "error" somebody wanted to correct. Using a microscope (which he normally employed to look for boll weevil eggs), Gardner made out the words "about six months pregnant" beneath the heavy black mark out. Strickland was not pregnant at the time of the alleged deal, nor was she overweight. If Coleman had really made the deal with Romona Strickland, how could he have been mistaken about such an unmistakable identifier? Conversely, if he had made the deal with somebody who really was pregnant, how did Strickland's name come to be on the indictment? It was hard to see how the prosecution in good conscience could simply "correct" the report and move ahead with Strickland's case, but they did so anyway.

Gardner showed Gupta a copy of the work he was most proud of:

the habeas writ he prepared for Joe Moore. It was the size of a small phonebook, with numerous appendixes attached to the back. "I wanted to tell the whole story of Tulia, from beginning to end," he told Gupta. Gardner's writ followed the basic structure of a legal document, and his instincts were sound. He identified most of the logical grounds for appeal and cited the correct case law to back them up. Yet the writ was unmistakably Gardner's work. It was peppered with bits of homespun wisdom, song lyrics, and lines from *Bartlett's Quotations*. On Coleman's performance in court, he wrote, "Reading Mr. Coleman's testimony and trying to understand the facts as he relates them is a bit like eating thin Jell-O with a fork, you just can't get a bite on it." On Moore's attorney Kregg Hukill: "Mr. Hukill was in a western cowboy drama set in a small Texas town. The good town folk have caught the bad guy and are going to give him a fair trial, then hang him. But this is a modern day Western cowboy drama, so the mob follows the modern script and gives the defendant a lawyer—then they hang him!" The document also referred to Coleman throughout as a "Liar, a Thief, and a Whoremonger."

Despite the humorous asides, it was clear to Gupta that Gardner was deadly serious about getting Moore out of prison. He had invested hundreds of hours in preparing the writ. He stunned Gupta by admitting that he spent many late nights poring over his law dictionary, sometimes frustrated to tears, as he struggled to get his thoughts down on paper. He obviously cared about Moore, which made it all the more difficult for her to ask Gardner to stop submitting motions on Moore's behalf. If he did not, she explained, Moore could lose his opportunity to file an amended habeas petition prepared by a team of experienced appellate lawyers. There was, of course, no such team at hand, but Gupta did not mention this to Gardner.

Gardner did not give her a straight answer that morning. He had been visited by quite a few out-of-town activists and reporters in the preceding year, and he had made it his habit—particularly if they were from New York—to goad them as much as possible, as a sort of test of their sensibilities. This typically involved presenting an enhanced version of his own redneck personality, complete with liberal use of racial epithets. But he gave Gupta a free pass. Something about her youthful earnestness and humility appealed to him. He loaned her all of his records, including his trial transcripts, which had cost him thousands of dollars to obtain, so that she could copy everything.

Gupta's next stop was the Swisher County courthouse. With an LDF intern in tow, she asked the clerk to pull the files for every defendant charged in the sting. If the clerk was surprised, she did not show it. In New York, clerks wandered through enormous rooms filled with hundreds of shelves to pull case files. In Tulia, the clerk showed Gupta into a tiny room with a single floor-to-ceiling shelving unit. "These are all our active cases," she said. "Help yourself." Gupta was struck again by the absurdity of it all. Tulia really was Mayberry, yet somehow a narc had taken credit for busting over forty drug dealers here. The pair spent the rest of the afternoon methodically copying the contents of each and every file on the office's only copier. By the time she headed back to New York, Gupta had a suitcase full of documents and a long story to tell George Kendall.

CHAPTER FOURTEEN

Doing Time

SHORTLY AFTER Gupta returned home, Blackburn called with big news. Tonya White, Donnie Smith's older sister, decided to turn herself in. Tonya was indicted at the same time as the rest of the Tulia defendants but was never arrested because she was living in Oklahoma at the time of the bust. Tonya was an unlikely suspect. She wasn't even living in Tulia when Coleman alleged that he bought cocaine from her. Beyond that, Tonya, a nurse's aide, had a reputation for being the straight arrow in the White family, the older sister who looked after her younger, wilder siblings as best she could. Her father Ricky called her "the squarest person I know."

When word got out that she was wanted in Tulia, Tonya was afraid to return. Now, after more than two years of exile, Mattie had persuaded her daughter to come back to Tulia and deal with the outstanding warrant. Zury Bossett, another out-of-town defendant whose indictment had been outstanding for years, was arrested over the summer after her warrant surfaced during a routine traffic stop. Blackburn convinced both women to let him take over their cases, the only two unadjudicated cases from the sting. It had been over a year since the Kareem White trial, and Coleman had not been back to Tulia. McEachern did not seem interested in prosecuting either case, not after the beating Coleman's reputation had taken in the national press since Kareem's trial.

But Blackburn had no intention of pleading out Tonya or Zury. After the disastrous Wafer suit, he was itching for another crack at Coleman and Stewart. He planned to file motion after motion, putting both of them on the stand in as many pretrial hearings as he could manage, grilling them on every last detail of the botched operation. He would have the national press covering every maneuver he made, every embarrassing thing Coleman said. By demanding a trial, Blackburn would force McEachern to make a decision: dismiss the cases and admit, in effect, that he no longer had confidence in Coleman, or stand by his man once and for all and take the cases to trial. It was a risky move for Tonya (even with no previous record, she was facing 2–20 years), but Blackburn convinced her and Mattie that it was the right thing to do. Beating Tonya's case, Blackburn told them, could be the thread that unraveled the fabric of the whole bust. While her brother Donnie would be paroling out soon, taking on McEachern now could be the last best chance to get her younger siblings, Kizzie and Creamy, out of the pen while they were still young.

Gupta was glad that Blackburn was getting back in the saddle. For her part, if she was going to convince her new bosses at the Legal Defense Fund to let her take on the Tulia cases, she had to work fast. Jason Williams, the nineteen-year-old defendant who got forty-five years in the second trial of the sting, had a habeas filing deadline of January 8, and it was already mid-November. Deadlines for the other defendants would fall one after the other in the weeks and months to come. And unless she filed an amended writ fast, the Court of Criminal Appeals was about to deny Gary Gardner's writ for Joe Moore. With over forty different case files and eight full trial transcripts, it was a lot of information to digest in a short time, and she wasn't sure if she fully understood the story.

Her ace in the hole was Tom Coleman. As a villain, he sold himself. Gupta typed up a memo summarizing Tim Hoffman's lengthy deposition of Coleman from Wafer's suit. Whatever the vagaries of his conduct in Tulia, clearly Coleman was a bad cop from central casting. It was enough for her supervisors at LDF to give Gupta the go-ahead. Gupta wrote letters to each of the defendants in prison, offering the LDF's services. She quickly received grateful responses from most of them. She fired off a notice to the CCA of her intent to amend Joe Moore's writ, just days before it was to be denied by the court. On January 7, she sent Jason Williams's habeas writ to the court. Drawing on the highlights of Gardner's research, the writ was a hastily assembled assault on Terry McEachern, alleging prosecutorial misconduct. It included a blow-by-blow reconstruction of Tom Coleman's background, documenting what the state knew or should have known about their star witness. Gupta focused particular attention on the Cochran County charge, relying on a key admission she found in Tim Hoffman's deposition of Sheriff Stewart. Though McEachern had previously insisted he didn't learn of Coleman's arrest until it came out in the courtroom, Stewart testified that he had told McEachern about it even before the cases went to the grand jury. If that was true, it was a clear Brady violation.

Gupta returned to Tulia the second week in January. She met with Alan Bean, who had been corresponding with many of the incarcerated defendants and had spent a good deal of time with their families. People were losing hope, Bean told her. Following the publicity, lawyers and activists came out of the woodwork to talk to them about the injustice of the sting, but nobody had filed a single piece of paper to help get their loved ones out of prison. Bean encouraged Gupta to talk to the family of Freddie Brookins Jr., whose parents, Fred Sr. and Patty, were active in the Friends of Justice.

As soon as she stepped into the Brookins' living room, Gupta felt good about the family. There were family photos everywhere she looked. She could hear grandkids chirping away happily down the hall, and occasionally a little boy tottered into the room to whisper something to Patty, a soft-spoken woman with a round face and a hint of Cherokee in her features. In his ball cap, work boots, and snug blue jeans, Fred Sr. seemed to exude a quiet, salt-of-the-earth confidence. In a slow and measured pace, his voice full of regret, he told the story of how he counseled his son not to take the plea bargain McEachern offered. Patty, who said very little, began softly crying as Fred described their son's sentencing. If Freddie hadn't taken his father's advice, he might have been paroled home already. Instead, he had another year at least before he was even eligible. To make matters worse, he had recently been moved from a unit in Brownfield, only an hour or so away from Tulia, to a unit in east Texas, on the other side of the state. After visiting him on a weekly basis for the past two years, they had not been able to see their son in over a month, and Gupta could see that it was killing them.

It was the saddest story Gupta had heard so far. And Fred Sr. told it with such earnestness that she herself was on the verge of tears. He was obviously angry, but he was not bitter—he kept emphasizing that the people of Tulia were good people, and he had always thought of Larry Stewart as a Christian man. In the back of her mind, Gupta began thinking of Fred Sr. as a potential spokesperson for the defendants. After an hour of visiting with Gupta, they were ready to turn their son's case over to her.

Donnie Smith made it back to Tulia that same week. He had been paroled after serving thirty months of his twelve-and-a-half-year sentence. Donnie had done his time at a unit in Colorado City, about 100 miles southeast of Lubbock. It was not known as a tough unit, and Donnie kept to himself for the most part and did his time quietly. Though he was just three hours from Tulia, Donnie received few visitors and little mail, aside from the occasional note from his mother or update from Alan Bean. Donnie had been curious about prison life ever since his older brother Cecil was sent away. "I learned a lot about how to make do with what you had," he said, like how to light a cigarette using a 220-volt outlet and a lead pencil or how to make coffee without a coffee pot. Toward the end of his stay, he attended a "coping skills" class for former drug addicts, which was supposed to teach him how to deal with the pressures of family life and how to apply for and keep a job.

There was no party for Donnie when he got home to Tulia, as his friends had promised him. He was completely broke aside from the $200 the state gives all parolees. He owed several thousand dollars in back child support, which continued to accrue every month while he was in prison. A cousin told him of a job opening with the city, and he went to the unemployment office to pick up an application. Two women behind the counter, both city employees, looked him over. "We're not hiring," they said in unison. He was later told that the city and county had a policy of not hiring applicants with criminal records. Out of frustration, he took a stack of applications and gave one to every friend he knew who had been busted.

By the end of February he had found a place to rent in Tulia and had gotten on at Excel. At $6.25 an hour, Excel paid more than he ever made in Tulia. He bought a used Honda and tried to concentrate on paying his bills and staying clean. After a few weeks, however, he began to see why turnover was so high at the plant. He was a boxer on the rib line, where his job was to catch thirty-five-pound cuts of ribs as they came down a conveyor line and toss them into cardboard boxes. The boxing station was designed for two employees, but Donnie always seemed to work alone. The pace of the work—grabbing the meat and hefting it into one of four different types of boxes depending on the cut—was wearing on his joints. Boxing was one of the lowest-paid, most menial jobs at the plant. Donnie was the only person on the line who spoke English, and the other workers shunned him. "You know why you have this shit job, don't you?" his supervisor, who was also Hispanic, told him one day. "It's because you're not Mexican." Donnie wanted to fight, but fighting would have cost him more than his job. He was a parolee, and people on parole can't get into fights.

Donnie still dreamed of his days as a sports hero. Not long after he got home, he went to eat at Tulia's best restaurant, the El Camino Dining Room. He hadn't been there since he was ten years old, when his baseball coach used to take the team out to eat after every victory. Donnie still looked hopefully for his team picture in the foyer, even though twenty-two years had passed. It all seemed fresh to him; he remembered every win, every home run, every touchdown. He still agonized over his failures too, like the punt he muffed that cost the Tulia High football team a crucial game. He still worried that everybody in Tulia remembered him for that one play, forgetting all the games he had won for that team and so many others. He thought he recognized the girl behind the cash register, but then he realized it was her younger sister. "You look just like her," Donnie said in his friendly way. "How's she doin'?" The girl, who was white and in her teens, looked uncertainly at Donnie, dressed in a sleeveless white athletic shirt, his tattooed arms rippling with muscles from years of prison workouts. She seemed dubious that her sister had even known somebody like Donnie.

Donnie's idols used to be sports heroes, but now the figures he admired most were black men like his father and Fred Brookins Sr., men with steady jobs and settled family lives and the respect of their neighbors. He had never felt further from achieving that ideal than he did when he got back to Tulia. He still held out hope for reuniting with his ex-wife Lawanda—Poopie, as he called her—even though she once came after him with a baseball bat following one of their many fights. He knew he had no future at Excel. He was just hoping to last long enough to get insurance. He had a perforated eardrum from a collision on the basketball court in prison, and it gave him chronic pain. A doctor at the prison infirmary had scheduled him for an operation, but as soon as he became eligible for parole the state seemed less interested in his health, and he never got his appointment. His coping skills counselor told Donnie he had to learn to ask for help when he needed it, so that he could get on his feet and be able to help other people in need. After a few months back in Tulia, he was dreaming daily of getting out of town, even if it meant leaving his family and friends behind. "You're on your own, that's what I learned," he said.

Vanita Gupta sat in her office on a bleak New York morning in early February and stared at a stack of files several feet high. After the initial euphoria of taking on the cases, reality had begun to set in. She had three dozen more writs to write, and the clock was ticking. Earlier in the month she had done a short presentation on Tulia for the American Bar Association. She closed with an appeal for pro bono assistance. "Have you tried the law school clinics?" somebody in the audience asked. She left exasperated. She didn't need students; she was barely out of law school herself. She needed lawyers.

Most of the nation's big law firms dedicated at least a few hours a year to pro bono work. The trick was in the pitch. When most people thought of civil rights litigation, they thought of the bread-and-butter work of the movement: voting rights, job discrimination, access to housing and services. They didn't usually think of getting alleged drug offenders out of prison. Gupta blanketed the nation's legal associations with her Tulia pitch. Her boss at LDF, Elaine Jones, began talking up Tulia at every opportunity. One afternoon Gupta got a message from a Des Hogan of the law firm of Hogan & Hartson. Her heart raced. Based in Washington, D.C., Hogan & Hartson was one of the top firms in the country, with over 1,000 attorneys worldwide. Could this be the founding partner—one of the most powerful lawyers in Washington—calling her? In fact Des Hogan was no relation to the founder of Hogan & Hartson, but he was an up-and-coming young lawyer. Just thirty-two, he was heading up the company's community services division, which handled pro bono work exclusively. He had been following the Tulia story in the *New York Times* and was a longtime fan of LDF, having studied Thurgood Marshall and fellow civil rights pioneer Charles Houston as one of the few white law students at Howard University, the nation's premier black college. Gupta persuaded Hogan to get on a plane to New York the next day, where she and George Kendall were hosting a meeting to pitch Tulia as a pro bono project to several big New York law firms.

Gupta seemed worried that nobody would attend, but Hogan was not surprised to find a healthy turnout of firm lawyers present. George Kendall's name had a lot of cachet, and the LDF was considered the gold standard when it came to civil rights work. "When LDF sends out an all-hands on deck message, people respond," Hogan said later. Gupta showed the group the Kunstler Tulia video and followed it with the hardest sell she could muster. The drug war had become a war on due process, she told them, and due process was a civil right just as important as the right to vote. The criminal justice system was the new battleground in the civil rights movement, and Tulia was the front line in that fight. Hogan was impressed with Gupta's presentation. She was passionate, but she also had incredible poise and confidence for a young attorney. She seemed unintimidated in the presence of Kendall and the older, more experienced firm lawyers.

In the weeks that followed, both Hogan & Hartson and Wilmer,

Cutler & Pickering, another prestigious firm based in D.C., agreed to work pro bono for the first four defendants whose writ deadlines were upcoming: Joe Moore, Chris Jackson, Jason Williams, and Freddie Brookins Jr. Gupta had her team. Now she needed a strategy.

Back in Tulia, things were not going well with Tonya White's case. The same team Blackburn assembled for Billy Wafer's civil suit had been hard at work on Tonya's case for months. At first, things seemed promising. Tonya was a great client. Tall and big-boned, she had a reputation for being plainspoken, sometimes to the point of rudeness, but she was also known as a responsible and reliable person. Unlike Billy Wafer, she did not have a history of drug use, and she had never been convicted of a felony. Blackburn believed her story from the start. He arranged for a polygraph, which Tonya passed easily.

Yet there were problems with the case, first and foremost with Tonya's alibi. Although Tonya visited her family in Tulia from time to time, she was positive she had been at home in Oklahoma City on the day of the alleged drug deal. Unfortunately she had little evidence to support her alibi. Like most of her codefendants, Tonya lived a remarkably record-free existence. She did not have any credit cards or bank accounts. She paid for almost everything, including her rent, with cash or money orders. Phone records showed that calls were made both to and from her Oklahoma City house around the time Coleman said she was in Tulia. Tonya lived alone, yet the records did not definitively prove that she had been at home. Blackburn managed to wrangle three pretrial hearings, but Judge Self presided over them with his customary skepticism. None of the hearings had produced much, and Self's signals about the admissibility of the theft charge and the background evidence collected by the team did not bode well for Tonya's chances at trial. Coleman, meanwhile, had paid an attorney to send letters to his old colleagues in Fort Stockton and Morton, threatening them with legal action if they continued to denigrate his reputation.

As the weeks wore down toward the trial date, a conflict that had been brewing for months came to a head. Blackburn had never hidden the fact that he thought of Tonya's case as a means to an end. Tulia, he believed, was going to be won or lost in the political arena, and this case, like Wafer's civil suit, was a way to keep the controversy in the national spotlight. Media attention had lately shifted from Tulia to a major police scandal in Dallas: a pair of crooked Dallas police department narcs had been caught in a scam in which they set up bogus cocaine busts in order to cash in on huge informant's fees. It seemed that half of all the cocaine seized in Dallas in 2001 was actually powdered gypsum, better known as Sheetrock. Dozens of defendants, mostly Mexican immigrants, were exonerated. If they were going to draw the nation's attention back to Tulia, they had to keep the pressure on the authorities in whatever way they could and hope for a break.

Yet, as attorneys, they also had a responsibility to their client. Indeed, they had all taken an oath before the Texas bar to put their client's interests above every other consideration. As the trial date grew closer, Chris Hoffman found himself emerging as the spokesperson for Tonya's interests. Hoffman, who was almost ten years younger than Blackburn and had little experience in criminal law, was beginning to have misgivings about Blackburn's strategy. If McEachern refused to back down, as he had shown no hint of doing thus far, Tonya would be tried in front of a Swisher County jury on essentially the same set of facts that her three siblings had been tried on. If that happened, there was every reason to believe that she would wind up in prison as well. Blackburn and McEachern were playing a game of brinksmanship that could cost an innocent woman twenty years in the pen.

Strictly speaking, the team was following Tonya's wishes. Both she and her mother, Mattie, had insisted that no deals be made. But Hoffman began to worry that Tonya did not have a realistic appreciation of her chances in court. Blackburn was a good trial lawyer, and the team had done a great deal more work on behalf of their client than any prior Tulia defendant had received, but in the end it still came down to a swearing match between Tonya and Coleman. Hoffman didn't understand how Mattie could be present for the travesty of her son Kareem's trial and still believe her daughter would get a fair shake in Swisher County. He made his last stand in a meeting at Blackburn's office in late March. It was time to ask McEachern for a deal, he told Blackburn. They had made their best effort, but it was a game that couldn't be won. Still, they had the polygraph and the phone records—they might be able to get McEachern to agree to probation. It would be a symbolic win for the prosecution, and another major setback for Blackburn's team, but at least Tonya could resume her life. If any of Mattie's kids could successfully complete a probation sentence without violating, it was Tonya.

But Blackburn was adamant: no deal of any kind. After the way the Wafer suit flamed out, losing this case would be a devastating blow. Although he had been cooperating with Gupta over the preceding months, privately he had little faith that her habeas plan would ever be successful. He was ready to make his last stand on Tonya's case, whatever the consequences. The meeting broke down into a shouting match, and Hoffman stormed out. In the days that followed he made a desperate attempt to lobby everyone he could think of to sway Blackburn. He called Gupta in New York, virtually in a panic. Gupta booked a flight to Amarillo for Tonya's court date, to provide moral support more than anything else.

In early April, Des Hogan made his first trip to Texas. In a series of conference calls over the preceding month, a division of labor had been established. Gupta and the LDF would officially represent Freddie Brookins Jr. and Jason Williams. Wilmer, Cutler & Pickering would write Joe Moore's writ, and Hogan & Hartson would take on Chris Jackson, who was being held at a unit ninety miles northeast of Austin. Hogan, the son of a former Catholic priest, was born and raised in Pittsburgh. His father, who left the priesthood to get married, was a staunch advocate for social justice at a time when the civil rights movement was the issue of the day. ("God and Thurgood Marshall and William Brennan were the three most important people in our house," Hogan recalled.) Hogan was tall and solidly built, with thick brown hair and watery brown eyes. He looked several years older than he was. As the head of the firm's community services division, he had been given the hard sell countless times by activists working on behalf of any number of unjustly incarcerated defendants. Once he reviewed the case file and met the defendant, however, he often found that their stories were not as compelling as advertised.

Over the course of a three-hour conversation with Jackson, a short, wiry young man with bags under his eyes, Hogan found that his new client's story held up well. Jackson, who lived about two hours away from Tulia in Pampa, had come to town in the summer of 1998 to attend a relative's funeral. Under Kareem White's urging, he decided to stick around for the summer and play softball for the Lobos. It turned out to be a fateful decision. Jackson did not claim to be an angel—he had several convictions on his record—but Hogan came away convinced that this time around Jackson had been railroaded. Jackson readily agreed to allow Hogan & Hartson to take over his case. Hogan was struck, however, by how little faith Jackson expressed in Hogan's ability to do anything for him. Hogan had done his share of prison interviews, and generally speaking his clients were happy to have anybody take an interest in their cases after their appeals ran out, particularly when they had a sentence as long as Jackson, who was serving twenty years. Jackson's original trial counsel,

Angela French, had been perhaps the worst of the court-appointed attorneys, and Jackson seemed to have given up on lawyers in general. After almost three years in prison, Jackson struck Hogan as a young man in a state of complete despair.

The next day Hogan caught a flight to Amarillo and drove to Tulia, where Gupta had set up a community meeting at Mattie White's house to discuss their progress on the cases. Hogan sat quietly as Gupta began to explain how the writ process was the first step in getting their loved ones out of prison. There were perhaps twenty people present. Though he did not speak except to introduce himself, Hogan privately hoped that none of them considered him the cavalry riding in to save the day. He certainly did not feel that way; in fact he felt they had just begun what would likely be a long, uphill battle to win new trials for the first four clients they were representing, much less the others whose cases they had not yet examined. It would be a long time before they even began to work on the cases of any of Mattie's kids. Yet Mattie and the other parents clearly believed in Gupta. They seemed star-struck by her air of confidence. Hogan himself was amazed at her poise, considering that she was less than a year out of law school. She somehow managed to win over both Blackburn and his team in Amarillo and Alan Bean and Gary Gardner's crew in Tulia. In a few months, she had planted herself squarely in the middle of a fight that had been going on for years. Hogan hoped for everybody's sake that she wasn't in over her head.

That afternoon, he drove to Plainview to meet with Paul Holloway. Hogan was impressed by the work that Holloway had done on behalf of his clients. Yet he was taken aback at how fatalistic Holloway seemed about the entire situation. Standing up for his clients had almost ruined him. When McEachern guessed, correctly, that Holloway supplied much of the damaging information in the original *Texas Observer* article about the busts, he had retaliated by refusing to give plea offers to any of Holloway's clients. Holloway earned a large part of his living from court appointments, but now he felt compelled to stop taking them. The whole game in indigent defense is to get your client as good an offer as possible from the state—if Holloway couldn't get them any deals whatsoever, then how could he represent them? Hogan was appalled. The first time he read about Tulia in the *Times*, he knew the legal system had failed in the Texas panhandle. Not until that moment in Holloway's office, however, did he fully realize how badly it was broken.

In addition, Holloway publicly criticized Judge Self, which did nothing to improve his standing at the courthouse. Recently Judge Miller, the other local judge, had announced his retirement, and one of McEachern's assistants was running to replace him. The prospect of a McEachern henchman becoming the only alternative to Judge Self was so depressing to Holloway that he was considering running for the vacant judgeship himself, quixotic though that idea may have been. A ninety-year-old veteran of Franklin Roosevelt's campaigns had volunteered to be his campaign manager. What Holloway really needed, Hogan thought, was not a campaign manager but a therapist.

Lately, Holloway said, even Jeff Blackburn had been beating up on him for his decision to share what he discovered about Coleman with Judge Self ahead of trial. Two years later Holloway was still agonizing over that decision. "I did everything I knew how to do," Holloway told Hogan. "And now I wonder if anything I did was worth doing."

CHAPTER FIFTEEN

The Tide Turns

Two weeks before Tonya White's trial date, Mattie met with Virginia Cave in Blackburn's office to discuss the case. Tonya, who was now living in Shreveport, Louisiana, had not yet made the drive up to Tulia, but she was still dead set on going to trial. She maintained an almost uncanny certainty that she would prevail, so much so that she made no provision for the very real chance that she would be in prison by the end of the month. The mood in Blackburn's office was not quite so sanguine. They desperately needed some way to bolster Tonya's alibi: a friend, a coworker, a visitor, anybody who could say he saw her in Oklahoma City on the afternoon of October 9, 1998.

Virginia, who was in her mid-thirties, was Blackburn's indefatigable scheduler and receptionist and had come to know Tonya's case forward and backward over the preceding six months. Two and a half years had passed since the day of the alleged incident, but Virginia pressed Mattie to come up with some detail they had missed about that day. Mattie mentioned that Tonya had missed some work that fall because she had gotten hurt. Virginia already knew that Tonya had been out of work at the time. It was bad luck for the defense because Coleman claimed he bought the cocaine from Tonya on a weekday afternoon, and Tonya had no timecard to prove otherwise. She had injured her back while moving an invalid patient at the hospital, Mattie recalled. Virginia perked up. Nobody had ever said that Tonya's injury was work related. "Did she get worker's comp?" Virginia asked. Mattie wasn't certain, but she thought Tonya may have gotten some money. Worker's comp usually paid weekly checks, and October 9 was a Friday—maybe Tonya had cashed a check somewhere that kept records. It was worth a try. Mattie promised to ask Tonya about it that afternoon.

A few hours later, Mattie called back and reported that Tonya did in fact have a checking account that fall at a Bank of America branch in Oklahoma City. She didn't keep it open very long and then forgot about it. Virginia immediately called the branch, and after getting Tonya to sign and fax a release, convinced a woman at the bank to cull through the records while she waited on the line. "Did you say October 9?" the woman asked. Virginia held her breath. "Yes, we have a record for that day," she said. The bank had deposited a worker's compensation check for $168 into Tonya's account. That in itself did not prove Tonya was actually present at the bank that day—but something else did. Tonya asked for eight dollars back in cash, which required her to sign a withdrawal slip. The bank had stamped it with the time and date: October 9, 1998, 11:13 A.M. Coleman had her in Tulia, roughly 275 miles away, at 10:15 A.M. Tonya had her alibi.

Gupta was out of her office until late that afternoon. When she checked her messages, she found that Blackburn had called her five times that day. She was tired and in no mood for another crisis, but she called him back anyway. Blackburn told her to sit down. After the call she ran through the halls of the Legal Defense Fund offices, screaming with excitement.

Blackburn's relationship with Terry McEachern had deteriorated to the point where the two could not be in the same room together, so

Chris Hoffman volunteered to drive to Tulia to tell McEachern what they had found. Hoffman met McEachern in the district attorney's office on the second floor of the courthouse. The office was small and sparsely decorated, as though McEachern spent as little time as possible there. "What've you got?" McEachern asked. Hoffman pulled out the photocopy of the cashed check and handed it across the desk. McEachern examined it for a moment. The time and date stamp clearly showed that Tonya was in Oklahoma City at or near the time of the alleged buy, as she claimed. If McEachern was taken aback, he did not show it. Hoffman next pulled out the phone records and the polygraph report. "I'm showing you all of this as a favor," he told McEachern. "You can't win."

McEachern picked up his phone and dialed Sheriff Stewart. To Hoffman's surprise, McEachern did not ask him to step outside, so he kept his seat and listened raptly as McEachern explained the significance of the new evidence to the sheriff. Hoffman could only hear one side of the conversation, but from McEachern's responses Stewart seemed to be asking whether the bank record was admissible in court. McEachern assured him that it most likely would be. Hoffman did his best to keep his poker face, but his disgust with Stewart was growing by the second. Here was irrefutable evidence that Coleman had fingered an innocent person, and Stewart was still trying to salvage the case. Now it began to sink in: these guys were never going to give up on Coleman. They were in too deep.

Five minutes later McEachern hung up. "I'll give her probation," he said. No deals, Hoffman replied. No probation, no deferred adjudication. It had to be outright dismissal or trial. McEachern chewed it over. He picked up the polygraph report again and examined it more closely. After a few moments he announced that he hadn't heard of the operator who conducted the test. He would have to check him out. Hoffman felt McEachern was stalling now, grasping at straws. He was going to walk out of here with a dismissal, he knew it.

McEachern called his own polygraph operator in Plainview, who vouched for the reputation of Hoffman's operator, as Hoffman figured he would. McEachern was out of ammo. "All right," he said.

In mid-June, Gupta flew to east Texas to visit Freddie Brookins Jr. Freddie was housed at the Terrell unit in Livingston, a small town not far from Huntsville, where the state's prison system was headquartered. A maximum security wing of the Terrell unit had recently become the new home of the state's 400 or so condemned prisoners, following an escape on Thanksgiving Day of 1998 from the old death row in Huntsville. (The execution chamber itself remained in Huntsville.) Even before it hosted death row, Terrell was notorious. It was considered one of the most violent, gang-infested units in Texas.

The problem wasn't just the inmates. In the late 1990s, driven in part by low guard pay and a booming economy, Texas prisons were suffering from a systemwide manpower shortage. Newly hired correctional officers, or bosses as they were called in Texas, started at just $19,000, and the turnover rate was staggeringly high. Desperate to fill staffing gaps as high as 10 percent at individual units, the agency began accepting virtually anyone who applied. All an applicant needed was a GED or a high school diploma. There were no height or weight requirements, and the minimum age was eighteen. Most welfare offices refer clients to day labor sites; at the food stamp office in Huntsville, welfare applicants are routinely given Texas Department of Criminal Justice (TDCJ) applications to fill out.

Recruits received just four weeks of training, or 160 hours, which ranked well below the national average. In theory, Texas correctional officers (COs) then received two weeks of on-the-job training. But many units were so shorthanded that they immediately stuck "new boots" in the chow hall, or some other low-responsibility task, rather than have them shadow working officers. Youth and inexperience were widely blamed for the dramatic increase in violent encounters between officers and inmates in the system. One of the most egregious incidents of guard brutality took place at the Terrell unit in October 1994, following a free-for-all brawl between inmates and officers. Over a dozen officers visited the cells of inmates involved and delivered retaliatory beatings, which resulted in the death of one inmate. Two officers were charged with murder.

At Brownfield, the panhandle unit he was first assigned to, Freddie adapted to life fairly well. He was beaten by three fellow inmates in the shower, though in other fights he gave as good as he got. One of his cell mates had hepatitis, and another had fried his brain by smoking formaldehyde-laced pot. But he learned to make do. Terrell was different, though. The place just seemed meaner. Right off the bat, he got on the wrong side of a boss who insisted on referring to black inmates as monkeys. "I'd appreciate it if you wouldn't call me that," Freddie told him one day. "And I told you to get your monkey ass in line," the boss shouted at him.

Freddie noticed that inmates from smaller towns like him tended to gravitate toward one another. It wasn't hard to tell which guys were from inner city Dallas and Houston. They would fight one another at the slightest provocation. Life at Terrell also included another big city phenomenon—a small population of black Muslims who met regularly. One afternoon Freddie was approached by a member and invited to attend a meeting. "It's black history month," the man said. "Why don't you come down here and try to get you some knowledge?" Freddie had run into the man on the unit before—he was from Lubbock—and he seemed like a fairly level-headed, likable person. Freddie reluctantly agreed to attend.

"Now I know a lot of your parents and grandparents have this *white* man up on the wall," the first speaker began. It took Freddie a moment to realize that he was referring to Jesus Christ. Christianity was the white man's way of keeping black people down, the man went on. Freddie had never heard anything like that before. It felt like he was at a KKK meeting, only with black people in charge. After ten more minutes in the same vein, Freddie decided he'd had enough. When he got up to leave, one of the Muslims moved to stop him.

"Oh, no brother, where you goin'? You can't leave from here," he said.

"Like hell I cain't," Freddie replied. "I'm not racist, man. I ain't gonna be up in here with y'all."

"But, brother you gotta understand—" the man began, but Freddie cut him off. "Where you comin' from, it ain't shit to understand," he said. And then he walked back to his station.

It wasn't just the Muslims who were obsessed with race. If life in Tulia was about race, prison was Tulia times ten. Among the inmates a kind of self-segregation ruled in every aspect of daily life: in the chow hall, the workout room, on work details, everywhere. The bosses accepted it as normal. Though he mostly kept to himself, Freddie would talk to whomever he pleased, and that made him unusual. He met a Hispanic inmate who was an expert tattoo artist. Freddie was fascinated by the intricacies of the craft—how the artist coated a sheet of paper with baby oil and held it over a candle flame, carefully scraping away the soot to be distilled into ink. He did some work on Freddie and the two became friends. Even more unusual was his willingness to associate with white inmates. Whites were the minority at Terrell, as they were at most Texas prisons. Some black inmates seemed to revel in the reversal of fortune this upside-down caste system brought them. Extortion of young white inmates—most often for cigarettes or commissary items—was a common practice. On more than one occasion, Freddie found himself intervening on behalf of a weaker white inmate.

"Why are you takin' up for these little white dudes, man?" one of the tormentors asked Freddie.

"Hell, why ya'll messin' with him?" Freddie replied. "He ain't done nothing to you."

"That's what he here for," the man said.

One afternoon a particularly hapless young white inmate refused to leave his cell. Freddie knew the kid was being leaned on daily by a group of black inmates. Desperate for protection, he was trying to get a disciplinary case and a short term in solitary, where his tormentors couldn't reach him. A five-man team of bosses geared up for a "cell extraction," an almost daily ritual at Terrell, and one of the most potentially violent. Freddie heard the kid pleading with the team, explaining why he wouldn't come out. It didn't help. As they were trained to do, the bosses went in gangbusters. They shot gas into the cell, then charged in and fell on the young man. Fully suited in gas masks and riot gear, the bosses could not be hurt. The same was not true for the inmate. They hog-tied him and dragged him screaming by his wrists out of his cell and down a flight of stairs. As Freddie and a half dozen other inmates looked on, the kid's shoulder broke with an audible pop.

Gupta met with Freddie in a four-by-eight cubicle with a solid Plexiglas window between them. They had to communicate through a pair of black telephones hanging from the wall. Gupta brought along a colleague from the Legal Defense Fund to shoot video footage of Freddie. After a few minutes of awkward introductions, it dawned on Gupta that Freddie assumed the photographer, who was perhaps twenty years older and six inches taller than she, was his attorney, not Gupta. Freddie was, if anything, even more polite than his father, but there was no mistaking the look of concern that crossed his face when Gupta explained that she was the one representing him.

If Freddie was expecting someone else, Gupta was also slightly perplexed by Freddie, at least at first. She expected somebody angry, but he was so quiet. He almost never raised his voice, and his expressionless face had such a flat affect that it was hard to guess what he was thinking. Jason Williams was the only other defendant Gupta had visited in prison so far, and though Freddie was just a few years older, she was struck by how much more mature he was than Jason. Freddie seemed to have done a lot of thinking about the meaning of what had happened to him.

Eventually Gupta was able to draw him out somewhat. He was bitter about the way his trial had gone, and Gupta understood why after reading his file. Freddie's attorney, Mike Hrin, had done very little investigating and had filed no pretrial motions. Still, there hadn't been much for Hrin to work with. Freddie told her about his alibi witness, the cousin who failed to show for him. Gupta promised to try to track him down.

When it was almost time to go, Gupta asked Freddie if he wanted to send a short video message home to Tulia. They shot a few minutes of Freddie telling his family that he loved them and thought of them every day. After the camera was turned off, Freddie finally lost his composure, and his eyes filled with tears.

Randy Credico spent the summer trying to lure national reporters back to Tulia, using the *New York Times* story on Tonya White's exoneration as his bait. In July, he landed his biggest catch ever: Bob Herbert agreed to come to Tulia. Herbert was one of the *New York Times'* biggest stars. He wrote a twice-a-week column on the op-ed page, the most widely read page in the most important newspaper in the world. Congressmen, Cabinet members, lobbyists, activists—anybody who needed to get a message out to America—waited in line to deliver hot tidbits to *Times* columnists in the hopes of getting their angle in front of millions of readers. Credico had been lobbying Herbert for months, inundating him with information about what had become his twin causes, New York's Rockefeller drug laws and the scandal in Tulia. Herbert didn't have time to sift through all of it. "I just need my 700 words," he told Randy.

When he finally bit on Tulia, however, he realized that 700 words wouldn't tell half of the story. In Tulia, Herbert spent a day with Alphonso Vaughn of the Amarillo NAACP, who took him to meet with Mattie White and Fred Brookins. His first column, dated July 29, 2002, and titled "Kafka in Tulia," was a huge hit, reaching number

1 on the paper's website tally of most e-mailed stories. Suddenly Tulia was the talk of New York. But Herbert wasn't done. Over the next month Herbert filed four more columns on Tulia, each more polemical than the last. He had tapped into the defendants' frustration: almost two years had passed since the story had first broken nationally, and yet nothing had been done. The district attorney and the sheriff were still in power, Coleman had never been called to task, and thirteen people were still locked up, some with no parole date in sight.

Herbert's columns ignited a second media frenzy in Tulia, this one even more furious than the first. *People* magazine did a lengthy profile of Mattie White and her family. Columnists and reporters all over the nation filed "Tulia, Two Years Later" stories. The popular cable channel Court TV began shooting what would become an hour-long special. Talk began to swirl about a made-for-TV movie, starring Alfre Woodard as Mattie White. Bill O'Reilly, the conservative TV host, became interested in the case and was surprisingly sympathetic. Blackburn began appearing on the show with some frequency, to his considerable delight. Most popular with the defendants' families was a BBC report by an avuncular English correspondent named Tom Mangold, which featured a lengthy interview with Tom Coleman himself. Ignoring the advice of his attorney, Coleman talked to Mangold for hours, answering questions about the operation with his peculiar blend of bluster and evasion. He did not come off well.

The new publicity paid dividends. In September, Gupta got a call from John Conyers, the veteran liberal congressman from Detroit. "Vanita," he told her, "I'm your new best friend. Tell me what I can do for you." Gupta was stunned. Six months ago she had been begging the bar association for assistance on a case few people seemed to remember; now a congressman was volunteering his help. By the time she hung up, Conyers had offered to call for congressional hearings on the case.

In Texas, meanwhile, Tulia threatened to become an issue in a

U.S. Senate race. John Cornyn, the Texas attorney general, was running against former Dallas mayor Ron Kirk to fill a rare empty seat in the Senate. As attorney general, Cornyn had carefully avoided the Tulia issue, despite calls for his office to investigate. It was an understandably sore spot for Cornyn. As the AG, he was nominally the top law enforcement officer in Texas, and Tulia happened on his watch. There was also the unfortunate fact that Cornyn posed for a photo with Coleman when the narc won the Officer of the Year Award. In the wake of the latest round of publicity, a helpful soul at the governor's office had discreetly removed the photo of Cornyn and Coleman from the website of the Texas Narcotics Control Program (TNCP).

Despite overtures from the ACLU and other organizations, the Kirk campaign was uninterested in making an issue of Tulia. As the first black mayor of Dallas, Kirk was one of the best-known black politicians in Texas. He was a corporate attorney by trade, and he was running a centrist campaign with a message of moderation and inclusiveness. Kirk had made some tentative inquiries into the issue early in the campaign, and state officials had contacted their man in Tulia, Delbert Devin, head of the Swisher County Democrats, to get the lowdown on how the issue played in the panhandle. Devin had told them, in essence, that it was all horseshit. There was no issue, as far as the locals were concerned.

Things were different now, however. Tulia was front and center on the national agenda, and it wouldn't do for either of the contenders to have no position on it. Plus, the election was winding down and Kirk was losing. He was looking for any issue to gain momentum. In late September, the Kirk campaign finally called Gupta. She was more than happy to give them the whole story of Tulia, but it was the photo of Attorney General Cornyn with Coleman that Kirk's people really wanted. General Corndog, as his detractors called him, shaking hands with a scruffy, ponytailed, and now thoroughly discredited narc—the possibilities for a negative TV spot were endless.

Blackburn was the last person to see the photo. Incredibly, he briefly found himself in possession of Tom Coleman's personal scrapbook. It was shown to him by an Amarillo TV news reporter, who had convinced Coleman to lend her the book for a story she was doing about the controversy. He called Gupta, giddy with the find. Blackburn never had a sit-down conversation with Coleman, and he doubted he ever would. But flipping through the scrapbook, knowing what he knew about the man's history, was an indescribable experience. Coleman had taken up with another single mother, a woman he had met in Amarillo, and there was a photo of her son, who looked to be about eleven years old, standing next to Coleman. They were wearing identical all-black tactical outfits of the sort favored by the jump-out boys, and both were pointing what appeared to be real guns at the camera. And, of course, there was the photo of Coleman in his finest hour, receiving the Officer of the Year Award from Attorney General Cornyn.

Unfortunately Blackburn, who was vacationing in Scotland when the Kirk campaign called, had returned the scrapbook months ago, and had failed to make copies of anything in it.

As it happened, Cornyn took the issue off the table by announcing that he was opening an official investigation into the matter, almost a year to the day after he was first asked to do so by the Texas ACLU. Kirk seemed to lose interest. The long shot Democratic gubernatorial candidate, Tony Sanchez, added a stop in Tulia to his bus tour of west Texas, for no other reason, it seemed, than that the town had been in the news lately. He had nothing of substance to say about the drug sting. But at least people were talking about Tulia in Texas again, if not actually doing much about the defendants who were still in prison.

In late September, Gupta took a week off to vacation in New Mexico with her fiancé. George Kendall called one morning with news about

Jason Williams, the young defendant for whom Gupta had filed the first habeas writ. If he was interrupting her vacation, Gupta knew that he must have heard something from the Court of Criminal Appeals. If the CCA looks favorably on a writ, it sends the case back to the original trial court for additional fact-finding, which is known as a remand. If a case is remanded, the CCA sends a letter explaining its decision to the defendant's attorney. In case of a rejection, it simply sends a preprinted postcard. Williams had received a postcard. Gupta was crushed. This meant that all four defendants would likely be rejected, since the facts were basically the same in all of their cases. Kendall tried to console her. They had figured all along on losing the state habeas appeal as an inevitable step along the road to federal court. But Gupta wanted to know why. How could any court, even the notorious Texas CCA, turn its back on a set of facts like these?

Back in New York, Gupta called the court to see if she could gather any intelligence. She was on fairly good terms with the deputy clerk who was handling the paperwork for the Tulia appeals. "What did we do wrong?" Gupta asked. The clerk seemed confused. "Jason Williams *has* been remanded to the original trial court," he told her. "Didn't you get the letter?" As Gupta listened incredulously, the clerk explained that the court had only dismissed the appeal for one of Williams's four cases—the one on which he received a sentence of probation—on procedural grounds; the other three had been remanded. The letter was on the way. Gupta hung up the phone glowing. She immediately called Des Hogan and told him the news and then hung up so he could call the same clerk and ask about Chris Jackson's writ. Hogan called back minutes later—Jackson's cases had been remanded as well.

PART FIVE

CHAPTER SIXTEEN

"The Dream Team"

THE LETTERS GUPTA and Hogan received were essentially the same. The Court of Criminal Appeals had sent the cases back to Judge Self's court and ordered him to answer two questions: first, whether the convictions in the cases in question were made solely on the basis of Tom Coleman's testimony and, second, whether the state erred by not turning over evidence that the defendants were entitled to have in preparing their defense. The defendants (or applicants as they are called in habeas proceedings) would have ninety days to gather facts in support of their claims. There was no word yet on the writs filed on behalf of Freddie Brookins or Joe Moore.

Such remands were rare in Texas. Blackburn privately suspected that the renewed media attention inspired by Bob Herbert's columns had shamed the CCA justices into action. Though it generated a lot of excitement in Tulia, as well as a new round of newspaper reports, the CCA's decision was a mixed blessing for Gupta and her team. On the one hand, it signaled that the highest court in Texas was at least willing to consider the possibility that their clients were entitled to new trials. On the other hand, the team still believed that their chances of winning at the state level were very slim; the cases would still be under the jurisdiction of Judge Self, who would have the final say over what form the fact-finding would take. Self was not obligated to hold a hearing of any kind if he did not deem it necessary. He could simply order the parties involved to review the testimony and evidence from the original trials and summarize the arguments for him in written briefs. Viewed from that perspective, the remands might only slow the team's progress toward federal court, where they felt their best chance for relief lay. Worse, once they arrived in federal court, the new judge would be required to give careful consideration to any findings of fact produced by the proceeding in Self's court. That too could wind up working against the team.

If the proceeding was going to happen in Self's court, however, Gupta was determined to make the best of it. She organized a series of conference calls with the teams from Hogan & Hartson and Wilmer, Cutler to hash out a strategy. Blackburn, despite his initial skepticism about the habeas plan, now joined the effort full-time. He had been working on Tulia for two years now, and he had no intention of being squeezed out by a bunch of out-of-town firm attorneys who had never set foot in a Texas courtroom. They planned to demand a full hearing, with a fresh examination of as many key witnesses as Self would allow. The "evidentiary record" from the trials of Jason Williams and Chris Jackson was exceedingly slim—their attorneys had done little if any investigating and found out nothing of importance about Coleman. Their only hope of getting a good result from the remands was to get Coleman, Stewart, and McEachern on the stand and under oath.

In the days following the remand orders, Gupta called Judge Self's office several times, hoping to get a sense of how he wanted to handle the proceedings. She left messages with Self's clerk, but the judge refused to call her back. Instead, he gave an interview to the *Amarillo Globe News*, in which he confirmed Gupta's worst fears. Self seemed to downplay the importance of the CCA's rare remand. He told the reporter that he did not believe a new hearing was in order; the matter could be settled with a "paper hearing," he said, in which each side submitted briefs summarizing their arguments.

Gupta was livid. In the weeks that followed, she filed motion after motion, seeking permission to depose witnesses, set guidelines for discovery, and, finally, to force Self to set a date for a real hearing. Still, nothing but silence from the judge. McEachern did not bother to respond to any of the team's motions either. He did not seem to be taking the habeas proceeding seriously. Finally, Self's clerk forwarded to Gupta a copy of an affidavit that McEachern had recently filed with the court. McEachern was now admitting that Sheriff Stewart had told him about Coleman's arrest just prior to the grand jury's indictment of the Tulia defendants, contradicting his earlier insistence that he had not known about the charges until several trials had already taken place. That would certainly help the team establish their Brady argument. But McEachern was now also claiming, among other things, that Tonya White's bank record was not definitive evidence of her innocence after all, that Billy Wafer had also failed to prove his innocence, and that Romona Strickland had flunked a polygraph test. The entire six-page affidavit was an incredible exercise in revisionist history, yet without the opportunity to cross-examine McEachern, there was no way to punch holes in his claims.

Gupta became increasingly convinced that a hearing—paper or otherwise—in front of Self would be pointless. He had already ruled several times on the admissibility of evidence about Coleman's background. He was even more unlikely to change his mind now that his judgment had come under national scrutiny, which was growing more intense by the day. Plus, Self was in the final weeks of a reelection campaign, running against a Plainview defense attorney who had been critical of the Tulia bust. Finding for the applicants now would be like admitting to the voters that he had made a mistake. He was heavily invested in preserving those convictions, and no amount of lawyering was going to overcome that.

As Gupta saw it, the answer was to force Self's recusal from the cases. She organized a conference call with Jeff Blackburn and Des Hogan, who had recently added two members of the firm to his team: Jenn Klar, a young woman fresh out of law school, and Mitch Zamoff, a former federal prosecutor in his mid-thirties with a great deal of courtroom experience. Everyone agreed that filing a motion to recuse Self would be a major gamble. If they took a shot at Self and missed, they would essentially be throwing themselves on his mercy in the proceeding that followed. Gupta had read all of the trial transcripts, and she knew how much McEachern relied on Self at trial. Now she lobbied hard: he had to go, or all their preparation for the hearing would be a waste of time. Hogan asked Jenn Klar to begin work on a potential motion, and Gupta agreed to begin researching the history of recusal case law in Texas. Of course, even if they did succeed in getting Self recused, there was no telling who would replace him. This was a huge decision, and nobody seemed ready to pull the trigger.

To make matters worse, Gupta's superiors at LDF were beginning to second-guess her judgment. Since Bob Herbert's columns had made Tulia a national cause célèbre, the senior attorneys had become much more interested in the case. Gupta had only been working at LDF for a little over a year, and now, after months of toiling in anonymity, she was suddenly at the helm of the organization's most important case. Gupta, who had been giving several interviews a week, was admonished to let LDF president Elaine Jones become the main contact person for the media. Her proposed recusal motion was brought up at an office-wide staff meeting, where senior attorneys discussed the pros and cons of the approach. Her closest adviser, George Kendall, remained hands-off, but everyone was waiting to see what her next move would be; any mistake she made was going to be parsed by the entire office. On November 6, Gupta received word that the Court of Criminal Appeals had remanded the case of Freddie Brookins Jr. as well. Three lives were now hanging in the balance.

With the recusal issue still undecided, Des Hogan returned to the panhandle in early November. He brought Jenn Klar with him, along with two other young Hogan & Hartson attorneys who had volunteered to work on the case, Tara Hammons and Adam Levin. The team had resolved to collect as many affidavits as possible from former associates of Coleman's. Their idea was to demonstrate what their clients' original trial counsels could have learned about Coleman, had McEachern and Stewart not conspired to conceal Coleman's arrest on the Cochran County charge and other information about his background. It was unclear whether or not Self would accept the affidavits as evidence, but they could prove useful if the case wound up in federal court down the road, as Hogan strongly suspected it would. After landing in Lubbock, the group split into two teams. Hogan and Tara Hammons headed west to Morton to meet with former Cochran County sheriff Ken Burke, other county officials, and some of Coleman's creditors. Jenn Klar and Adam Levin headed south for Pecos County to track down Coleman's old associates in Fort Stockton.

On the way to Morton, Hogan stopped in the small town of Levelland, about twenty miles west of Lubbock, to interview Chris Jackson's original trial attorney, Angela French. He wanted to get her files on the case and better establish what, if anything, she had learned from McEachern prior to Jackson's trial. He also had to start assembling evidence that French had provided Jackson with ineffective assistance at trial. It was a common ground for appeal, and defense attorneys were used to being asked such questions by appellate attorneys. Still, it was a delicate task, particularly in a case like this one, in which the railroading of the defendants—and the general ineffectiveness of the state's indigent defense system—had become a national story.

French had been dodging Hogan's phone calls since he first took on Jackson's case, and after he read the trial transcript, he understood why. She had not filed a single pretrial motion on Jackson's behalf, and her examinations of the state's witnesses had been short and painfully confused. French did not have a formidable reputation as a litigator. A colleague of French's told Hogan that he observed French getting strategic advice from her husband, an athletics coach, during a first-degree felony trial. Jenn Klar discovered online that a brief French had authored had once been featured in the humor section of the State Bar of Texas website. In the brief, French asked a judge to push back a trial date for one of her clients citing, among other reasons, the fact that "Counsel's dog ate all her 'decent' pairs of shoes; and counsel needs more time to purchase replacements."

Hogan and Hammons drove to French's office, which was in a small strip mall. Hogan walked in, identified himself, and asked to see French, whereupon her secretary immediately got up and closed the door to French's personal office. "She's not here," the secretary said. After an unsuccessful two-hour stakeout of French's home and office, the pair caught up with their quarry late that afternoon in the hallway of the county courthouse, where French was visiting with a client she had just plead out. Hogan stepped up and introduced himself.

"Oh, great—sorry I missed you this morning," French said. She was a shapely blond woman with pretty eyes and a coquettish manner. "Let me just finish up with my client and I'll meet you out front in a bit." Hogan and Hammons retired to the front steps of the courthouse to wait. Fifteen minutes later, Hogan sent his partner in to check on French's progress. "She's gone," Hammons reported. On a hunch, the pair hurried around to the back of the courthouse, just in time to catch French sneaking down the back steps. She reluctantly agreed to a twenty-minute meeting. What she had to say confirmed much of what Hogan suspected. Jackson's case was her first felony trial ever, and she admitted being in over her head. McEachern had told her nothing about Coleman's arrest. She felt bad about the way things had gone, and she wanted to help Chris out, she said. Hogan told her he would prepare an affidavit summarizing what she had told them, and she agreed to sign it when she received it. Hogan did not have high hopes that she would be a cooperative witness.

The next day, the pair drove up to Morton to meet with Ken Burke, the former Cochran County sheriff whom Coleman had so frequently maligned in court. Burke was now out of law enforcement, having been defeated in the last election. When Hogan reached his wife at home, she told him Burke was unavailable; he was "out plowing the back forty." Hogan figured he was getting the runaround again. It turned out, however, that Burke really was on his tractor that morning. He called Hogan back and arranged to meet him at the courthouse. "I want Jay Adams to be there too, though," Burke said. Adams was the county attorney, the man Paul Holloway had met with so long ago to collect the file on Coleman's charges. It was Adams himself who witnessed Coleman stealing the gas, but Holloway had warned Hogan not to expect much cooperation from him. His main concern seemed to be that Coleman would sue Cochran County, as he had threatened to do on many occasions since leaving Morton.

Hogan and Hammons met Burke in a room at the county courthouse. Burke was in his late seventies but very hale. He wore a big belt buckle and a cowboy hat. Hoping to get as much done as possible before Adams arrived, Hogan began asking Burke questions about Coleman as Hammons quietly removed her laptop and began typing notes. Burke explained that he hired Coleman because somebody in town knew his father and recommended him for the job. Burke didn't do much of a background check on him. Coleman proved to be a cocky, irresponsible deputy, and right off the bat Burke began having problems with him. Still, Burke felt sorry for Coleman and found himself cutting his new deputy a lot of slack, in part because Coleman seemed to view the sheriff as a father figure of sorts. That all ended after Coleman left, and Burke discovered how much money he owed all over town. Burke considered what Coleman had done in Morton to be worse than simply being irresponsible with his money; he considered it theft.

Before Burke could expound on Coleman's shortcomings, Jay Adams stalked into the room. He was a big man, and he loomed over Hogan like a high school principal trying to intimidate a freshman. In his hand was a copy of the new *Texas Monthly*, which contained a story about Tulia. He slapped it down on the desk in front of Hogan and pointed to a row of prison mug shots illustrating the story.

"Which one of these is your boy?" Adams demanded. Hogan pointed to Jackson's photo. "Is he one of the guilty ones, or is he one of the innocent ones?" Adams asked.

Hogan replied without hesitation. "I have every reason to believe what he says, and no reason to believe what Tom Coleman says," he said.

Adams didn't reply. Instead he turned to Burke and warned him that getting involved could be a major headache for the county. He insisted on reviewing any affidavit Burke filed before it was notarized. Hogan assured him that they would bring it by his office as soon as they were done.

After Adams left, Hogan interviewed Burke for two hours about Coleman's time in Morton. When the interview was done, Hammons typed up a summary of Burke's comments in affidavit form and the three walked over to Adams's office so he could review it. Among other things, Burke asserted that he had caught Coleman lying not just about his unpaid bills, but about several other subjects as well, which nicely supported the team's efforts to establish that Coleman was a habitual liar. Burke also stated that in his opinion, based on his experience with Coleman as an employee, Coleman was "incapable" of performing the undercover work he claimed to have done in Tulia. Burke's affidavit was pure gold, but it would be useless if Adams refused to sign off on it. Adams stared at the affidavit for ten minutes. It was clear he would have preferred to let sleeping dogs lie. He looked warily at Hogan and then turned to Burke. "If this is what you want to do," he finally said, "it's okay with me."

In conference calls throughout the week, the team continued to wrestle over the wisdom of the recusal motion. Gupta lay awake at night all week trying to decide what to do. She had read and reread the draft motion a million times, but they still didn't seem to have enough ammunition to force Self to act. Still at the office after 10:00 one evening, she got an e-mail from Gary Gardner. The two had been talking or e-mailing at least once a week since her first trip to Tulia. Gardner was remarkably knowledgeable about the clients and their cases, and even when he had nothing useful to contribute, he kept her spirits up.

"Go check your fax machine," Gardner wrote. Gupta heard it whirring to life even as she read Gardner's e-mail. The fax was a copy of a letter Judge Self had written to the *Tulia Herald*, published in the October 31 edition. As Self's reelection campaign ground down toward election day, Gardner, Alan Bean, and Charles Kiker had been relentlessly hounding the judge about Tulia in the letters page of the *Herald* and the Plainview paper. Gardner had submitted a particularly incendiary piece to the *Herald* in recent weeks, charging Self with deliberately suppressing admissible evidence about Coleman to protect the convictions in the sting. The editor of the *Herald* had refused to run Gardner's letter, so Gardner resubmitted it as a paid advertisement, only to have it trashed again. At the last minute, however, Kareem White's girlfriend Chandra Van Cleave, who worked at the *Herald*, had Gardner send her another copy and personally laid it in on the letters page. She had been on bad terms with her boss, a staunch supporter of the bust, since beating her own indictment in the sting, and she secretly relished Gardner's bashing of Self and McEachern.

After reading this one, Self finally had enough. "Until now, I have ignored Alan Bean's and Gary Gardner's attacks against me," Self's letter to the editor began. Gupta couldn't believe her eyes as she read on. Self stood by his rulings, he wrote, noting that the local Court of Appeals had supported his decision. The letter concluded in high dudgeon. "The truth is: my name is on the ballet [sic], not Tom Coleman's; in the 4 1/2 years I have been on the bench, I have presided over hundreds of trials, not just the trials involving Tom Coleman; and, more than 90 percent have been upheld by the Court of Appeals." Gardner, who found the letter uproariously funny, had highlighted and annotated it for Gupta with his own pithy comebacks. He loved Self's bluster and bravado—it was the reason he goaded him so relentlessly in the first place. But Gupta knew the letter was a serious matter. The judge was commenting publicly on the very matter the CCA had directed him to reconsider, and his vigorous public defense of his initial rulings bordered on an ethical breach. Gupta called Gardner and excitedly explained his unintended act of genius. Gardner laughed and laughed.

For the purposes of the recusal memo, Gupta could not have scripted Self's comments better herself. Or so she thought, until Gardner sent her another letter a couple of days later. This one was taken from an article in the *Amarillo Globe News* that appeared on November 7, a few days after Self won reelection. Of his support among Swisher County voters, Self was quoted as saying, "I think this shows that they're partly tired of all the talk about the drug bust. I think it's also that the voters in Swisher County believe their officials do their jobs properly and act within the law." Self had as much as admitted his own bias against the applicants in the habeas proceeding that was now before him. Now there was no question—it was time to roll the dice and go after Judge Self. Hogan and Gupta inserted Gardner's discoveries into the recusal motion and mailed copies to Judge Self and the Court of Criminal Appeals in Austin.

On November 14, Gupta and Hogan each got letters on Ed Self's letterhead. He was recusing himself from the cases, effective immediately, and had officially requested that a new judge be assigned to take his place. There was no explanation attached. "I don't think the defense would have ever been satisfied, regardless of what ruling I made," Self told the Amarillo paper the next day. Tulia, it seemed, had become more trouble than it was worth. Gupta called everyone she knew in Tulia with the news. It was a brand-new day for the team. The state habeas process, which had seemed like a road bump on the way to federal court, suddenly meant something. Without Self at the helm, anything was possible.

Five days later, the team got word that a semiretired judge from Dallas named Ron Chapman had been assigned to take Self's place. Blackburn seemed to think it was good news. Chapman was the last Democrat to win election to the Dallas area Court of Appeals; in fact, by the time he retired in 1999, he was the last Democrat holding a countywide office in Dallas. He tried to extend his luck with a run for Congress but was defeated, just a few weeks before getting the Tulia assignment. The secret to his longevity was his centrism: he was pro-gun and pro-death penalty, but also pro-choice. Now he mostly did professional arbitration for a living and heard an occasional case as a visiting judge. Gupta immediately began researching his published judicial opinions to get a feel for his tendencies as an appellate judge.

It was a bad turn of events for Terry McEachern. Worse still was an incident that took place a few days later. The day after Thanksgiving, McEachern was pulled over by the police near Ruidoso, New Mexico, a popular ski town a few hours drive from Tulia. He was with a woman who was not his wife, and he was drunk. After failing a field sobriety test, McEachern was taken to the station, where he declined to take a Breathalyzer test. McEachern, who had made his reputation in part on the relentless prosecution of DWI cases, told the officers that he did not trust the machines. He admitted to drinking, however, and he also told them he had taken a Valium, which a doctor had prescribed for back pain. For McEachern, the timing could not have been worse. "The Tulia prosecutor," as he had come to be known in the media, was now a national figure of sorts, and the next day the arrest was all over the wires. McEachern announced that he planned to fight the charge. Word got back to Blackburn in following weeks that McEachern was strangely paranoid about the bust. He was privately accusing Blackburn of setting him up somehow.

Blackburn had more big news. The previous fall, in Tonya White's case, he had convinced Judge Self to let him test five random samples of powdered cocaine evidence allegedly purchased by Coleman. It was the same test that Paul Holloway and Tom Hamilton had unsuccessfully sought so long ago, to support their theory that the evidence against their clients was nothing more than heavily diluted eight balls mixed by Coleman himself. Even with Self's approval, however, McEachern had managed to stall the testing all winter, until after White's bank record alibi was discovered and the case was dismissed. Now, a year later, Blackburn had finally obtained a report from the chemist, and the results were compelling. Cocaine is normally cut to somewhere in the range of 50 percent purity for sale on the street. The purity of the tested samples ranged from 3 percent to 12 percent. Doing a line of this so-called cocaine would barely numb your nose. If five random samples had all turned up bunk, Blackburn had no doubt that virtually all of the eight balls were worthless. It didn't prove beyond a doubt that Coleman had diluted the coke himself, but it certainly seemed a more plausible explanation than the alternative, which was that forty-seven different cocaine dealers had all conspired together to sell him bunk cocaine. Paul Holloway's hunch, it seemed, had been right all along.

The test results were a tremendous boost for the team, though they kept the report a secret for the time being.

By the end of November, the team still had not heard anything from Judge Chapman, though Gupta and Hogan had been calling and e-mailing him regularly. They had only thirty days left until the deadline set by the Court of Criminal Appeals for fact-finding, and they were starting to panic. Chapman seemed to be no more interested in the process than Judge Self had been. Hogan and Gupta began burying Chapman's office in paper, filing motion after motion in an attempt to make a complete record for what they anticipated would be their next step: federal court. Then, on Christmas Eve, Blackburn got a call from Chapman. He had been out of town, taking an extended break after the disappointing end to his hard-fought congressional campaign. He had long ago requested an extension of the CCA's deadline for the habeas proceeding, which he assumed everybody involved had guessed already. Instead he came home to a mountain of paper on his desk, all about the Tulia cases.

"What is the matter with these people?" he asked Blackburn, exasperated. He chatted informally with Blackburn for half an hour. He'd already read a good deal about Tulia in the press, including some things that disturbed him greatly. Before he hung up, he asked Blackburn to assure his "firm friends" that they would be getting a full hearing, with all the time they needed to examine witnesses. Chapman was just the kind of fair-minded, impartial judge they had been hoping for, and Blackburn called Gupta immediately, excited with the news. It appeared that their clients, after three-and-a-half long years of waiting, were finally going to get their day in court.

Shortly after the new year began, the team from Wilmer, Cutler & Pickering got word that Joe Moore's case was about to be remanded as well. They now joined Gupta, Blackburn, and the members of the Hogan & Hartson team in preparation for what everybody anticipated would be a joint proceeding involving four applicants: Jason Williams, Chris Jackson, Freddie Brookins Jr., and Moore. In recent months, several of the other Tulia defendants had paroled out, and the list of those still incarcerated was down to the sixteen who had received the lengthiest sentences. Gupta had recently received news from Freddie that he had made parole as well. He was due to be released sometime in June. It was a tremendous relief, particularly since Freddie's Brady case was arguably the weakest of them all, since his trial had come later than the other three applicants. But Gupta was not interested in winning parole for Freddie—she wanted him exonerated. Freddie and his family represented everything that was good about Tulia to Gupta, and at the same time everything that was hopeless. She wanted him not just to get out of prison but to make it, to succeed in life. Parole would not free him from the stigma of a felony conviction, which would make him ineligible for financial aid for college, among other restrictions. Worse, while he was on parole—which could last for over a decade—he would be at the mercy of Sheriff Stewart and McEachern, who could have him sent back to prison for violating any of a laundry list of parole requirements.

There were now over a dozen attorneys working on the cases. The Wilmer team was being led by a senior partner named Ted Killory. A tall, handsome Harvard Law graduate in his late forties, Killory looked like he played tennis with senators in Nantucket on the weekends. He spent much of his time advising wealthy individuals, and he was known as a master negotiator. Because Des Hogan's team had already done much of the legwork in the panhandle, the attorneys from Wilmer applied themselves to the legal side of the case. Led by Bill White and a young associate named Mark Oh, they began researching the case law for a massive brief outlining all of their legal arguments.

Exhaustive research and pretrial preparation was what clients paid for when they hired a top-tier law firm. Still, despite Chapman's extension, by the standards of firm attorneys there was not much time to prepare for the hearing, even with the small army of associates, legal assistants, and clerks at the team's disposal. In the weeks that followed, Jenn Klar, the young Hogan & Hartson associate, methodically examined every trial transcript and distilled vast amounts of information into a series of memos for the team. She produced the most detailed chronology yet of Coleman's law enforcement career, including a summary of everything that was known about the gas charge in Cochran County. She catalogued over two dozen examples of apparent perjury from Coleman's trial testimony and produced a ten-page memo detailing other inconsistencies in his testimony that tended to support the theory that he had fabricated cases in Tulia. She was working fourteen hours a day on the case, logging so many hours that her supervisor, looking over her time sheets, became alarmed and told her to slow down.

One afternoon in January, however, Klar came into Des Hogan's office in tears. She had been reading Kareem White's trial transcript and had just come to the account of his polygraph test, in which he admitted he had sold drugs in the past. Now she was in crisis. Bookish and polite, Klar was a self-described "suburban Virginia girl." She had never been around drugs and had never represented a criminal defendant. "Des, I think some of these people are guilty," she said.

Hogan shut the door to his office. "Jenn, some of these people were involved with drugs," he said. Many of them had prior records—Gupta had made that very clear from the first day she spoke with Hogan about the cases. And a few of the defendants, like Donnie Smith, had actually admitted to getting crack cocaine for Coleman. This fact was also no secret, though it seemed to have gotten lost in the second round of national press coverage launched by Bob Herbert's columns in the *Times*. Reporters loved stories of wrongfully convicted defendants; at the same time, deadlines and time constraints made them notoriously averse to nuance, and that was a problem with this story. Some of the Tulia cases, like Tonya White's, were obvious cases of actual innocence. But what category was Donnie

Smith in? Yes, he had admitted to making several small crack deliveries; but he had also been forced to plead guilty to much more serious powder deliveries, cases that he still insisted were bogus. He was not innocent in the sense that most people would use that word, yet he also had clearly not gotten due process of law, and that was true for virtually all of the defendants. The bottom line was that without corroboration, only Tom Coleman could say definitively which of the cases he made were real, and which were fabricated.

Hogan knew it was an issue they would have to deal with, and quite possibly very soon. Thanks in part to Bob Herbert's prodding, the FBI had kick-started a long moribund investigation of the Tulia sting and had interviewed almost all of Coleman's targets in recent months. Blackburn and Gupta had been picking up bits and pieces of what had been discussed in the interviews. It seemed that most of the defendants still maintained their innocence, but around a half dozen of them had admitted to getting crack for Coleman. What the FBI was hearing from the defendants seemed to coincide in one respect with Coleman's case reports: he claimed to have made about a dozen crack buys from six different people. Considered on their own, the crack buys (along with a few modest marijuana purchases) presented the outlines of a plausible undercover investigation in a small town like Tulia, and half a dozen arrests was probably about what Sheriff Stewart and Coleman's supervisors at the task force expected him to make. The problem, of course, was that Coleman also claimed to have bought around 100 eight balls from these six defendants, and 40 more besides. Those had always been the most suspect cases, all the more so now that Blackburn had finally confirmed that most, if not all, of the powdered cocaine was bunk. Tabulating the money Coleman spent for each of his buys in Tulia, the team calculated how much he could have stolen if each of the powder cases was bogus: around $18,000.

The team had never asked for an FBI investigation, just as it had never asked reporters to portray Tulia as a case of forty-seven choir-boys and girls arbitrarily targeted for wrongful prosecution. If an embarrassing FBI report on the case were to become public in the middle of the habeas proceedings, however, there was a good chance that reality and image were going to collide in a very ugly way, and all of their clients—not just the few who had admitted to selling crack—were going to suffer for it. Hogan could just imagine the field day that McEachern would have if he got his hands on that report. It would be all the vindication he needed in the eyes of his constituents, and it could prove very damaging in court, despite its irrelevance to the vast majority of cases Coleman filed in Tulia.

In mid-January, Judge Chapman called for a preliminary meeting of the parties in Tulia. It was the team's first face-to-face meeting with Chapman, and several crucial decisions would be made, including what types of evidence the team would be allowed to collect and present to the judge. Chapman had given no indication of how he wanted to proceed, but the team decided to go for broke. They would try to sell Chapman on giving them a full range of discovery, including the ability to take depositions from a wide range of witnesses. Common in civil suits, depositions were rare in habeas hearings, where a defense attorney was fortunate if he even got to call a witness to the stand, much less interrogate him for six hours before the hearing even started.

McEachern would surely object. It would be the first time the team traded arguments with McEachern, and Gupta wanted as much muscle and talent in the room as she could get. Des Hogan and Mitch Zamoff flew in to represent the Hogan & Hartson team, and Bill White came on behalf of Wilmer, Cutler. George Kendall, Gupta, and Blackburn rounded out the team. After countless conference calls, this was the first time Gupta met Mitch Zamoff or Bill White in person. They were both young partners in their respective firms. Zamoff, the former federal prosecutor, was tall, lean, and intense, with an angular face and clean-shaven head. He was a marathoner, and he looked the part. White, on the other hand, was a well-fed, well-paid securities lawyer. He could not run a marathon to save his life, but his investigative credentials were almost as impressive as Zamoff's—he had spent eight years in the enforcement division of the Securities and Exchange Commission and had interrogated his share of white-collar criminals. Together with Kendall, who had argued cases in front of federal appeals courts on numerous occasions, it was an experienced, formidable group.

The preliminary meeting was to take place in open court, and about a dozen spectators were in the gallery as the proceeding began, including Alan Bean, Gary Gardner, and several family members of the four applicants. Though everyone knew Gupta and Blackburn, it was the first time most of the observers had seen the other attorneys, the group some in Tulia had begun to call "the dream team." McEachern arrived with both of his assistant prosecutors, Mark Hocker, a stout young man with a crew cut, and Kelley Messer, who had carefully coiffed brown hair and a deceptively disarming smile. Charlotte Bingham, Blackburn's old nemesis from Billy Wafer's civil suit, had been retained by the county once again. If the convictions were reversed, Swisher County would probably be sued, so Bingham had an acute interest in the proceedings.

Judge Chapman entered in his black robe and took his chair at the top of the dais. He was in his early sixties, with a receding hairline and big, thoughtful eyes behind glasses. He had barely introduced himself when McEachern stood up and demanded that the courtroom be cleared. His face was red, and he was so angry that he was visibly shaking. "I'm not gonna allow this to be turned into a circus so that I can be politically assassinated," he said, waving his arm in the direction of Bean and Gardner. Chapman called all of the attorneys up to the dais, and after a brief discussion, the team agreed to move the proceeding into the judge's chambers.

Zamoff made the team's pitch for depositions. "We'll need these powers to help us narrow the range of issues involved here," Zamoff argued. In fact, the opposite was true. They planned to follow every trail they knew about, and any new ones they could find in the time Chapman allotted them. They would subpoena every person whom Hogan and his team had visited on their drive through the panhandle and turn the hearing into a blow-by-blow recreation of Tom Coleman's embarrassing history in law enforcement. They would depose all of the state's witnesses, McEachern included.

The team waited anxiously as Chapman turned to McEachern for a response. But McEachern said nothing. It suddenly dawned on Hogan that this might have been the first habeas hearing in which McEachern, in his sixteen years as a prosecutor, had ever participated. The habeas process was not taken seriously in Texas; people who were sent to prison generally didn't come back, at least not until their parole date came up. It seemed that McEachern did not know how a habeas hearing was supposed to be conducted any more than Gary Gardner did. Apparently nobody else present for the state did either.

Without a peep from McEachern, Chapman sided with the team. They could subpoena a wide range of witnesses and documents, and they could conduct depositions. "Let's just get all of the evidence into the record," Chapman said, and let the Court of Criminal Appeals decide what was what. It was a huge victory for the team.

More than anything, McEachern seemed worried about the new round of publicity the hearing would surely bring. Between Tulia and his DWI charge, it seemed every time he turned on the news his name was being trashed for one reason or another. He asked Chapman to impose a gag order from that afternoon forward—nobody from either side would be able to discuss the cases with anyone until the proceedings were complete. George Kendall stood up and gave an impassioned speech on behalf of open courtrooms, decrying "secret hearings" as unconstitutional and un-American. McEachern, never much of an orator, was overmatched. The hearing date was set for March 17, and the courtroom would be open to the public.

In mid-February, the team began receiving documents in response to their subpoenas. Garry Smith, the attorney who had represented Coleman in the Cochran County theft charge, had turned over his entire file on the case. Though his dealings with Coleman were protected to some degree by attorney-client privilege, he had been surprisingly forthcoming, even including handwritten notes he had made on the case and records of correspondence and phone calls to and from Coleman. The team also received two boxes of documents from the task force and Sheriff Stewart's office. There were stacks and stacks of incident reports filed by Coleman, a copy of the Amarillo police department employee manual, copies of Coleman's time sheets, and miscellaneous material of limited value. There was also a folder filled with mug shots. Ever since Tonya White's trial, Blackburn had been trying to obtain from Sheriff Stewart the photos that were supposedly used to help Coleman identify his suspects. Stewart claimed that he had gone to great lengths to make sure Coleman's identifications were correct, but Blackburn suspected that Stewart simply handed Coleman a photo of whatever name Coleman inquired about. A more professional method would have been a "photo lineup," in which an officer is shown several suspect photos without names on them and is asked to pick out the perpetrator. Stewart's assistant had always insisted that no records had been kept of which photos Coleman had been shown during his investigation. The folder they now received was labeled "Photos that may or may not have been shown to Tom Coleman."

Gupta searched the boxes in vain for the report of the polygraph that Coleman had supposedly been given by the task force as a condition of returning to work in Tulia following the settlement of the

Cochran County charges. It was a linchpin of the state's defense of Coleman; Stewart testified in the Wafer suit that he had relied almost entirely on the polygraph in deciding to keep Coleman on the job. Yet Stewart himself admitted that he had never actually seen the test results, and now the state seemed strangely evasive about turning the charts over to the team. Could Commander Amos have been lying about conducting a polygraph in the first place?

Des Hogan and his team called everybody they had contacted on their November visit to Texas, trying as best they could to get commitments to testify in person at the upcoming hearing. Although they had the power to subpoena witnesses, as a practical matter participation was voluntary. If somebody simply failed to show up in Tulia for the hearing, the odds of the team having him arrested in some far-off county and hauled in to court in time to testify were slim.

Jenn Klar interviewed both Carol Barnett, Coleman's ex-wife in Pecos County, and Carla Bowerman, his old girlfriend in Morton, the woman whose sudden departure prompted Coleman to resign his job as a Cochran County deputy in the middle of his shift. Bowerman was so terrified of Coleman that she refused to submit an affidavit. She wanted nothing more to do with him. Barnett had been more cooperative. Now, however, she would not agree to come to Tulia to testify in person for the hearing, despite Klar's efforts to persuade her. She filed an affidavit explaining that she was afraid for her life and the safety of her children.

After striking out twice, Klar got lucky. Back in November, Klar and her team had collected a half dozen affidavits from Coleman's old Pecos County associates but were never able to track down a key witness, former Pecos County sheriff Bruce Wilson, who had hired Coleman for the deputy job in Iraan. In late February, Klar finally got Wilson on the phone. Nobody had ever interviewed Wilson about

Coleman's history in Pecos County—not the task force, not Sheriff Stewart, not even Paul Holloway or any of the attorneys who followed his leads. By now Wilson had heard from a number of his colleagues about Coleman's current troubles and the impending hearing in Tulia. Klar, for her part, had learned that Wilson was an old friend of Coleman's father, which was how Coleman got the Pecos County deputy job in the first place. She did not have high hopes that Wilson would cooperate.

Once Wilson began talking, however, Klar sensed there was something different about him. He was certainly not afraid of Coleman, nor did he seem to despise him as many of Coleman's former colleagues apparently did. Klar could sense that he was reluctant to get involved, yet once she started asking questions he seemed incapable of giving an evasive answer. He was the honest cop of the Ranger myth, the real deal. Coleman had always claimed that his ugly divorce from Carol Barnett forced him to leave Pecos County, but Wilson said this wasn't true. "Coleman left before I could fire him," he told Klar. Wilson confirmed Barnett's version of events: that Coleman left town abruptly, leaving his patrol car parked at his house and taking one of his kids with him, without Barnett's knowledge. Further, he left significant debts in Iraan when he left town, which had still not been repaid. The whole story was similar to what transpired just a year later in Morton. Wilson reluctantly agreed to testify at the hearing if subpoenaed.

The first week in March, the two sides met in Amarillo to conduct depositions. Blackburn had secured a nicely appointed conference room at a downtown law firm for their use. Bill White of Wilmer, Cutler was there, as well as Hogan, Gupta, and Blackburn. McEachern showed up accompanied by Charlotte Bingham, whose sour disposition made her the least favorite member of the team from the defense perspective. She was usually swaddled in a floor-length black overcoat, which she seldom removed, even in court. Blackburn had taken to calling her "fetus face."

Perhaps realizing that he was in over his head, McEachern had recently hired a Lubbock attorney named Rod Hobson to help him prepare for the hearing. The defense team met him for the first time at the depositions. At first blush, Hobson did not cut an intimidating figure. He stood no higher than McEachern's shoulder, and he wore a pair of wraparound sunglasses on a cord around his neck, which, together with his well-tanned face, made him look like he had just come from a beach volleyball game.

In fact Hobson was a fierce competitor, a skilled litigator with a well-earned reputation for making the legal process as unpleasant as possible for his opponents. He once defended a man who had been falsely accused of rape by his ex-girlfriend, who happened to be the daughter of the local judge. At trial, the victim tearfully described a variety of deviant sex acts that the defendant had supposedly subjected her to, the abhorrent details of which had the predictable effect on the plainsmen—and plainswomen—of the jury. Hobson skillfully turned the proceedings around, however, after his client told him that a portion of the woman's account closely mirrored a scene from a movie the two of them had once watched together. It seemed the pair were regular patrons of a porno shop. Hobson subpoenaed the woman's rental history and brought the film in question into court with him, along with a representative sampling of some of the more colorfully titled selections he found on the list. By the end of the day, the alleged victim's credibility was in tatters, and Hobson's client was acquitted.

The team decided to depose Coleman's supervisors at the task force, Jerry Massengill and Lieutenant Mike Amos, as well as Terry McEachern. They already had a lengthy deposition of Stewart from Blackburn's lawsuit on behalf of Billy Wafer, and they decided to leave

Coleman alone until the hearings, to preserve an element of surprise. Massengill was the first to be deposed, and Bill White did the questioning. Almost immediately, Rod Hobson set a confrontational tone. He objected frequently, raising his voice as though he were in front of a jury and threatening to call the judge when questions of procedure arose. The deposition threatened to turn into a shouting match between him and Blackburn.

After some preliminary questions, Bill White steered the deposition to Coleman's hiring. Massengill announced that he had some notes in his pocket that might help him remember things better, if White would allow him to take them out. "Sure. Absolutely," White immediately replied. Anything a witness brought to a deposition was fair game for the other side to examine as well, and White was eager to see what was in Massengill's pocket. Massengill had taken notes during his initial background check of Coleman, he explained. Later, after Coleman's background became an issue in the original sting trials, Lieutenant Amos had asked him to summarize those old notes. A copy of the handwritten summary was what he had with him today. The original notes themselves, he told White, should have been in the boxes of discovery documents that Amos handed over for the hearings.

White was reasonably sure that no such notes had been turned over by the task force. Massengill was about to give them something new. Hobson looked pained. He clearly had not been aware of the existence of the notes, and now he called for a brief recess to look them over. When he was done, he reluctantly handed the notes over to White. The others on the team peered over White's shoulder as he read them. They quickly saw why Hobson's face had fallen. As Massengill looked on nervously, White marked the document "Massengill Exhibit One" and handed it back across the table. He asked Massengill to read aloud from the third bulleted entry in the notes. Massengill read:

Item three. Chief Deputy Cliff Harris advised he supervised Tom Coleman. Tom Coleman was hired as a resident deputy for however they pronounce that. Tom became involved in a custody battle over his children. Tom was accused of kidnapping the children. No charges ever came out of it. Tom lost custody to the children. Tom was too gung ho and became a discipline problem, had possible mental problems and applied for other jobs. It was believed that Tom had worked in Midland, Texas and had walked off the job in a small community in the Panhandle.

McEachern looked oblivious, but the rest of the prosecution team blanched visibly. Gupta struggled to contain her emotions. She had always known that Amos, Massengill, and Stewart were negligent in their background check; they even failed to contact Coleman's most recent prior employer, Cochran County Sheriff Ken Burke, who did his best to warn future employers off of Coleman. But this was far worse than she ever expected. Massengill was now admitting that they hired somebody described by his own supervisor as having "possible mental problems" and then turned him loose to make unsupervised, uncorroborated drug buys in cases that put dozens of people in jail, some of them for decades.

It was hard to fathom. In terms of the upcoming hearing, however, it was almost too good to be true. Massengill's notes meant that the task force had known Coleman was a bad actor from day one, and now they were in the record for the judge and everyone else to read. And there was more. One of Coleman's own references, a Texas Ranger from Odessa named Bullock, had told Massengill that "on the job Tom needed constant supervision, had a bad temper and would tend to run to his mother for help." At the next break in the deposition, Gupta and her colleagues ducked outside and began furiously dialing the rest of the team to tell everybody what they had learned.

*

The next day, the team deposed Terry McEachern, whose strategy seemed to be selective memory loss. Again and again, he testified that he did not remember when he learned various facets of Coleman's story. The deposition went in circles, with little of value gained by the team. McEachern did say something that alarmed Gupta considerably. He had just recently discovered, he claimed, that some marijuana was found on the day of the arrests in Tulia, back in July 1999.

In all the years that had passed, the state never contested an assertion that was virtually always made in press coverage of the Tulia bust—that no drugs of any kind were found during the initial roundup. Now McEachern was suggesting that was not true, though he would not say exactly what he was referring to or which defendant was implicated. Hogan asked McEachern if anybody had actually been charged with possession cases stemming from the day of the bust. "Well, I didn't find out until very recently," McEachern replied.

"So the answer is no?"

"The answer is, I don't know whether I'm going to charge them or not," McEachern answered ominously. "I just found out about it and I'll look at the case."

Gupta called McEachern the next morning to get a feel for his resolve. Although he had come to despise Blackburn, McEachern had always been polite to Gupta. He even included her in his periodic mass e-mailings, which usually consisted of corny jokes and bland homilies. McEachern was not his usual blustery self on the phone. He obviously had not enjoyed being interrogated for six hours by her colleagues. His cross-examination in the upcoming hearings, which were now less than two weeks away, would be even harsher, and it would take place in front of a gallery full of Swisher County voters and reporters. He had seemed despondent during his deposition, and in fact his overall mental and physical health appeared to have declined precipitously since his DWI arrest.

Gupta played on his affection for her, suggesting that she could see him as the victim of circumstances. "Say you were taken in by the task force and Coleman," she urged him, though she did not really believe that was true. "Say you were lied to and now you want to set the record straight with new trials." He couldn't do it, he told her. Gupta began to wonder for the first time if McEachern was really in charge anymore. She knew his position had become tenuous in Swisher County, especially after his DWI arrest. There were rumors that the commissioner's court was looking to take away his authority to prosecute, giving it instead to the county attorney. And there was a growing fear that the drug sting might wind up costing the county even more money than it already had. Gupta tried one last tack. She reminded McEachern that Joe, Chris, Jason, and Freddie were just the first four clients. There were still twelve more locked up, and Gupta had other big law firms lined up to work pro bono on behalf of the next set of clients that needed habeas work, she said. It was the truth. "Even if you win this one, you know we'll be back," she said.

"Vanita, my hands are tied," McEachern said.

Amos had done a polygraph of Coleman after all. The state finally turned over the report, and Blackburn sent it to Eric Holden, a polygraph expert in Dallas. Holden had written the manual used by the state police, and his opinion was gold in Texas. He concluded that Coleman's polygraph was junk. The Amarillo police department examiner had conducted only two tests, not the accepted minimum of three, and had used an antiquated machine, without following the proper verification procedures. But worse than that, the charts, according to Holden's expert opinion, had simply been scored wrong.

Whereas the Amarillo operator had given Coleman a "plus 7," meaning he had passed with ease, Holden gave the same chart a score of "minus 2," meaning "inconclusive, leaning toward deception." Coleman's reactions were strangely flat and his heart rate was unusually elevated, Holden noted. Such readings made conclusions about the subject's veracity difficult to draw and usually suggested some sort of physical problem, possibly including drug use. In any event, there was no way a reasonable operator could have found Coleman to have been definitively truthful from these charts, Holden said. "An examiner who got these results without further testing," he told Blackburn, "would want to put them away in a closet and hope no one ever asked him about them."

Blackburn thought about how many times Stewart and Amos and McEachern had relied on that polygraph to justify their continued faith in Coleman, despite the mountain of evidence undermining his credibility. So many people had lost so much because of what was on those charts, and it was all a sham—as Amos must have known all along, which explained his reluctance to let them go. The team added Holden to the list of possible witnesses for the hearings.

The boxes started arriving a few days before the attorneys did. By Saturday morning, March 15, there were perhaps two dozen of them, piled in rows in Blackburn's living room. They were full of big black binders containing the accumulation of months of research and preparation by the firms: every trial transcript, every motion, every document related to the Tulia sting, all carefully indexed and cross-referenced. The firm attorneys had left nothing to chance; they even FedExed a box full of pens, legal pads, and paper clips, as though they were planning a trip to a land with lawyers and courts but no office supply stores.

On Sunday, the day before the hearings were to start, Gupta and

Blackburn hauled everything over to the rendezvous point, the Comfort Suites motel a few miles from Blackburn's office. By 10:00 A.M. they had turned the second floor conference room into a war room. Six long folding tables had been pushed into a large rectangle and covered with black evidence binders, stacks of manila files, and laptop computers. The team from Hogan & Hartson arrived first. By noon, Des Hogan, Mitch Zamoff, and Jenn Klar had joined Gupta and Blackburn in the war room. Two other young Hogan & Hartson associates, Tara Hammons and Adam Levin, also made the trip down. The Wilmer, Cutler team, led by Ted Killory and Bill White, arrived a few hours later. They brought three young associates with them, Winston King, Anitra Cassas, and Mark Oh. With George Kendall, Gupta, and Blackburn rounding out the lineup, the team would arrive in court on Monday with thirteen attorneys.

Gupta called them all together for a meeting at 7:30 that evening in the war room. Despite countless conference calls over the preceding year, it was the first time all of the attorneys had met in person. Judge Chapman had not set a time limit on their presentation, but they wanted to get through all of their witnesses, except for McEachern, by Friday, when the hearings would likely break for a week at least. They planned to examine McEachern when Chapman reconvened the hearings to hear the state's side of the case. They had a lot of witnesses to call in just five days, and they would handle the examination in turns, moving as quickly as possible. It turned out that Rod Hobson would not be assisting McEachern with the hearings; he had apparently booked a Hawaiian vacation for the same week well before McEachern had hired him to help prepare for the depositions. In his place, McEachern hired a Dallas attorney named John Nation. He had yet to make an appearance on the case, and the team knew very little about him, except that he was a former prosecutor with some experience in appellate work. The team also learned that McEachern had filed a last-minute subpoena to the Department of Justice. They could only speculate that he was trying to obtain the interviews conducted in recent months by the FBI. There was no way to know if he had been successful.

The discussion turned to opening statements, and how to present the legal basis underlying their case that their clients deserved new trials. Bill White had prepared a brief citing all of the relevant case law for the judge. It was an impressive brief, summarizing some two dozen cases in support of the team's arguments. McEachern was now conceding that he knew about Coleman's arrest prior to the trials, but he would likely argue that he did not know any of the other damning information about Coleman, such as the material in Massengill's background check notes. Precedent had firmly established, however, that every member of the "prosecution team"—which included police officers—was subject to the requirements of the Brady doctrine, not just the prosecuting attorney. Police officers and district attorney's investigators could not circumvent the state's responsibility to provide the defense with potentially exculpatory evidence simply by conspiring to keep the information from the prosecuting attorney. In this case, the team was prepared to argue, Coleman, McEachern, and Stewart had all conspired to keep useful information from defense attorneys.

The other argument McEachern had successfully made during direct appeals was that the state had no duty to turn over evidence to the defense that would not have been admissible in court. Since Self had eventually ruled the theft charge—as well as the information about Coleman's checkered law enforcement career in general—inadmissible, it was therefore not Brady material, and the state's failure to provide it to defense attorneys was irrelevant, McEachern argued. The team planned to rebut this by arguing first that Self was mistaken when he ruled the evidence was inadmissible, and second, that the original appellate court had misinterpreted the case law on the subject. The lone case McEachern had cited in his rebuttal was a rela-

tively recent Texas Court of Criminal Appeals decision known as
Lagrone. In Lagrone, the CCA found that while the prosecution may
have failed to reveal information in its possession to the defense, the
failure was irrelevant to the outcome of the case because the material
would have been inadmissible in court under the rules of evidence.
But Lagrone was an aberration in case law. Most of the relevant
precedents, including rulings from the U.S. Supreme Court and prior
rulings from the CCA itself, held that admissibility was irrelevant
when it came to assessing what should properly be considered Brady
material. It was not up to prosecutors to decide before trial what evidence was admissible and what was not; that was a ruling to be made
by judges. In other cases, appellate judges had noted that certain
kinds of Brady evidence, while inadmissible in itself, could nevertheless lead to the discovery of evidence that was admissible. Exculpatory
evidence was often accumulated in this kind of piecemeal fashion; one
appellate judge had used the metaphor of peeling away the layers of
an onion.

Tom Coleman's examination would of course be the climax of the
proceedings, and the job was given to Mitch Zamoff by acclamation.
Zamoff had been studying Jenn Klar's memos on inconsistencies in
Coleman's testimony in preparation. Klar had recently augmented
this work by analyzing Coleman's statements in two lengthy television
interviews. Even after he had been burned time and again by the news
media, Coleman seemed unable to resist getting in front of a camera.
The team had obtained the entire unedited transcript of Coleman's
interview with Tom Mangold of the BBC, which ran for several
hours. Coleman could not be prosecuted for any possible perjury
from the original trials, since the statute of limitations had run out.
But Zamoff planned to grill Coleman on each of the inconsistencies,
of which there were many.

Coleman's trial and deposition testimony was also filled with accusations that other people—his critics—had told lies about him. In the

documents turned over by the state, the team found a sort of enemies list, apparently prepared by Coleman. For each of his critics, Coleman listed something that he or she had allegedly done wrong. The purported offenses were often similar to those of which he himself had been accused. The team was planning a visual aid to help illustrate this phenomenon. It was a large chart listing every person Coleman had ever accused of lying about him and his or her motivation for doing so. Blackburn had gleefully labeled it the "wheel of persecution" exhibit. "Let's spin the wheel and see who's lying on you, today, Tom!" he joked.

The chart demonstrated the sheer volume of people, many of them law enforcement officers, who would have to be lying in order for Coleman's testimony to be true. Gathered together in one place for the first time, it made a powerful impression. And the team had prepared much more, the kind of investigation that only deep-pocketed law firms could have completed in such a short period of time: two thick binders of exhibits, careful analyses of past testimony from all of the state's witnesses, graphs that indicated how many cases Coleman had made from month to month, and how much money he had spent in Tulia. They had Coleman's personnel records, including a grade report reflecting that he had once failed a course on evidence and investigations at a junior college in Odessa. They even knew what he scored on his GED exam (the bare minimum). It was a dream come true for Blackburn to see it all in one place, lined up in neat black binders, all loaded for bear. Just walking around the war room, with all of the attorneys gathered in one place, busily finalizing exhibits and examination outlines, made him feel giddy.

Before the team members retired to their rooms to read over their exam notes and prepare for the next morning, Gupta stood up and thanked them for their hard work. She hadn't had a full night's sleep in weeks. The daily paper in Austin had run a column that morning by an African American columnist identifying Tulia as the new front line in the civil rights movement and taking Jesse Jackson to task for focusing his energies that week instead on trying to get a woman into the Augusta, Georgia, country club that hosted the Master's golf tournament. Gupta solemnly read a portion of it to the team. "Just as Jasper put Texas on the international map as the spot for a modern-day lynching," she read, "Tulia has become synonymous with race-based justice." They had gotten the day in court they wanted, and they had the attention of the nation. There was nothing left to do but make their case.

CHAPTER SEVENTEEN

The Hearing

THE TEAM ARRIVED at the Swisher County courthouse a little before 8:00 A.M. on Monday morning in a caravan of rented SUVs. There were already two satellite trucks in the parking lot, and a small knot of reporters watched as the attorneys marched up the steps, grim-faced in their dark suits and sunglasses, hauling boxes and briefcases stuffed with binders and file folders. They looked like TV-drama FBI agents, coming to investigate crop circles or some other strange phenomenon that had carried them far from their urban element.

Gupta and Kendall headed for the jail adjacent to the courthouse to visit their clients before the hearing got under way. Sheriff Stewart allowed them all to gather in a cramped office on the first floor, just down the hall from his own office. Freddie Brookins and Jason Williams had been delivered to the jail the previous day and were wearing street clothes brought to them by their families. Joe Moore and Chris Jackson had just arrived and were wearing the jail's orange inmate jumpsuits. Sheriff Stewart had not wanted the inmates to appear in court at all, but Gupta had insisted on it. She didn't want the judge, or for that matter her own team, forgetting what this hearing was all about. Still, she was careful not to build up her clients' expectations for the hearing. She realized now that she needn't have worried. They were grateful to be back in Swisher County near their families and friends, but none of them seemed to be as excited as Gupta about the upcoming proceedings. Being back in the county jail revived the bitter memory of their original trials. Despite the fact that they now had a new judge and new attorneys, it was hard for them to imagine that the results were going to be any different. Gupta reminded them that they would be face-to-face with Stewart, McEachern, and Coleman again, men whose actions they had stewed about for years. They had to do their best not to grimace or react in any way in front of the judge, she warned them, no matter what they heard the witnesses say.

The courtroom filled slowly that morning. By the time Judge Chapman took the bench at 9:00 A.M., perhaps thirty-five spectators, virtually all of them black, had quietly taken seats in the gallery. Like guests at a wedding, they filled half of the courtroom, seeming to leave the other side—in vain as it turned out—for supporters of Terry McEachern and Larry Stewart. Judge Chapman had expected a larger turnout, especially considering the sizable contingent of media representatives, who now filled two rows of the gallery. The attention of the nation was focused on this little panhandle courthouse, but where were the local folks?

Sheriff Stewart had been expecting more people as well, and he had extra officers on hand to maintain order. Now he leaned against the wall just inside the door of the courtroom, hands clasped behind his back, looking over every new person who entered. The Tulians among them nodded deferentially as they squeezed past him, but most of the out of town press and visitors had no idea who he was and ignored him, as though he were a bailiff. He looked as if he were not sure what he was supposed to be doing.

There was barely room for all thirteen of the applicants' attorneys in the attorney's well. McEachern had brought everyone at his disposal, including Mark Hocker and Kelley Messer, his two assistant prosecutors, and Charlotte Bingham, wrapped in her customary trench coat. McEachern's special prosecutor, John Nation, nodded and shook hands with each member of the team. With his prim smile, red face, and male-pattern baldness, Nation bore a strong resemblance to Les Nesman, the anally retentive newsman on the 1980s sitcom *WKRP in Cincinnati*.

The four applicants were seated in the jury box to Chapman's left. They listened attentively as the judge cleared his throat and addressed the attorneys gathered in the well. "In reaching the decisions that I have been asked to make in these cases, I want to reiterate, and I think the lawyers know this already, that the Court feels bound by the specific language in each individual's order remanding these cases from the Court of Criminal Appeals," Chapman said. The most important thing, he instructed the attorneys, was the time line of the original trials: he wanted to know what the district attorney had learned about Coleman's background, when he knew it, and when, if ever, the information became available to the various defense attorneys of the four applicants. In reviewing the trial record, Chapman said, he had noted that the process of uncovering Coleman's background and record had been ongoing, beginning with Joe Moore's trial and continuing up to Freddie's, some two months later.

The brevity of Chapman's address seemed to add portent to every point he made. Was he trying to warn the defense team that he wasn't interested in the mountain of information they had collected about Coleman, if it wasn't material that McEachern could have been expected to know? Was he setting the stage for a possible decision to grant relief to some of the applicants but not others?

Blackburn spoke first. From the morning of the bust, when the news cameras were rolling, to the trials of the applicants, the state had created an image of the Tulia operation, he told the court, speaking without notes in a calm, confident voice. "And what we are going to be able to show you through facts," he said, "is that the image that they created and put together for themselves began to overtake the reality of what had really happened later on." The district attorney and the sheriff and Coleman's commanders at the task force became so wedded to that image, Blackburn argued, that they could not abandon it in the face of mounting problems with the cases. "It was a devotion to that image and a need to carry it through these trials, the trials of these four men, that ultimately landed them in prison and that also led the state at various times and in various ways to not only create a false impression to the jury, not only create a false impression to the public, but also withhold critical evidence so that that impression, which we will prove false . . . would sustain them and would keep this process going."

Gupta followed Jeff with a summary of what was known about Coleman's history: his failings in Pecos and Cochran counties, the theft charge, the altered and inconsistent offense reports in the Tulia investigation, the successful alibi evidence brought forward by some defendants. Unlike Blackburn, she read her comments from a prepared text, lifting her eyes intermittently to look in the judge's direction. She sounded nervous.

Mitch Zamoff summed up the team's opening and quickly demonstrated why the team considered him their ringer in the courtroom. Barely glancing at his notes, he delivered a stinging indictment of the prosecution team's failure to disclose what they knew about Coleman and an impressive summary of the relevant case law. His tone was strident, and he spoke with the air of authority that comes from prosecuting scores of defendants on behalf of the federal government. He made it clear from the outset who was on trial today. "Your Honor, I respectfully submit that the nature and the cumulative power of the Brady evidence that was not disclosed in this case is really quite startling. We will prove, your Honor, that had the proper Brady disclosures been made here that six law enforcement witnesses, including two former sheriffs, a deputy sheriff, and a chief of police, would have testified at these gentleman's trials that the only witness against them, the only uncorroborated witness against them, had a reputation for dishonesty. A *reputation* for dishonesty, your Honor. Not that he lied once, not that he lied a few times, but that he lied as a matter of course and that he was known in his community for lying. Essentially, that he had no credibility."

The state was going to argue that the evidence was inadmissible, Zamoff continued, but that was wrong for several reasons. Specific instances of misconduct could be introduced to show motive or bias of a witness, he argued, and Coleman had plenty of motive to testify. "He was a law enforcement officer who, to say the least, had an extremely tainted record. His last two deputy jobs had ended in turmoil with his sheriffs believing he had no integrity, he had no reliability, and deeming him unfit for rehire. He was facing criminal charges for theft, criminal charges for abusing his power as a law enforcement officer.... He had substantial motive to try to make high-profile cases that did not exist... in order to try to salvage his career and repair a tarnished reputation in the law enforcement community."

Texas case law also recognized that defendants have the right to introduce evidence to correct false or misleading testimony of prosecution witnesses, Zamoff told the court. "This was a prosecution where there was repeated bolstering by the prosecution, I submit because they knew there was no corroboration for this officer." Zamoff quoted from one of the trial transcripts in which Lieutenant Amos referred to Coleman as "a real exceptional officer." "Now, I am not sure how that testimony even makes itself into the record, frankly, in a case like this," Zamoff said dismissively. "But, certainly, if the prosecution is going to talk about how exceptional this guy is, the defense is entitled to the information and to put on the evidence that would allow them to rebut that false impression. If he was exceptional, Judge, he was exceptional in terms of his dishonesty and his unreliability and not in any other way."

At Freddie Brookins's trial, Zamoff went on, Amos had testified that given the opportunity he would hire Tom Coleman again. "Well, I am startled by that statement for a number of reasons. But, certainly, it is not the type of bolstering statement that a defendant should be prevented from testing."

"Finally, Judge, in each and every one of these trials . . . the prosecution boasts about the background check that it did on Tom Coleman," Zamoff continued, motioning toward McEachern, seated just three feet in front of where he was standing. "Again, it is extremely abnormal for that type of a subject to arise in a drug prosecution. But I am at a loss to understand how the prosecution can rely on a background check and use a background check to disadvantage defendants and then not disclose anything about what the background check revealed, not give the defense the opportunity to challenge the background check.

"In this case, Judge, we are going to prove that the background check was a sham. It was negligent at its very best. And it either did disclose or should have disclosed an absolute mountain of Brady evidence."

McEachern was noticeably red-faced by the time Zamoff took his seat. John Nation had watched impassively and didn't take a single note, not even during Zamoff's whirlwind summary of the relevant case law. Now he stood and addressed the judge. "May it please the court," he began carefully. In his way, with his bow tie and his excruciatingly correct manner, he was as alien to the country lawyer tradition as the D.C. firm attorneys were with their expensive shoes and thousand-dollar briefcases. "We believe that the record showed that these defendants, one and all, were guilty exactly as charged in the indictment, that the jury verdicts were certainly warranted in these cases, and that there is no showing of factual innocence and there is no showing of insufficient evidence," he said. The defense may not like the fact that Coleman had no corroboration for his cases, Nation said, but that did not matter now. Nothing they collected against Coleman in the preceding months would have changed the outcome of the cases, he said.

Moreover, even if McEachern had given the original trial attorneys the information he knew about Coleman—or if they had uncovered similar evidence themselves—it would not have been admissible in the first place, Nation argued. As expected, he cited the Lagrone case, the only precedent he mentioned in his five-minute opening statement. To be sure, the Court of Criminal Appeals had ruled in Lagrone, the state had an affirmative duty to turn over Brady material to the defense. Blackburn grimaced as Nation read the relevant portion in his school-marmish voice: "However, the prosecution has no duty to turn over evidence that would be inadmissible at trial." The research the defense team put together may be impressive, Nation suggested, but the Court had to keep it in perspective. "This is not a trial of Tom Coleman or a trial of Mr. Terry McEachern, although certainly the Court and the public . . . could be forgiven for getting a mistaken impression this week on that," he said. "The narrow issue that is drawn here," Nation summed up, "is were any of these facts that the habeas counsel claim are exculpatory, were they in fact exculpatory, did in fact the prosecution have any duty to disclose them?"

The courtroom was deathly silent as Nation sat down.

Des Hogan called the team's first witness, Ori White, the district attorney from Fort Stockton in Pecos County. White was very familiar with Coleman's character. As a private attorney he had represented Carol Barnett in her divorce from Coleman. As DA, he also knew many of Coleman's old law enforcement colleagues from Pecos County. White had testified in the Kareem White case about Coleman's reputation for truthfulness, though he was only allowed to give the standard one-word assessment, in this case "bad." He repeated that assessment under questioning from Hogan. But Hogan wanted more. He asked for specific examples of Coleman's behavior, at which Nation sprang up.

"I am going to object to specific instances of conduct, your honor," he said. It was a crucial moment. The defense team had the goods on Coleman. Ori White and Bruce Wilson, their leadoff witnesses, had told them things about Coleman nobody had yet heard, things that would ruin Coleman before any jury. But if Chapman would not allow the team to go into lines of examination that were of debatable admissibility in a normal trial, then much of what they had collected on Coleman would never see the light of day, and a huge portion of their research and strategy was worthless.

Chapman's ruling came with only a moment's hesitation: "The objection will be overruled. You may answer."

There was a collective sigh from the defense team. White testified that Coleman had a very bad temper and a reputation for being violent, and that during the custody trial he was concerned not only for his client's safety but also for his own.

"What steps, if any, did you take to try to ensure your safety?" Hogan asked.

"I wore a bullet-proof vest to the final hearing," White said.

A murmur rippled through the gallery. As Hogan moved on to Coleman's poor reputation in the Pecos County sheriff's office, Nation tried in vain to derail the examination with hearsay objections. Chapman overruled him without even looking up. The feeling of exhilaration in the gallery was palpable—it was not the prosecution that was accustomed to being overruled in the Swisher County courthouse. Chapman was not Ed Self, and this was not going to be a repeat of the Kareem White trial.

Hogan then steered the examination to the performance of White's fellow prosecutor, Terry McEachern. "Now, if you found out—as a DA, if you found out that one of your peace officers had been arrested while he was doing an undercover operation," he asked, "would you do an investigation to find out the details of what that arrest was about?"

McEachern glared at White as he formulated his answer. "I would consider that to be Brady material, and I would—I would have to disclose it," White replied, "and I would have to do an investigation to find out whether my undercover officer was an honest person."

Finally, Hogan asked White why he had agreed to come and testify against Coleman in Kareem White's case, and again in the present hearing.

"I felt that if the convictions or the evidence would be solely based on just Tom Coleman," White replied, "that there was a serious question in my mind that it would be proper to convict those individuals based on his testimony alone."

When Hogan sat down, John Nation stood up to cross-examine White. Nation, having come so late to the process, knew very little about Coleman's background or what had transpired in the original trials of the applicants. "Mr. White," he began, and paused, his face screwing up slightly. Nation suffered from Tourette's Syndrome, a condition he controlled with medication; even so, his face betrayed a noticeable tic when he was deep in concentration. "Ordinarily questions of the credibility of witnesses are for juries to decide, aren't they?"

"Once you start the trial, that is true," White conceded.

"As far as you are aware, there is no requirement in Texas law that a undercover officer's testimony be corroborated by any specified list of factors?"

"No, sir."

"Certainly there is no requirement in law," Nation went on, "that an undercover officer be corroborated by a tape or video recording of the transaction?"

"He can be convicted on the voice of one person," White replied.

"Right. And as a DA, of course, you don't get to choose your witnesses, do you?"

"No, sir."

"And you understand that other people may have different views of Mr. Coleman's reputation or different opinions about him?"

"It certainly is possible."

With that Nation took his seat.

By the time Hogan called former Pecos County sheriff Bruce Wilson to the stand midmorning, the gallery had begun to fill up. It was apparent that very few white Tulians would be attending the hearings, and black spectators began to fill both sides of the courtroom.

Wilson, who was in his early sixties, had retired in 2000 after thirty-three years with the Pecos County sheriff's department, the last sixteen as sheriff. About six feet tall and slim, with thinning silver-gray hair, high cheekbones, and a long, narrow face, Wilson was a west Texas sheriff from central casting. He wore a gray western-style blazer, a blue tie, boots, and crisp new blue jeans. With his lips pressed together in a thin frown, he listened carefully to each of Hogan's preliminary questions and gave terse, economical answers. He hired Tom as a deputy in 1989, he said, because he was close friends with his father, Joe Coleman, who died of a heart attack two years later.

"What was Joe Coleman's reputation as an officer?" Hogan asked. At the mention of Coleman's father, Wilson inhaled deeply and seemed to choke up a bit. "One of the best," he answered after a pause. Was he trustworthy? "Whatever he told you, you could bank on," Wilson said. The entire courtroom knew what was coming next. Was Tom Coleman a good officer, Hogan asked? Wilson looked down at his hands, clearly having second thoughts about what he was about to do. "No," he said softly. Hogan was moving slowly now, pitching his questions in a soft voice as though a sleeping baby were in the next room. He had a career west Texas lawman on the verge of tears. Was Coleman trustworthy, Hogan asked? A half minute passed in utter silence as Wilson, still thinking about his loyalty to Joe Coleman, struggled to compose himself.

"I don't know how to say it," he finally said. "No, I don't trust him."

Once that line had been crossed, Wilson began volunteering stories about Tom, some of which even the defense team had never heard. How the deputy had denied threatening two women in the tiny town of Iraan where he was stationed, only to have a humiliating tape recording of the incident played before him in the sheriff's office. How a woman had taken to lying down in the backseat of her son's car to see if Coleman really was pulling her son over several times a day, as the boy had complained. (He was.) How the citizens of Iraan had convened a town hall meeting, attended by over 100 persons, on the subject of getting Deputy Tom Coleman out of their town. How people had come to Wilson seeking help in getting Coleman to pay his bills. How Coleman had accidentally shot out the windshield of his own patrol car with a shotgun, while he was seated in it. When Wilson finally stepped down, after a perfunctory cross-examination by the state, the courtroom buzzed the way courtrooms do on TV dramas, and even Judge Chapman seemed stunned by what Wilson had said.

The team assembled in the private back room at the El Camino Dining Room for lunch. Spirits were high. Ori White and Bruce Wilson—especially Wilson—had been devastating witnesses, and Hogan handled them perfectly. Chapman was giving plenty of latitude and he seemed involved, taking copious notes at various points. Yet the mood was tempered by the revelation that Chapman seemed unfamiliar with the relevant case law. He had told the team during opening statements that he had not received Bill White's most recent brief, summarizing the most important cases. Did he know what an aberration the Lagrone case really was? Even if Chapman wanted to side with their clients, he would have to justify his findings to the ultraconservative Court of Criminal Appeals, and the team could not expect him to do it without a sound legal basis. They would have another chance to argue the law at the end of the hearing, when both sides would submit written summaries to the judge. "We're going to have to write his opinion for him, every single aspect of it," Gupta said.

It was the first trip to Tulia for many of the attorneys, and some were having trouble making the adjustment. The menu at the El Camino presented an unexpected obstacle. Could the fajitas be served without the meat? They could, though it was fair to say it had never happened before. Was there herbal tea on the menu? There was not. Cappuccino was available, but it was premixed and vanilla flavored. It was also, in the estimation of the young Hispanic waitress, "nasty." In the end there was no time to eat, and the team rushed back to the courthouse with their meals in boxes.

When the applicants returned to the jury box after lunch, Joe Moore was wearing his customary overalls over a white dress shirt, which had been delivered to him during the break by Gary Gardner. He cracked a smile for the first time as he visited with Gupta and Kendall just before the hearing reconvened. The team began the afternoon by calling two more of Coleman's old law enforcement colleagues, both from Fort Stockton. Juan Castro, the Fort Stockton chief of police, had described Coleman in an affidavit as a "paranoid gun freak." Now, under examination by Adam Levin, the young Hogan & Hartson associate, he recounted how officers had to be present when Coleman collected his kids from Barnett's house for visitation because she was so afraid of him. Nation did not return to the hearing after lunch, and McEachern's young assistant prosecutor, Mark Hocker, had taken over cross-examination duties. When he got his turn with Castro, Hocker produced a copy of Tom Coleman's criminal history, taken from a database commonly referred to as the TCIC/NCIC. It was clean, as Castro acknowledged, which meant he had no convictions. But not only that, Hocker insisted: didn't it also mean that Coleman had never been arrested? Didn't state law require that arrests be reported and entered into the database? It certainly did, Castro replied.

Gupta couldn't believe what she was hearing. It was one thing for McEachern to wave Coleman's blank criminal history report around in front of an unsuspecting jury, as he had in previous trials, knowing full well that Coleman had in fact been arrested, right here in Swisher County. McEachern would have his chance to explain that later in the hearing. But now Hocker was waving it in front of Chapman, even though he knew the defense team had not only a copy of the theft indictment but also proof of the arrest made by Sheriff Stewart himself. Hocker had inadvertently brought up an embarrassing question the defense planned to raise themselves: Why hadn't Stewart reported the arrest? Did he try to cover up the incident? It was an egregious tactical error by Hocker, one that Larry Stewart would pay for later.

Next came Sam Esparza, a veteran Pecos County sheriff's office narcotics investigator who had been a colleague of Coleman's at the department. Esparza, a muscular man in his late forties with a gruff voice and tough manner, had submitted an affidavit testifying that he had caught Coleman lying on several occasions. Under questioning by Adam Levin, he now described an incident in which he asked Coleman, at that time a rookie deputy, to ride along with him to serve an arrest warrant on a man accused of sexually assaulting two little girls. Coleman was eager to come along—a little too eager, as Esparza discovered. "He immediately went to his patrol car, opened the trunk to his car, and started pulling out assault weapons," Esparza testified. "I asked him what he was doing and he said, 'Well, isn't this a felony warrant?' And I said, 'Yeah, it is, Tom, but you are not going to need all that firepower.'" Esparza knew the suspect and was certain that he would come quietly, he explained. It was a simple matter of driving ten miles into the country to pick him up. On the ride out, however, Coleman was so agitated and excited about the impending action that Esparza ordered him to wait in the car while he made the arrest. But

Coleman could not stay put; he was like a kid at Disneyland. As Esparza predicted, the man offered no resistance whatsoever to being arrested. As he was about to put the cuffs on, however, Esparza was startled to find Coleman at his elbow, his hand resting on his gun. Esparza had to order him back in the car. "[I] just told the sheriff he was going to have to keep an eye on this guy," Esparza said.

Esparza also testified that he considered Coleman a racist. He recounted an incident in which Coleman told him he didn't consider Esparza to be a "Mexican," because he didn't look or sound or act like one. "You just better get used to it," Esparza had told Coleman. "I am of Mexican descent and I am proud of it. . . . And if it bothers you, tell me now because I will just go drop you off at the sheriff's office and that will be the last of that." Esparza said that was the last time he ever rode with Coleman.

Esparza testified that Tom Coleman's father, Joe Coleman, had been a mentor to him. "He taught me a lot and I just—I had a world of respect for him. He was a hell of a man," Esparza said. Why then, Levin asked, was he testifying here today against Joe Coleman's son? Now it was Esparza's turn to stifle his emotions.

"Because I am a law enforcement officer and people like Mr. Coleman are a bad representation—," he began, before Hocker cut him off with an objection.

"I don't condone the type of behavior that this man displays as far as from a peace officer," Esparza said when he was allowed to finish his answer.

On cross-examination, Mark Hocker drew derisive laughter from the gallery with a clumsy attempt to get Esparza to admit having an affair with Coleman's wife, as Coleman had apparently alleged. The judge had now heard several hours of essentially unrebutted allegations about Coleman's character, and Hocker was clearly running out of ideas to stop the bleeding. McEachern, however, seemed uninterested in taking over for his young assistant. While Charlotte Bingham scribbled an occasional note and passed it over to Hocker, McEachern for the most part sat quietly, absently chewing his fingernail or resting his head on the palm of his hand.

The rest of the afternoon was devoted to testimony from Coleman's creditors in Cochran County: the hardware store, the bank, the grocery store, the auto supply store. The team had subpoenaed them all and felt pleasantly surprised with how many people showed up. It seemed Morton hadn't yet forgiven Coleman, despite his payment of restitution. Burned time and again by Coleman, each of them now told a familiar story, which inevitably included some version of the same refrain: he was a law officer, so we figured he was trustworthy. The testimony seemed to have a powerful effect on the few white Tulians present: the witnesses from Morton were small-town plainsmen, just like them, who knew that a man who didn't pay his debts and wouldn't keep his word was about as low as you could get. Ironically, the testimony seemed to have the opposite effect on some of the black observers. If they identified with anyone in the stories of bad credit and broken promises that afternoon, it was the perpetually broke Tom Coleman, who came across as nothing if not scrappy and resourceful in avoiding his responsibilities for so long.

The last creditor was a propane dealer named James Holleyman, who testified that, after weeks of calling, he had finally reached Coleman on the phone to collect on a bill that was three or four months overdue.

"And what did he say?" Des Hogan asked.

"He said bring me 200 more gallons and I will pay you for it next Friday," Holleyman replied, and the courtroom tittered in grudging admiration of Coleman's gumption.

*

The next morning, Lieutenant Amos, Coleman's commander at the task force, took the stand. Amos was a key witness, and the team had prepared dozens of questions about Coleman's hiring, his methods in Tulia, and, crucially, how and when the Cochran County charge against Coleman was discovered. It would be a lengthy exam, and the team planned to handle Amos in turns, beginning with Gupta. A career Amarillo police department detective, Amos had headed the task force for most of its history. He had a military bearing and a tendency to speak in the cop jargon of J. Edgar Hoover–era narcs. Gupta began with a document the team had discovered in the task force files. It was a letter from the governor's office allowing the task force a one-month extension to fill a grant-funded undercover position—Coleman's as it turned out—after which the money would have to be returned to the state. It seemed that Stewart, after hounding the task force for years to put an undercover man in Tulia, was having trouble finding somebody to do the job. By the time Coleman walked through his door, time was running out to fill the position. Gupta asked Amos to read aloud from a note he had scrawled to Jerry Massengill at the bottom of the letter. "Jerry, you need to finish your background on the candidate out of Swisher County as soon as possible," Amos read.

Gupta turned to the subject of Massengill's background check. The team had already put Massengill's notes—the bombshell they had collected during his deposition—into evidence, but Gupta wanted Amos to read the most damaging portions out loud, in front of Judge Chapman and the four applicants that Coleman had put away for so long. She pointed to Massengill's summary of what he had learned from Cliff Harris, the chief deputy in Pecos County. In a thick panhandle accent, Amos read what Harris had to say: that Coleman was a discipline problem, that he was "too gung ho," that he had been accused of kidnapping his son in a custody battle, that he had walked off the job on a sheriff in the panhandle, and—worst of all—that he had, in Harris's words, "possible mental problems."

Gupta paused to let this sink in. "Okay. Based on what you just read, the task force was then on notice that a former employer of Coleman's thought he was—he had possible mental problems and was a disciplinary problem; is that right?" she asked.

"That is correct," Amos replied.

Amos testified that Coleman had blamed his problems in Pecos County on the nasty divorce he was going through, though he seemed hazy about the details of Coleman's explanation. Other than visiting with Coleman, Gupta asked, did he follow up on these allegations? Amos replied that he did not.

"Why didn't you?" Gupta asked.

"Well, after visiting with the sheriff and various people that had been contacted, [Sheriff Stewart] was made aware of it. And, like I said, Tom had explained some of the circumstances surrounding this incident, if I remember correctly." Although he had not been in the courtroom for Monday's daylong examination of Coleman's well-documented mendacity, Amos seemed suddenly conscious of how lame this explanation must have sounded to the judge and the whisperers in the gallery. "And the bottom line was the sheriff made the decision to hire Tom Coleman," he added.

At the prosecution table, McEachern sat with his head resting forlornly on his hand. Nation was focused intently on Amos, his face screwed up as though he had just swallowed something bitter. A line had been crossed: Amos was turning on Stewart. Charlotte Bingham began furiously scribbling notes and passing them to Nation.

Next Gupta had Amos read aloud Massengill's account of his conversation with a Texas Ranger named Bullock, who reported that Coleman "needed constant supervision, had a bad temper, and would tend to run to his mother for help."

"Did it raise any concerns," Gupta asked, "that Ranger Bullock had stated that Tom needed constant supervision?"

"Not really," Amos replied. A lot of new hires needed close supervision, he said. But Coleman was hired specifically to work alone in a "deep cover" capacity, Gupta pointed out. There was, of course, no good answer to that. All Amos could do was repeat what was becoming something of a mantra: he had shared all of the background information with the sheriff, and it was the sheriff who decided to hire Coleman.

Gupta was not ready to move on just yet. She noted that Massengill had never successfully contacted Pecos County sheriff Bruce Wilson. "Did you ever try to call Sheriff Wilson up yourself after you realized that he hadn't been contacted?" she asked.

"No."

"And did you instruct Sergeant Massengill to do that?"

"I don't recall instructing him to do so, no."

"Okay, so despite the fact that you had heard from Chief Deputy Cliff Harris that Coleman had possible mental problems and was a disciplinary problem, is it your testimony then that you—neither you nor the sergeant contacted anybody else from Pecos County?"

"No, we did not," Amos grimly replied.

Massengill had also failed to contact Cochran County sheriff Ken Burke, though he had apparently gotten in touch with somebody in the office, who reported that Coleman was "loyal" and "highly motivated." Massengill had failed to record this person's name.

"So according to your testimony, then, there was one call placed to somebody whose name you don't recall in Cochran County and then another call placed to Sheriff Ken Burke who never returned your call and who you were never able to get in touch with; is that correct?"

Amos was getting hammered and Nation jumped in, arguing that Gupta's questions were repetitive. She moved on to the subject of how Amos became aware of the theft charges against Coleman and how he dealt with them. Amos recounted the story of the meeting with Coleman and Stewart, in which they confronted Coleman with the warrant. Again, Amos characterized the decision of how to deal with Coleman as Sheriff Stewart's responsibility, not the task force's. Gupta then showed Amos a copy of Coleman's TCIC/NCIC history, the same document Mark Hocker had referred to the day before.

"Does it indicate any arrests on that sheet?" Gupta asked.

"No, it does not," Amos replied.

"You just testified that the sheriff arrested Tom Coleman. Why does the report not indicate an arrest?"

"I don't know," Amos said.

Shortly thereafter, the hearings broke for lunch.

In the mostly empty courtroom prior to the restart of the hearing, Gupta, Hogan, Kendall, and Blackburn huddled with their clients. They seemed in much better spirits, but they were angry about what they had heard that morning. It was the first time they had heard about the revelations in Massengill's notes. Cynical as he had become about Sheriff Stewart, Freddie still couldn't believe what Amos had read aloud to the court. They had known all along that Coleman was a bad apple, even before they hired him. They had known and they had turned him loose in Tulia anyway.

That afternoon, Gupta, Blackburn, Killory, and Hogan took turns grilling Amos about Coleman's operation in Tulia: the botched identifications, the dismissed indictments, the lack of corroboration for his buys. The issue of Coleman's alleged racism also came up. Amos had admitted in his deposition that he had personally disciplined Coleman for using the word "nigger" around the office, and that he had attempted to get Coleman to make some buys outside of the black community when it became apparent that his operation was almost entirely focused on black suspects. The team suspected that Amos had volunteered both stories in his deposition in order to burnish the task force's image a bit in advance of the hearing. Now he tried to downplay Coleman's use of the word, insisting that he did not consider Coleman a racist.

There was no way to put a positive spin on what was in Massengill's notes, however. Despite Nation's futile objections, the attorneys read them into the record over and over again as the afternoon wore on, painting a picture of unfathomable irresponsibility and negligence on the part of Massengill, Amos, and Stewart. Coleman's hiring was a civil suit waiting to happen, and the team wanted to make sure that Charlotte Bingham knew it. Late that afternoon, Killory summarized the negative information in Massengill's notes for perhaps the tenth time—"that Mr. Coleman was too gung ho, that he was a discipline problem, that he had possible mental problems, that he lost custody of his children, not paying his bills, and he kidnapped his son for several weeks." Then, with his perfect elocution and his suave Harvard bearing, he crystallized the utter failure of Coleman's supervisors with a few well-crafted questions.

"And you understood at the time of those allegations that those allegations were being made by a supervisory law enforcement person for whom Mr. Coleman had worked as a law enforcement officer, correct?"

"That was my understanding, yes, sir," Amos replied.

"Okay. And is it—am I correct from your prior testimony, and correct me if I am wrong, please, that in response to those allegations, apart from your conversation with Mr. Coleman himself, you never asked anyone about those allegations; is that correct?"

"I did not, no sir."

"Okay. And I believe I correctly heard you that apart from the conversation you and Mr. Massengill had with Mr. Coleman about all of these allegations from his former supervisor, that you are not aware of any member of the prosecution team actually talking to anyone else in Pecos County about those allegations; is that correct?"

"Not to my knowledge, no, sir. That is correct."

"And am I correct that Mr. Coleman's only response, the only response that you have testified to today was in response to all those allegations—his rebuttal evidence, shall we say—was that he was having marital problems at the time?"

Nation made a last futile attempt to pull Amos out of the fire. "Your honor, I object. We have been all over this before." Chapman overruled.

"You may answer," Killory said.

Amos didn't look like he wanted to answer. Earlier, Gupta had read a portion of his testimony from one of the trial transcripts, in which Amos had characterized Coleman as "a real exceptional officer." Amos had gamely tried to stand by that assessment. "He done the job we asked him to," he had told Gupta. Now, after almost seven hours on the stand, the fight seemed to have gone out of him.

"I remember marital problems," he said. "And there may have been some other things discussed, but that is basically what I recall."

That evening the team convened in the war room at the Comfort Suites for a postmortem on the day's events. The mood was cautiously optimistic. Amos had provided plenty of good material, and the opposing team seemed to be in disarray. Seated so close to McEachern and his colleagues, it was hard to miss the grim stares that passed between them. At one point during his cross-examination of Amos, an irritated Nation had instructed Charlotte Bingham to quit passing him notes.

The subject on everyone's mind, however, was something said outside of court. During a break in the hearings, Judge Chapman had chatted with two young women from San Francisco who were making a low-budget documentary about Tulia. Blackburn called them the "8 MM-and-a-dream girls." Word had gotten back to the team that Chapman had told the filmmakers not to necessarily expect the same ruling in the each of the four cases. It could only mean that he thought Freddie Brookins's Brady claim was weaker than that of his three coapplicants because his trial came last and more information about Coleman was, in theory at least, available to his attorney.

Chapman seemed to think, mistakenly, that Paul Holloway and Tom Hamilton had shared their research on Coleman with Freddie's attorney, Mike Hrin, or that Hrin had somehow gotten wind of what came out in Billy Wafer's hearing or Donnie Smith's trial, which had both been held the week before Freddie's case went to court. The team had taken a deposition of Hrin for the hearings and could use it to rebut Chapman's mistaken impression, but Gupta was still anxious. Denying at least one applicant's claims might make a nice out for Chapman, if he worried about being perceived as too permissive in his handling of the proceedings. But not Freddie, Gupta thought. She knew that to the rest of the team, getting new trials for three of the four would be a victory worth celebrating, but for her, this would all be for nothing if he didn't get exonerated.

If Chapman didn't like Freddie's Brady claim, Gupta now argued, what about his ineffective assistance of counsel claim? Freddie's original trial attorney, Mike Hrin, had given Freddie only a token defense. This came out in Hrin's deposition, but Gupta now felt sure that Chapman hadn't read it. "We should put Hrin on the stand and show Chapman how little he did," she said.

But the rest of the team was not convinced. The examination of Amos had taken longer than anticipated, and it was becoming evident that the witness list would have to be pared down if they were going to get their whole case presented by Friday. If there wasn't time to put Hrin and the other trial attorneys on the stand, the team would simply have to emphasize their ineffectiveness in their closing brief to Chapman and hope he read it carefully.

The discussion turned to the batting order of the remaining witnesses. Stewart, Coleman, and McEachern were the big three still to be examined. McEachern would go last, that much was clear. They wanted to have every bit of Brady information out on the table before they confronted McEachern with his failure to reveal what he knew to the defendants. And the team had long assumed that Coleman would be the climax of the proceedings. "The whole thing depends on whether Chapman hates Tom Coleman or not, so he's the kicker," Zamoff said. "Get Coleman up there and go for the jugular." But Amos's decision to blame Stewart had changed the picture somewhat. Stewart was looking worse and worse as the hearing progressed, and the importance of his examination was growing. They had already established the negligence of the task force in hiring Coleman. If they could also prove that Stewart had actively conspired to conceal Coleman's arrest, it would go a long way toward implicating the whole prosecution team in the miscarriage of justice, not just one renegade racist cop. Nation's pathetic "you don't get to pick your witnesses" defense of McEachern had to be demolished, and the best way to do it was to paint a picture of a conspiracy in which everyone, McEachern, Amos, and Stewart, actively sought to cover for Coleman, in order to protect their own reputations and to get the convictions they wanted.

Getting to Stewart would not be easy, Blackburn warned them. Blackburn alone among the team had been present when the sheriff was deposed in the Billy Wafer suit. Deposing Stewart had been like sawing through concrete with a hacksaw; he may not have been flashy, but he wasn't going to be the one to wear down first. With his preacher's confidence and his "if you say so" nonanswers, you were more likely to get him to bring a six-pack to the Church of Christ picnic than concede a point. He had always stood by Coleman, had always insisted that he'd had no reason to doubt Coleman's honesty. Getting him to say otherwise now, with the nation watching and his own reputation hanging in the balance, would take a masterpiece of an examination. Mitch Zamoff retired to his room to study Stewart's prior testimony and Jenn Klar's memos.

Wednesday morning began with the conclusion of Lieutenant Amos's testimony. The team then called Jerry Massengill, Coleman's direct supervisor at the task force. Massengill's testimony, most of which covered familiar territory, failed to reveal any bombshells, and his laconic answers—particularly his string of "don't recall's"—were unsatisfying. Nation seemed to be taking an unduly long time during his cross-examination, almost as if he were purposely trying to run out the clock on the defense team. His questions were less than inspired. "Now, occasionally police officers in small towns have little disputes, do they not?" he asked at one point, referring to Coleman's poor reputation with prior law enforcement colleagues.

The energy in the gallery was low when Chapman called a lunch break. Gary Gardner and his brother Danny were giddy as they headed out to the parking lot, however. They had just heard that Larry Stewart was likely to go on that afternoon. Gary rushed off to complete an errand before the entertainment began, and Danny went to find some lunch.

Danny Gardner resembled a smaller, more modest version of his older brother. When Danny was a kid, he recalled, Larry Stewart drove the school bus, though he was just a high school student himself. It was not an uncommon practice in farming country in the 1950s, where many kids logged years behind the wheel of a tractor or farm truck by the time they earned their driver's license. Still, it was a position of honor for Stewart. Only the most responsible and upright young man could be trusted with Swisher County's future, not to mention one of the school district's most expensive assets. Even then, Danny remembered, Larry Stewart was thought of as a man apart.

And that was still how the town thought of him, which was why so few white people had come to the hearing, Danny said. "They don't want to hear about it," he said. That had been the attitude since the beginning. And no matter what happened in the hearings, Stewart's job was safe. "The people in Tulia will put him right back in," Danny said, shaking his head.

*

Those who were present for Larry Stewart's testimony, which began Wednesday afternoon and stretched across much of Thursday, witnessed a side of their sheriff few had ever seen. It was not a side that Zamoff was surprised to see, however. He had read Stewart's deposition in the Billy Wafer case, and he was struck by how well Stewart performed as a witness. There seemed to be two Stewarts. One, the farmer-turned-lawman, was humble and pious, direct and plain—the public persona that had led Bob Herbert to refer to him in the *New York Times* as a "not particularly bright bulb." This Stewart had prevailed in the original trials, when deferential court-appointed attorneys, conscious of the sheriff's popularity with the hometown juries, had treated him with kid gloves. Under hostile questioning in his deposition, however, another side of Stewart came out. He spoke with the grammar and diction of a man who prided himself on his education; he did not say "seen" instead of "saw" or "done" instead of "did," as most plainsmen of his generation did. When he felt insulted, he countered by becoming even more polite. Like an exasperated flight attendant, he had perfected a way of saying "sir" that made the honorific sound like an insult. Zamoff was also impressed by the sheriff's agility under questioning. This Stewart could be cagey and abrasive—even, when the occasion demanded, Clintonesque in his ability to turn a phrase and parry a leading line of questioning.

Stewart took a seat in the witness chair a little after 2:00 P.M., placing his white hat on the railing beside him. He wore a gray blazer over a white western shirt and a black tie, and he had on wire-rim glasses with squarish, slightly tinted lenses. With his long knobby fingers draped over his bony knees, he had the look of a basketball player waiting at courtside in a seat too small for his frame. Stewart answered Zamoff's preliminary questions in a tone of fatherly tolerance, his face placid and blank. Zamoff's manner quickly became brusque. With his suit hanging loosely off of his lithe frame, he looked like a cat waiting to pounce at Stewart's first hint of evasiveness. It didn't take long. Zamoff brought up the subject of Coleman's reports and asked if it was ever appropriate for an officer to amend a police report by simply scratching out words. He was alluding to the mysterious redaction of Romona Strickland's original offense report.

"Well, it's not something I think would be the most desirable way to do it," Stewart replied evenly.

"I'm not talking about desirability," Zamoff shot back. "I'm asking you what is proper police procedure?"

Stewart declined to take the bait. "Well, I think that would depend on the situation," he replied, friendly and polite as ever.

"When would it be acceptable to do that?" Zamoff asked.

"If the change were made with the department or the prosecutor all knowing about it, I don't see that it would be a problem," Stewart replied. "I think there could be circumstances when it would be acceptable. Generally I would say it is not."

It was the kind of nonanswer that Zamoff had expected, after reading his deposition. He took the opportunity to let Stewart know that this examination was going to be different; if he failed to answer a question, he was going to get ten more.

"Well, what I want to do, sir, is I want to identify every circumstance when you think that would be acceptable," Zamoff said.

"You asked for every instance that would be appropriate?" Stewart said.

"You said there were some circumstances. I'd like to identify those circumstances."

There was a pause. "I've identified one," Stewart replied, testily, "and right now I can't think of any others, sir."

"Okay. Here's what I'm going to ask you to do," Zamoff began dryly, "before the end of this examination I'd like you to tell me, and you can stop me at any point, if you can think of any other circumstances."

The unmistakable sarcasm and disrespect had a palpable effect on the gallery. Sheriff Stewart, one of the most powerful officials in the county, was being treated like any other witness—worse, like a defendant in a criminal case. In eleven years as sheriff of Swisher County, he had been laughed at behind his back, dressed down by the mothers of defendants, even had his trigger finger bitten half off by a drunken Mexican. But nobody had ever failed to respect his badge inside his own courthouse.

Zamoff moved on to Tom Coleman's hiring. Stewart had always publicly stood by Coleman, but now he would not concede that he had made the decision to hire him in the first place.

"It was a joint decision," he said.

"Well, that's funny, because the task force officers who have been here," Zamoff said over Nation's objection, "have said that was your decision alone."

"I had to hire someone that was acceptable to them," Stewart countered.

Stewart testified that his job was simply to check Coleman's standing with TCLEOSE, the state licensing agency for peace officers, and that the task force had committed to doing the background check. Stewart had called TCLEOSE to verify that Coleman was a licensed officer, but he had never actually obtained his official file, so he had not seen the documents in the evidence binder that Zamoff laid before him now: letters from a half dozen creditors about bad debts, a notice of Coleman's wages being garnished for unpaid child support, and the letter from Cochran County sheriff Ken Burke urging future employers to avoid Coleman. Stewart testified that he was not aware that TCLEOSE kept such records in their files or that he was allowed to view them. As a result he knew only what Coleman had told him about the debts during his initial interview.

Stewart testified that his only other participation in the background check was to call Texas Ranger Larry Gilbreath, one of Coleman's references, and that Gilbreath had given Coleman a good recommendation. Gilbreath did mention that there had been some problems in Cochran County, Stewart said, but he had not been specific about what they were, and Stewart had never followed up to find out. Coleman himself had told him he'd left some debts in Cochran County and that he probably would not get a good recommendation from the sheriff there, Stewart said. Nobody had ever called Burke, however, so Stewart was never made aware of Burke's side of the story. It seemed Coleman had also told Stewart during his job interview that he'd had a conflict with Jay Adams, the county attorney, as well, but Stewart hadn't investigated that further, either.

Yet Massengill and Amos had both testified that they shared with Stewart all of the background information they had collected on Coleman—including the damaging portrayal in Massengill's notes. How could it be then, Zamoff now asked, that Stewart had testified, as he did in Freddie Brookins's trial, that he did not recall Massengill telling him about any negative information uncovered in the background check? As a witness in the current proceeding, Stewart had not been allowed in the courtroom for the previous days' testimony, but he had read both Amos and Massengill's depositions. He knew what was in Massengill's notes about Coleman, and he knew that the judge had by now heard all of it in detail. Zamoff was calling him a liar.

"I don't specifically remember [saying] it," Stewart responded carefully, "but I believe I did see that in one of the transcripts, yes, sir."

In that same trial, Zamoff reminded Stewart, the sheriff was also asked if, subsequent to hiring Coleman, he had learned anything "negative or marginal" about the officer. Zamoff now read Stewart's dubious response aloud to the court: "With what I know right now today, I do not believe it's negative."

"Do you remember being asked that question and giving that answer?" Zamoff asked.

"It's in the transcript. I'm sure I did say it. Yes, sir," Stewart replied icily. He knew where this was headed.

"Now let's talk about what Sergeant Massengill told you about his research on Tom Coleman," Zamoff began, with obvious relish. "Do you remember a conversation in which he told you that one of the people he called said that Tom Coleman needed constant supervision on the job?"

In light of his dubious testimony in Freddie's trial, Stewart had little choice but to testify now that he did not. "I'm not saying he didn't give me that information. I do not remember it," he said.

"Would you view that as a positive comment, that an officer needs supervision?" Zamoff asked.

"I don't know that it would be positive or negative. I think it's a statement of fact, maybe," Stewart replied.

"If you could just answer my question it would be helpful," Zamoff said. He had been handling Stewart as if he were a criminal suspect from the beginning, and now Stewart was starting to sound like one. "Do you view it as a positive comment that an officer needs constant supervision?"

"It's probably not a positive comment," Stewart finally conceded.

"When you testified here that there was nothing negative in Tom Coleman's background," Zamoff said, pointing to the page from Freddie's trial transcript, "were you aware of this fact that someone said he needed constant supervision?"

As Freddie stared down at him from the jury box, less than ten feet away, Stewart began to stumble over his words. "I think I told you a while ago: I don't remember that conversation, so I don't know—can't say that I was aware of it. I don't remember that specific information at the time that I testified to that."

The examination went on in this vein for several excruciating minutes, with Stewart continuing to deny recalling any of the negative comments from Massengill's notes, and only grudgingly admitting, sometimes after considerable goading by Zamoff, that they were in fact not positive evaluations of Coleman's work or character.

Later Zamoff read to the court a quote that Stewart had given to the *Tulia Sentinel* immediately after the bust: "The officer went to great lengths to be sure that all suspects were correctly identified. He is a man of integrity and professionalism. He upholds the law, and that includes using every means to properly identify every suspect." Later in the same article, Stewart was quoted as saying, "The officer swore under oath, and I truly believe that he has correctly identified every subject."

"It turns out that you were wrong about that; is that correct?" Zamoff said.

"It appears so, yes, sir," Stewart replied.

By the time Chapman halted the hearing for the evening, Stewart was visibly angry. Zamoff was just getting started.

President Bush began his invasion of Iraq that evening, March 19, 2003, and the TV in the war room showed tiny lights arcing across a darkened cityscape and the herky-jerky images of correspondents reporting by videophone. It added to the somber tone of the meeting. Zamoff had Stewart right where he wanted him, and he had yet to face the biggest question of all: his handling of Tom Coleman's arrest. But it was far from clear whether Chapman was coming around. Yet another ex-parte comment from the judge had gotten back to the team. Chapman had told a reporter that much of the information uncovered was not admissible, and that it was a close call. And he had again mentioned the time line—suggesting that more information was available to Freddie's attorney than to the other three applicants. At least the judge indicated at the close of the day's testimony that he would like to hear from the original defense attorneys. Gupta was confident that Mike Hrin would bolster Freddie's case—he had learned nothing from the prosecution team except what he had been able to pry out of Massengill on the stand. Gupta relished the thought of getting Hrin up on the stand just to ask him how he felt in retrospect about Stewart's testimony in Freddie's trial, which was looking more and more like perjury. Still, they were running out of time. They wanted at least a day and a half for Coleman, which meant they had to start his exam tomorrow afternoon. Zamoff would have to close his trap on Stewart quickly.

The next morning the courthouse parking lot was packed with cars, and four satellite trucks had set up shop not far from the front entrance. Word had gotten around that Coleman's testimony was likely to start sometime today, and reporters were clustered around the courthouse steps, hoping to get a shot of him arriving at the courthouse. The gallery was packed when Chapman arrived, and there was a tense energy in the courtroom. Stewart was called back to the stand, and Zamoff quickly steered his interrogation to the arrest of Tom Coleman. Stewart testified that the first time he learned charges had been filed against Coleman was when he received a Teletype from Cochran County on August 7, 1998.

"Do you believe, sir, that Tom Coleman knew about those charges prior to that date?" Zamoff asked.

Nation immediately objected. He knew where Zamoff was headed: Coleman's waiver of arraignment, signed some two months before his arrest. He was going to try to force Stewart to admit that Coleman was dishonest. "Objection to the question calling for speculation, Your Honor," he said. Chapman instructed Stewart to answer.

"I don't have any personal knowledge, sir, that he knew about it," he replied carefully.

Zamoff left the matter dangling for the time being and asked Stewart to describe in detail his arrest of Coleman. Stewart said he got the warrant on a Friday and immediately called Lieutenant Amos in Amarillo to discuss it. Since Coleman didn't work on weekends, the two agreed to wait until Monday to deal with the problem. On Monday, Stewart drove to Amarillo to meet with Mike Amos, Jerry Massengill, and the Amarillo chief of police about the matter. Coleman was called in. His reaction to the warrant, according to Stewart, "was one of surprise and disbelief." Stewart decided that rather than suspend Coleman, he would give him a week of vacation, "to offer him the opportunity to see what it was about."

Now Zamoff placed an exhibit binder in front of Stewart and referred him to document number five, a copy of Coleman's waiver of arraignment, dated May 30, 1998.

Didn't this mean, Zamoff asked, that Coleman and his attorney had full knowledge of the charges on May 30, 1998?

"This document as it's presented does indicate that they knew about it, yes, sir," Stewart replied.

"What do you mean by 'as it's presented'?" Zamoff demanded. "I mean, this is a document. I mean—"

"This is a document," Stewart interrupted. "Yes, it indicates that."

"And if it's true, sir, that Tom Coleman knew about these charges in May of 1998 as exhibit five indicates, it would reflect very poorly on his credibility that he didn't tell you anything about it until you showed up with an arrest warrant. Is that fair to say?" Zamoff asked.

"I would have expected him to say something to me, yes, sir."

That wasn't good enough for Zamoff. "Do you think it would reflect poorly on his credibility," he demanded again, "for him to know about these charges in May, not say anything about it to you, and pretend he's surprised when you arrest him in August?"

"I don't know about his credibility," Stewart replied. "I think it would make me question, you know, why he didn't tell me about it."

"Well, credibility is sort of related to honesty, isn't it?"

"Yes, sir. I think it is, yes."

"And you would expect an honest officer working for you to let you know if he had been charged with a crime, wouldn't you?"

"That's correct, sir."

"And if Tom Coleman knew that he had been charged with a crime in May, June, July, and part of August and never told you, that would be dishonest, wouldn't it?"

Stewart still could not bring himself to say it. "It would—it would—yeah, probably would be."

"What's the—why do you say 'probably'?" Zamoff lashed back. "What is potentially not dishonest about that?"

"I don't know what—without knowing all the circumstances and without knowing exactly what he was thinking, all I can say is 'Yeah, that probably would be.' You know, I don't know what was going on in his mind. But yes—"

"What other circumstances—I'm sorry," Zamoff interrupted.

"I don't have a specific circumstance, sir," Stewart replied coldly. "I'm telling you that, yes, I think that dishonesty is a possible answer to that along with some other possible answers."

"What are the other possible answers?"

Here was where Stewart, in his deposition in Billy Wafer's suit, had brought up Coleman's unlikely story of the blank waiver of arraignment. He seemed reluctant to do that again now, in front of Judge Chapman, with Zamoff asking the questions. "I don't have any specific. I'm saying that there probably are some possibilities."

"Well, I mean, we're here, we're testifying about—"

"Right."

"—you know, how you feel about particular situations, and I'm asking you today: Do you think that would be honest or dishonest?"

"It appears to be dishonest," Stewart replied.

That was the best Zamoff was going to get from Stewart for the time being, and he moved on to the actual details of the arrest itself. As Stewart recounted the discussion, Amos's position was that Coleman could not continue his investigation while these charges were hanging over his head. Strictly speaking, however, Coleman was

Stewart's employee. Stewart had hired him, so he was Stewart's man to fire. The sheriff had to make a decision about how to proceed. It wasn't just the money and time that were on the line. It was also Stewart's judgment. He had sized Coleman up and pronounced him good. Firing Coleman now meant admitting that he had been wrong about the man's character all along, and judging a man's character was what being sheriff was all about. If Coleman was no good, then perhaps Stewart was no good either. There in the offices of the Amarillo police department, Stewart made his decision.

Judge Chapman listened with rapt attention as the sheriff described the steps he took next. The warrant from Cochran County had specified a $3,000 cash bond. Had Coleman been arrested on the spot in Amarillo, he would have been required to appear before a magistrate in open court for a bond hearing, which would have created a public record of his arrest. Stewart sidestepped that with a call to Swisher County judge Harold Keeter, who gave Stewart permission to issue Coleman a personal recognizance, or PR, bond, for which no cash or hearing would be required.

Of course, the arrest would have to take place in Swisher County for that ploy to work. Stewart got in his cruiser and drove back down I–27 toward Tulia. Massengill followed behind, with Coleman in the passenger seat. Shortly after the tandem entered Swisher County, somewhere around Happy, Stewart pulled over to the side of the highway. In the afternoon heat, with the tractor trailers whizzing anonymously by, the three men sat in the air-conditioning of Stewart's car and hastily conducted the most unusual arrest of the sheriff's twenty-year career. There would be no bond hearing, no trip to the Swisher County courthouse, no calls to Cochran County to get to the root of the matter. Coleman was to take a week's vacation to get the matter "resolved," after which he could return to duty. The paperwork filled out and the bond executed, the two cars slipped back onto I–27, their secret intact.

Until now. "Let's go through the history of exactly what happened and see if we can figure out a little bit more about the details of this incident," Zamoff said. He produced a Teletype from Cochran County which objected to the PR bond and noted that Stewart had failed to have Coleman sign his fingerprint card. It was a crucial omission, because without the signed card, Cochran County could not report the arrest to the statewide database where criminal records were maintained. Stewart now insisted that it was an oversight, and that Cochran County never returned the card so that it could be completed correctly.

Stewart sat stone-faced and silent as Zamoff approached and handed the sheriff a piece of paper. It was Coleman's blank TCIC form, his "clean record" that McEachern had alluded to in the original trials and that Hocker had waived in front of the judge on Tuesday. Zamoff asked Stewart to read what it said. "No identifiable record," the sheriff read.

Zamoff held the document up at arm's length, displaying it to the courtroom. "Now, this has been causing me a great deal of confusion," he said, his voice rising. "How is it that if Tom Coleman was arrested, and every single person in this room knows he was arrested, including yourself, that you're able to create a criminal history sheet that makes it look like he wasn't arrested?"

Nation rose to object to Zamoff's tone, but Stewart's blood was finally up and he didn't need Nation's help.

"Sir," he began, his voice dripping with menace. "I don't create anything. I didn't create this sheet. I don't create his record. That's what you asked me about, how was I able to create this?" Now he was almost shouting. "Is that what you asked me?"

In the heated exchange that followed, Stewart insisted that Cochran County had never returned the incomplete fingerprint card to him to have it signed by Coleman, so it was their fault, not his, that the arrest never made it into the database.

Zamoff pointed out that Stewart could have simply created a new card and forwarded it over. "My issue for today is that whether you created a new one or got him to sign an old one or did anything, you did nothing to provide the information requested from Cochran County that would allow them to initiate the reporting process, that being the fingerprint card, correct?"

"I did nothing further. That's correct, sir."

"So now today we have this report that the State is waiving around here at this hearing which shows that Tom Coleman was never arrested, when we all know he was. That's the result of what happened here, so that if some defense lawyer wants to go look up Tom Coleman or request his record, they're going to get that which makes it look like he was never arrested; is that your understanding of what that document would show?"

Stewart agreed it was true.

Zamoff now turned to the dismissal of the charges against Coleman. At the beginning of his exam, Zamoff had gotten Stewart to testify that in order to continue working in Swisher County, Coleman had to satisfy Stewart that he had not committed the crime of which he was accused. Zamoff referred Stewart to the dismissal order in the exhibit binder, and noted that it indicated, "Restitution has been made."

"All right," Zamoff began. "What is it about this motion to dismiss or this dismissal that assured you he did not commit the crime?"

"I don't know that there's anything here that assures me that the offense did not occur," Stewart replied. Stewart testified that Coleman had never actually shown him the dismissal order, and that he did not realize at the time that Coleman had paid restitution for the gas he was accused of stealing.

"Your principal concern was just that [the charges] were resolved so you could get him back on the street; isn't that true?" Zamoff asked.

"I believe that's correct, yes, sir," Stewart answered. He was beginning to wear down.

Zamoff announced that he just had a couple more areas to cover, and Chapman called for a brief break. When the teams returned, however, Zamoff unexpectedly passed the witness.

Nation was caught off guard. He rose and began gathering his notes. He spent an hour going over once again Stewart's reason for hiring Coleman, the nature of undercover work, and the division of labor on the background check, bolstering as best he could Stewart's performance on the job. Then he turned to Zamoff's accusations.

"I want to move to some of the questions you were asked by opposing counsel. Were you trying to—Would you have done anything unethical to keep Tom Coleman on the streets after his arrest simply not to jeopardize the operation?"

"Absolutely not," Stewart replied.

"Was convicting these four defendants so important to you that you would have kept Tom Coleman on no matter what?"

"No, that's not correct."

Nation pointed out that Coleman had made over a hundred cases.

"Well, if you had become convinced that Tom Coleman was a liar and a criminal, would you have been willing to throw each and every one of these cases he made out?"

"Yes, sir."

"Without a second thought?"

"Yes, sir."

"No matter what—how much political heat it would have caused you or may have caused you in this county?"

"Yes, sir."

Zamoff quietly jotted down notes on this exchange. It was exactly what he needed for his big finish with Stewart.

After lunch, Nation made a brief attempt to discredit the Cochran County authorities, noting that the charges had been filed just before the statute of limitations ran out. He brought up the polygraph test, which Stewart described, once again, as his main reason for believing that Coleman did not commit the theft. Then he passed Stewart back to Zamoff.

Zamoff rose and buttoned his coat. He got Stewart to admit that he had never previously encountered a case where a county attorney made false allegations about a cop in a sworn affidavit, and that Jay Adams had in fact filed a report about the gas theft shortly after he witnessed it, even though the case was not filed for some time. Then he came back to the subject of Coleman's honesty.

"Now sir, you testified that if you were convinced Tom Coleman was a liar you would throw these cases out. Do you remember that?"

"I believe so, yes, sir."

"Do you stand by that statement?"

"I think so."

"Well, it causes me to ask this question: Why haven't these cases been thrown out?"

"I think the reason is because I don't believe that at this point."

Once again, Zamoff referred Stewart to the waiver of arraignment, the date Coleman signed it, his failure to inform Stewart, and his feigned surprise when confronted with the warrant.

"And you don't think based on that information that he lied to you?"

"I don't think that's a lie in the sense that would affect the cases, no, sir," Stewart replied carefully.

"Well, if he lied to you, that would affect his credibility, wouldn't it?"

"In a sense, yes, sir."

"Well, in what sense wouldn't it?" Zamoff demanded.

As the four applicants watched from their seats in the jury box, Stewart struggled to recount Coleman's explanation for the discrepancy—that he had signed a blank waiver of arraignment because he feared that charges might soon be filed. He hadn't known for certain he would be charged when he signed the waiver, Coleman had told

Stewart; it was a precautionary measure. So, technically speaking, Stewart suggested, it was possible that he had still not learned of the charges by the time Stewart received the arrest warrant.

"Is that what he told you, that he actually didn't know about these charges even though—"

"That's what I understand his attorney testified to."

"Well how about Tom Coleman, did he tell you that he actually didn't know on May 30, '98 that he knew of these charges?"

"I believe that's what I understand, yes, sir."

"Well, what did he tell you?"

"About?"

"This."

"About this waiver?"

"Yes."

"His attorney testified—"

"Sir, I don't mean to interrupt you, but my question is: What did Tom Coleman tell you about this?"

"I don't know if we've ever discussed this. If we have, my recollection is that he would testify the same—or told me the same thing his attorney did, that this was a document he signed because there were some things going on and they didn't know where it was going, and this would save him a trip back to his attorney's office if it came to that."

"Well, is the testimony that the attorney didn't tell him after this happened?" Zamoff asked, referring to the actual filing of the charges.

"I don't know what the testimony would be," Stewart replied.

Stewart was clearly getting exhausted and flustered. Zamoff continued to hammer away, trying to force Stewart to admit that Coleman was a liar. After Stewart parried a couple more questions, Zamoff made his final push.

"Okay, but I'm asking you, sir, because you said if you were convinced somebody is a liar these cases would be dropped. Do you find that story plausible that there was some blank waiver signed by Coleman...and he didn't know about the charges and his lawyer never told him before August of '98?" he asked, pointing his finger at Stewart. "Do *you* find that plausible?"

"Again, you know—Yes, that's hard to believe, but I have heard this, his lawyer testified to that," Stewart said. Now Zamoff almost had him.

"It's hard to believe for you, though, isn't it?" he asked.

"Yes, sir," Stewart finally said. "It's a little bit hard to believe."

During the recess, the team huddled around Zamoff, congratulating him. Stewart's testimony, particularly during Zamoff's devastating redirect, had been some of the most compelling the judge had heard so far. Chapman had seemed acutely interested, particularly in the details of Stewart's arrest of Coleman, about which he had taken the time to ask some questions of his own. But there was no time to celebrate. They would call Coleman next. It was 1:30 in the afternoon, and Zamoff would have about three and a half hours to work with. It was not nearly enough time to cover the outline he had prepared for Coleman, but it was enough to get started.

Coleman had spent the morning out of sight, waiting in a small office just outside the entrance to the courtroom. Word had gone out that Coleman was the next witness, and there was not a single empty seat in the gallery as the attorneys returned from the recess. It was a sea of mostly black faces, except for the first two rows, which were now even more packed with reporters. After Judge Chapman had taken his seat at the dais, Zamoff called for Coleman, and the gallery immediately went silent. Coleman came in dressed in a black leather jacket over a blue shirt and a black tie and made his way to the witness chair, his eyes carefully cast straight ahead. He nodded to the judge, took his seat, and was sworn in.

Zamoff began with a few questions about Coleman's law enforcement background. He had planned to then read from the deposition testimony of all of his old law enforcement colleagues, to get Coleman's reaction to their allegations. As it turned out, however, Coleman didn't wait to hear what they had to say about him; he immediately went on the attack. When Zamoff asked him why he left Pecos County, he replied, "I had a conflict with a deputy named Sam Esparza for having an affair with my wife."

According to Coleman, Carol Barnett was the source of much of his trouble in the mid-1990s. He'd had to quit his deputy job in Pecos County because she worked at the sheriff's office as well, and there was too much bad blood between them to work together. After Coleman moved to the north Texas town of Sherman, he got a job as a jailer at the nearby Denton County sheriff's office, but marital problems had forced him to quit that job as well, he said. Barnett had filed a restraining order against Coleman, and he lost his job because of it, he said. His next stop was Cochran County, where he worked for only a year.

"And why did you leave there?" Zamoff asked.

"Various reasons," Coleman replied.

"Why don't you tell us what those reasons were."

Coleman responded with a long, rambling account of some confiscated marijuana that went missing from the evidence vault. He tried to report it—first to the chief deputy, Raymond Webber, then to Sheriff Ken Burke, and finally to the county attorney, Jay Adams—but nobody would listen to him, he said. He finally told Jay Adams that if any evidence from his own cases went missing, he was going to call the Texas Rangers. "And he told me if I called the Texas Rangers that I was going to be fired," Coleman said.

Coleman's story, in which he neatly implicated all three of his chief critics from Cochran County, prompted some hoots from the rear of the gallery. Coleman pretended he didn't hear them. He sat slightly hunched forward in his seat, staring at Zamoff, with his forehead wrinkled and his head cocked slightly to one side, as though he were having trouble hearing.

"And what was it about this sequence of events that caused you to feel compelled to leave your job?" Zamoff asked.

"Well, first off, we have missing marijuana; second off, the sheriff's driving around town in a personal vehicle that the county bought the tires for that he got out at the county barn," Coleman replied. "Several other little things, and it's just like 'Am I going to stay here and live like this, or I'm just going to go down the road?' And I chose to go down the road."

Zamoff offered Coleman the opportunity to list any other reasons he left, and each open-ended question resulted in another lengthy story. He said he had caught Raymond Webber, for example, in a compromising position with a female inmate late one night at the jail. It was a story not too dissimilar from the circumstances under which Coleman himself was terminated from what would prove to be his last law enforcement job, in Ellis County, where the DA had discovered he was having sex with a task force snitch. Zamoff just let him go on at length, without stopping him to ask questions. Coleman did not mention his debts, or the fact that his live-in girlfriend had left him, which was the reason he gave for leaving on the actual night of his sudden departure, according to the dispatcher who was on duty that night.

When Coleman was done, Zamoff produced a copy of his farewell letter to his Cochran County coworkers, written the night he left town. Coleman did not look happy to see it. Zamoff directed him to read the first page, in which Coleman began by thanking Sheriff Burke for the job, but telling him he had to move on. "You're a pretty good person. I have enjoyed being your friend. I wish you well and hope you can win the election in November, 1996," Coleman finished reading.

"Okay. Now this sheriff who you're writing to at this time, this is the same person who you claim you had a confrontation with about the marijuana; is that correct?" Zamoff asked.

"Uh-huh."

"And this is the same sheriff who you claimed you had a confrontation with about the tires and this vehicle issue?"

"Uh-huh."

"And all of that happened before this letter was written; is that correct?"

"Uh-huh," Coleman replied.

"All right," Zamoff said, "Now, if you turn the page it seems to be some words of wisdom, or whatever you want to call it, for other people in the department. Is that fair to say?"

"I guess so," Coleman replied. He was reading ahead and frowning. Zamoff had him read his advice for Raymond Webber: "Just hang in there. You'll wake up one of these days. I have faith in you."

The letter went on to list four or five other co-workers, each of whom Coleman had offered some advice. "And you didn't hesitate in this letter here to make suggestions of how people could improve themselves if you thought that they had some deficiencies; is that fair to say?" Zamoff said dryly.

"There was a lot of problems in that department," Coleman replied, drawing another round of tittering from the gallery.

Coleman's risible farewell letter had set a kind of farcical tone, especially in comparison to Zamoff's dramatic confrontation with Stewart that morning. Zamoff seemed content with it. "Now, after resigning from Cochran County, where did you go next?" he asked, then interrupted Coleman before he could answer. "I guess resigning is really the wrong word for it. After *leaving* Cochran County, where did you go next?"

Zamoff ran through a list of subject areas, each setting up questions he planned to ask the next morning. Was theft still a crime, even if restitution was made? Coleman admitted it was. Was it proper to scratch out a portion of a report? It was not. Shouldn't reports always include the time of day a crime took place, and shouldn't descriptions of suspects include more than just their race and sex? He peppered his

questions with veiled insults of Coleman, referring to his work in
Tulia as an "alleged investigation" and his buys as "cases you claim
you made." The mood in the gallery was giddy. They were watching a
virtuoso at work. The four applicants, meanwhile, sat and stared at
Coleman, for the most part expressionless.

Zamoff began a line of questions about Coleman's hiring for the
Tulia job in January of 1998. Coleman said he was pessimistic about
his chances after the interview. When he was called a few weeks later
and offered the job, he said, his response had been, "Did you do the
background?" Coleman didn't think he'd get the job, he said, because
he'd told Amos, Massengill, and Stewart that he'd left debts in
Cochran County and that he probably would not get a good recommendation from Sheriff Burke. Zamoff asked whether or not he'd
informed his new employers about the possible theft charges, which
Coleman admitted he'd known might be filed since the fall of 1997. "I
believe they were. I can't totally recall. That was a long time ago," he
said. Nobody had ever asked him to respond to the allegations that he
needed "constant supervision" or had "mental problems" before or
after he was hired, he said.

Zamoff quizzed Coleman about his unpaid debts in Cochran
County. "You know, at your deposition, you testified that a man ain't a
man unless he pays his bills?" Zamoff said.

"That's right."

"That's kind of a funny thing for you to say, isn't it?"

"Yep. And you've never been behind on your bills?" Coleman
retorted.

"Well, you're being asked the questions today, sir," Zamoff
replied.

This drew yet another appreciative response from the gallery, and
a bit later Mark Hocker rose to scold them. "Your Honor...could we
get an instruction to the gallery that this is a courtroom and not a
church and we don't need amen shouted out?" he said disdainfully.

Chapman gently admonished the audience to maintain their decorum.

Zamoff turned to Coleman's methods in Tulia. Coleman conceded that he had no corroboration for his buys, but he said that he had been searched three or four times, and did not feel safe wearing a wire. Zamoff pointed out that there was no record of those searches in Coleman's reports. He also raised a point that some of the original defense attorneys had made to Terry McEachern long ago. In cases where Coleman made more than one buy from the same person, presumably building a level of trust, why hadn't he worn a wire during the later buys? Coleman admitted that he could have done that, he just chose not to. If he'd had it over again, he might have done it differently, he said.

"And you probably would have requested fingerprints from any of the drugs that were allegedly sold to you; is that correct?" Zamoff continued.

"That would have been—it wouldn't have been applicable," Coleman replied.

"Well, fingerprints are evidence, correct?" Zamoff asked.

"You use fingerprints for identification. If you know the person that you're buying from, why should I get fingerprints?" Coleman responded.

"Well, the reason you do it, sir, I would suggest, is that it provides corroboration for one person's word," Zamoff replied in an exasperated tone. "Did you ever consider that?"

"No, I didn't consider it," Coleman replied in a small voice. It was obvious he was telling the truth.

It was getting close to five o'clock and Zamoff was running out of time. "You've said in an interview, sir, that you gave with a television station that 'The most important thing is if I say you sell dope to me, I better be damn sure who you are because you're fixing to go to prison,'" Zamoff read. "Do you remember saying that?"

Coleman replied that he'd only been wrong about one person, Yul Bryant. He amended that to two when Zamoff reminded him of Romona Strickland, but he denied that Tonya White or Billy Wafer were bad cases.

Zamoff pulled out a page from a transcript of an interview Coleman had given to Tom Mangold of the BBC. Strictly speaking, under the rules of evidence, Mangold himself should have been there to testify about it in order for it to be used in court, but Zamoff hoped to bluff it by McEachern's team.

Zamoff read Mangold's question to Coleman: "That's right, but you got it wrong in four cases?"

"And they're not in prison are they?" Coleman had replied.

"You got it wrong in four cases?" Mangold had persisted.

"That's right," Coleman had replied.

When Zamoff was done reading the exchange, he turned to Coleman. "So you are agreeing that you got it wrong in four cases or are you changing that today?" he asked.

"Let me just read this a minute," Coleman replied.

"Anything you want to change about your testimony?"

"There were some mess-ups in four cases, yes, sir," Coleman finally conceded.

Nobody from the state was objecting to Zamoff's use of the transcript, so he pressed on. "Now if you look at the last page of this transcript that I've given you, the very last page, there's a comment you made in there that I want to ask you about," he said. "Down around two-thirds of the way down you said, 'I hope I don't have nobody in jail that ain't (chuckle) supposed to be in jail. I mean, God, that would be bad.'"

"I want to ask you two things about that. First, I'm not sure why you chuckled. I mean, what is funny about that comment?"

"I don't remember I chuckled. I don't know. I don't remember," Coleman replied. "Let me—Can I ask a question?"

"I don't believe this is the time for that, sir," Zamoff replied dismissively. He had Coleman reeling now. "Now, secondly, you're not sure if everyone you locked up deserves to be in jail; is that fair to say?"

"I'm pretty sure," Coleman replied.

"But you're not totally sure?"

"I'm pretty sure."

"Well, that's admitting that you're not totally sure, right?"

"I'm totally sure," Coleman finally said.

Shortly thereafter, Chapman recessed court for the evening.

That night the team assessed the situation in the war room. Zamoff had landed a few good blows on Coleman, but the questioning seemed to go in circles at times, with Coleman simply denying what somebody else had claimed about him or adjusting his earlier testimony to better fit the facts. Bruce Wilson, Ori White, and the others had all seemed much more believable than Coleman, but it still came down to a swearing contest, as many of the original trials had. They had plenty of examples of Coleman apparently lying in the original trials, but Coleman had always managed to find a way to explain away the inconsistencies. What they needed to do was catch him in a new lie on the stand, with Chapman and everybody else watching.

Coleman's arrest in Tulia was the key. He had backed himself into a corner with his claim that he didn't know about the charges until Sheriff Stewart discovered the warrant. Even if the waiver of arraignment he signed had been blank, as he'd claimed, there was still the issue of the attorney he had hired, Garry Smith. Surely, once Coleman had actually been charged, Smith would have contacted Coleman to let him know. Coleman had claimed in his deposition that Smith never did. Thanks to their subpoena powers, the team had obtained documents that seemed to indicate that Coleman and his attorney had in fact been in steady contact about the charges for months before Stewart found out about them. The records were buried deep in the exhibit binder, and Zamoff suspected that with so many documents to look through, nobody from the state had even glanced at them yet. There was no way to know if Coleman was aware they had obtained Smith's records. He had told so many unlikely stories over the years, any one of them could be his undoing. If Zamoff could get him to repeat his claim that he had never been in touch with Smith, this was going to be the one.

Friday morning began with a surprise witness. Instead of Coleman, a sober-faced middle-aged woman with short, curly hair took the stand. Adam Levin, the young Hogan & Hartson associate, stood up to examine her. Her name was Paula Gerik, and she was the communications supervisor at the Cochran County sheriff's office. She was responsible, she said, for the county's use of the state criminal records database, and for sending fingerprint cards into the DPS, the state police agency, so that arrests could be entered into the database. The day before, during his recross-exam of Sheriff Stewart, John Nation had sought to absolve Stewart of the blame for Coleman's arrest not appearing on his criminal record, laying it instead on Cochran County authorities. Even if Stewart had submitted Coleman's fingerprint card without a signature, Cochran County could still have entered the arrest in the database, Nation had argued. Stewart, for his part, had suggested that Cochran County was to blame for failing to return the blank signature card to his office. Levin strongly suspected that both of those contentions were false. He had immediately slipped out of the hearing and phoned the Cochran County sheriff's office. After a brief conversation with Gerik, he'd had a subpoena drawn up and rushed down to Morton.

Under questioning from Levin, Gerik testified that she recalled receiving an arrest record for Tom Coleman from Swisher County, and that the fingerprint card had indeed been unsigned. She had called Stewart's office on August 12, 1998, to complain. Gerik still had her handwritten call logs from the day in question, which Levin now entered into evidence. It seemed she was a meticulous record keeper. She had called again on August 13 and talked to Linda Swanson, Stewart's assistant, who asked her to send back the fingerprint card, so that she could have Coleman sign it. "So here's the question: Did you mail Mr. Coleman's unsigned fingerprint cards back to Swisher County?" Levin asked.

"Yes, sir, I did."

"And did you ever hear from Swisher County again . . . about the fingerprint card?" Levin asked.

"No, sir, I didn't," Gerik replied.

Without that signed signature card, Gerik testified, there was no way to notify DPS of the arrest, and therefore no way to put the charge on Coleman's record. It was Sheriff Stewart who was responsible for Coleman's arrest remaining a secret. It had always been Stewart.

Levin passed the witness. Nation had been staring at Gerik with a sour frown on his face throughout her testimony. Now he stood and examined the phone logs.

"All right. Now who told you that you could not mail, you could not notify DPS or otherwise cause NCIC and TCIC to reflect an arrest unless you have all this information?" he asked.

"Because we had tried before, and we have sent one in with an unsigned fingerprint card and all they did was mail it back to us," Gerik replied matter-of-factly.

Nation then made the mistake of questioning her credentials. "Ma'am, as part of your training for your office, have you ever gone to TCIC school?" he asked.

"I have been to two forty-hour ones, and every two years we have an update of sixteen hours," she replied. Mrs. Gerik was a woman who knew what she knew. Nation made a couple more halfhearted attempts to absolve Stewart and then sat down.

Gerik stepped down and Zamoff called Tom Coleman back to the stand. Coleman eyed Zamoff wearily as he climbed back into the witness chair. He looked like a boxer who didn't want to answer the bell. Zamoff began with a line of questions about Coleman's tenure in Pecos County under Bruce Wilson.

"[W]ould you agree that while you were working in Pecos County, you caused some trouble for the sheriff?"

As Coleman recalled things, it was the other way around. He had always insisted on doing his job the right way, writing tickets to whomever he stopped regardless of who it was. Wilson, on the other hand, had a tendency to play favorites and cut people slack, and that had caused friction between them. Coleman admitted that he had left town abruptly. As he had when he left Cochran County, however, he found time to leave a note behind. Zamoff drew it out and read a portion of it. It was addressed to Sheriff Wilson.

"I won't ever forget you and all the shit you had to put up with while I was here," Zamoff read.

Zamoff asked what Coleman had meant by "all the shit."

"All the disagreements that I had with the sheriff," Coleman replied.

"And this had nothing to do with the town meeting that he had to attend because people were complaining about you?" Zamoff asked.

"Probably."

"And the incident where he says he caught you lying about a tape-recorded incident with some women, did it have anything to do with that?"

Coleman said he remembered the incident, but that he had never heard any tape recording of it, and he denied lying about it to Wilson.

Zamoff read some more from the letter. "I love law enforcement, but will never get to be a cop again after leaving this department like this," he read. "What did you mean by that?"

Coleman mentioned the friction he'd had with Wilson over favoritism, and what he termed his "lunatic" ex-wife, who was bent on seeing his career ruined. He felt sure that Wilson would not give him a good recommendation when he applied for future jobs, he said.

Zamoff moved on to the subject of the theft charges in Cochran County. Coleman immediately said he did not learn of the charges until August 7, 1998. "Well, first let's talk about what you did and then we're going to talk about what you knew and when," Zamoff began. He directed Coleman to the charging documents in the evidence binder, charging Coleman with theft and misuse of government property. They were dated May 6, 1998.

"And you are saying here today that the first time this was brought to your attention was, I guess, when you were arrested by Sheriff Stewart in August of 1998?" he asked.

"August, yes, sir," Coleman replied.

Zamoff then walked Coleman through the offense report, in which Chief Deputy Raymond Weber noted discrepancies in fuel statements for the patrol vehicles, one for May 18, 1996, and one for May 29, 1996, the day Coleman left Cochran County. It seemed Coleman's county-issued card had been used twice for fill-ups on each of those days. There was also a statement from county attorney Jay Adams, alleging that he saw Coleman with his own eyes filling his personal vehicle from the county pumps on May 18, 1996, at about 4:37 in the afternoon.

It wasn't true, Coleman claimed. Another deputy could have used his gas card to fill their patrol car, he said, which would explain the double fill-ups. What about Jay Adams's eyewitness account? Zamoff asked. Also false, Coleman said.

"This is entirely made up, you weren't even there?" Zamoff asked.

"Looks to me like," Coleman replied.

"And of course the computer printout which shows that the card charged out to you was in that gasoline pump at 4:37 on that date, that doesn't convince you you were there either?" Zamoff asked.

"No. I imagine they got their computer printouts and all their little deals together to put the times together," Coleman said.

"Wait. You think they did what?" Zamoff asked. Coleman repeated his assertion.

"So the whole thing is just a whole made-up, frame-up job?"

"I believe so."

Coleman suggested it was all done just before the statute of limitations to get him to pay back the $7,000 he owed to merchants in Morton. Zamoff pointed out that Adams's offense report was dated June 13, 1996, just a few weeks after the incident. Coleman suggested it had been forged.

"So basically the deal in Cochran County, as you see it, is that Adams is lying under oath?" Zamoff asked.

"Yes, sir."

"Burke is lying?"

"Yes, sir."

"Weber is lying?"

"Yes, sir."

When Coleman intimated that he might file charges against them for the alleged slander, Zamoff pointed out that five years had now passed.

"But you're just waiting for the right time?" he asked.

"You can say that," Coleman replied.

Zamoff now shifted to the question of when Coleman first learned about the charges filed against him in Cochran County. Though he'd been unsure the day before, Coleman was now positive that he hadn't mentioned any possible charges looming during his interview for the

Tulia job in January 1998. Had he known they were coming, he said, he would have told them about it.

"And if you had found out about it after January, like February or March or April or May, you would have come right out and told those guys right then, right?"

"True," Coleman replied.

"Because that's the kind of dishonesty if you didn't tell them, that would be cause for you to get fired, correct?"

"True."

Zamoff now directed Coleman to his testimony in a postconviction hearing for Cash Love, held in Tulia on April 12, 2000. Love's attorney, Van Williamson, had only recently learned that Coleman was arrested, and he was trying to get his client a new trial based on that information. Zamoff read from Williamson's questioning of Coleman about the charges: "In any case the exact date that we . . . know for a fact that you knew about it . . . is the date that you signed the waiver of arraignment, which is May 30, 1998?" Coleman had answered, "Yes, sir."

"That's after you consulted with your attorney and retained counsel?" Williamson had asked. Zamoff read Coleman's answer: "Yes, sir."

"Do you remember being asked those questions and giving those answers?" Zamoff asked.

Coleman admitted that he went to see his attorney, Garry Smith, in May, and that Smith had him sign a waiver.

"And the waiver is a waiver of what?" Zamoff asked.

"Of possible problems in Cochran County," Coleman replied.

"The document is called a waiver of possible problems, what is it?" Zamoff responded mockingly.

"No it was a waiver of judgment or something where he would have to take, he would take care of the problem in Cochran County," Coleman replied. "I imagine you have that waiver," he added balefully. That piece of paper had become his bane.

"Well I have it, but before we talk about it, I would like to know what you're saying. What are you saying you signed on May 30?"

"A waiver," Coleman replied.

"And what was on it?"

"Nothing."

In the exchange that followed, Zamoff demanded to know exactly what was on the waiver, and Coleman insisted he would not answer until he saw the document in the exhibit binder.

At an impasse, Zamoff referred Coleman back to his testimony in Cash Love's hearing. "Okay. But this testimony here where you say you knew about the charges in May 1998. You're saying this is false?"

"I'm not saying it's false," Coleman replied.

Zamoff read the exchange from the transcript again. "[I]s that true or false?" he demanded.

"My answer to that question is I didn't know anything about the charges until August 7, 1998," Coleman said. He seemed to have received some coaching since his last round with Zamoff; after his long, rambling responses of the previous afternoon, somebody seemingly told him to stick to his story and give up as little information as possible.

But Zamoff just hammered him harder. "No, sir. The first excerpt I read you, page 24, 'Would you agree with me that it was sometime in May of 1998? Yes, sir,'" Zamoff read, stabbing his finger at the transcript in front of Coleman. "True or false?"

"False," Coleman finally replied.

Zamoff now drew out the waiver of arraignment. "I need to understand more about how this document is blank," Zamoff said, placing it in front of Coleman's face. "I mean this document is a computer-generated document. It has three paragraphs on it, signatures, a caption—what was on it when you signed it?"

"My answer is this document was blank when I signed it."

"Well, was the case number on it? See at the top, the very top there where it says number 5701, was that on it?"

"I don't recall."

"Well, if it was on it, you would have known you had a case, right?"

"My answer is this document was blank when I signed it," Coleman said in a flat voice. The examination had taken on the tone of a prisoner interrogation.

"Well, that's not the question I asked you. The question I asked you was, If you saw this number, you would know you had a case?"

"Yes."

"So it must have been blank, right, or else you would have known you had a case?"

"Must have."

"Must have, it wasn't on there," Zamoff said mockingly. "How about State of Texas versus Tom Coleman, was that on there?"

"I don't recall."

"Well, if you saw this, you would have known you had a case, right, because it's Texas versus Coleman?"

"I don't recall."

"Well, I'm asking you what you know if you see the State of Texas versus Tom Coleman, would you know if you had a case?"

"I don't recall," Coleman repeated for the third time.

"It's not a question about memory," Zamoff said, his voice rising. "It's a question about sitting right here. If you see a piece of paper with State of Texas versus Tom Coleman, does that mean you have a case against you?"

"Yes, sir," Coleman replied.

Zamoff went methodically through the rest of the document, forcing Coleman to repeat his dubious claim—"this document was blank when I signed it"—over and over again until it became like a weight around his neck.

"And I take it once the charges were filed, your attorney was instructed to tell you, right?" Zamoff asked.

"Yes, sir," Coleman replied.

"Because he's your man, right, he's your man on these charges?"

"I hired him, yes, sir."

"Okay. And you have to know because if you get charged, you've got to notify your superior officers, correct?"

"Correct."

Zamoff then directed Coleman's attention to a letter from Garry Smith to the prosecuting attorney on the case dated June 1, 1998. The letter referenced the cause number for the case against Coleman and included a copy of the waiver of arraignment.

"And it's signed Garry Smith and cc Mr. Tom Coleman," Zamoff read. "You see that?"

"Uh-huh."

"So certainly when you got this letter, even if the waiver of arraignment was blank when you signed it, when you got this letter on or near June 1, '98, you know there's a case?"

"I never got this letter," Coleman replied. It had gone to his mother's house in Midland, he claimed, because that was the only address Smith had for him.

If Coleman didn't know charges were filed against him in May, then why, Zamoff asked, had Coleman hired an attorney that same month?

"I figured Cochran County was going to ask me to pay those bills, something, I knew I was going to have problems in Cochran County," Coleman replied.

"Why? It's been two years, what happened?"

"I don't know. That's my question, why. It's been two years."

"That's everyone's question."

"Uh-huh. Why—never mind."

"So you have no explanation—just after two years you decide it's time to walk into Garry Smith's office and hire him?"

"Yes, sir."

"And it's just a coincidence we're supposed to believe that you did that the same month the charges were filed against you?"

"True."

"Just a coincidence?"

"True. That's true."

"And we're also supposed to believe from the time this waiver of arraignment gets filed, which is actually on June 1, 1998, until August 7, 1998, he never makes contact with you and you never try to contact him?

"True."

Zamoff directed Coleman to the next exhibit in the binder, a letter from Garry Smith to Coleman dated July 20, 1998, in which Smith referenced the case and discussed bond arrangements.

Again, Coleman claimed he never got the letter. Zamoff pointed out that Smith seemed to assume that Coleman already knew about the case in the letter.

"But you said you had no idea there was a case," Zamoff said.

"The answer to this question is I didn't know there was a case until August 7, 1998," Coleman replied.

Zamoff pressed on, ignoring Coleman's denials. He was rapidly approaching the moment when he planned to close the noose on Coleman. He pointed to the bottom of the letter.

"And he says, please give me a call regarding this matter at your earliest convenience. Do you see that?"

"Uh-huh."

"Okay. But you never did that because you never got this letter?"

Everybody on the defense team knew what the next exhibit was—copies of Garry Smith's telephone messages from Coleman. Gupta and Blackburn leaned forward in their chairs, struggling to control their body language. This was it. Coleman was either going to lie on the stand in front of Chapman, or he was going to catch on to Zamoff's trap and wriggle out of it.

"Is that right?" Zamoff asked.

"Correct," Coleman said.

For a split second, nobody on the defense team was sure what they had heard. Coleman had been saying "uh-huh" and "true" all morning. Then it registered. "Correct." Coleman was saying yes. They had done it. Coleman had committed perjury, live and in person, in front of Judge Chapman, with a gallery packed full of witnesses, and the man from the *New York Times* in the front row and four satellite trucks waiting outside.

Exultant, Zamoff directed Coleman to turn the page in his exhibit binder. There they were, photocopies of a handful of pages from a "While You Were Out" pad, each recording an incoming phone message to Garry Smith's office. The first one was from Tom Coleman. It was dated July 23, just three days after Smith sent Coleman the letter.

"That reflects you called him three days after that letter was sent, doesn't it?" Zamoff asked.

Coleman looked like he wanted to crawl under the witness chair. "I've called him, but I didn't make contact with him. He wasn't there," he said.

"Just five minutes ago you said you never tried to make contact with him in that period. Are you now changing that testimony?"

"Yes, sir, I'm changing that testimony. Yes, I tried to contact him, but I never talked to him between May and August 7, 1998."

"And again, sir, we're supposed to believe it is just a coincidence that three days after he sent you a letter asking you to give him a call regarding this matter, you just happened to call his office?"

"I was calling to check in," Coleman replied feebly.

There was a low murmuring from the gallery. Zamoff hadn't just beaten Coleman, he had crushed him. On the dais, Chapman's body language had begun to betray him. He had shifted further and further away from Coleman, who was seated on his immediate left, until, by the time Zamoff had sprung his trap, he was almost out of his chair.

Coleman became increasingly petulant as Zamoff moved through other instances of apparent perjury from previous trials, including his testimony in Billy Wafer's revocation hearing that he had never been arrested. When Zamoff noted that Coleman had an obligation to report his arrest to TCLEOSE, Coleman replied that he had not been aware of that fact until he received a letter from the agency years after his arrest. Prior to that letter, he said, he'd never had any contact with TCLEOSE about the matter.

"Okay. And you never tried to call them and bring it to their attention or anything like that?" Zamoff asked.

"No, sir," Coleman replied.

Zamoff then had a VCR wheeled into the courtroom and played a videotape of an interview Coleman had given to an Amarillo TV station. Coleman watched, humiliated, as the interviewer asked him why he had never reported his arrest to TCLEOSE. His response was that he had called TCLEOSE to inquire about it and they had told him it was not his responsibility to do so. He was either lying to the reporter on the videotape, or he was lying to Zamoff now. Coleman had given so many accounts of his behavior in Tulia over the years, he could no longer keep track of them.

With Coleman floundering, Zamoff landed another serious blow. "Did you know that the purity of the drugs that you claim you bought down here was very, very low?" he asked.

"I heard that, yes, sir," Coleman replied.

"I mean in some cases it was less than 10 percent pure, have you heard that?"

"Uh-huh."

"And I take it, that is much lower than normal street narcotics, correct?"

That was of course correct, and it was the kind of thing a professional narc would be expected to know. Coleman could have made an effort to explain away the purity—he could have said, for example, that some dealers in Tulia tried to rip him off—but he seemed not to have any fight left in him. "No, it's about the way it is. It's what you buy," he claimed.

"Have you heard the theory, sir, that you took undercover money that you were given to buy drugs and that you put some of that money in your pocket and kept it?" Zamoff asked.

"Yeah, I heard that theory," Coleman replied.

"All right. And have you heard the theory that you took some of that money . . . and instead of coming to Tulia, you went up to the Amarillo area and bought narcotics there?"

"I also heard that one too," Coleman replied in a tired voice.

"And have you heard the theory that once you bought these narcotics, which were the typical amount of purity, you took a cutting agent and you cut those drugs up into many impure servings and turned that into evidence as if you bought it from the defendants in these cases?"

"I also heard that theory."

"That you're able to make one eight ball into several eight balls and pretend that you made many buys against many different people. Have you heard that?"

"I heard that."

"Because if that's not true, you have to believe that there are about forty-five drug dealers in a town of only about 5,000 people, is that correct, if your buys are all correct?"

"They are correct," Coleman replied, halfheartedly. "And it's true."

Just before lunch, Zamoff turned to Coleman's use of the word "nigger." He read a portion of a BBC interview transcript in which Coleman denied using the word. Coleman now admitted to Zamoff that this was untrue, and said he used the word with his friends and family. There followed this exchange:

Q: Oh, so you have used it with your friends and family?

A: Yes, sir.

Q: Okay.

A: It's kind of a—go ahead.

Q: I'm sorry. What were you going to say?

A: Nothing.

Q: No, please finish your answer. It's kind of what?

A: It's kind of a greeting.

Q: It's kind of a greeting between you and your family and friends?

A: No, it's just a greeting.

Q: It's like a greeting? You use it—I mean pretend I'm your family member and tell me how you use it.

Coleman hesitated, and then said, "I would have—my friends would come over and they knock on the door and I open the door, and they say"—at this he made an expansive gesture and bugged his eyes out slightly, raising his voice—"What's up, nigger?"

The courtroom exploded in incredulous laughter. The judge looked at the ceiling. Hocker raised his voice, asking Chapman to silence the crowd, but Chapman waved him off. "It's not necessary," he said. Now the hearing really had become a farce, but it was not the gallery that had caused that to happen, or the defense team. It was Coleman.

When the crowd had quieted down, Coleman went on to testify that he did not consider the word to be a term of racial prejudice "in this day and time."

When Zamoff brought up Sam Esparza's accusation that Coleman had made racist comments to him when the two were on patrol, Coleman shook his head and smiled, in a poor simulation of disbelief. Zamoff asked him why that was funny. "Just is," Coleman said. "All the things they can come up with." Shortly afterward the hearing recessed for lunch, and the halls of the courthouse echoed with excited conversation and hilarity.

*

The team assembled in the back room at Dorothy's, a café just off the courthouse square. As soon as the door was closed, they all began talking at once. They had expected a slaughter, but the impact of seeing Coleman with his back to the wall had left them all slightly stunned. "We have just seen the most amazing three hours of testimony we've ever seen or ever will see," Adam Levin said to nobody in particular. Gupta held her face in her hands as her colleagues looked around the room from person to person, trying to get a sense from one another of whether they had really seen and heard what they had just witnessed. "I have a lot of experience in civil and criminal law and I have never seen anybody so demonstrably false," Ted Killory said.

"He admitted he perjured himself," Gupta said. "He's got to be in front of a U.S. attorney on perjury charges. We'll get the transcript."

"One thing's for sure—" Bill White said, "the civil case is done." Even Charlotte Bingham would have to concede that somebody was going to pay for hiring this man. Then it seemed to dawn on everybody at once: maybe this hearing was done too. The state's star witness was in tatters, and McEachern's neck was next on the block. If he was ever going to concede, he would do it now. With barely a word from Gupta, Killory was already hustling out the door, headed back to the courthouse.

An hour later, the gallery filed back into the courtroom for the scheduled resumption of the hearing. The 1:00 hour came and went, and still no sign of the judge. At 1:30 the reporters in the front row were beginning to speculate about what was going on in the judge's chambers. Periodically Gupta or George Kendall came out of the back room and visited with their clients in a hushed whisper. Just before 2:00, Chapman came out and announced that the hearing was over for the day and would reconvene in nine days, on April 1. With that, he turned and left. The defense team members were mysteriously absent as reporters scrambled to get a quote about the strange halt in the proceedings. Nation and Hocker made a brief appearance. Smiling primly as if nothing unusual were afoot, Nation announced that the state was ready to begin its case at any time. "I believe we'll be able to show a broader picture of Mr. Coleman, and we fully intend to answer all the issues that have been raised," he said. With that, the state team disappeared as well.

CHAPTER EIGHTEEN

Negotiation

THE SECRET NATION was hiding was a big one. During the lunch break, Killory had caught up with Chapman alone in his chambers. He asked the judge to take a message to McEachern for him: the team was ready to offer the state a chance to stop the hearings, come to the table, and talk about a settlement. Coleman still had at least four more hours on the stand. This was a chance for McEachern to stop the bleeding while he still could. If he didn't take this opportunity now, Killory said, the papers were going to be calling Tulia the Birmingham or Selma of this generation. After Coleman's display on the stand that morning, Chapman seemed to think the time was ripe as well. As Killory waited alone in the hall, the judge visited with McEachern and his team in the district attorney's office. After twenty minutes, Chapman stepped out into the hall and beckoned Killory inside. "They want to talk," he said. Mitch Zamoff had by now returned to the courthouse as well, and he joined Killory in McEachern's office.

McEachern's entire team was inside the office, and the place was in disarray. It seemed they had been discussing the possibility of a settlement among themselves at lunch. McEachern's assistant Kelley Messer was almost in tears, she was so angry. The team had watched her shaking her head in disbelief as Zamoff questioned Coleman about the purity of the cocaine that morning, and clearly she still believed that all of the defendants were guilty. Bingham was obviously not ready to stop fighting either. McEachern, however, was in a shambles. Complaining of back trouble, he was laid out on the floor along one wall of the room. "If I had known Coleman was going to get up there and say all that I never would have let things get this far in the first place," he mumbled. It was way too late for that.

He listened with resignation as Killory and Zamoff made their pitch. Any settlement, they argued, should be global, applying not just to these four applicants but to every defendant charged in the sting, including everybody who was still in prison. The state would have to confess error and join the defense in petitioning the CCA to throw out the convictions, and then promise not to retry any of the defendants. In exchange, the defense would agree to discuss limiting the county's liability for monetary damages. It was an outline for total victory, years before Gupta, Blackburn, or any of the defense team had ever imagined possible.

Nation, whose job would be to rehabilitate Coleman on the stand if the hearing did resume, seemed receptive. But he had very little invested in the outcome of these cases compared to the rest of the state's team. Bingham immediately objected to including those defendants who had pleaded guilty. She also seemed to feel, despite what had transpired with Coleman on the stand that morning, that the cases were still good, and that the CCA would never endorse letting all of the defendants off the hook. Killory gently reminded Bingham that if they resumed the hearing, McEachern would quite possibly be the next witness called to the stand. He did not appear, at the moment at least, to be up to the task. Chapman proposed that the two sides take a week to see if they could hammer out a deal. McEachern reluctantly agreed, though he demanded absolute secrecy from the defense team. Chapman ordered them to reconvene on the Monday after next in Tulia. If they could reach a deal, then he would announce it in court on Tuesday morning, April Fools Day. If not, then the hearing would continue, beginning where they had left off, with Coleman on the stand again.

Immediately after Judge Chapman made his surprise announcement to the court, Gupta and Kendall headed for the jail to meet with their clients and tell them the news. They were elated, but there was an important decision to be made. If the team was going to push for a global settlement, all four of the applicants had to agree to it. The other twelve defendants still in prison had nothing to lose by going global, but these four did. It was their hearing that had forced the state to come to the bargaining table, and it was entirely possible that the state might offer the four of them new trials, while leaving the others to fend for themselves. If that happened, Gupta explained, she needed to know how the four of them wanted her to respond. If they told McEachern it was all or nothing and he rejected the deal, it might mean they would have to resume the hearing when the two sides reconvened in Tulia in nine days' time. Were they willing to demand a global settlement, even if it meant potentially taking their own freedom off the table?

Joe Moore spoke up first. What Coleman had done was wrong, he said. If this was the best chance to make it right for everybody, he was willing to take his chances on restarting the hearing if it came to that. Freddie quickly agreed, and then Chris Jackson, but Jason Williams was nervous about saying one way or the other. He was just twenty-three years old, and he was serving a forty-five-year sentence. He would not be eligible for parole until he was at least thirty. For the first time, he felt like he might actually get out, and now his lawyer was asking him to do something that sounded like taking a step backward. He looked at Joe Moore. "This might be Creamy and Cash and them's only chance," Moore told him. "We need to do this now." Williams reluctantly agreed.

That afternoon the team met in the jury room on the second floor to begin drafting a proposed settlement to show the state. They carefully avoided speaking to any reporters, and there was no mention of the potential settlement in media coverage of the day's events, which focused on Coleman's outlandish testimony and apparent perjury. On Saturday, their secret still intact, the attorneys returned home. On Monday, Zamoff e-mailed a proposal to McEachern and Bingham. Bingham wrote back that the state had "significant concerns" with some of the provisions, but she offered no counterproposal. Tuesday came and went, and still there was no word from the state team.

On Wednesday night, Blackburn had a long conversation with Rod Hobson, who had returned from Hawaii and read a rush transcript of the previous week's proceedings. He realized now, he told Blackburn, that there was a great deal about the story he had never heard. He'd been stunned by the number of witnesses and the amount of evidence the team had collected; McEachern had given him no sense of the freight train that was bearing down on him when he was hired. Hobson had also been taken aback by the testimony of the state's witnesses—not just Coleman but also Commander Amos and Sheriff Stewart. He had his first glimmer of doubt about the state's case during the depositions, when Amos seemed unwilling to give Hobson a copy of Coleman's missing polygraph charts. Still, he'd had no real reason to believe that Stewart and Coleman were liars. Reading their testimony now had begun to bring out the indignant defense lawyer in him. He was still technically a special prosecutor working for McEachern, but like a torpedo that has missed its target, he was beginning to turn back toward the people who had hired him. He told Blackburn that a global settlement was the only just resolution he saw as a prosecutor, and he would talk to McEachern about it. But Bingham was another matter, he warned Blackburn. She was going to be the sticking point.

By Friday, it had become apparent that McEachern's team had not come to a consensus about a course of action, and the defense team prepared to head back to Tulia without an agreement. They would have to try to hash it out at the courthouse on Monday. The defense team informed Judge Chapman that they were prepared to restart the hearings on Tuesday, if necessary, and sent him a list of witnesses they intended to call.

The team set up shop in the jury room adjacent to the courtroom on Monday morning. The entire team returned, dressed in their court clothes. They brought a laser printer with them so they could quickly print out settlement language, and plenty of snacks and drinks for what they anticipated would be a long day of negotiations. The state team assembled in McEachern's office, joined this time by Sheriff Stewart. Killory and Zamoff met with McEachern and Bingham in the courtroom to begin the discussions. Bingham did all of the talking for the state team. Both sides agreed that some defendants still in prison would not be covered by any global settlement. Two of the defendants who were still in prison, a pair of identical twins named Landis and Mandis Barrow, had been on probation for a crime committed in Amarillo at the time of the sting in Tulia, and had been sent to prison not by McEachern but by an Amarillo judge who had revoked their probation. The team would have to negotiate separately with the authorities in Amarillo for their release. Daniel Olivarez, one of Paul Holloway's original clients, was also at the mercy of the Amarillo district attorney, since one of his sting cases had allegedly taken place in Amarillo. Cash Love's case, meanwhile, had been stuck for over a year in the Amarillo appeals court, which had yet to rule on Van Williamson's contention that Love's 361-year sentence had been improperly applied by Judge Self. He could not get any habeas relief until the appeals court made a ruling of some kind. That left twelve incarcerated defendants, five of whom had pleaded guilty. Bingham was still insisting that those who plead out were not eligible for relief of any kind. She wanted to hear some direction from the Court of Criminal Appeals on the matter, or to see some case law that supported the defense argument that it didn't matter how the defendants had plead. After an hour or so of preliminary discussions, the negotiators returned to their respective camps to discuss the progress with their colleagues.

Midmorning, Bingham appeared at the door of the jury room and asked for Gupta. "We've got a problem," she said, though her tone was oddly triumphant. She handed Gupta a police report, which she said Sheriff Stewart had just brought to her attention. When Gupta read the top of the report her heart froze: it was for Freddie Brookins Jr. The charge was possession of marijuana. This was the mysterious unadjudicated offense that McEachern had darkly alluded to in his deposition. According to the report, a portion of a marijuana cigarette had been found in Freddie's wallet when they were booking him in. It was a tiny amount of pot, but it could be a felony, Bingham said, if they decided to charge Freddie with attempting to smuggle it into the jail. "Even if we let Freddie go," she said, "Stewart will just have him rearrested."

"You cannot be serious," Gupta said. Bingham shrugged her shoulders, a familiar look of smug satisfaction on her face. Gupta had long suspected that things had gotten personal between Freddie and Sheriff Stewart, who seemed to resent the team's portrayal of Freddie as an upright and unjustly accused young man. This latest development confirmed it for her. Gupta took the unwelcome news back to the team in the jury room.

Shortly thereafter, Hobson came into the room. His face was grim. In the ongoing internal debate on the state side, Hobson, and to a lesser degree Nation, had been the main proponent of settling the cases. He was impressed by Freddie and cited his story in particular to rebut Kelley Messer's and Bingham's continued insistence that everybody was guilty as charged. Then Stewart arrived with this new incident report. It did not change Hobson's opinion of Freddie, nor did it seem likely to change public opinion about Coleman's operation in Tulia; it was, after all, less than a gram of pot, and still the only contraband recovered during the arrest of forty-seven alleged cocaine dealers. Messer had immediately taken it as evidence that Freddie was guilty as charged, however, and the incident seemed to have renewed the state's willingness to fight. Bingham in particular seemed to have the idea that if they just stuck together long enough, the firm attorneys would grow weary of the time and expense of pursuing the hearing and cut their losses. McEachern, the ostensible captain of what had become a rudderless ship, seemed to be listening to her.

Killory and Zamoff returned to the courtroom after lunch for another negotiating session. Bingham and McEachern sat down at one of the attorney's tables across from them. Bingham seemed to feel she had somehow gained the upper hand since the morning session. Negotiating like this was what she did for a living, and she was good at it, though it was normally her client's money at stake, not the lives of incarcerated men and women. Killory, who did not believe in antagonizing his opponents, had been cordial from the outset. Now, however, he laid out the team's position in the starkest possible terms. The next witness on the stand, he pointed out, was Terry McEachern. By the time Zamoff was done with him, Killory said, it wouldn't just be these convictions that would be in jeopardy; it would be McEachern's bar license.

Before Bingham could interject, Killory reminded them both that in Joe Moore's case, as in most of the other trials, Judge Self had ordered McEachern to turn over the criminal records of any of his witnesses, as the defense had requested. "I have the transcript from Joe Moore's trial in which Terry stood up," Killory said, "having sworn to do his duty as a prosecutor, and lied to the court and to Judge Self by saying his law enforcement people of course had no arrest records and so they would be exempted from that." McEachern stared levelly back at Killory and said nothing. Nor should Bingham think she could outlast the firms, Killory said. "If our people are still in prison come next week," he said, "It will be the last thing I do if it takes me years to pursue this. There will be no end to the resources we will throw at this matter. And if you choose to put Terry in the dock, that's up to you. But whatever you saw on the stand with Tom Coleman was just a shadow of what you're going to see with Terry," he said. "That was just a warm-up."

McEachern hadn't said a word during Killory's speech. Now he and Charlotte stepped into the judge's chambers, a room just off the courtroom. Killory and Zamoff could hear Bingham's voice rising and falling, and McEachern shouting back at her. He seemed to have found his voice at last. When they returned a few minutes later, Bingham reported in a clipped and angry voice that the state was ready to agree in principle to a global settlement. McEachern did not want to face Zamoff. He was throwing in the towel.

For the next several hours, the two teams exchanged drafts of possible settlement language, with Bingham carefully vetting every line. At five o'clock the courthouse employees went home for the evening, leaving the two teams alone on the second floor. Night fell and still the deliberations dragged on. Figures could be seen passing back and forth in front of the large plate glass jury room window, which cast a dim light over the front entrance to the courthouse. Around nine o'clock, Blackburn stepped outside to smoke a cigarette. It would be over soon; they were just haggling over commas and clauses. The settlement would be global. Bingham had agreed to $250,000 to be split among all of the sting defendants. The state would confess error with respect to the Brady material and would stipulate that Coleman was simply not a credible witness under oath. Every single indictment

Coleman made in Swisher County would be vacated, and the state would not seek new trials for any of them. All charges would be dropped, including the eleventh-hour charge against Freddie. In exchange, the defendants agreed not to sue the county. They could still sue the task force, however, and Blackburn planned to, in a big way. At long last, the state was throwing Coleman to the wolves, and there was excited talk among the team of having Coleman arrested for perjury the next day, if he showed his face at the courthouse. They had won.

Blackburn was exultant. The whole town square was quiet as he stalked across the deserted courthouse parking lot. Spotting the Swisher County centennial monument, he walked over and sized it up. It was a six-foot slab of polished granite that stood under a tree less than a hundred feet from the courthouse. He had always hated its self-congratulatory inscription: "Law, Order, Education, and Christian Principles have sustained this county for 100 years." He unzipped his pants and began urinating on it. Just then a car pulled onto Second Street and began heading toward the square. Caught briefly in its headlights, Blackburn quickly zipped up his pants and scurried back toward the courthouse steps.

Tuesday morning, Chapman called the Court of Criminal Appeals to inform them of the proposed settlement and to ask for permission to bond the applicants out on their own recognizance until a decision was reached about their cases. Chapman wanted the four applicants released immediately, in the courtroom, with their families present. The answer from the CCA was an unequivocal "no." The four applicants would remain locked up along with the rest of the sixteen while the justices considered their fate.

Tuesday afternoon, the gallery of the second floor courtroom filled once again with spectators and reporters for what everybody assumed would be the second half of Coleman's examination, though Coleman had not been spotted entering the courthouse that morning. Both sides had maintained a near absolute silence about the ongoing negotiations, and neither the reporters nor the Tulians who packed the gallery knew what to expect. McEachern and Bingham sat to one side of the well, glowering and silent. Hobson visited with Gupta and Blackburn, as Nation chatted amiably with the applicants sitting in their accustomed spot in the jury box. A little after 1:00 P.M., Chapman came out and took his seat at the dais. "I'm pleased to be able to disclose at this time that following serious and lengthy discussions, a settlement agreement has been reached in this case," he announced to a perfectly quiet courtroom. Both sides stipulated that Tom Coleman was not a credible witness, he explained. All Swisher County convictions would be vacated, and each of the applicants would be entitled to a new trial. However, the entire agreement was subject to approval by the Court of Criminal Appeals, he added. With that, the hearing was adjourned. There was stunned silence in the courtroom. It was finally over. Or was it? Nobody was sure how to interpret that last sentence. Were they free, or not?

One thing was for certain: Gary Gardner and Alan Bean and the defendants' families had been right about Tom Coleman. He was a liar, after all. As he left the courtroom with the rest of the crowd, Alan Bean's father-in-law Charles Kiker stuck his head inside the door of an office off the hallway, where Stewart was seated behind a desk, his arms folded across his chest. "Are you going to resign now?" he asked Stewart.

"You take a hike," Stewart told him.

Immediately after the announcement, Gupta and Kendall went to the Kikers' for a meeting with family members of the defendants. Gary Gardner and his wife Darlene, Alan and Nancy Bean, Mattie White, her sister Connie, Thelma Johnson, Anita Barrow, and Billy Wafer were there. "This means you get to carve thirty-six more notches on your gun, doesn't it Vanita?" Gardner laughed. He was right. Technically the settlement agreement still had to get the approval of the Court of Criminal Appeals. But the state had confessed error, Gupta explained, which rarely ever happened in habeas petitions. It meant that both sides were calling for a new trial. The CCA would all but have to set them free, though nobody could say how long they would take to act. First the team had to produce a document called a finding of fact, listing everything that had come out at the hearing. It would take some more dickering with the state's team to get the language acceptable to both sides. Chapman seemed to feel that some insurance was needed in the finding of fact to induce the CCA to give its blessing. He passed the defense team some language that he wanted included, a rare move for a judge to make. "Tom Coleman is the most devious, nonresponsive law enforcement witness that this court has encountered in twenty-five years on the bench," he wrote. It became a widely quoted line.

"Terry McEachern needs to feel the heat too," Billy Wafer said. Fred Sr. nodded. "There's a bigger picture here," he said. "This has been goin' on for years in Plainview, but nobody ever stuck up for themselves." Patricia Kiker had overheard a cop outside of the courtroom saying all of the defendants would be back in prison eventually anyway. Indeed, it was unclear how much of the day-to-day information revealed in the hearings had made it out into Tulia at large. Very few white Tulians had attended in person, and the TV news coverage tended to condense the confusing sequence of events so much that it was difficult for casual observers to get the full picture of what had gone wrong and who was responsible, even if they wanted to. The *Tulia Herald*, for its part, all but ignored the hearings. The sum of the paper's coverage in the March 27 issue was a three-column-inch story, in which McEachern was quoted as saying the hearings were going "about like he expected."

CHAPTER NINETEEN

Out the Front Door

ON APRIL 24, a grand jury in Tulia indicted Tom Coleman on three counts of aggravated perjury. Presenting the information to the jurors were Rod Hobson and John Nation, whom McEachern asked to stay on as special prosecutors long enough to try the charges against Coleman. McEachern was apparently ready to make Coleman a scapegoat, but Sheriff Stewart was not done fighting. He insisted that Hobson allow him to testify before the grand jury, but his appearance was not enough to outweigh what was in the transcripts of Coleman's disastrous hearing testimony. It was all there in black and white. Each perjury count carried a possible sentence of two to ten years in prison.

There were no indictments for Sheriff Stewart or Terry McEachern, though neither fared well in the published summary of the hearing. After considerable negotiation between the two sides, the findings were finalized on May 1 in a document titled "Joint Stipulated Findings of Fact and Conclusions of Law." In addition to fourteen separate cases of apparent perjury by Coleman in the hearing itself, the document listed several examples of "misleading testimony" by Stewart and McEachern in the original trial transcripts. On the list was Stewart's dubious testimony in Freddie Brookins's trial about the absence of "negative information" in Coleman's background check, about which Zamoff had grilled him during the hearing. The document also cited his testimony in Freddie's trial that he did not recall why Coleman left Cochran County, and his statement in Cash Love's trial that he "never had any trouble with Coleman."

McEachern, meanwhile, was singled out for testifying in multiple trials that none of the state's witnesses had criminal records and in a postconviction hearing for Cash Love that he had no knowledge of Coleman's arrest prior to Love's trial, a statement that he offered at the time to back up with a signed affidavit, if necessary. This was "directly contradictory," the findings noted, to his later deposition testimony, in which he admitted learning of the arrest even before any of the defendants were indicted. The findings also included this unfortunate quote from McEachern in Kizzie White's trial: "We brought forth . . . the most outstanding law enforcement officer of the year. If you can't believe him, well, then, who can you believe?"

Finally the document took Stewart to task for his unusual way of arresting Coleman. "The methods used by Sheriff Stewart and other members of the Swisher County Sheriff's office regarding the arrest and release on bond of Coleman on the Cochran County warrant," it read, "were used to conceal it from public knowledge and possibly were in violation of the Texas Code of Criminal Procedure."

The findings were signed and sent to the Court of Criminal Appeals on May 1, placing the defendants' fate officially in the hands of the CCA. Taken together, the findings were a devastating indictment of the convictions, and there was little question that the CCA would sign off on the settlement agreement, though there was no timetable for action and no way to tell how long the justices would take to rule on Chapman's recommendations. The defendants were in limbo.

In late May, however, the Texas Legislature passed a bill specifically authorizing Judge Chapman to grant bond to the defendants. Notoriously conservative, especially on criminal justice issues, Texas legislators from both parties had nevertheless come to view Tulia as an embarrassment to the state. With every major paper in the state editorializing in favor of the bond bill and the Texas ACLU carefully shepherding it through the legislative process, the measure made it to the governor's desk and into law at a breakneck pace. The governor, meanwhile, announced that he was directing the Texas Board of Pardons and Paroles to examine the cases and consider the defendants for pardons, which would make the wait for the CCA's judgment unnecessary. Chapman scheduled a court date for the afternoon of June 16, 2003, in Tulia to grant the defendants bond and release them.

June 16 was a beautiful summer morning in Tulia, with a striking blue High Plains sky and a light breeze blowing. The parking lot of the courthouse was once again filled with satellite trucks, and the local restaurants with out-of-towners in fancy suits. A large crowd milled about on the lawn outside the courthouse, waiting for a glimpse of the defendants. Alan Bean and Gary Gardner were happily giving interviews and introducing reporters to family members of defendants. Gardner kept shouting the word "fan-tastic!", which his wife Darlene had encouraged him to use instead of "bullshit" when talking to reporters. A few Texas state legislators had made the trip to Tulia as well, and they were happily working the crowd, shaking hands and congratulating family members. Around eleven, a buzz went through the crowd as a long white prison bus was spotted pulling into the the side parking lot of the courthouse. Two burly guards in gray uniforms and sunglasses disembarked and led the thirteen defendants out of the bus and up the side stairs of the courthouse. Squinting in the sunlight, the defendants nodded and smiled in response to the many shouted greetings and lifted their cuffed hands to wave awkwardly at their friends and family.

Inside, the courtroom was filled to capacity. Every member of the defense team was there, as well as Gupta's boss from the Legal Defense Fund, Elaine Jones, and many other activists from Austin and New York and Washington, D.C. Finally, when all thirteen of the defendants were in the jury box, Chapman entered and called the packed courtroom to order.

"Your Honor, it is a tragedy that brings us all together here today," Mitch Zamoff began. "Tom Coleman is a cancer," he continued. "His disregard for the oath, his disregard for the rights of citizens, and his disregard for the well-being of the very community he was assigned to protect should sadden and outrage every upstanding member of the law enforcement community." Larry Stewart stood by the door with his hands behind his back, watching impassively. Chapman had diagnosed that cancer, Zamoff summed up, and now it was time for him to cure it.

After Zamoff sat down, Ted Killory stood and addressed the court. "I would ask everyone to pause for a moment, anyone who questions whether what we are doing today is the right thing," he began. "The Bible says, 'Do unto others as you would have done unto yourself.' And in this case, I think if all involved in the process: the sheriff, the original prosecutor, and others, had just stopped and paused and said, 'I am about to put these gentlemen in prison based on the testimony of a man who I know to be a liar, to have a checkered past, to have been chased out of prior law enforcement jobs, [who] I know to be a man who uses racial epithets when talking about people of color.'"

"None of us came to Tulia to make Tulia out to be a racist place," he continued. "We don't believe that to be the case. What we do believe [is] that sometimes we are all creatures of our own upbringing." He asked whites in Tulia to consider for a moment how they would have responded to the sting if their positions had been reversed—if the authorities had been black and the defendants white, and the arresting officer a known racist. "I think you would say that is just not fair. That is not what I would want the justice system to do to me. And yet that is what happened here, Your Honor."

When the defense team was finished, Chapman praised both the defense attorneys and the special prosecutors for their work in reaching a settlement. He recalled the day he was assigned to the cases. "I began to sense that the largest complaint that these defendants had was that no one had listened to them, that they had not had a full and impartial hearing of their claims," he said. His intent was merely to provide a forum for such a hearing, "letting as much light shine on these events as possible," he said. Then he turned to address the men and women in the jury box. "There are a great number of people—not just limited to your attorneys or the Court—who have a great deal of time, effort, and faith in each of you invested in these proceedings," he began. "Your families and loved ones are counting on you; and others in Texas or elsewhere—who are or may someday find themselves accused under similar circumstances—are counting on you," he said. "I hope—no, I implore you—to commit . . . to living your lives within the law, to live lives that the Lord would have you do." With that, he told them they were free to go.

A cheer erupted in the courtroom as friends and family members in the gallery surged toward the jury box. A gaggle of photographers, waiting patiently outside the door for Chapman to conclude the proceedings, burst into the room and spilled around the lawyer's well to get close to the hugs and kisses. Donnie pushed his way through the crowd to be the first to hug Creamy and Kizzie. A beaming Ricky White was right behind him, in a silk shirt, long shorts, and ball cap, all in matching polka dots.

Freddie pushed in the opposite direction, toward Fred and Patty and Terry and Serena. For the first time in years, there were no bars or Plexiglas between Freddie and the people he loved. Joe Moore's booming voice could be heard laughing and hollering above the crowd.

Outside the courthouse, at the bottom of the steps, a much larger crowd was waiting. The television news crews were camped out, ready to pounce on the defendants when they came through the doors. Gupta hustled all of the defendants into the jury room for a last-minute pep talk. Jason Williams looked nervously out the jury room window at the large crowd below. Gupta told them they didn't have to talk to any reporters if they didn't want to, but she wanted Joe and Freddie, at least, to say something at the press conference.

Gary Gardner was waiting on the steps when Joe Moore stepped out into the sunlight. A dozen cameras snapped away as Gardner grabbed Moore's arm and hoisted it in his fist. The picture of the two of them side by side and grinning was on the front page of the Amarillo paper the next morning. Ted Killory, the only person in the crowd taller than Joe Moore, shepherded his client about by the shoulders as though he feared he might be rearrested the moment he stepped onto the courthouse lawn. Vanita stayed close to Freddie and his family as the mob migrated over toward the Swisher County centennial monument for a news conference. Flanked by state senators, family members, friends, and attorneys, Freddie stepped in front of the mike and told the world how happy he was to be free again.

Later the crowd moved to the basement of the memorial building for a big barbecue lunch and celebration. There were huge plates of ribs and sausage, with beans and coleslaw and bread. A podium had been set up at one end, with a large "Welcome Home" banner hung behind it. As everyone ate, Alan Bean rose and began calling various people to the front of the room to speak. Charles Kiker spoke of the need for repentance among the powers that be in Tulia before the healing could start. "I don't see the sheriff here," he noted, to applause. Thelma rose to thank the "dream team" and defend them from the grumblings about "Yankee attorneys" that had been heard around Tulia in recent months. "We love you," she said. "Yankee or not you're people and darn good people." She invited everybody out to the Lobos softball game scheduled for later that night.

By the time Gary Gardner came to the podium several hours later, the room was mostly empty, as many of the defendants had moved outside to smoke and breathe the fresh air and find their friends, and the reporters and cameramen had followed them. He had asked to be allowed to speak first, since he was the first in Tulia to speak out publicly against the bust, back in December 1999, and he had never stopped thinking of the fight to free the defendants as his own personal struggle. It had long since been decided, however, that Gardner, with his tendency to say whatever he pleased regardless of the setting or audience, was not the ideal spokesman for the Friends of Justice. So he sat, his typed speech in his fist, and listened to state officials speak first and then a host of others, some of whom he knew had joined the fight only at the eleventh hour, when victory was near.

In the end he decided that having the last word was enough. He stepped up to the podium, said a few words to the mostly empty room, and then closed the proceedings the way a thousand other gatherings had ended in the memorial building. "Stack the chairs, store the tables, and turn out the lights," he said. "This party's over."

The celebration continued down at the softball field that evening. Dozens of relatives had come to town to see the much-anticipated release, and the black side of the bleachers was packed with chanting fans in high spirits. The Lobos were playing an experienced team, a mostly middle-aged white squad with a few Hispanic members. A warm day had turned into a mild summer night, and a pleasant breeze kept the mosquitoes at bay. Many of the defendants were at the park, though none had joined the game. They stood alongside the dugout in twos and threes, slapping hands with friends and cousins they had not spoken to in years. Donnie Smith had been an on-again, off-again member of the team, but when the other team went ahead 13 to 8 with just six outs to play, he inserted himself into the game in place of the left fielder, a youngster who had already made a couple of errors. He immediately made a nice running catch to end a rally. Then in the bottom of the inning he sparked a Lobos comeback with a two-run double that rolled all the way to the wall. Now everybody was chanting and cheering, Tonya White loudest of all, as batter after batter for the Lobos ripped the ball into the outfield. Even the umpire, a skinny Hispanic teenager, seemed to get caught up in the fervor, calling several close plays in the Lobos' favor. When Tony Powell cleared the bases to put the Lobos ahead 16 to 13, the entire team poured out of the dugout, and the fans went wild. Donnie had to lie down on a picnic table after racing around to score on Powell's big hit. His heart was racing wildly, and he looked briefly like he might pass out. In the top of the next inning, however, he fired a perfect strike from deep left field to catch a runner coming too far around second on a double. Only a handful of men in Tulia could have made that throw. It was a thing of beauty.

But the Lobos magic didn't last. In their last at-bat, the opposing team tied the game, helped by an error in center field, then went ahead on a mammoth two-run homer that sailed deep into the darkness. After an intentional walk to Kent Brookins, the Lobos went quietly in the bottom of the seventh, and the game was over.

That night it seemed like the town of Tulia had somehow returned to the summer of 1999, before anyone had ever heard the name Tom Coleman, watched tape of their loved ones being taken to jail on the six o'clock news, or listened to their lives being discussed on the *O'Reilly Factor* and *Court TV*. All over town, sons and daughters and brothers and sisters and boyfriends and girlfriends were reunited under the same roof for the first time since that July morning four years before when everything turned upside down. For Joe Moore, it seemed like time had turned back even further. Thelma's son David had moved into Moore's old house on South Dallas Street after paroling out on his manslaughter conviction, so Joe moved in with Thelma in her Housing Authority apartment. David's teenage daughter was in the apartment as well, since her father could not be near children, even his own, as a condition of his parole. After twenty years of living alone, Moore was together again with the woman he still called his wife and a child who called him "grandpa," back with people who cared about him and needed him around. He knew he would be coming into some money soon from the settlement, and he was already planning how best to put it to use, to get something going again, to get back on his feet.

Freddie spent the evening at home with his parents and Terry and Serena. He knew all of his old friends would be out partying tonight, celebrating a day many thought would never come. He didn't have the slightest urge even to crack a beer. If he was going to celebrate, he would do it in his old bedroom with the door closed, jumping on the bed and shouting out loud. He knew his dad would be watching him closely over the next few days, to see if he had changed, if he had grown hateful in prison. He wished things could turn back to the way they used to be in Tulia, when he was still in high school and everybody got along—or so it had seemed to him. But he knew in his heart that things would never be the same again.

On Briscoe Street a party was breaking out. It seemed to blow in out of nowhere, like an April thunderstorm sweeping down off the plains at forty miles per hour. One car pulled up and then another, the drivers hollering out as friends and relatives were spotted leaning under porch lights or poking heads through the screen doors of the Housing Authority duplexes and small frame houses that lined the street. Then a Cadillac came moving too fast up the narrow street, the driver's arm swinging wildly outside the window, music thumping from oversize speakers in the backseat. He pulled abruptly into a driveway, cranked the stereo as loud as it would go, and leaped out of his door, already dancing before his feet hit the street. He was immediately joined by a half dozen young women, some in their jeans and T-shirts, others dressed to the nines in long leather boots and short skirts, on their way to a night out in Amarillo.

A crowd of several dozen materialized, and an utterly quiet panhandle night was transformed into a scene from the old TV show *Soul Train*, with sickly yellow streetlights and hard dirt lawns in place of colored strobes and parquet floors, and dancers moving their bodies to the sounds of Fifty Cent and Eminem instead of Earth, Wind, and Fire and Donna Summer. Young men gave each other one-armed street hugs and laughed and drank and fired their empty bottles into the open field at the end of the block. The Swisher County Memorial Building sat dark and empty not 1,000 feet away; its maps of cavalry campaigns and Indian battles might as well have documented the history of the moon for all they mattered to the twenty-first-century residents of Briscoe Street.

Donnie Smith leaned against the hood of a car with a beer in his hand, surveying the action. He was in charge of his kids that night, and the two young boys—Sid, 11, and Shaquille, 10—hovered around their dad and eyed the scene with a quiet deference. One of Donnie's favorite Fifty Cent songs, "21 Questions," came on, to the dancers' vocal approval. He had just begun to explain the meaning of the words when he was interrupted by a young man to whom he owed money. The sum was six dollars, and the man was insistent, but Donnie didn't have it. He couldn't go anywhere in Tulia anymore without running into someone he had wronged in some way, large or small. Donnie smoothed things over with another promise, but he seemed chastened by the exchange, at least briefly. "I know where I should be—in the pulpit of that church," he said, referring to the possibility, which he considered from time to time, of becoming a minister. "But I'm not ready—I love pussy too much, man. I'm a heterosexualist, man!" he said, looking chagrined as he noticed Sid at his elbow.

He had a new plan for making money, he said. He wanted to get his commercial driver's license and become a long-haul trucker. "I don't want no manual labor no more man, I'm tired of working that," he said. He liked the idea of seeing the country and not being tied down to any one place. "Just drive for a while, ya know. Unload the truck. Or let somebody else unload the truck, ya know what I'm sayin', and get me another load and be gone." An out-of-town organizer had promised to help Donnie apply for a grant to cover the tuition for truck driving school. If that didn't work, Donnie said, he had a plan to open a barbershop in South Dallas. He had recently driven there to visit a friend for a few days and wound up staying for two weeks, in no small part because he'd pawned his car for dope money while he was in town. He was enthralled by the idea of South Dallas, an entire neighborhood, a town really, of nothing but black people and black-owned businesses. Plenty of people with money, plenty of nightlife. And lots of barbershops. "Already got the lot picked out," he said.

"Dad, if you move to South Dallas are we comin' with you?" Sid asked. Donnie regarded him for a moment, unsure of how to respond. "I hope so, boy," he said.

EPILOGUE: SUMMER 2005

ON AUGUST 22, 2003, Texas Governor Rick Perry signed pardons for thirty-five of the Tulia defendants. The pardons covered everyone who was actually convicted in Swisher County on cases filed by Coleman, though the governor's move still left Landis and Mandis Barrow and Daniel Olivarez in prison and in a state of legal limbo. (Cash Love was ordered released shortly after his co-defendants got out.) On the same day the pardons were announced, Jeff Blackburn filed a civil rights lawsuit in federal court in Amarillo on behalf of the legal team, seeking monetary damages. Defendants named in the suit included not only Amarillo, as the host city for the Panhandle Regional Narcotics Trafficking Task Force, but also every one of the thirty cities and counties that belonged to the task force. Swisher County was named as well, despite the settlement reached in March. That deal, in which Charlotte Bingham had worked so diligently to protect the county from civil liability, applied only to those defendants who had actually been convicted in the sting. The team had chosen Blackburn's clients Tonya White and Zury Bossett (who were never convicted) as plaintiffs for the federal suit, which effectively put Swisher County back on the hook.

*

It was not a good summer for Terry McEachern. In June he was convicted on his DWI charge in Ruidoso. Local network news stations in
Amarillo and Lubbock obtained the police video of McEachern's field
sobriety test and played it on the air several times. Shortly thereafter,
the State Bar of Texas began to investigate McEachern's role in the
Tulia scandal. McEachern appealed to the Swisher County Commissioner's Court for financial assistance in defending himself in his fight
with the state bar, but the county declined to come to his aid. County
Judge Harold Keeter called the bar suit a "personal" matter. Despite
his mounting troubles, McEachern threw his hat in the ring for
another term as district attorney the following spring. His opponents
were the Plainview city attorney and a local defense attorney. After
seventeen years as district attorney, during which time he'd rarely had
a serious challenger, McEachern came in a humiliating third in the
primary, garnering less than a quarter of the vote. He would be
returning to private practice at last, assuming he retained his bar
license.

The day after McEachern's defeat, on March 10, 2004, in
response to the suit filed by Tonya White and Zury Bossett, the city
of Amarillo agreed to a global settlement that applied to every defendant Coleman accused in the sting. A $5 million cash payment would
be split among the defendants, who retained the arbitration services
of Judge Chapman to divide the money fairly among them. As a condition of the settlement the city of Amarillo agreed to cease participation in the task force, effectively disbanding it altogether.

As a further condition, Commander Michael Amos agreed to take
early retirement from the Amarillo police department. A month later
a separate agreement was reached with the remaining cities and counties in the task force, which agreed to pay a total of $1 million to the
defendants.

The scandal in Tulia had a profound effect on narcotics enforcement, not just in the panhandle but across Texas. Immediately after

the story broke in June 2000, Texas task forces were under the microscope, and it didn't take long before another major scandal surfaced. In April 2001 the Texas ACLU announced it had found "another Tulia" in the central Texas town of Hearne, where dozens of cases had been dismissed after a task force snitch admitted fabricating cases. Attorneys from the national ACLU's Drug Policy Litigation Project filed suit, making Hearne, and Byrne grant–funded task forces generally, their top priority nationally.

As in Tulia, the defendants in Hearne were virtually all black, and the cases were mostly for delivery of small amounts of powdered cocaine. In this case, however, the cases were not made by an officer, but by a young black man working off a drug case of his own. The task force had supplied him with a list of names, buy money, and a handheld tape recorder, designed to be carried in a shirt or jeans pocket. The story went from bad to worse after ACLU investigators learned that the snitch, who had a history of drug abuse and mental illness, had failed a lie detector test prior to the arrests being made. The local district attorney, who was also the head of the task force, pressed ahead with the prosecutions anyway, only dismissing the remainder of the cases after the snitch's poor performance on the stand in the first case resulted in a mistrial. The snitch later claimed that task force officers coerced him into fabricating cases by threatening him with a lengthy prison sentence and bodily harm if he refused. Prior to the scandal breaking, the district attorney abruptly resigned from the task force. Later, the commander and several of the agents left as well.

Pressing their case with the scandals in Tulia and Hearne, the Texas ACLU pushed two reform bills through the Texas legislature in 2001. One bill made termination notices in the files of police officers open to the public. The second measure sought to raise the standard of evidence in undercover narcotics work by requiring that all cases be corroborated, whether by audio, video, or other means. At the insis-

tence of prosecutors, it was amended to require corroboration only for
cases made by confidential informants (like the snitch in the Hearne
case), but not for those made by licensed officers. The Tulia scandal
and the organizing it inspired also gave impetus to an effort to reform
the indigent defense system in Texas. The main achievement of the
Fair Defense Act of 2001 was to limit the discretion of judges, which
had resulted in a patchwork of appointment systems that varied from
court to court. Providing attorneys for poor defendants remains the
responsibility of individual counties, but each county is now required
to have a written system for appointing attorneys that applies to all
courts in the county. Among other things, the systems must assign
attorneys to defendants in a timely manner (usually within 4 to 6 days
of arrest), provide an impartial method for assigning cases to attorneys,
set minimum qualifications for attorneys, and clearly establish hourly
compensation rates and criteria for the hiring of expert witnesses and
private investigators. The new law also provided for the first time a
modest level of state funding for indigent defense, which advocates
have managed to gradually increase in subsequent sessions.

In 2002, Texas governor Rick Perry announced that he was
assigning supervision of the state's Byrne grant drug task forces to the
Texas Department of Public Safety (DPS), the state police force. The
transition has been a bumpy one. When DPS narcotics captains made
preliminary visits to their new charges, they discovered that many of
the task forces were in disarray. At one outfit in the San Antonio area,
for example, evidence was missing from 20 percent of the unit's case
files, forfeiture cash was not properly accounted for, and commanders
had "little contact or supervisory control" over some of their agents.
The DPS crafted new rules for the task forces, bringing them more in
line with established procedures for state police narcs. The use of
masks in the serving of arrest warrants was banned, and procedures
for control of evidence and use of confidential informants were tight-
ened. Some task force commanders refused to accept the new com-

mand structure and simply shut down their operations rather than submit to the new rules. A few announced that they would forgo Byrne grant money to avoid DPS oversight. These "renegade" task forces subsisted for a few years on their own asset forfeiture accounts—some had accumulated huge hoards prior to the takeover—until the state legislature in the summer of 2005 finally forced them to comply with DPS rules or fold altogether.

Budget cuts brought further changes to the program in Texas and around the nation. As the war on terror became the issue of the moment in Washington, the Byrne program became the target of budget cutters looking for ways to assign more Department of Justice money to "first responders" to prepare for future emergencies. President Bush cut the program completely in his proposed budget in 2003, only to have it rescued by Congress, albeit at considerably reduced funding levels. The cuts forced the governor's office in Texas to deny grant renewals to several of the state's task forces and reduce payments to others.

The multimillion dollar settlement of the Tulia suit had an even greater impact on the program. The idea that cities and counties could be liable for misdeeds that occurred outside of their jurisdictions simply by virtue of being a member of a regional task force set an alarming precedent that rippled through the state's rural areas. Over the next year, nine task forces across the state disbanded, many citing unacceptable liability risks and higher insurance premiums. In the subsequent lawsuit in Hearne, a federal judge reinforced the precedent set by the Tulia settlement, ruling in effect that all political entities in a task force were at least potentially liable for malfeasance committed by its agents, regardless of where the acts in question occurred. By the time the Hearne suit was settled for an undisclosed amount in June 2005, there were just twenty-five task forces left in Texas, down from a late 1990s high of close to fifty.

*

The resolution of the Tulia cases seemed for a time like it might bring changes in Swisher County as well. At the urging of Randy Credico, a multiracial "reconciliation committee" was formed shortly after the release of the defendants to give opponents of the sting and defenders of the sheriff a chance to open a dialogue with one another. In an unexpected twist, Credico had lately begun spending time with Sheriff Stewart—eating dinner and attending church with his family—and had begun telling reporters that he, Blackburn, and others had been too hard on Swisher County. Sheriff Stewart attended the press conference announcing the formation of the reconciliation committee, though he seemed content to let Credico do the talking on his behalf.

Credico's efforts notwithstanding, there was no consensus in Tulia about whether or not justice was served by the settlement. Ike Malone, the black community's most outspoken defender of the bust, left town shortly before the defendants were released. Even months after the settlement, many in Tulia still seemed to believe that Coleman had been guilty of nothing more than faulty record keeping. Gary Gardner, for his part, was not done fighting. He announced that he would be running for sheriff against Stewart, who he felt had managed to escape largely unscathed from the whole episode despite his central role in the events that led to the scandal. Gardner had no real chance of winning, but it gave him a venue to keep pounding away at Stewart, McEachern, and Self. Alan Bean and the Friends of Justice turned their attention to other communities having trouble with drug task forces; Alan, Nancy, Charles Kiker, Fred Brookins Sr., and Thelma Johnson became traveling consultants of a sort, even visiting Washington, D.C., to speak on Capitol Hill.

Donnie Smith spent part of the summer of 2003 in a rehab facility in Abilene, along with a handful of other defendants from the sting who had fallen back into their old ways and were in danger of being rearrested before the pardons could be issued by the governor's office. He remained in Abilene for a few months after completing rehab, working and staying clean, but returned to Tulia when the settlement checks came in July 2004. Like many of the defendants, the first thing he bought was a nice new truck. Young black men cruising around Tulia in new SUVs and nice new clothes became a common sight that summer, which caused no small amount of grumbling in certain circles.

Donnie never opened his barbershop in Dallas. The settlement money—much of which went to his kids for past due child support—didn't last long. Before long he fell back into his old lifestyle. He was arrested in Plainview and served a little time in jail. When he got out, nobody in Tulia seemed to know where he had gone or what his plans were.

Freddie Brookins enrolled in classes at Amarillo College, as his father had long hoped he would. He and Terry bought a house in Tulia together and had a baby of their own. Fred Sr., though he had long since qualified for retirement, continued working nights at the packing plant. He and Patty spent a lot of time watching their grandkids, as both Terry and Freddie spent their days studying and working toward their degrees.

Jeff Blackburn's name and face were all over the news in the months following the settlement. The Texas Criminal Defense Lawyers Association named him Lawyer of the Year. He got back all of his expenses, plus a hefty fee, in the settlement, though he found that the fight had left him too exhausted to enjoy it. His health had deteriorated so severely over the previous year that he checked himself briefly into the hospital with bleeding ulcers. When he got out, he left for a long visit to Ireland. After he returned home in the fall of 2004, he used some of his settlement fee to start an innocence project—a sort of law clinic in which students work on correcting miscarriages of justice through post-conviction work—at Texas Tech University in Lubbock.

Vanita Gupta spent much of her time in the months following the settlement traveling back and forth between New York and Louisiana, where a team of Legal Defense Fund attorneys, led by George Kendall, had won a new trial for an inmate named Wilbert Rideau, who was serving a life sentence for a killing he committed in 1961, at the age of 19. It was the third time the conviction had been set aside, each time because of prosecutorial misconduct, but the state of Louisiana opted to try him again. In 1993, *Life Magazine* had named Rideau, the editor of the nationally recognized *Angolite* prison magazine, "the Most Rehabilitated Prisoner in America," and his case became a referendum on whether incarceration in America was really about rehabilitating offenders, or merely punishment.

A film production company obtained Gupta's life rights in the winter of 2003, and the well-known actress Halle Berry announced she was interested in playing Gupta (or a "composite character" that sounded an awful lot like Gupta), prompting another round of media buzz about Tulia. A few months later, Gupta was awarded the Reebok Human Rights Award, one of the most prestigious international awards for public service. She suddenly found herself in great demand as a speaker at conferences, and she traveled widely, telling the story of Tulia to a variety of audiences. On January 15, 2005, Wilbert Rideau's fourth trial ended in a verdict of manslaughter—not murder—and he was released, after forty-four years in prison.

That same week, after many postponements, Tom Coleman finally stood trial for perjury. The trial, which lasted five days, was held in Lubbock, with Rod Hobson and John Nation acting as special prosecutors. One of the three counts against Coleman was dropped prior to trial, leaving two alleged instances of perjury: first, his statement at the habeas hearing that he did not know he had been indicted for theft until Sheriff Stewart found the arrest warrant, and second, his denial at the hearing that he had stolen gas from Cochran County in the first place.

Hobson was thoroughly prepared and put on his usual good show for the jury. At one point, he called Sheriff Stewart to the stand and grilled him on his testimony in the March 2003 hearing and in the original trials. Frustrated by Stewart's evasive answers, Hobson angrily announced that the sheriff needed to retain an attorney before the questioning could continue—strongly suggesting that in his opinion Stewart's testimony was coming close to perjury. The judge took Hobson's request seriously, and Stewart appeared the next day with an attorney. A chastened Stewart tried to rationalize his testimony in Cash Love's trial that he "never had any trouble with Coleman" by suggesting he was referring to a lack of citizen complaints against him. (Nobody in Tulia, of course, knew that Coleman worked for Stewart.) Coleman's arrest, he argued, didn't qualify as trouble, since it was dealt with in a week.

"If it was dealt with in a week what are we doing here?" Hobson asked.

"I've wondered that myself," Stewart replied dryly.

"You still don't know, Sheriff, do you?" Hobson replied.

There were no Texas Rangers present to testify on Coleman's behalf this time. Coleman's mother did take the stand in his defense, however, and her testimony, while combative and contradictory of some of her son's own claims, almost allowed Coleman to wriggle free once again. Cochran County Attorney Jay Adams, who had offered eyewitness evidence against Coleman in the gas theft back in 1996, had described Coleman in his statement as wearing a light-colored cowboy hat. Coleman's mother protested that he always wore a black hat, and she brought forth a selection of photos, including some of Coleman as a boy, each of which portrayed her son in a black hat. Despite the seemingly incontrovertible credit card records—which showed a gas charge made to Coleman's county-issued card at roughly the time he was witnessed filling up by Adams—the jury seemed to buy the black hat defense, acquitting Coleman on one of the two perjury counts. On the second charge, however, they found him guilty. Coleman hid his face in his hands as the verdict was read. With a felony conviction, his law enforcement career was definitively over. Coleman was sentenced to ten years' probation.

With his settlement cash, Joe Moore bought a modest house in town that had been derelict for years and a house out in the country on a small piece of land. He spent most of his time at the ranch house, where he began once again to raise his hogs and calves. This time he added a large vegetable garden. Not that he imagined it would make him any money; he just wanted to grow something on his own land. One hot summer afternoon he sat in the bleachers at the softball field in Tulia, watching the Lobos play ball and enjoying the fresh air. A toddler in a pink blouse, her hair tied up in tiny cornrows, tottered over and flopped down in his lap. The girl was so young she hadn't even been born when Moore went to prison. "Who's little girl is this?" he asked, laughing. "Look like she's yours," somebody behind Moore said. He had missed a lot over the four years he had been locked up, though in some ways it seemed like he had never left. "You know they say Tom Coleman was Lawman of the Year and Jeff Blackburn was Lawyer of the Year, but they both didn't know what they was getting in to," he said, shaking his head.

Squinting in the sunlight, he looked around him at the cloudless blue sky, the low line of houses that marked the southern edge of town, and the open plains beyond them.

"They messed with the wrong town," he said, shaking his head again. "Tulia, man."

APPENDIX: TULIA DEFENDANTS

During his undercover operation in Tulia, Tom Coleman claimed to have made at least 117 purchases of illegal drugs from 47 different defendants. Listed below are the names of the defendants, along with their age at the time of arrest, their race, the specific deliveries for which they were charged, their sentences, and when and if they were released. (Not every alleged purchase resulted in a case being filed, so the charges listed below do not add up to 117.) All of the powder cocaine cases listed below, with the exception of one, were for amounts between one and four grams of cocaine, making them second degree felonies. Coleman's alleged July 27, 1998 purchase from Cash Love—5.4 grams of powder cocaine for $300—was the largest single purchase in the operation. At least twenty-one of the forty-seven defendants were accused of selling drugs to Coleman in a "drug free zone" within 1000 feet of a school or park, making the charges first degree felonies, punishable by up to 99 years in prison. Thirty-five of the 47 defendants were pardoned by the governor. This included every defendant who was actually convicted on charges made by Coleman in Swisher County. Of the remaining twelve defendants on this list, nine either had their charges dismissed prior to trial or were placed on deferred adjudication, which means no final conviction was entered against them. A tenth defendant was a juvenile at the time of his crime, so the conviction will not remain on his adult record. The remaining two, Landis and Mandis Barrow, were already on probation for an unrelated crime at the time of their arrest in the

Coleman sting, and were sent to prison as a result of this probation being revoked. They were never convicted on the Coleman charges, and therefore were not eligible for pardons. They remained incarcerated as of June 2005.

Dennis Mitchell Allen, black, 34
Delivery of powder cocaine on April 12, 1999, April 22, 1999 and May 3, 1999
Pled to 18 years prison, Feb. 15, 2000
Released in settlement on June 16, 2003
Pardoned by governor on August 22, 2003

James Ray Barrow, black, 31
Delivery of powder cocaine on Oct. 1, 1998 and Dec. 9, 1998
Pled to 10 years probation, May 23, 2000; probation revoked
Released in settlement on June 16, 2003
Pardoned by governor on August 22, 2003

Landis Barrow, black, 22
Delivery of marijuana on Sept. 3, 1998; delivery of powder cocaine on Dec. 2, 1998
On probation for previous offense; probation revoked
Sentenced to 10 years in prison, Jan. 21, 2000
Still incarcerated

Leroy Barrow, black, 59
Delivery of powder cocaine on Oct. 1, 1998, and Sept. 24, 1998; delivery of simulated controlled substance, Oct. 9, 1998; delivery of marijuana on Sept. 14, 1998
Pled to 10 years probation, March 9, 2000
Pardoned by governor on August 22, 2003

Mandis Charles Barrow, black, 22
Delivery of cocaine on Sept. 3, 1998; delivery of marijuana on June 23, 1998
On probation for previous offense; probation revoked
Sentenced to 10 years in prison, May 10, 2000
Still incarcerated

Troy Benard, black, 29
Delivery of powder cocaine on May 24, 1999
Pled to 10 years in prison, March 24, 2000
Released on parole
Pardoned by governor on August 22, 2003

Zury Bossett, black, 20
Delivery of powder cocaine on August 21, 1998
Charges dismissed on July 23, 2002

Fred Wesley Brookins, Jr., black, 24
Delivery of powder cocaine on April 5, 1999
Sentenced to 20 years in prison, Feb. 18, 2000
Released in settlement on June 16, 2003
Pardoned by governor on August 22, 2003

Yul Eugene Bryant, black, 31
Delivery of powder cocaine on May 5, 1999
Case dismissed on Feb. 15, 2000

Eddie Cardona, Hispanic, 41
Delivery of marijuana on March 29, 1999
Case dismissed

Marilyn Joyce Cooper, black, 39
Delivery of powder cocaine on Feb. 12, 1999
Pled to three days in county jail, March 24, 2000
Pardoned by governor on August 22, 2003

Armenu Jerrod Ervin, black, 19
Delivery of powder cocaine on May 3, 1999, March 7, 1999, March
    5, 1999, and March 1, 1999
Pled to 10 years probation, April 13, 2000
Pardoned by governor on August 22, 2003

Michael Fowler, black, 28
Delivery of powder cocaine on Nov. 20, 1998
Pled to five years' probation, April 20, 2000
Pardoned by governor on August 22, 2003

Jason Paul Fry, black, 25
Delivery of powder cocaine on Jan. 8, 1999, Dec. 29, 1998, and Dec.
    7, 1998
Pled to three years in prison, March 22, 2000
Pardoned by governor on August 22, 2003

Vickie Fry, black, 27
Delivery of powder cocaine on May 21, 1999
Pled to five years' probation, March 22, 2000
Pardoned by governor on August 22, 2003

Willie B. Hall, black, 38
Delivery of powder cocaine on Aug. 5, 1998, Sept. 21, 1998, Sept. 28,
    1998, Oct. 14, 1998, and Dec. 2, 1998; delivery of crack cocaine on
    Aug. 20, 1998; and delivery of marijuana on Aug. 20, 1998
Pled to 18 years in prison, Jan. 19, 2000
Released in settlement on June 16, 2003
Pardoned by governor on August 22, 2003

Cleveland Joe Henderson, Jr., black, 25
Delivery of powder cocaine on Feb. 22, 1999
Pled to five years' probation, April 4, 2000
Pardoned by governor on August 22, 2003

Mandrell L. Henry, black, 24
Delivery of powder cocaine on July 23, 1998, and July 21, 1998
Pled to two years in state jail, Jan. 12, 2000
Pardoned by governor on August 22, 2003

Christopher Eugene Jackson, black, 27
Delivery of powder cocaine on May 12, 1999, May 19, 1999, and
    June 4, 1999
Sentenced to 20 years in prison on Jan. 12, 2000
Released in settlement on June 16, 2003
Pardoned by governor on August 22, 2003

Denise Kelly, black, 29
Delivery of powder cocaine on May 19, 1999
Pled to one year in state jail, March 16, 2000
Pardoned by governor on August 22, 2003

Etta Kelly, black, 23
Delivery of simulated controlled substance, June 14, 1999
Pled to three years' deferred adjudication

Eliga Kelly Sr., black, 62
Delivery of crack cocaine on Dec. 21, 1998 and June 29, 1998; delivery of powder cocaine on June 25, 1998; delivery of marijuana on Aug. 25, 1998
Pled to 10 years probation, March 8, 2000
Agreed to testify as a state's witness
Pardoned by governor on August 22, 2003

Calvin Kent Klein, white, 22
Delivery of powder cocaine on June 16, 1998
Pled to 10 years in prison, probated for five years, Dec. 29, 1999; Probation revoked
Released in settlement on June 16, 2003*
Pardoned by governor on August 22, 2003
*Though Klein was released on June 16, he was almost immediately required to return to jail to continue serving time on an unrelated charge.

Jonathan Loftin, white, 16
Charged in juvenile court with delinquent conduct for delivery of marijuana May 14, 1999, and delivery of powder cocaine on May 24, 1999
Sentenced to boot camp for juvenile offenders

William Cash Love, white, 25
Delivery of powder cocaine on June 25, 1998, June 29, 1998, July 7, 1998, July 21, 1998, July 27, 1998, Aug. 21, 1998, and Sept. 3, 1998; delivery of marijuana on May 21, 1998
Sentenced to 361 years in prison, Jan. 29, 2000
Pardoned by governor on August 22, 2003

Joseph Corey Marshall, black, 23
Delivery of powder cocaine on Nov. 25, 1998, Dec. 9, 1998, and Dec. 24, 1998
Pled to 10 years' probation, March 24, 2000
Pardoned by governor on August 22, 2003

Laura Ann Mata, Hispanic, 23
Delivery of powder cocaine on Dec. 2, 1998
Pled to five years in prison, Sept. 2, 1999
Released on parole
Pardoned by governor on August 22, 2003

Vincent Dwight McCray, black, 38
Delivery of powder cocaine on April 19, 1999, April 26, 1999, and
    June 4, 1999
Pled to three years in prison, March 15, 2000
Released on parole
Pardoned by governor on August 22, 2003

Joe Welton Moore, black, 58
Delivery of powder cocaine on Oct. 9, 1998, and delivery of crack
    cocaine on Aug. 24, 1998
Sentenced to 90 years in prison, Dec. 15, 1999
Released in settlement, June 16, 2003
Pardoned by governor on August 22, 2003

James Moreno, Hispanic, age unknown
Delivery of powder cocaine on Jan. 4, 1999; delivery of simulated
    controlled substance (cocaine) on Jan. 8, 1999
Charges dismissed, Nov. 15, 1999

Daniel G. Olivarez, Hispanic, 20
Delivery of marijuana on May 21, 1998; delivery of powder cocaine
    on July 15, 1998, and April 27, 1998
Pled to 12 years in prison, March 22, 2000*
Released on parole
Pardoned by governor on August 22, 2003
*Though Olivarez's Swisher County convictions were thrown out in
    the June 16, 2003 settlement, he also had charges in Potter County
    (Amarillo) that were made by Coleman as well. The Potter County
    district attorney declined to participate in the settlement, and
    these charges were not covered by the governor's pardon. For this
    reason, Olivarez was not released until his parole in June 2005, 22
    months after his pardon.

Kenneth Ray Powell, black, 40
Delivery of powder cocaine on Dec. 21, 1998, Jan. 4, 1999, Jan. 25,
  1999, Feb. 8, 1999, and March 1, 1999
Pled to 10 years probation, March 22, 2000
Pardoned by governor on August 22, 2003

Benny Lee Robinson, black, 24
Delivery of powder cocaine on March 7, 1999, and April 12, 1999
Pled to deferred adjudication, June 14, 2000
Deferred adjudication revoked
Released in settlement on June 16, 2003
Pardoned by governor on August 22, 2003

Finaye Shelton, black, 25
Delivery of powder cocaine on Dec. 29, 1998, and Feb. 22, 1999
Pled to five years' probation, March 9, 2000
Pardoned by governor on August 22, 2003

Donald Wayne Smith, black, 31
Delivery of crack cocaine on June 29, 1998; delivery of powder
  cocaine on July 7, 1998, Sept. 21, 1998, Nov. 3, 1998, Nov. 11,
  1998, and Nov. 23, 1998
Sentenced to two years' state jail for the crack delivery on Feb. 16,
  2000
Plead to 12-and-a-half years (to run concurrently with first sentence)
  on the remaining charges on Feb. 26, 2000
Released on parole
Pardoned by governor on August 22, 2003

Lawanda Smith, black, 25
Delivery of powder cocaine on Oct. 14, 1998, Oct. 23, 1998, Nov. 3,
  1998, and Nov. 16, 1998
Pled to three years' deferred adjudication, July 27, 2000

Yolanda Yvonne Smith, black, 26
Delivery of powder cocaine on Dec. 14, 1998, Dec. 24, 1998, and
  Jan. 18, 1999
Pled to six years in prison, March 24, 2000
Released on parole
Pardoned by governor on August 22, 2003

Romona Lynn Strickland, black, 26
Delivery of powder cocaine on Feb. 12, 1999, and March 15, 1999
Pled to $2,000 fine, June 20, 2000
Pardoned by governor on August 22, 2003

Timothy Wayne Towery, black, 27
Delivery of powder cocaine on Oct. 14, 1998, Oct. 23, 1998, Nov. 9,
    1998, Nov. 16, 1998, Nov. 23, 1998, Nov. 30, 1998, and Dec. 7,
    1998
Pled to 18 years in prison, Jan. 19, 2000
Released in settlement on June 16, 2003
Pardoned by governor on August 22, 2003

Chandra Leah Van Cleave, white, 22
Delivery of powder cocaine on Feb. 8, 1999
Dismissed on April 28, 2000*
*Van Cleave plead guilty on the same day to an unrelated charge for
possession of crack cocaine and was sentenced to three days in the
county jail.

Billy Don Wafer, black, 42
Delivery of powder cocaine on Jan. 18, 1999
Case dismissed on Jan. 4, 2001

Kareem Abdul Jabbar White, black, 24
Delivery of powder cocaine on March 15, 1998, July 15, 1998, Sept.
    28, 1998, Nov. 23, 1998, and Dec. 14, 1998
Sentenced to 60 years in prison, Sept. 8, 2000
Released in settlement on June 16, 2003
Pardoned by governor on August 22, 2003

Kizzie R. White, black, 23
Delivery of crack cocaine on July 21, 1998, July 30, 1998, Aug. 5,
    1998, Aug. 25, 1998, and Sept. 16, 1998; delivery of powder
    cocaine Sept. 24, 1998; delivery of marijuana on July 9, 1998
Sentenced to 25 years in prison, April 7, 2000
Released in settlement on June 16, 2003
Pardoned by governor on August 22, 2003

Tonya Michelle White, black, 30
Delivery of powder cocaine on October 9, 1998
Case dismissed on April 9, 2002

Alberta Stell Williams, black, 49
Delivery of powder cocaine on August 27, 1998 and August 31, 1998
Pled to ten years in prison, March 9, 2000
Released on parole
Pardoned by governor on August 22, 2003

Jason Jerome Williams, black, 19
Delivery of powder cocaine on Sept. 3, 1998, April 22, 1999, May 5,
    1999, and April 19, 1999
Sentenced to 45 years in prison, Jan. 14, 2000
Released in settlement on June 16, 2003
Pardoned by governor on August 22, 2003

Michelle Williams, black, 30
Delivery of powder cocaine on Nov. 9, 1998, Nov. 11, 1998, and May
    17, 1999
Pled to two years in prison, April 14, 2000
Completed sentence and released
Pardoned by governor on August 22, 2003

NOTES

A Note on the Sources

I have been reporting on Tulia for the past five years. Most of that reporting appeared in a magazine called *Texas Observer*, where I first broke the story in June 2000. This book is informed by over 100 interviews. I was fortunate to have complete access to the team of postconviction attorneys—the "Dream Team"—during the decisive hearing in March 2003 that reversed most of Tom Coleman's convictions. I also attended one of the original hearings at which Tom Coleman testified, a probation revocation hearing for Mandis Barrow held in May 2000. For other scenes of hearings or trials depicted in this book, I have relied on interviews with participants and court transcripts. Many of the original trial attorneys provided deposition testimony as part of the habeas proceeding, which was also helpful. Of course, I benefited from the impressive collection of documentary evidence put together by the postconviction attorneys in preparation for the March 2003 hearing.

Prologue

This account draws on my own in-person reporting of the March 2003 hearing in Tulia, as well as interviews with the attorneys for the applicants, the applicants themselves, and their family members.

Coleman was named Task Force Officer of the Year in an August 6, 1999, press release from the governor's office. In the text, I mentioned just a few of the media reports filed over the years on Coleman and Tulia, which are too numerous to list here. My story in *Texas Observer*, "The

Color of Justice," ran June 23, 2000, and was the first investigative piece on Tulia. Stories by Jim Yardley of the *New York Times* and Hector Tobar of the *Los Angeles Times* followed on October 7, 2000. CNN's first story aired on October 10, 2000. These three reports spawned countless follow-ups in print, radio, and television outlets across the country. A report by producer Melissa Cornick for the ABC program *20/20* aired on December 4, 2000. Greg Cunningham of the *Amarillo Globe News* did a lengthy series on the scandal in March 2001. He and Betsy Blaney of the Associated Press covered the story from the panhandle for several years. Tom Mangold reported on Tulia for the BBC program *Correspondent* in early March 2003. The CBS News program *60 Minutes* featured Tulia in its season premier on September 28, 2003. Court TV's one-hour special, *Railroaded in Texas* by producer Gordon Platt, aired on October 30, 2003.

CHAPTER ONE

My account of July 23, 1999, the morning of the bust, is drawn from interviews with law enforcement officers who were present, including Department of Public Safety officer Jackie Gunnels, Tulia Police Chief Jimmy McCaslin, and Sheriff Larry Stewart, as well as interviews with defendants who were arrested that morning and their family members. (Sheriff Stewart subsequently decided not to make himself available for interviews for this book.) Contemporary newspaper accounts in the *Tulia Herald*, *Tulia Sentinel*, and *Amarillo Globe News* were also helpful. Footage of the actual morning of the arrest was carried by Amarillo network news. The video, which showed handcuffed defendants being led into jail in various states of undress, was reused in many subsequent reports.

CHAPTER TWO

Two locally produced histories of Swisher County were indispensable in researching this chapter: *Swisher County History*, compiled by Grace Evans in 1968, and *Windmilling: 101 Years of Swisher County History*, published by the Swisher County Historical Commission in 1978. The Panhandle-Plains Historical Museum at West Texas A&M University in Canyon has many useful Swisher County files, as does the Center for American History at the University of Texas–Austin. Billie Sue Gayler gave me a helpful tour of the holdings of the Swisher County Archives and Museum in the Swisher Memorial Building in Tulia. References to election results in Swisher County are from records in the Swisher County Courthouse.

Several books were helpful for a general overview of panhandle history and customs. Jane Kramer's *The Last Cowboy* has a great take on changes in the cattle economy and west Texas generally in the post–World War II period. Two books by the historian David Edwin Harrell Jr., *Southern Evangelicals*; and *White Sects and Black Men*, were useful for understanding the importance of religion in the Texas panhandle. Legendary *Tulia Herald* editor H.M. Baggarly's work has been collected in two books: *Texas Country Editor* (1966) and *The Texas Country Democrat* (1970). The book *Richard West's Texas*, particularly the section titled "Perryton: The Panhandle," is a well-written and thoughtful look at the traditional economy of the region. Frederick Rathjen's *The Texas Panhandle Frontier*, Byron Price's *The Golden Spread*, and John C. Dawson's *High Plains Yesterdays* are general histories of the panhandle. A. G. Mojtabi's *Blessed Assurance* in an interesting look at the mind-set of plainsmen and Amarilloans in particular. On the same subject, two *Texas Observer* articles by Buck Ramsey were helpful, "Letter from Amarillo," April 17, 1970 and "Is Amarillo Ready for Self Government?" December 8, 1967.

The We the People saga was well covered in the national media. See, for example, "Three Tulia Residents Face Trial," *Dallas Morning News*, July 26, 1993; "Three Sentenced in West Texas Tax Protest," by Bill Lodge, *Dallas Morning News*, September 27, 1994; "Eleven Indicted in Conning of Coloradoans," by Sue Lindsay, January 24, 1995, *Rocky Mountain News*; "The Reluctant Citizens: Bruised and Bitter," by David Jackson, *Chicago Tribune*, May 17, 1995.

Swisher County was one of the fastest shrinking counties in Texas in 2002, according to the Census Bureau's county-by-county estimates for that year. An informative interview with Hale County Extension Agent Dirk Aaron, in which he explained, among other things, the history of the Conservation Reserve Program, helped me understand why this is happening in the Texas panhandle and across the plains. The *New York Times* published an insightful series of articles by Timothy Egan and Peter T. Kilborn on the Great Plains in December 2003, and another on rural poverty in December 2002, also by Timothy Egan.

I benefited from interviews with many local people about the culture of Tulia and the panhandle, including some current and former Tulians who asked that their names not appear in this book. Alan Bean has made himself an authority on Tulia history, spending many hours immersed in old copies of the *Tulia Herald* from H.M. Baggarly's era. I benefited from many hours of conversation with him. Gary Gardner had in his possession an actual copy of the anti-Baggarly flyer mentioned in this chapter, as well as many other gems from the region's past. Jeff Blackburn is an authority on the history of Amarillo and its many characters. Former Texas Rural Legal Aid (TRLA) attorney Bill Beardall also provided particularly helpful insights into the culture of the panhandle. Beardall and his colleagues founded what became the Plainview chapter of TRLA, which fought a legendary battle against the growers and their law enforcement and government supporters in the area on behalf of farm workers.

CHAPTER THREE

My account of Joe Moore's trial is based on court transcripts, a deposition of Kregg Hukill taken in preparation for the habeas hearing in March 2003, and interviews with Moore and Thelma Johnson, who attended the trial. Interviews with members of the Wilmer, Cutler & Pickering team that represented Moore after his conviction, particularly Bill White, Winston King, and Ted Killory, were also helpful. The short history of the Flats in this chapter draws primarily on Moore's recollections, as well as those of others who grew up in the old neighborhood, including Thelma Johnson, Mattie White, and Ricky White.

CHAPTER FOUR

My account of Gary Gardner's life is based on interviews with Gardner, his wife Darlene, his brother Danny, and others friends and family members in Vigo Park. The story of Gardner's ancestors and the founding of Vigo is also outlined in *Swisher County History*.

The story of Turnaround America and Hermann Wrice's career has been well covered. See, for example, "Drug Foe Who Made His Mark Here Dies," *St. Petersburg Times*, March 15, 2000. My account of antidrug marches is from interviews with Irene Favila, who participated in one march, as well as contemporary coverage in the *Tulia Sentinel* (especially editorials in the October 12, 1995, and October 26, 1995, issues) and the *Plainview Daily Herald*. Wal-Mart's underwriting of drug investigations was reported in "Smith Convicted for Dealing Drugs," *Tulia Sentinel*, March 20, 1987.

My account of Tulia's drug testing program comes from interviews with school board members, including Gary Gardner and Scott Burrow, as well as coverage in the *Tulia Herald* and *Amarillo Globe News*. Gardner's suit became a national story as drug testing generally became an issue around the country. See, for example, "They Decided to Fight the System When Ordered to Take Drug Tests," *Congressional Quarterly Researcher*, November 20, 1998. The extended quote from school board member Sam Sadler is from a transcription of an audio recording made of the school board meeting at which the policy was approved. Results of tests in Tulia were reported in the *Tulia Sentinel* on July 29, 1999.

CHAPTER FIVE

This chapter is based chiefly on interviews with Paul Holloway, Tom Hamilton, Brent Hamilton, and Jay Adams. Though he gave several interviews for my earlier coverage of the story in *Texas Observer* and *Texas Monthly*, Terry McEachern declined to cooperate for book interviews.

I also had the benefit of extensive research done by the habeas attorneys in preparation for the March 2003 hearing, which included two large exhibit binders collecting virtually every relevant document in the case. These included Coleman's farewell note to Sheriff Burke referenced in this chapter, as well as records of all of his debts in Cochran County, and the garnishment of his paycheck for past due child support. They also included records pertaining to his arrest, his waiver of arraignment, and the subsequent plea agreement that settled the charges filed against him in Cochran County. The habeas team also compiled all of Tom Coleman's hearing and trial testimony into one indexed volume, which was a very useful reference.

Paul Holloway and Brent Hamilton provided me with copies of many of the documents they collected early in their research on Coleman. Holloway's memos, in which he summarized his findings, were particularly useful.

The best research on the system of indigent defense in Texas is summarized in a December 2000 document called the *Fair Defense Report*. The research was done by an Austin-based nonprofit called Texas Appleseed, led by former Texas Rural Legal Aid Attorney Bill Beardall. At the time of the report, Texas had nothing that could be called a "system" of appointing attorneys to represent poor defendants. Each judge in Texas had complete discretion over how attorneys were appointed in his or her court. Texas was one of only a handful of states in the nation that allocated no state funding for indigent defense: it was entirely the responsibility of county governments.

This method of appointing defense counsel, more than any other single aspect of the Texas criminal justice system, probably comes closest to the root cause of the state's poor national (and international) reputation for justice. Particularly in rural counties, the report found, the pressure on judges to keep costs down resulted in compensation that was generally poor and sometimes completely inadequate. Even in urban areas like Houston, rules varied widely from court to court. How quickly an attorney was appointed, how much money he or she would earn, and whether or not money for private investigators and expert witnesses was available—in short, how effectively a defendant was going to be represented in court—depended entirely on which court in Houston a defendant's case was arbitrarily assigned to. The report found that Texas was near the bottom in overall spending on indigent defense and that judges' authority to make indigent defense appointments gave them too much economic power over the local bar in many cases.

I relied also on interviews with Texas ACLU director Will Harrell and Bill Beardall in reporting this chapter. Beardall's work produced a good deal of state-level news coverage. See for example a package of articles published July 16, 2000, in the *Dallas Morning News*. Another *Dallas Morning News* story, "Quality of Justice: Defenses in Question," September 10, 2000, catalogues instances of questionable representation in death penalty cases.

CHAPTER SIX

This chapter is based primarily on interviews with Paul Holloway, Tom Hamilton, Brent Hamilton, and Billy Wafer, along with transcripts of court proceedings in Wafer's case. The portrait of Coleman is drawn from interviews with Coleman's ex-wife Carol Barnett, in which she recounted not only what she told Holloway during the conversation described in this chapter, but also much more about her past dealings with Coleman, his personal history, and his reputation in the community and in law enforcement generally. This account was augmented by interviews with his former Pecos County law enforcement colleagues Larry Jackson and Cliff Harris. Much of what Carol Barnett had to say about her ex-husband is backed up by documents collected by Paul Holloway and Tom and Brent Hamilton, including a 1994 report prepared by an investigator at a judge's request during Coleman's divorce from Carol Barnett. The document, titled "Social Study Investigation," is an assessment of Coleman and Barnett's fitness as parents, and it summarizes a number of interviews conducted by the investigator with Coleman's friends and colleagues.

Barnett's allegations are also supported by documentary evidence collected by the habeas team in preparation for the March 2003 hearing in Tulia. Extensive testimony about Coleman's personal life and career is found in the transcripts of the hearing itself, in which a host of former law enforcement colleagues, associates, and creditors appeared to testify about Coleman's past behavior.

After my initial story for the *Texas Observer* in June 2000, Tom Coleman declined my requests for interviews. He has, however, responded at one time or another to most of the allegations made against him over the years, both in court and in press interviews. His court testimony consists of the transcripts of the original trials in which he testified, his lengthy deposition on June 29, 2001, in Billy Wafer's lawsuit, and his testimony in the March 2003 hearing in Tulia. I have also been able to review transcripts of his comments from a series of press interviews, including an interview with KAMR Channel 4 in Amarillo, which aired in 2002, a March 2003 interview with Tom Mangold of the BBC, a September 28, 2003, interview with *60 Minutes*, and a March 2005 interview with Todd Bensman in *D Magazine*.

CHAPTER SEVEN

My account of the White family is based primarily on interviews with Donnie Smith, his parents Ricky and Mattie White, his sister Tonya White, his brother Cecil Jackson, and a number of Donnie's friends in Tulia. The discussion of Tulia's troubled sports heroes draws mainly from interviews with Cecil Jackson, Ricky White, Ricky's brother-in-law Melvin Tatum, and Fred Brookins Sr., as well as court records. Estimates of black male graduation rates are from an informal calculation by Nancy Bean, who teaches at Tulia High.

The account of Donnie's trial is from court transcripts, as well as interviews with Donnie, his attorneys Tom and Brent Hamilton, Mattie White, and other friends and family members.

Chapter Eight

The story of the Brookins family is based principally on interviews with Freddie Brookins Jr., his parents, Fred Brookins Sr. and Patty Brookins, his brother Kent Brookins, his wife Terry Basaldua, and a number of Freddie's friends in Tulia. The account of his trial is based on interviews, as well as court transcripts. His attorney Michael Hrin was deposed prior to the March 2003 hearing in Tulia and provided an account of his preparation for trial, strategy, and reactions to the state's case. I also benefited from interviews with Vanita Gupta, who represented Freddie in his habeas appeal, as well as the other habeas attorneys working on the Tulia cases generally.

For the record, Fred Brookins Sr., who has worked at the Excel meat-packing plant in Plainview for over twenty years, did not characterize the facility as an excessively dangerous or particularly undesirable place to work. Some of the best reporting on the dangers of meatpacking in general is Karen Olsson's coverage of the IBP plant in Amarillo, including "On the Line at IBP," May 22, 1998 and "The View From Outside," November 9, 2001. Plainview city councilwoman Irene Favila also provided helpful background on the hiring practices of the Excel plant in Plainview.

Chapter Nine

Gardner's research into the Tulia sting produced many lists, memos, letters, affidavits, and newspaper clippings, all of which he shared with me. My account of the work of the Friends of Justice is based on interviews with the participants. My account of Coleman's reputation in Pecos County and Cochran County draws on the same sources I cited in Chapter 6, "Officer of the Year."

My account of Randy Credico's career is from interviews with Credico, as well as a documentary about his life by director Laura Kightlinger, titled *Sixty Spins Around the Sun*. The effort to reform New York's Rockefeller drug laws has been thoroughly covered in the *New York Times* and elsewhere. In 2004 the New York state legislature finally softened the laws somewhat, though they were not repealed. See "Easing of New York Drug Laws Takes Effect," *New York Times*, January 13, 2005. The best overview of the Rockefeller laws and their impact is Jennifer Gonnerman's 2004 book *Life on the Outside*, which tells the story of

Elaine Bartlett, a first-time drug offender who was sentenced to twenty-five-years-to-life under the Rockefeller laws.

My account of Kareem White's trial is based on court transcripts. His polygraph test and the events surrounding it were thoroughly discussed on the record in a pretrial hearing. I also relied on interviews with Kareem's attorney Dwight McDonald, as well as interviews with Alan Bean, Gary Gardner, Randy Credico, and others who attended the trial.

The *Dallas Morning News* broke the story of Terry McEachern's prosecution of Felipe Rodriguez. See "Retarded Man Released from Jail," by Brooks Egerton, *Dallas Morning News*, August 8, 2000. The case of David Stoker is covered in detail in "Flawed Trials Lead to Death Chamber," by Steve Mills, Ken Armstrong, and Douglas Holt, *Chicago Tribune*, June 11, 2000.

Chapter Ten

My account of the ACLU "war orphans" press conference is from my own in-person reporting. For a partial listing of the initial round of national media coverage of Tulia following the initial investigative story in *Texas Observer*, see my notes for the Prologue.

The discussion of racial attitudes in this chapter draws on numerous interviews with white and black Tulians, though not everybody was willing to speak on the record. The story of the rodeo clown in the 1950s was told to me by Johnny Nix. Election records referred to in this chapter are from records held at the Swisher County Courthouse.

The information about farm subsidies comes from a variety of sources. According to numbers maintained by the U.S. Department of Agriculture and compiled by the Environmental Working Group, a government watchdog organization, the total value of Swisher County's farms is $264,279,000. County farmers received $136,007,848 in subsidies from 1995 to 2003, or slightly more than half of the total value of their operations. In neighboring Hale County, farmers have received roughly $251 million in subsidies over the same period, or about 74 percent of the total value of the county's farms.

My account of the Lobos is based primarily on interviews with Fred Brookins Sr., Ricky White, Mattie White, Thelma Johnson, and Kent Brookins. The history of law enforcement in the Flats draws on interviews with Joe Moore and others who grew up in the old neighborhood, as well as court records and accounts in *Swisher County History*. Many people, both white and black, remembered the Flats as a lawless place, but paradoxically also as one in which local law enforcement historically took little interest, often declining to prosecute even serious crimes that took place in the neighborhood.

Details of the Kareem White and Ricky White Jr. rape allegations are from court records and interviews, primarily with Kareem's attorney Paul Holloway and Ricky White Sr. David Johnson's manslaughter trial was reported by Lili Ibara in the October 25, 2002, *Texas Observer* and in the *Tulia Herald*. Dr. Ralph Erdmann's downfall was widely reported. See, for example "Autopsy Record of Pathologist Who Quit Raises Many Eyebrows," by Roy Bragg, *Houston Chronicle*, March 8, 1992. My account of the Jamie Moore rape case is from interviews with Gary Gardner and court records from the case, including statements given by Moore and his accuser.

CHAPTER ELEVEN

This chapter draws on my past reporting in *Texas Observer* on drug task forces in Texas, including "Zero Tolerance," October 29, 1999, "The Law West of the Pecos," December 10, 1999, "The Color of Justice," June 23, 2000, and "The Numbers Game," October 26, 2001. The latter article, a critical examination of a troubled task force in Chambers County in rural southeast Texas, focused in part on the racially disparate impact of task force operations. This task force, like many in Texas, devoted almost all of its undercover work to street-level crack purchases. In a jurisdiction that was 10–12 percent African American, 57 percent of the task force's cases over a five-year period involved black suspects. African Americans make up just 12 percent of the Texas population but account for 70 percent of all drug offenders admitted to state prison, according to 2001 figures of the National Corrections Reporting Program.

The best investigative reporting of the careers of Gary Painter and Clayton McKinney appears in a series of *Texas Observer* articles by Nick Johnson and David Armstrong, including "Have Badge, Will Travel," October 18, 1991, and "Drugs, Stings, and Profits," May 22, 1992. These articles in turn drew in part on reports in the *Nimby News*, by Alpine reporter Jack McNamara, who has covered the west Texas drug war for many years.

Details of the Texas Rangers' 1998 investigation of the Permian Basin Drug Task Force are from an official report by Ranger Curtis D. Becker, assisted by FBI agent Dan Kennerly. The report is a compelling read, and the lack of indictments against Permian Basin Task Force members is difficult to explain. At the time, Odessa District Attorney John Smith placed the blame on John Neal, the assistant attorney general who presented the information to the grand jury. Smith told the *Odessa American* that the AG's office seemed more interested in making the whole embarrassing scandal disappear as quickly as possible than in following up on the allegations in the Rangers' report.

Information about the origin of the Byrne grant program comes from newspaper accounts, including "Drug Gang Chief Charged in Officer's Killing," by William G. Blair, *New York Times*, August 24, 1989, and "Bush and Dukakis Trade Accusations Over Crime," by Andrew Rosenthal, *New York Times*, October 21, 1988.

The best research on the Byrne grant task forces has been done by Scott Henson and his team of researchers at the Texas ACLU. The organization's December 2002 report, *Too Far Off Task*, catalogued seventeen recent Byrne grant task force scandals in Texas. A follow-up report in May 2004 called *Flawed Enforcement* detailed racial disparities in Byrne grant task force operations. See also Terence Dunworth, Peter Haynes, and Aaron J. Saiger, *National Assessment of the Byrne Formula Grant Program*, June 1997. Yearly funding figures are from the Bureau of Justice Assistance Annual Reports. David B. Muhlhausen of the Heritage Foundation assessed the effectiveness of the Byrne Grant in congressional testimony on March 21, 2002, in a statement titled, "The Homeland Defense: Assessing the Needs of Local Law Enforcement."

General statistics about the Texas drug war are from *State of Texas: Profile of Drug Indicators*, Office of National Drug Control Policy Drug Policy Information Clearinghouse, August 2004, and Texas Department of Criminal Justice statistical summaries available on the agency website. Black admissions for drug offenses represented 81 percent of the growth of Texas' use of prison for drug offenses between 1986 and 1999, according to Jason Ziedenberg and Vincent Schiraldi, *Race and Imprisonment in Texas*, Justice Policy Institute Policy Brief, 2005. The statistic that in Texas, almost one out of three young black men (29 percent of the black male population between 21 and 29) are in prison, jail, parole, or probation on any given day is from Dana Kaplan, Vincent Schiraldi, and Jason Zeindenberg, *Texas Tough? An Analysis of Incarceration and Crime Trends in the Lone Star State*, by the Center on Juvenile and Criminal Justice. The same report also notes that blacks in Texas are incarcerated at a rate seven times greater than whites.

General U.S. prison statistics are from *Bureau of Prison Statistics: Prison*

Statistics, U.S. Department of Justice, Office of Justice Programs. According-
ing to a July 2002 report from that office titled *Prisoners in 2001*, drug
offenses account for nearly two out of five of the blacks sent to state
prison, and more blacks are sent to state prison for drug offenses (38 percent) than for crimes of violence (27 percent). Although the proportion
of drug users who are black is estimated to be from 13 to 15 percent,
blacks account for 36 percent of all drug arrests and 63 percent of those
convicted of drug crimes in state prisons. Allen J. Beck of the Bureau of
Justice Statistics (BJS) reported in August 2000 that Texas for the first
time had the nation's largest incarcerated population under the jurisdiction of its state prison system.

CHAPTER TWELVE

My account of Charles Sturgess's arrest is from a Texas Rangers report by
Garth Davis, which included a witness statement from the young man
involved and a list of the contraband seized when Sturgess's truck was
searched. My account of the history of vice in Swisher County is from
interviews with longtime residents, in particular Johnny Nix, Jeff Bivens,
and Gary Gardner. My account of Driskill House is from interviews with
director Greg Culwell and longtime resident Bobby Keeter, as well as literature from the facility. My account of Bobby Keeter's life is based primarily on interviews with Keeter at Driskill House and court records.

Money for rehab in Texas had dried up over the last ten years. Governor Ann Richards, a recovering alcoholic, had an ambitious program for
more substance-abuse treatment programs for prison inmates when she
took office in 1991. She and Lieutenant Governor Bob Bullock, also a
recovering alcoholic, outlined a program with 14,000 treatment beds at a
cost of about $160 million per year. Funding for drug treatment became
an issue in Richards's 1994 reelection campaign against Republican challenger George W. Bush. Bush said treatment programs were unproven,
and on a campaign stop said, "Incarceration is rehabilitation." He vowed
to take $25 million out of Richards's program and use it to "get tough"
on juvenile crime.

When Bush won, the 1995 legislature cut Richards's program from
14,000 beds to 5,300. In 1997 Bush signed a law that sentences first-time
felons convicted of possessing a gram or less of cocaine to a minimum of
180 days and a maximum of two years in a state jail. Under Richards,
first-time offenders received automatic probation with drug counseling.

Public spending on drug rehab has continued to dwindle under Bush's successor, Governor Rick Perry. Only 36 of the state's 557 hospitals have special units to treat chemical dependency, a total of 538 beds. My account of Tulia's locked MHMR office is from an interview with Stacey Tarbet, who works for an MHMR-funded drug rehab facility in Plainview. Tarbet also identified for me a list of panhandle rehab facilities that closed in recent years as a result of budget cuts.

CHAPTER THIRTEEN

The circumstances of Coleman's firing from the Waxahachie task force were described in a report to TCLEOSE by task force project director Joe Grubb, who is also the local district attorney. According to the report, a task force snitch accused Coleman of "inappropriate sexual contact." She passed a lie detector test. Coleman refused to submit to one and was fired. A source close to the task force, who asked not to be identified by name, confirmed that the "contact" was a consensual sexual relationship between Coleman and the snitch.

My account of Jeff Blackburn's life is drawn primarily from interviews with Blackburn, as well as interviews with his friends and colleagues. My account of the depositions in Billy Wafer's civil suit is taken from the transcripts of the depositions, as well as interviews with Blackburn, Chris Hoffman, and Billy Wafer. Coleman's account of the blank waiver in Kizzie White's motion for new trial is from a transcript of his testimony. My account of Vanita Gupta's life is from interviews with Gupta herself. The Delma Banks case is summarized on the NAACP Legal Defense Fund website. Gupta's work at LDF was funded by a Criminal Justice Fellowship from the Open Society Institute, the George Soros–funded nonprofit that has funded a wide range of criminal justice reform efforts, including drug policy reform. Roy Criner's case was widely covered; see, for example, "Court Shouldn't Keep Innocent Men in Jail," by Robert Hinton, *Dallas Morning News*, August 27, 2000. Michael C. Hall's story "And Justice for Some" in the November 2004 issue of *Texas Monthly* is a thorough and well-written overview of recent CCA decisions.

The account of Romona Strickland's case is from interviews with her attorney Eric Willard and Gary Gardner.

CHAPTER FOURTEEN

I reported on the Texas prison guard shortage in a *Texas Observer* article called "The Gray and the White," March 31, 2000. News clips on the notorious reputation of the Terrell Unit include "Mother Probes Son's Death in Prison," by Allan Turner, *Houston Chronicle*, June 4, 1995, and "Transfer of Prison Officials Called 'Routine,'" by Stephen Johnson, *Houston Chronicle*, January 11, 1995.

My account of Tonya's case is from interviews with Jeff Blackburn, Chris Hoffman, Virginia Cave, Tonya White, and Mattie White. My account of Des Hogan's trip is from interviews with Hogan.

CHAPTER FIFTEEN

The account of Tonya White's exoneration is based on interviews with Jeff Blackburn, Chris Hoffman, Tonya White, Mattie White, and Virginia Cave.

In late June 2002, the Supreme Court ruled in a 5–4 decision that random drug testing of students involved in extra-curricular activities was constitutional. At the time, the Tulia school board's appeal of Gary Gardner's successful suit was still pending before the Fifth Circuit Court of Appeals, but the facts in the case before the Supreme Court were so similar that the ruling effectively made the issue moot. Gardner had lost. "I still think I was right," Gardner said after the ruling. "But after the Supreme Court rules against you, who you gonna call? Ghostbusters?"

CHAPTER SIXTEEN

The account of Angela French's representation of Chris Jackson is based on interviews with Des Hogan, as well as material contained in the ineffective assistance of counsel portion of Jackson's habeas writ and a Dec. 19, 2002 affidavit by Dwight McDonald. French provided two affidavits describing her work on Chris Jackson's behalf and answered questions in a deposition taken in advance of the hearing in Tulia in March 2003. Ken Burke's account of Tom Coleman's career is based on interviews with Des Hogan, as well as Burke's affidavit, which was filed as evidence in the March 2003 hearing in Tulia.

The account of Gary Gardner's letter to the editor about Judge Self is based on interviews with Gardner, Chandra Van Cleave, and Vanita Gupta. Self's responses are documented in a recusal motion filed by Gupta and others on behalf of their clients. Ron Chapman's background is from a memo prepared by LDF staff about his career and published decisions. Details of McEachern's DWI arrest are from published media reports and records of his arrest.

The account of the ongoing FBI investigation into Tulia is from interviews with members of the habeas team and defendants interviewed by FBI agents. The state team did not obtain any information from the FBI about the investigation in time to use it for the March 2003 hearing.

The account of the depositions taken prior to the hearing are based on interviews with the habeas attorneys, as well as court transcripts of the proceedings. The account of the habeas team's preparation for trial is from my contemporaneous in-person reporting as well as interviews with the attorneys.

Chapter Seventeen

The account of the hearings is from my in-person reporting, both in court and at preparation sessions, meals, and meetings of the attorneys the week of the hearings. I also relied on the court transcripts of the hearing, as well as interviews with the attorneys and the voluminous files they collected in preparation for the hearing.

Chapter Eighteen

My account of the negotiation is drawn primarily from interviews with members of the habeas team who were present. I also had the benefit of interviews with Rod Hobson, who provided insight into the state team's strategy and reactions during the crucial week leading up to the final negotiation session, as well as on the day of the negotiation in Tulia that led to the settlement.

Chapter Nineteen

This account is based on my in-person reporting of release day, as well as interviews with defendants, their family members, and friends.

Epilogue

Daniel Olivarez was released on parole in June 2005. Vanita Gupta continued to work with the Amarillo authorities to secure the release of Landis and Mandis Barrow, though they remained incarcerated as of this writing.

The possible demise of the Byrne grant program is discussed in "Signs of Drug-War Shift," by Kris Axtman, *Christian Science Monitor*, May 27, 2005, and other press reports.

As of June 2005, the FBI still considered its Tulia inquiry to be an "ongoing investigation" and refused to release anything to the public or media. After Coleman was indicted for perjury, however, Rod Hobson was given a draft report of the investigation's findings. As a special prosecutor, he felt obligated to share this with Coleman's defense, which he did. In September 2004, a couple of months before Coleman's perjury conviction, the report was leaked to a reporter in Dallas named Todd Bensman, who published a report on WFAA television in Dallas (and later, in March 2005, in *D Magazine*) noting essentially what Blackburn and Gupta had anticipated from their own inquiries: eight defendants had admitted to selling crack cocaine to Coleman. Apparently nobody admitted to selling powder cocaine to Coleman, according to Bensman's report. The remainder maintained their innocence.

As the first report to detail the findings of the FBI investigation, Bensman's story qualifies as a scoop. But the angle of his piece—that Tulia is a case of the media run amok in its persecution of an innocent cop—does not hold up. Bensman was apparently unfamiliar with the defense theory of the cases—that Coleman fabricated powder charges, in some cases out of whole cloth, and in others against defendants against whom he made legitimate crack buys—or of previous coverage of Tulia, including my own, which reported that more than one defendant admitted getting crack for Coleman. Bensman singled out two FBI interviews in particular, with Alberta Williams and Daniel Olivarez, in which each admitted to getting crack for Coleman—in Olivarez's case "3-4 ounces" of crack, according to Bensman's account of the FBI report. That would have put Olivarez on the hook for the largest quantity of cocaine purchased by Coleman in the entire eighteen-month operation. The problem is that Coleman never reported making a single crack buy from Olivarez. According to Coleman's own police reports, he made four separate buys from Olivarez, all eight balls of powder, with a combined weight of less than 11 grams. If Coleman really bought 3 to 4 ounces (or 84 to 112 grams) of crack from Olivarez, then where is the missing evidence? The Williams and Olivarez FBI interviews, as described by Bensman, actually support the defense theory of the cases, rather than undermine it. The FBI apparently never followed up on this question, and Bensman seems unaware of the issue. His report produced very little follow-up coverage.

ACKNOWLEDGMENTS

This project would not have been possible without a Soros Justice Fellowship from the Open Society Institute. I would like to thank the staff at OSI, particularly Gara LaMarche and Kate Black, for their continued interest in this project and their support, even after my fellowship was over. Likewise, this book would never have been written without the opportunity provided me by *The Texas Observer*, where I first reported on the story in 2000. I appreciate the continued support of all of my colleagues there, in particular my former editor Lou Dubose, who suggested that I head to west Texas in the first place, and *Observer* board chair Molly Ivins, whose encouragement I will never forget.

This project builds on the work of many dedicated activists and organizers. The Texas ACLU was the first organization to understand the significance of Tulia, and has done more work than any group I know of to educate the public and elected officials about the shortcomings of the Byrne Grant drug task force program in Texas and across the country. They have been a great resource for me in writing this book, and I would particularly like to thank Will Harrell and Scott Henson for their assistance. I would also like to thank the staff of the NAACP Legal Defense and Education Fund, particularly Vanita Gupta, for making herself available, not only for interviews, but also as a resource for documents and other fact-checking material. Her work, and the work of all of the attorneys who devoted time to this case, has been an inspiration to me. I would particularly like to thank Jeff Blackburn for his hospitality in Amarillo and his patient participation in the reporting of this book.

I would like to thank the Tulia defendants and their families, particularly Joe Moore, Thelma Johnson, Donnie Smith, Ricky White, Mattie White, Freddie Brookins, Jr. and his parents Fred, Sr. and Patty, for opening up their lives to me.

I would also like to thank Peter Osnos, publisher of PublicAffairs, who believed in this book from the very beginning. My editor, David Patterson, kept this project on track and out of the weeds. I had considerable help in researching this book. Nobody knows the documentary record of Tulia better than Jenn Klar, formerly of Hogan & Hartson, and I thank her for her time and energy in helping me ensure that this book is factually accurate. In Tulia, Alan Bean and Gary Gardner knew the issues and characters involved better than anybody else and provided countless invaluable insights. Will Potter and Mollie McGraw also provided research assistance on the drug war in Texas. Bill Blakeslee, an experienced private investigator (and my father), helped me locate hard-to-find people free of charge, and provided constant encouragement throughout this project, as did my mother, Lynda Blakeslee.

Debbie Nathan, Karen Olsson, Lou Dubose, Simon Green, and Dan Green read early drafts of this book and provided helpful comments and encouragement. Simon Green, of Pom, Inc., also provided expert representation. My wife, Karen Poff, read the manuscript many times and listened to countless stories about people she had never met and places she was unlikely to ever go. Her unflagging enthusiasm and good humor are the best endorsement for matrimony I know of.

Much of this book was written at two libraries: the Austin Public Library's John Henry Faulk Central Library and the Tarlton Law Library at the University of Texas-Austin. I would like to thank the courteous and efficient staff of both of these facilities, and in particular the reference staff at the Faulk Central Library, who provided timely assistance with fact checking.

My hosts during most of my trips to Tulia were Mani and A.G., proprietors of the clean and comfortable Lasso Motel on Highway 87. I recommend it.

I would also like to thank the following people, in no particular order, for their assistance over the years: Julie and John Thornton, Danette Chimenti, Paul Holloway, Brent Hamilton, Tom Hamilton, Van Williamson, Barbara Markham, Kathy Mitchell, Ann Del Llano, Jack McNamara, Gary Oliver, Michael King, Barbara Belejack, Charlotte McCann, Julia Austin, Jake Bernstein, Rosie Bamberger Chavez, Robert

Bryce, Char Miller, Alan Pogue, Ed Lieck, Molly Ivins, Nancy Bean, Charles Kiker, Patricia Kiker, Darlene Gardner, Danny Gardner, Colby Gardner (for giving me his seat), Johnny Nix, Greg Cunningham, Des Hogan, Winston King, Rod Hobson, Ann Richards, Christine Hefner, Tom Mangold, Justin Manask, Lili Ibara, Billy Wafer, Randy Credico, Graham Boyd, Jennifer Gonnerman, Betsy Blaney, Dirk Aaron, Greg Culwell, Rick Hubbard, Emmett Benavidez, Evan Smith, Pam Colloff, Jim, Nova, and Kristen Poff, Paul Stekler, Merrill Feitell, and the staff of the Tulia Public Library.

INDEX

PublicAffairs is a publishing house founded in 1997. It is a tribute to the standards, values, and flair of three persons who have served as mentors to countless reporters, writers, editors, and book people of all kinds, including me.

I.F. STONE, proprietor of *I. F. Stone's Weekly*, combined a commitment to the First Amendment with entrepreneurial zeal and reporting skill and became one of the great independent journalists in American history. At the age of eighty, Izzy published *The Trial of Socrates*, which was a national bestseller. He wrote the book after he taught himself ancient Greek.

BENJAMIN C. BRADLEE was for nearly thirty years the charismatic editorial leader of *The Washington Post*. It was Ben who gave the *Post* the range and courage to pursue such historic issues as Watergate. He supported his reporters with a tenacity that made them fearless and it is no accident that so many became authors of influential, best-selling books.

ROBERT L. BERNSTEIN, the chief executive of Random House for more than a quarter century, guided one of the nation's premier publishing houses. Bob was personally responsible for many books of political dissent and argument that challenged tyranny around the globe. He is also the founder and longtime chair of Human Rights Watch, one of the most respected human rights organizations in the world.

For fifty years, the banner of Public Affairs Press was carried by its owner Morris B. Schnapper, who published Gandhi, Nasser, Toynbee, Truman and about 1,500 other authors. In 1983, Schnapper was described by *The Washington Post* as "a redoubtable gadfly." His legacy will endure in the books to come.

Peter Osnos, *Publisher*